SUPER 10

CBSE Class 12

Physics

2023 Exam Sample Papers

with 2021-22 Previous Year Solved Papers, CBSE Sample Paper & 2020 Topper Answer Sheet

DISHA™
Publication Inc

DISHA Publications Inc.

45, 2nd Floor, Maharishi Dayanand Marg,
Corner Market, Malviya Nagar, new Delhi -110017
Tel: 49842349/ 49842350

Edited By
Govind Thakur

Typeset By
DISHA DTP Team

Buying books from DISHA

Just Got A Lot More Rewarding!!!

We at DISHA Publication, value your feedback immensely and to show our apperciation of our reviewers, we have launched a review contest.

To participate in this reward scheme, just follow these quick and simple steps:
- Write a review of the product you purchase on Amazon/Flipkart.
- Take a screenshot/photo of your review.
- Mail it to *disha-rewards@aiets.co.in*, along with all your details.

Each month, selected reviewers will win exciting gifts from DISHA Publication. Note that the rewards for each month will be declared in the first week of next month on our website.

https://bit.ly/review-reward-disha.

Write To
Us At

feedback_disha@aiets.co.in

Contents

PHYSICS (CODE NO. 042)

Unit	Title	No. of Periods	Marks
I	**Electrostatics** Chapter–1: Electric Charges and Fields Chapter–2: Electrostatic Potential and Capacitance	26	16
II	**Current Electricity** Chapter–3: Current Electricity	18	
III	**Magnetic Effects of Current and Magnetism** Chapter–4: Moving Charges and Magnetism Chapter–5: Magnetism and Matter	25	17
IV	**Electromagnetic Induction and Alternating Currents** Chapter–6: Electromagnetic Induction Chapter–7: Alternating Current	24	
V	**Electromagnetic Waves** Chapter–8: Electromagnetic Waves	04	18
VI	**Optics** Chapter–9: Ray Optics and Optical Instruments Chapter–10: Wave Optics	30	
VII	**Dual Nature of Radiation and Matter** Chapter–11: Dual Nature of Radiation and Matter	08	12
VIII	**Atoms and Nuclei** Chapter–12: Atoms Chapter–13: Nuclei	15	
IX	**Electronic Devices** Chapter–14: Semiconductor Electronics: Materials, Devices and Simple Circuits	10	7
	Total	160	70

Unit I: Electrostatics   26 Periods

Chapter-1: Electric Charges and Fields

Electric Charges; Conservation of charge, Coulomb's law-force between two point charges, forces between multiple charges; superposition principle and continuous charge distribution.

Electric field, electric field due to a point charge, electric field lines, electric dipole, electric field due to a dipole, torque on a dipole in uniform electric field.

Electric flux, statement of Gauss's theorem and its applications to find field due to infinitely long straight wire, uniformly charged infinite plane sheet and uniformly charged thin spherical shell (field inside and outside).

Chapter-2: Electrostatic Potential and Capacitance

Electric potential, potential difference, electric potential due to a point charge, a dipole and system of charges; equipotential surfaces, electrical potential energy of a system of two point charges and of electric dipole in an electrostatic field.

Conductors and insulators, free charges and bound charges inside a conductor. Dielectrics and electric polarisation, capacitors and capacitance, combination of capacitors in series and in parallel, capacitance of a parallel plate capacitor with and without dielectric medium between the plates, energy stored in a capacitor (no derivation, formulae only).

Unit II: Current Electricity   18 Periods

Chapter-3: Current Electricity

Electric current, flow of electric charges in a metallic conductor, drift velocity, mobility and their relation with electric current; Ohm's law, V-I characteristics (linear and non-linear), electrical energy and power, electrical resistivity and conductivity, temperature dependence of resistance.

Internal resistance of a cell, potential difference and emf of a cell, combination of cells in series and in parallel, Kirchhoff's laws, Wheatstone bridge.

Unit III: Magnetic Effects of Current and Magnetism   25 Periods

Chapter-4: Moving Charges and Magnetism

Concept of magnetic field, Oersted's experiment.

Biot - Savart law and its application to current carrying circular loop.

Ampere's law and its applications to infinitely long straight wire. Straight solenoids (only qualitative treatment), force on a moving charge in uniform magnetic and electric fields.

Force on a current-carrying conductor in a uniform magnetic field, force between two parallel current-carrying conductors-definition of ampere, torque experienced by a current loop in uniform magnetic field; Current loop as a magnetic dipole and its magnetic dipole moment, moving coil galvanometer-its current sensitivity and conversion to ammeter and voltmeter.

Chapter-5: Magnetism and Matter

Bar magnet, bar magnet as an equivalent solenoid (qualitative treatment only), magnetic field intensity due to a magnetic dipole (bar magnet) along its axis and perpendicular to its axis (qualitative treatment only), torque on a magnetic dipole (bar magnet) in a uniform magnetic field (qualitative treatment only), magnetic field lines. Magnetic properties of materials- para- dia and ferro - magnetic substances with examples, Magnetization of materials, effect of temperature on magnetic properties.

Unit IV: Electromagnetic Induction and Alternating Currents   24 Periods

Chapter-6: Electromagnetic Induction

Electromagnetic induction; Faraday's laws, induced EMF and current; Lenz's Law, Self and mutual induction.

Chapter-7: Alternating Current

Alternating currents, peak and RMS value of alternating current/voltage, reactance and impedance, LCR series circuit (phasors only), resonance; power in AC circuits, power factor, wattless current.

AC generator, Transformer.

Chapter-8: Electromagnetic Waves

Basic idea of displacement current, Electromagnetic waves, their characteristics, their transverse nature (qualitative ideas only).

Electromagnetic spectrum (radio waves, microwaves, infrared, visible, ultraviolet, X-rays, gamma rays) including elementary facts about their uses.

Chapter-9: Ray Optics and Optical Instruments

Ray Optics: Reflection of light, spherical mirrors, mirror formula, refraction of light, total internal reflection and optical fibres, refraction at spherical surfaces, lenses, thin lens formula, lensmaker's formula, magnification, power of a lens, combination of thin lenses in contact, refraction of light through a prism.

Optical instruments: Microscopes and astronomical telescopes (reflecting and refracting) and their magnifying powers.

Chapter-10: Wave Optics

Wave optics: Wave front and Huygen's principle, reflection and refraction of plane wave at a plane surface using wave fronts. Proof of laws of reflection and refraction using Huygen's principle. Interference, Young's double slit experiment and expression for fringe width (no derivation final expression only), coherent sources and sustained interference of light, diffraction due to a single slit, width of central maximum (qualitative treatment only).

Chapter-11: Dual Nature of Radiation and Matter

Dual nature of radiation, Photoelectric effect, Hertz and Lenard's observations; Einstein's photoelectric equation-particle nature of light. Experimental study of photoelectric effect.

Matter waves-wave nature of particles, de-Broglie relation.

Chapter-12: Atoms

Alpha-particle scattering experiment; Rutherford's model of atom; Bohr model of hydrogen atom, Expression for radius of nth possible orbit, velocity and energy of electrons in his orbit, hydrogen line spectra (qualitative treatment only).

Chapter-13: Nuclei

Composition and size of nucleus.

Mass-energy relation, mass defect, binding energy per nucleon and its variation with mass number, nuclear fission, nuclear fusion.

Chapter-14: Semiconductor Electronics: Materials, Devices and Simple Circuits

Energy bands in conductors, semiconductors and insulators (qualitative ideas only)

Intrinsic and extrinsic semiconductors- p and n type, p-n junction

Semiconductor diode - I-V characteristics in forward and reverse bias, application of junction diode-diode as a rectifier

UNMATCHED QUESTION BANK for CLASS 12

Includes

- NCERT Exercises - Intext & Chapter End
- NCERT Exemplar - MCQs & Subjective Qns.
- Past 15 Years CBSE Board Questions from 2008-2022.

Divided Chapter-wise | **Fully Solved** | **Step-by-Step Detailed Solutions**

15 Chapters	16 Chapters	13 Chapters	16 Chapters
300+ MCQ	300+ MCQ	300+ MCQ	300+ MCQ

More than 80% of the Questions* in NEET/ JEE Main 2022 were asked from these Books

(* – same or similar Questions)

4/ 5 level of Exercises

NCERT based Topicwise MCQs	Exemplar & Past Questions – Covers 7 yrs NEET/ JEE Main	Matching, Statement & A–R Type MCQs
Skill Enhancer MCQs		Numeric Answer Qns in Physics, Chemistry & Mathematics

1st Book with 5 Unique Features

NCERT Locater	NCERT + NEET/ JEE Main PYQs in One Liner Format	Tips/ Tricks/ Techniques ONE-LINERS
2 & 4/ 5 Statements, Matching & AR MCQs	100% Solutions	

CBSE SAMPLE QUESTION PAPER (THEORY)
SESSION : 2022-2023

Time Allowed : 3 Hours   **Max. Marks : 70**

General Instructions

1. There are 35 questions in all. All questions are compulsory.
2. This question paper has five sections: Section A, Section B, Section C, Section D and Section E. All the sections are compulsory.
3. Section A contains eighteen MCQ of 1 mark each, Section B contains seven questions of two marks each, Section C contains five questions of three marks each, section D contains three long questions of five marks each and Section E contains two case study based questions of 4 marks each.
4. There is no overall choice. However, an internal choice has been provided in section B, C, D and E. You have to attempt only one of the choices in such questions.
5. Use of calculators is not allowed.

SECTION-A

1. According to Coulomb's law, which is the correct relation for the following figure?

    (a) $q_1\,q_2 > 0$ (b) $q_1\,q_2 < 0$ (c) $q_1\,q_2 = 0$ (d) $1 > q_1/q_2 > 0$

2. The electric potential on the axis of an electric dipole at a distance 'r from it's centre is V. Then the potential at a point at the same distance on its equatorial line will be
     (a)   2V   (b) $-V$ (c)   V/2   (d)   Zero

3. The temperature (T) dependence of resistivity of materials A and material B is represented by fig (i) and fig (ii) respectively. Identify material A and material B.

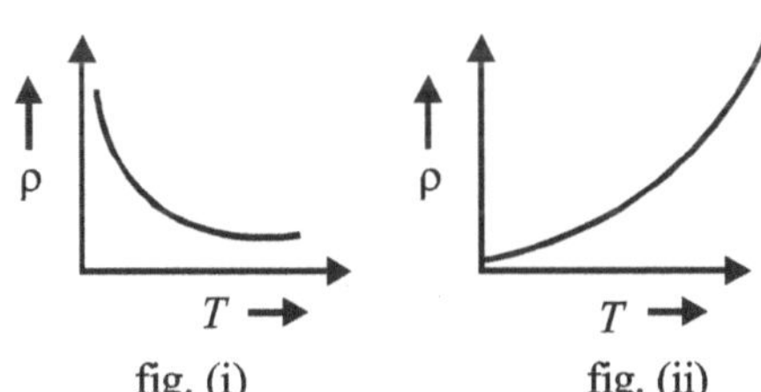

fig. (i)   fig. (ii)

  (a)   material A is copper and material B is germanium   (b)   material A is germanium and material B is copper
  (c)   material A is nichrome and material B is germanium   (d)   material A is copper and material B is nichrome

4. Two concentric and coplanar circular loops P and Q have their radii in the ratio 2:3. Loop Q carries a current 9 A in the anticlockwise direction. For the magnetic field to be zero at the common centre, loop P must carry
     (a)   3A in clockwise direction   (b)   9A in clockwise direction
     (c)   6 A in anti-clockwise direction   (d)   6 A in the clockwise direction

5. A long straight wire of circular cross-section of radius a carries a steady current I. The current is uniformly distributed across its cross-section. The ratio of the magnitudes of magnetic field at a point distant a/2 above the surface of wire to that at a point distant a/2 below its surface is
     (a)   4 : 1   (b)   1 : 1   (c)   4 : 3   (d)   3 : 4

6. If the magnetizing field on a ferromagnetic material is increased, its permeability
   (a) decreases
   (b) increases
   (c) remains unchanged
   (d) first decreases and then increases

7. An iron cored coil is connected in series with an electric bulb with an AC source as shown in figure. When iron piece is taken out of the coil, the brightness of the bulb will

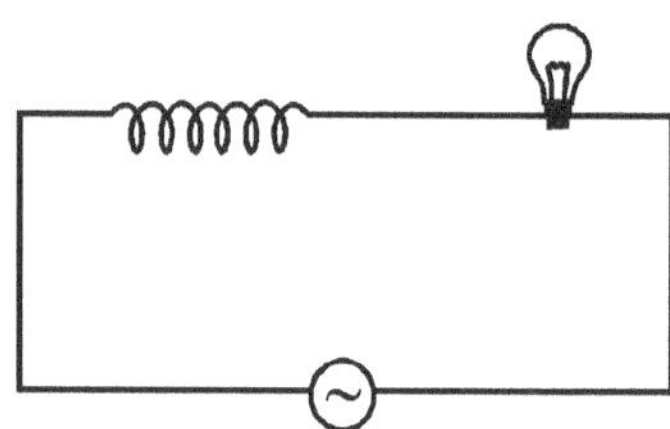

   (a) decrease
   (b) increase
   (c) remain unaffected
   (d) fluctuate

8. Which of the following statement is NOT true about the properties of electromagnetic waves?
   (a) These waves do not require any material medium for their propagation
   (b) Both electric and magnetic field vectors attain the maxima and minima at the same time
   (c) The energy in electromagnetic wave is divided equally between electric and magnetic fields
   (d) Both electric and magnetic field vectors are parallel to each other

9. A rectangular, a square, a circular and an elliptical loop, all in the $(x\text{-}y)$ plane, are moving out of a uniform magnetic field with a constant velocity $\vec{v} = v\hat{i}$. The magnetic field is directed along the negative z-axis direction. The induced emf, during the passage of these loops, out of the field region, will not remain constant for
   (a) any of the four loops
   (b) the circular and elliptical loops
   (c) the rectangular, circular and elliptical loops
   (d) only the elliptical loops

10. In a Young's double slit experiment, the path difference at a certain point on the screen between two interfering waves is $\dfrac{1}{8}$ th of the wavelength. The ratio of intensity at this point to that at the centre of a bright fringe is close to
   (a) 0.80
   (b) 0.74
   (c) 0.94
   (d) 0.85

11. The work function for a metal surface is 4.14 eV. The threshold wavelength for this metal surface is :
   (a) 4125 Å
   (b) 2062.5 Å
   (c) 3000 Å
   (d) 6000 Å

12. The radius of the innermost electron orbit of a hydrogen atom is 5.3×10^{-11} m. The radius of the n = 3 orbit is
   (a) 1.01×10^{-10} m
   (b) 1.59×10^{-10} m
   (c) 2.12×10^{-10} m
   (d) 4.77×10^{-10} m

13. Which of the following statements about nuclear forces is not true?
   (a) The nuclear force between two nucleons falls rapidly to zero as their distance is more than a few femtometres.
   (b) The nuclear force is much weaker than the Coulomb force.
   (c) The force is attractive for distances larger than 0.8 fm and repulsive if they are separated by distances less than 0.8 fm.
   (d) The nuclear force between neutron-neutron, proton-neutron and proton-proton is approximately the same.

14. If the reading of the voltmeter V_1 is 40 V, then the reading of voltmeter V_2 is

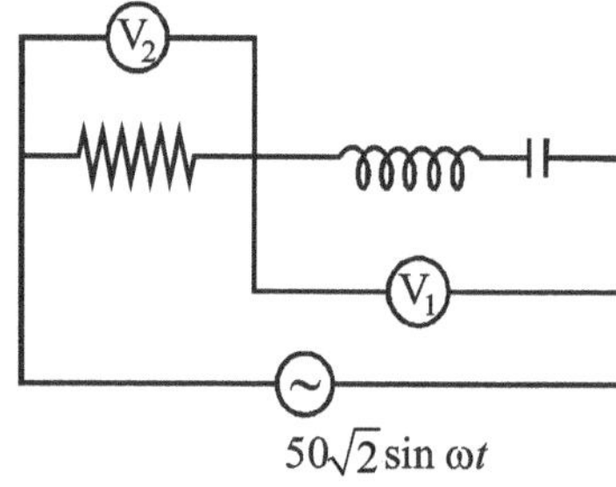

   (a) 30 V
   (b) 58 V
   (c) 29 V
   (d) 15 V

15. The electric potential V as a function of distance X is shown in the figure.

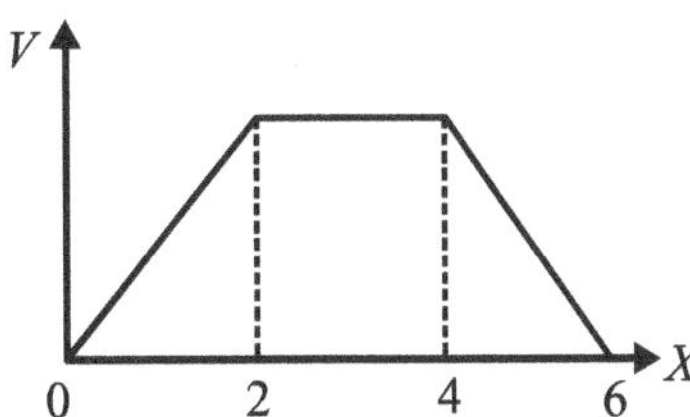

The graph of the magnitude of electric field intensity E as a function of X is

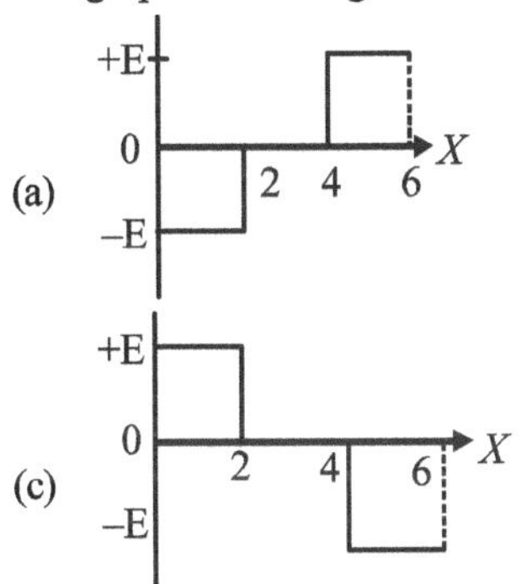

(a)

(c)

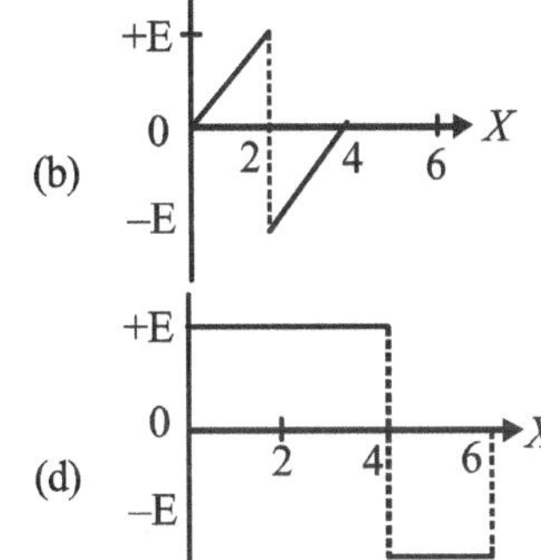

(b)

(d)

16. Two statements are given-one labelled Assertion (A) and the other labelled Reason (R). Select the correct answer to these questions from the codes (a), (b), (c) and (d) as given below.
(a) Both A and R are true and R is the correct explanation of A
(b) Both A and R are true and R is NOT the correct explanation of A
(c) A is true but R is false
(d) A is false and R is also false
Assertion (A): The electrical conductivity of a semiconductor increases on doping.
Reason (R): Doping always increases the number of electrons in the semiconductor.

17. Two statements are given-one labelled Assertion (A) and the other labelled Reason (R). Select the correct answer to these questions from the codes (a), (b), (c) and (d) as given below.
(a) Both A and R are true and R is the correct explanation of A
(b) Both A and R are true and R is NOT the correct explanation of A
(c) A is true but R is false
(d) A is false and R is also false
Assertion (A): In an interference pattern observed in Young's double slit experiment, if the separation (d) between coherent sources as well as the distance (D) of the screen from the coherent sources both are reduced to 1/3rd, then new fringe width remains the same.
Reason (R): Fringe width is proportional to (d/D).

18. Two statements are given-one labelled Assertion (A) and the other labelled Reason (R). Select the correct answer to these questions from the codes (a), (b), (c) and (d) as given below.
(a) Both A and R are true and R is the correct explanation of A
(b) Both A and R are true and R is NOT the correct explanation of A
(c) A is true but R is false
(d) A is false and R is also false
Assertion (A): The photoelectrons produced by a monochromatic light beam incident on a metal surface have a spread in their kinetic energies.
Reason (R): The energy of electrons emitted from inside the metal surface, is lost in collision with the other atoms in the metal.

SECTION-B

19. Electromagnetic waves with wavelength
(i) λ_1 is suitable for radar systems used in aircraft navigation.
(ii) λ_2 is used to kill germs in water purifiers.

(iii) λ_3 is used to improve visibility in runways during fog and mist conditions.

Identify and name the part of the electromagnetic spectrum to which these radiations belong. Also arrange these wavelengths in ascending order of their magnitude.

20. A uniform magnetic field gets modified as shown in figure when two specimens A and B are placed in it.

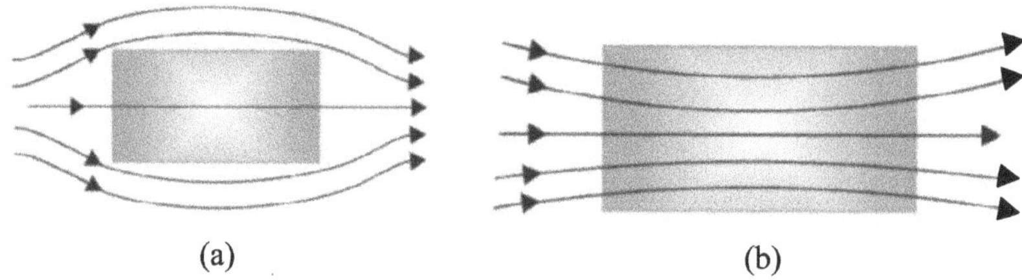

(a)   (b)

(i)   Identify the specimen A and B.

(ii)   How is the magnetic susceptibility of specimen A different from that of specimen B?

21. What is the nuclear radius of ^{125}Fe, if that of ^{27}Al is 3.6 fermi?

OR

The short wavelength limit for the Lyman series of the hydrogen spectrum is 913.4 A^0. Calculate the short wavelength limit for the Balmer series of the hydrogen spectrum.

22. A biconvex lens made of a transparent material of refractive index 1.25 is immersed in water of refractive index 1.33. Will the lens behave as a converging or a diverging lens? Justify your answer.

23. The figure shows a piece of pure semiconductor S in series with a variable resistor R and a source of constant voltage V. Should the value of R be increased or decreased to keep the reading of the ammeter constant, when semiconductor S is heated? Justify your answer

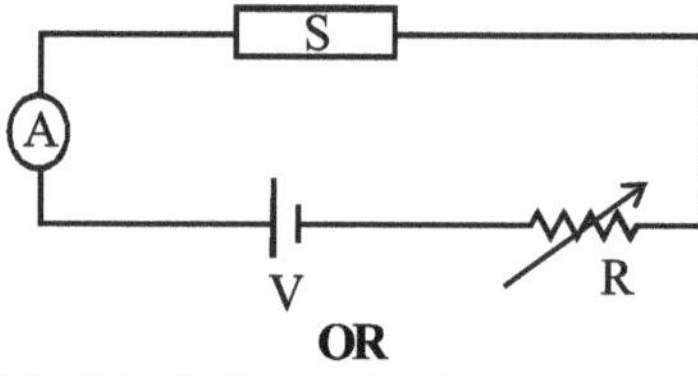

OR

The graph of potential barrier versus width of depletion region for an unbiased diode is shown in graph A. In comparison to A, graphs B and C are obtained after biasing the diode in different ways. Identify the type of biasing in B and C and justify your answer.

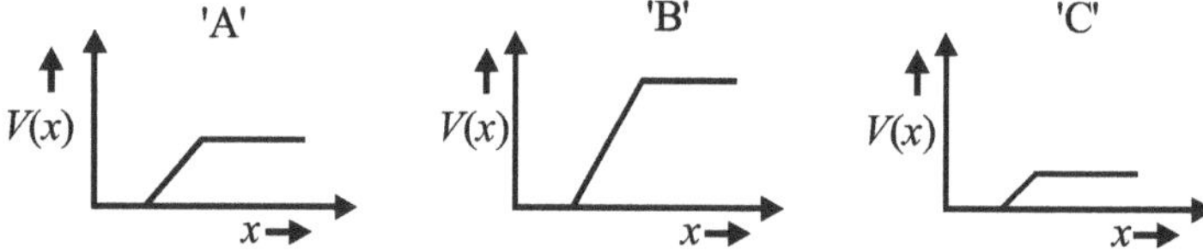

24. A narrow slit is illuminated by a parallel beam of monochromatic light of wavelength λ equal to 6000 Å and the angular width of the central maximum in the resulting diffraction pattern is measured. When the slit is next illuminated by light of wavelength λ', the angular width decreases by 30%. Calculate the value of the wavelength λ'.

25. Two large, thin metal plates are parallel and close to each other. On their inner faces, the plates have surface charge densities of opposite signs and of magnitude 17.7×10^{-22} C/m^2. What is electric field intensity E:

(a)   in the outer region of the first plate, and

(b)   between the plates?

SECTION-C

26. Two long straight parallel conductors carrying currents I_1 and I_2 are separated by a distance d. If the currents are flowing in the same direction, show how the magnetic field produced by one exerts an attractive force on the other. Obtain the expression for this force and hence define 1 ampere.

27. The magnetic field through a circular loop of wire, 12cm in radius and 8.5Ω resistance, changes with time as shown in the figure. The magnetic field is perpendicular to the plane of the loop. Calculate the current induced in the loop and plot a graph showing induced current as a function of time.

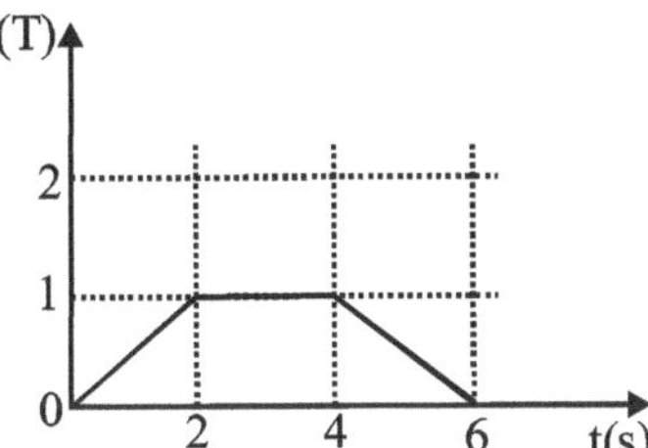

28. An a.c. source generating a voltage $\varepsilon = \varepsilon_0 \sin \omega t$ is connected to a capacitor of capacitance C. Find the expression for the current I flowing through it. Plot a graph of ε and I versus ωt to show that the current is ahead of the voltage by $\dfrac{\pi}{2}$.

OR

An ac voltage $V = V_0 \sin \omega t$ is applied across a pure inductor of inductance L. Find an expression for the current i, flowing in the circuit and show mathematically that the current flowing through it lags behind the applied voltage by a phase angle of $\dfrac{\pi}{2}$. Also draw graphs of V and i versus ωt for the circuit.

29. Radiation of frequency 10^{15} Hz is incident on three photosensitive surfaces A, B and C. Following observations are recorded:

Surface A: no photoemission occurs

Surface B: photoemission occurs but the photoelectrons have zero kinetic energy.

Surface C: photo emission occurs and photoelectrons have some kinetic energy.

Using Einstein's photo-electric equation, explain the three observations.

OR

The graph shows the variation of photocurrent for a photosensitive metal

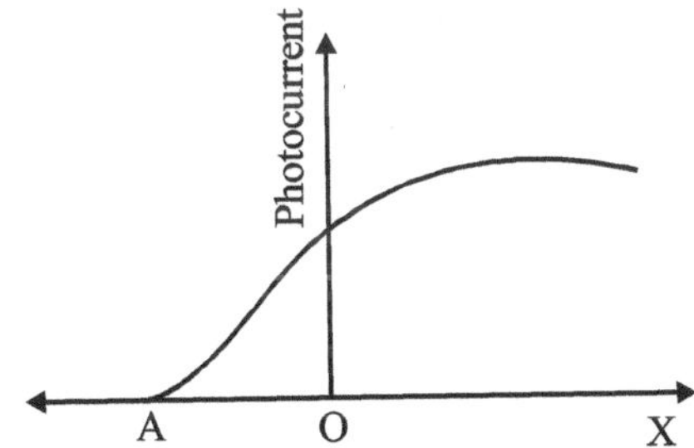

(a) What does X and A on the horizontal axis represent?

(b) Draw this graph for three different values of frequencies of incident radiation υ_1, υ_2 and υ_3 ($\upsilon_3 > \upsilon_2 > \upsilon_1$) for the same intensity.

(c) Draw this graph for three different values of intensities of incident radiation I_1, I_2 and I_3 ($I_3 > I_2 > I_1$) having the same frequency.

30. The ground state energy of hydrogen atom is -13.6 eV. The photon emitted during the transition of electron from n = 3 to n = 1 state, is incident on a photosensitive material of unknown work function. The photoelectrons are emitted from the material with the maximum kinetic energy of 9eV. Calculate the threshold wavelength of the material used.

SECTION-D

31. (a) Draw equipotential surfaces for (i) an electric dipole and (ii) two identical positive charges placed near each other.

(b) In a parallel plate capacitor with air between the plates, each plate has an area of $6 \times 10^{-3} \text{m}^2$ and the separation between the plates is 3 mm.

    (i) Calculate the capacitance of the capacitor.

    (ii) If the capacitor is connected to 100V supply, what would be the charge on each plate?

(iii) How would charge on the plate be affected if a 3 mm thick mica sheet of k = 6 is inserted between the plates while the voltage supply remains connected ?

OR

(a) Three charges –q, Q and –q are placed at equal distances on a straight line. If the potential energy of the system of these charges is zero, then what is the ratio Q:q?

(b) (i) Obtain the expression for the electric field intensity due to a uniformly charged spherical shell of radius R at a point distant r from the centre of the shell outside it.

(ii) Draw a graph showing the variation of electric field intensity E with r, for r > R and r < R.

32. (a) Explain the term drift velocity of electrons in a conductor. Hence obtain the expression for the current through a conductor in terms of drift velocity.

(b) Two cells of emfs E_1 and E_2 and internal resistances r_1 and r_2 respectively are connected in parallel as shown in the figure.

Deduce the expression for the
(i) equivalent emf of the combination
(ii) equivalent internal resistance of the combination
(iii) potential difference between the points A and B.

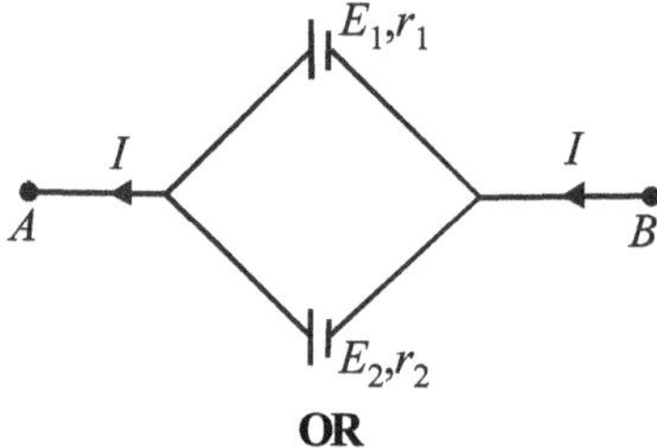

OR

(a) State the two Kirchhoff's rules used in the analysis of electric circuits and explain them.

(b) Derive the equation of the balanced state in a Wheatstone bridge using Kirchhoff's laws.

33. (a) Draw the graph showing intensity distribution of fringes with phase angle due to diffraction through a single slit. What is the width of the central maximum in comparison to that of a secondary maximum?

(b) A ray PQ is incident normally on the face AB of a triangular prism of refracting angle 60° as shown in figure.

The prism is made of a transparent material of refractive index $\dfrac{2}{\sqrt{3}}$. Trace the path of the ray as it passes through the prism. Calculate the angle of emergence and the angle of deviation.

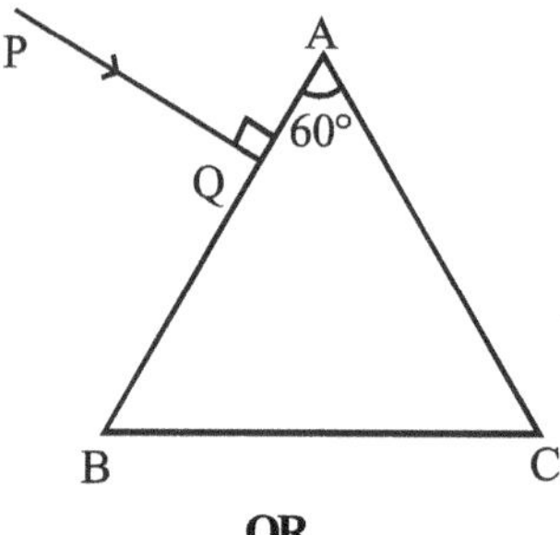

OR

(a) Write two points of difference between an interference pattern and a diffraction pattern.

(b) (i) A ray of light incident on face AB of an equilateral glass prism, shows minimum deviation of 30°. Calculate the speed of light through the prism.

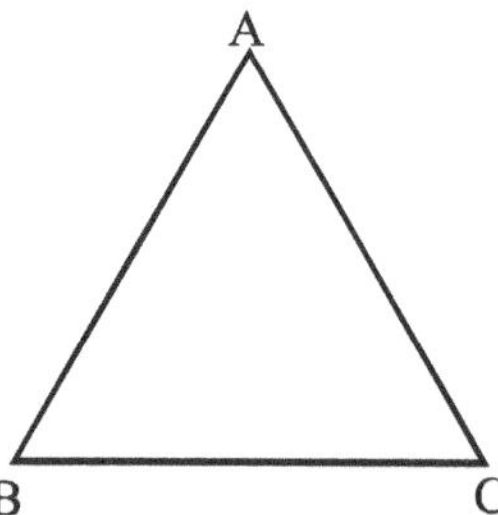

(ii) Find the angle of incidence at face AB so that the emergent ray grazes along the face AC.

SECTION-E

34. **Case Study :**
Read the following paragraph and answer the questions.
A number of optical devices and instruments have been designed and developed such as periscope, binoculars, microscopes and telescopes utilising the reflecting and refracting properties of mirrors, lenses and prisms. Most of them are in common use. Our knowledge about the formation of images by the mirrors and lenses is the basic requirement for understanding the working of these devices.
(i) Why the image formed at infinity is often considered most suitable for viewing. Explain
(ii) In modern microscopes multicomponent lenses are used for both the objective and the eyepiece. Why?
(iii) Write two points of difference between a compound microscope and an astronomical telescope
OR

(iii) Write two distinct advantages of a reflecting type telescope over a refracting type telescope.

35. **Case study: Light emitting diode.**
Read the following paragraph and answer the questions.
LED is a heavily doped P-N junction which under forward bias emits spontaneous radiation. When it is forward biased, due to recombination of holes and electrons at the junction, energy is released in the form of photons. In the case of Si and Ge diode, the energy released in recombination lies in the infrared region. LEDs that can emit red, yellow, orange, green and blue light are commercially available. The semiconductor used for fabrication of visible LEDs must at least have a band gap of 1.8 eV. The compound semiconductor Gallium Arsenide – Phosphide is used for making LEDs of different colours.

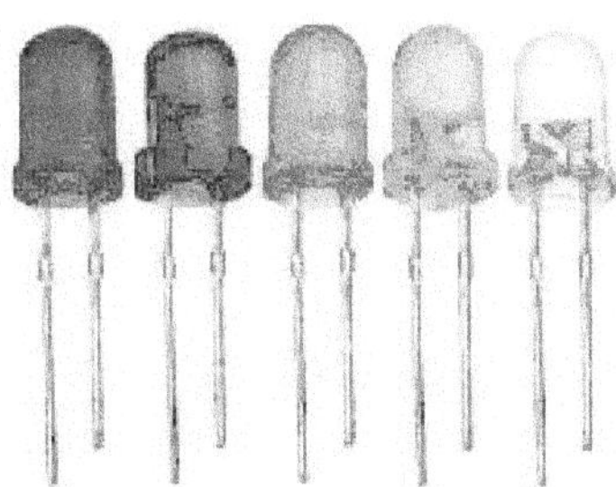

LEDs of different kinds
(i) Why are LEDs made of compound semiconductor and not of elemental semiconductors?
(ii) What should be the order of bandgap of an LED, if it is required to emit light in the visible range?
(iii) A student connects the blue coloured LED as shown in the figure.
The LED did not glow when switch S is closed. Explain why ?

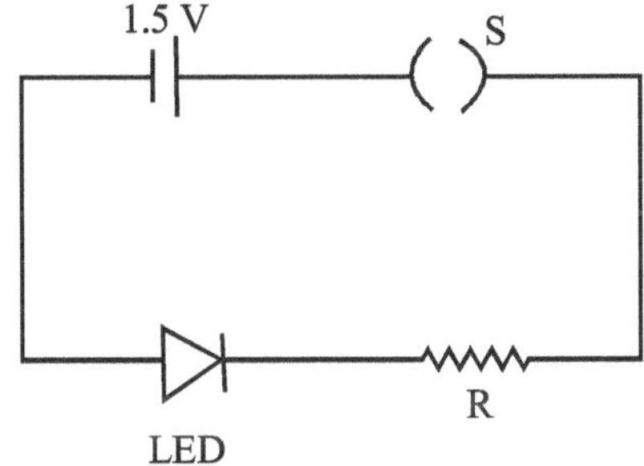

OR

(iii) Draw V-I characteristic of a p-n junction diode in
(i) forward bias and (ii) reverse bias

SOLUTIONS

1. **(b)** $q_1q_2 < 0$ [1 mark]
2. **(d)** Zero   [1 mark]
3. **(b)** Material A is germanium and material B is copper   [1 mark]
4. **(d)** 6A in the clockwise direction   [1 mark]
5. **(c)** 4:3   [1 mark]
6. **(a)** Decreases   [1 mark]
7. **(b)** Increase   [1 mark]
8. **(d)** Both electric and magnetic field vectors are parallel to each other.   [1 mark]
9. **(b)** The circular and elliptical loops   [1 mark]
10. **(d)** 0.85   [1 mark]
11. **(c)** 3000 Å   [1 mark]
12. **(d)** 4.77×10^{-10} m   [1 mark]
13. **(b)** The nuclear force is much weaker than the Coulomb force.   [1 mark]
14. **(a)** 30 V   [1 mark]
15. **(a)**   [1 mark]
16. **(c)** A is true but R is false   [1 mark]
17. **(c)** A is true but R is false   [1 mark]
18. **(a)** Both A and R are true and R is the correct explanation of A   [1 mark]
19. λ_1 - Microwave   [½ mark]

    λ_2 - ultraviolet   [½ mark]

    λ_3 - infrared   [½ mark]

    Ascending order - $\lambda_2 < \lambda_3 < \lambda_1$ [½ mark]
20. A - diamagnetic   [½ mark]

    B - paramagnetic   [½ mark]

    The magnetic susceptibility of A is small negative and that of B is small positive.   [1 mark]
21. From the relation $R = R_0 A^{1/3}$, where R_0 is a constant and A is the mass number of a nucleus   [½ mark]

    $$R_{Fe}/R_{Al} = (A_{Fe}/A_{Al})^{1/3}$$
    $$= (125/27)^{1/3}$$ [½ mark]
    $$R_{Fe} = 5/3 \, R_{Al}$$
    $$= 5/3 \times 3.6$$ [½ mark]
    $$= 6 \text{ fermi}$$ [½ mark]

    OR

    Given short wavelength limit of Lyman series

    $$\frac{1}{\lambda_L} = R\left(\frac{1}{1^2} - \frac{1}{\infty}\right)$$

    $$\frac{1}{913.4 \,\overset{\circ}{A}} = R\left(\frac{1}{1^2} - \frac{1}{\infty}\right)$$ [½ mark]

    $$\lambda_L = \frac{1}{R} = 913.4 \, Å$$ [½ mark]

    For the short wavelength limit of Balmer series
    $n_1 = 2, n_2 = \infty$ [½ mark]

$$\frac{1}{\lambda_B} = R\left(\frac{1}{2^2} - \frac{1}{\infty}\right)$$

$$\lambda_B = \frac{4}{R} = 4 \times 913.4 \, Å$$ [½ mark]
$$= 3653.6 \, Å$$

22. $$\frac{1}{f} = (\mu - 1)\left(\frac{1}{R_1} - \frac{1}{R_2}\right)$$ [½ mark]

    $$\frac{1}{f} = \left(\frac{\mu_m}{\mu_w} - 1\right)\left(\frac{1}{R_1} - \frac{1}{R_2}\right)$$ [½ mark]

    $$\frac{\mu_m}{\mu_w} = \frac{1.25}{1.33}$$

    $$\frac{\mu_m}{\mu_w} = 0.98$$ [½ mark]

    The value of $(\mu - 1)$ is negative and 'f' will be negative. So it will behave like diverging lens.   [½ mark]
23. To keep the reading of ammeter constant value of R   [1 mark]

    should be **increased** as with the increase in temperature of a semiconductor, its resistance **decreases** and current tends to increase.   [1 mark]

    OR

    B - reverse biased : In the case of reverse biased diode   [½ mark]
    the potential barrier becomes higher as the battery further raises the potential of the n side.   [½ mark]
    C - forward biased : Due to forward bias connection the   [½ mark]
    potential of P side is raised and hence the height of the potential barrier decreases.   [½ mark]
24. Angular width $2\varphi = 2\lambda/d$ [½ mark]
    Given $\lambda = 6000$ Å
    In Case of new λ (assumed λ' here), angular width decreases by 30%   [½ mark]
    New angular width $= 0.70 \,(2\varphi)$ [½ mark]
    $2\lambda'/d = 0.70 \times (2\lambda/d)$
    $\therefore \lambda' = 4200$ Å   [½ mark]
25.

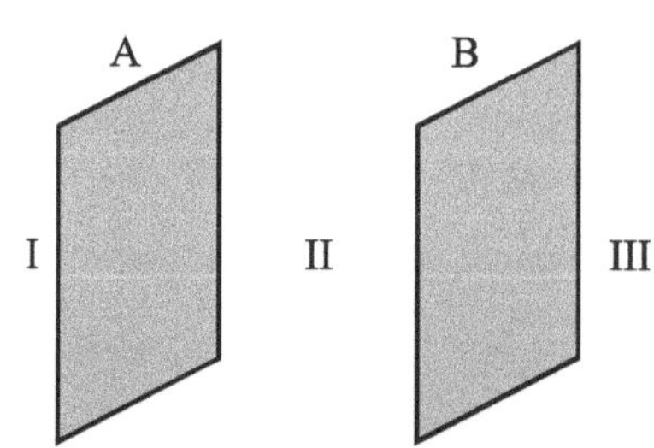

Surface charge density of plate A $= +17.7 \times 10^{-22}$ C/m^2
Surface charge density of plate B $= -17.7 \times 10^{-22}$ C/m^2

(a) In the outer region of plate I, electric field intensity E is zero. [½ mark]

(b) Electric field intensity E in between the plates is given by relation [½ mark]

$$E = \frac{\sigma}{\epsilon_0}$$

Where,
ϵ_0 = Permittivity of free space = $8.85 \times 10^{-12}\,N^{-1}\,C^2\,m^{-2}$

$$\therefore E = \frac{17.7 \times 10^{-22}}{8.85 \times 10^{-1}}$$ [½ mark]

Therefore, electric field between the plates is 2.0×10^{-10} N/C [½ mark]

26. Diagram [½ mark]

Derivation [1/½ marks]

The ampere is the value of that steady current which, when maintained in each of the two very long, straight, parallel conductors of negligible cross-section, and placed one metre apart in vacuum, would exert on each of these conductors a force equal to 2×10^{-7} newtons per metre of length. [1 mark]

27. Area of the circular loop = πr^2
= $3.14 \times (0.12)^2\,m^2 = 4.5 \times 10^{-2}\,m^2$

$$E = -\frac{d\varphi}{dt} = -\frac{d}{dt}(BA) = -A\frac{dB}{dt} = -A \cdot \frac{B_2 - B_1}{t_2 - t_1}$$ [½ mark]

For $0 < t < 2s$

$$E_1 = -4.5 \times 10^{-2} \times \left\{\frac{1-0}{2-0}\right\} = -2.25 \times 10^{-2}\,V$$

$$\therefore I_1 = \frac{E_1}{R} = \frac{-2.25 \times 10^{-2}}{8.5}\,A = -2.6 \times 10^{-3}\,A = -2.6\,mA$$ [½ mark]

For $2s < t < 4s$,

$$E_2 = -4.5 \times 10^{-2} \times \left\{\frac{1-1}{4-2}\right\} = 0$$ [½ mark]

$$\therefore I_2 = \frac{E_2}{R} = 0$$

For $4s < t < 6s$,

$$I_3 = -\frac{4.5 \times 10^{-2}}{8.5} \times \left\{\frac{0-1}{6-4}\right\}\,A = 2.6\,mA$$ [½ mark]

	$0<t<2s$	$2<t<4s$	$4<t<6s$
E(V)	−0.023	0	+0.023
I(mA)	−2.6	0	+2.6

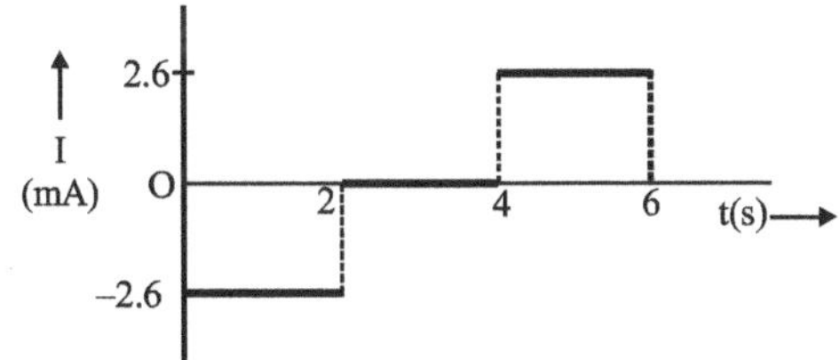

28. Derivation [2 marks]

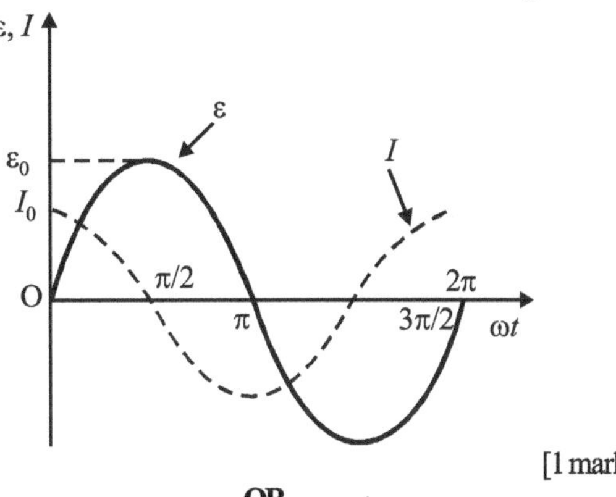

[1 mark]

OR

Derivation [2 marks]

[1 mark]

29. From the observations made (parts A and B) on the basis of Einstein's photoelectric equation, we can draw following conclusions:

1. For surface A, the threshold frequency is more than 10^{15} HZ, hence no photoemission is possible. [1 mark]

2. For surface B the threshold frequency is equal to the frequency of given radiation. Thus, photo-emission takes place but kinetic energy of photoelectrons is zero. [1 mark]

3. For surface C, the threshold frequency is less than 10^{15} Hz. So photoemission occurs and photoelectrons have some kinetic energy [1 mark]

OR

(a) A - cut off or stopping potential [½ mark]
X - anode potential [½ mark]

(b)

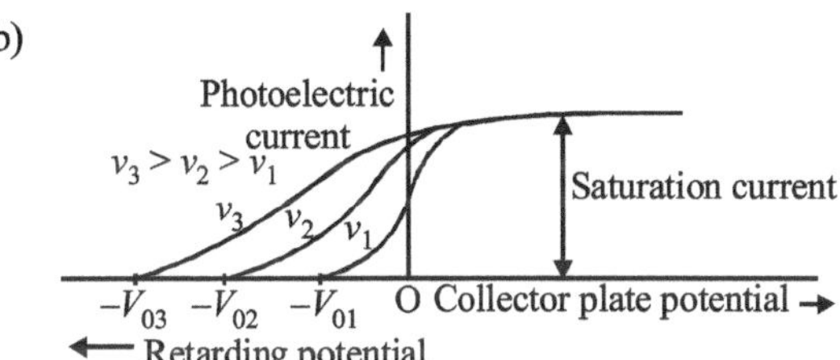

[1 mark]

Figure Variation of photoelectric current with collector plate potential for different frequencies of incident radiation.

(c)

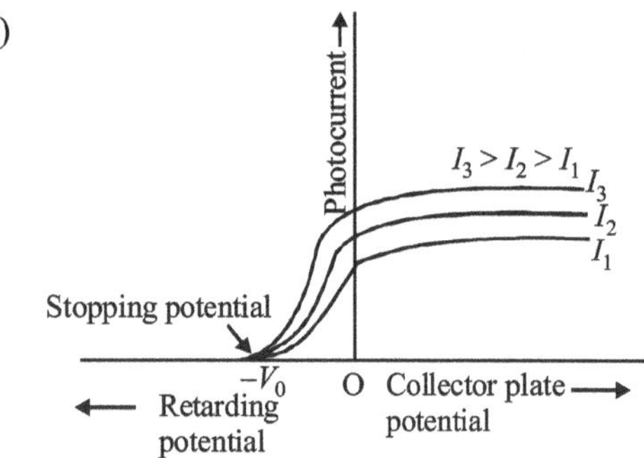

[1 mark]

Figure Variation of photocurrent with collector plate potential for different intensity of incident radiation.

30. For a transition from n = 3 to n = 1 state, the energy of the emitted photon, [1 mark]

$$hv = E_2 - E_1 = 13.6\left[\frac{1}{1^2} - \frac{1}{3^2}\right] eV = 12.1 \text{ eV}.$$ [½ mark]

From Einstein's photoelectric equation,
$$hv = K_{max} + W_0$$
$$\therefore W_0 = hv - K_{max} = 12.1 - 9 = 3.1 \ eV$$ [½ mark]
Threshold wavelength,

$$\lambda_{th} = \frac{hc}{W_0} = \frac{6.62 \times 10^{-34} \times 3 \times 10^8}{3.1 \times 1.6 \times 10^{-19}} = 4 \times 10^{-7} \text{m}$$ [1 mark]

31. (a)

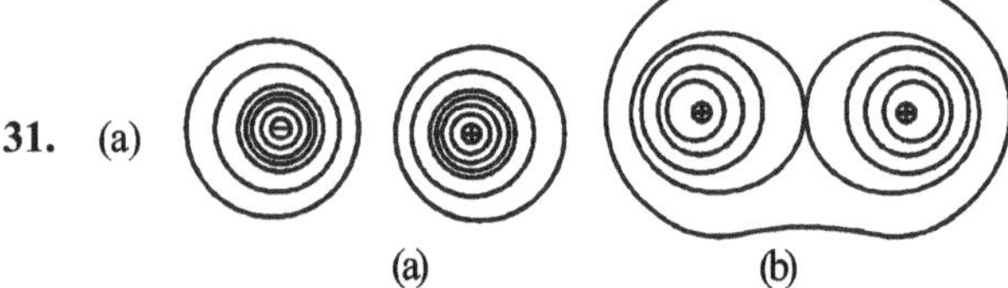

(a)   (b)

Figure 2.11 Some equipotential surfaces for (a) a dipole, (b) two identical positive charges.

Here, A = 6×10^{-3} m^2, d = 3mm = 3×10^{-3}m [2 marks]

(b) (i) Capacitance, C = $\in_0$A/d = (8.85 × 10^{-12} × 6 × 10^{-3}/3 × 10^{-3}) = 17.7 × 10^{-12} F [1 mark]

(ii) Charge, Q = CV = 17.7 × 10^{-12} × 100 = 17.7 × 10^{-10}C [1 mark]

(iii) New charge Q' = KQ = 6 × 17.7 × 10^{-10} = 1.062 × 10^{-8} C [1 mark]

OR

(a) Diagram [½ mark]

$$\frac{K(-q)Q}{x} + \frac{kQ(-q)}{x} + \frac{k(-q)(-q)}{2x} = 0$$ [1 mark]

$$\frac{-2kqQ}{x} + \frac{kq^2}{2x} = 0 \text{ or } \frac{kq^2}{2x} = \frac{2kqQ}{x}$$

$$q = 4Q \text{ or } \frac{Q}{q} = \frac{1}{4}$$ [½ mark]

(b) Electric field due to a uniformly charged thin spherical shell:

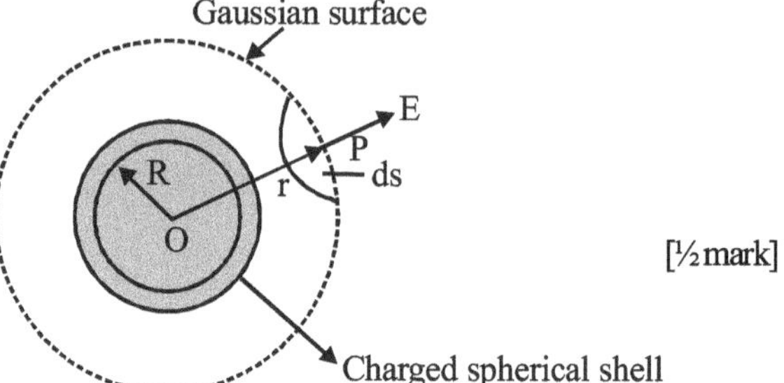

[½ mark]

(i) When point P lies outside the spherical shell: Suppose that we have calculate field at the point P at a distance r (r > R) from its centre. Draw Gaussian surface through point P so as to enclose the charged spherical shell. Gaussian surface is a spherical surface of radius r and centre O.

Let $\vec{E}$ be the electric field at point P, then the electric flux through area element of area $\vec{ds}$ is given by
$$d\varphi = \vec{E} \cdot \vec{ds}$$ [½ mark]
Since $\vec{ds}$ is also along normal to the surface
$$d\varphi = E \, dS$$
∴ Total electric flux through the Gaussian surface is given by

$$\varphi = \oint Eds = E\oint ds$$

Now, $\oint ds = 4\pi r^2$ ...(i)
$$= E \times 4\pi r^2$$
Since the charge enclosed by the Gaussian surface is q, according to the Gauss's theorem,

$$\varphi = \frac{q}{\in_0}$$ ...(ii) [½ mark]

From equation (i) and (ii) we obtain

$$E \times 4\pi r^2 = \frac{q}{\in_0}$$ [½ mark]

$$E = \frac{1}{4\pi \in_0} \cdot \frac{q}{r^2} \text{ (for r > R)}$$ [½ mark]

(ii) A graph showing the variation of electric held as a function of *r* is shown below.

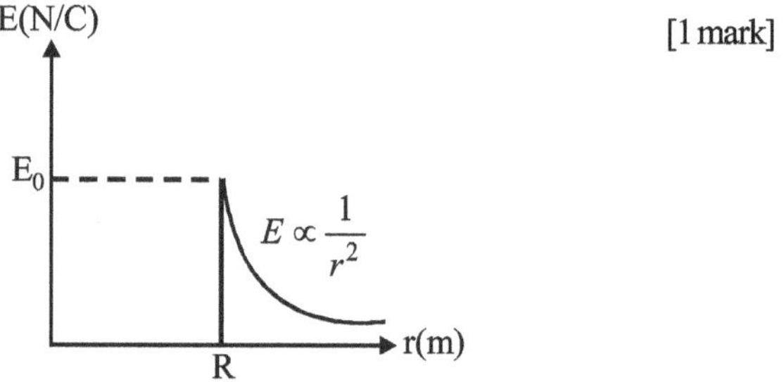

[1 mark]

32. (a) **Drift velocity:** It is the average velocity acquired by the free electrons superimposed over the random motion in the direction opposite to electric field and along the length of the metallic conductor. [2 marks]

Derivation $I = neAV_d$

(b) Here, $I = I_1 + I_2$ ...(i)

Let V = Potential difference between A and B.

For cell ε_1

Then, $V = \varepsilon_1 - I_1 r_1 \Rightarrow I_1 = \dfrac{\varepsilon_1 - V}{r_1}$ [3 marks]

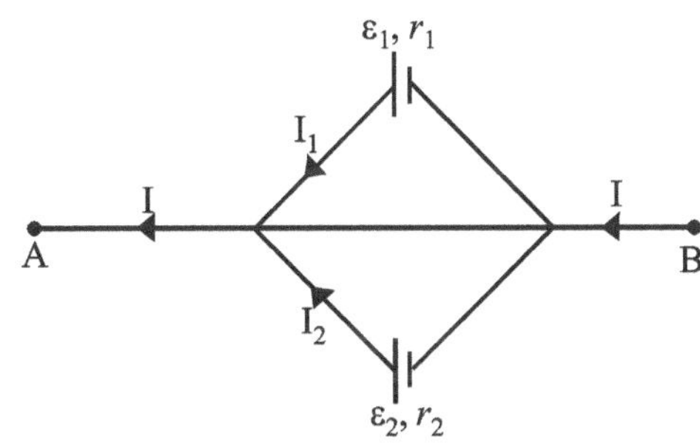

Similarly, for cell ε_2 $I_2 = \dfrac{\varepsilon_2 - V}{r_2}$

Putting these values in equation (i)

$$I = \frac{\varepsilon_1 - V}{r_1} + \frac{\varepsilon_2 - V}{r_2}$$

or $I = \left(\dfrac{\varepsilon_1}{r_1} + \dfrac{\varepsilon_2}{r_2}\right) - V\left(\dfrac{1}{r_1} + \dfrac{1}{r_2}\right)$

or $V = \left(\dfrac{\varepsilon_1 r_2 + \varepsilon_2 r_1}{r_1 + r_2}\right) - I\left(\dfrac{r_1 r_2}{r_1 + r_2}\right)$ ...(ii)

Comparting the above equation with the equivalent circuit of emf 'ε_{eq}' and internal resistance 'r_{eq}' then,

$V = \varepsilon_{eq} - I r_{eq}$ ...(iii)

Then

(i) $\varepsilon_{eq} = \dfrac{\varepsilon_1 r_2 + \varepsilon_2 r_1}{r_1 + r_2}$

(ii) $r_{eq} = \dfrac{r_1 r_2}{r_1 + r_2}$

(iii) The potential difference between A and B

$V = \varepsilon_{eq} - I r_{eq}$

OR

(a) Junction rule: At any junction, the sum of the currents entering the junction is equal to the sum of currents leaving the junction. [1 mark]

Loop rule: The algebraic sum of changes in potential around any closed loop involving resistors and cells in the loop is zero. [1 mark]

(b) Derivation [3 marks]

33. (a)

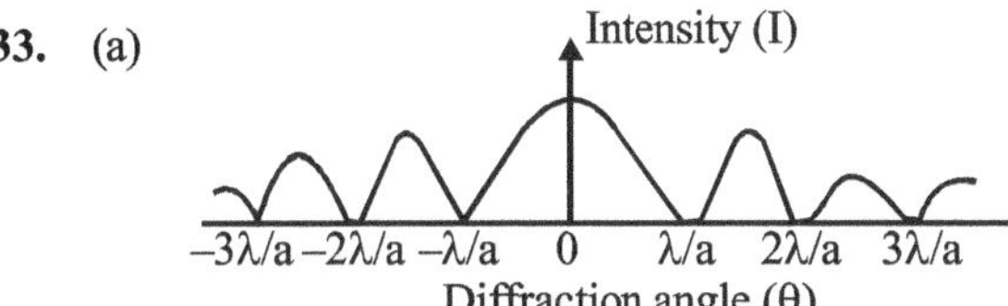

[1 mark]

Width of central maximum is twice that of any secondary maximum [1 mark]

(b)

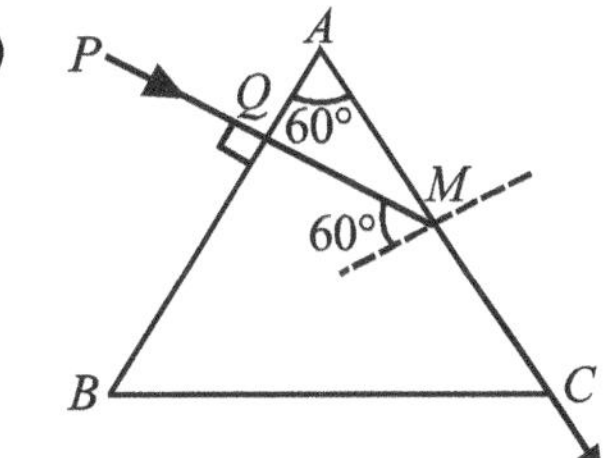

Given : $\angle A = 60°$, $\angle i = 0°$

At M : $\sin C = \dfrac{1}{\mu} = \dfrac{\sqrt{3}}{2} = \sin 60°$

$\therefore$ C = 60° [1 mark]

So the ray PM after refraction from the face AC grazes along AC.

$\therefore$ $\angle e = 90°$

From $\angle i + \angle e = \angle A + \angle \delta$

or $0° + 90° = 60° + \angle \delta$

$\therefore$ $\delta = 90° - 60° = 30°$ [1 mark]

OR

(a) (i) The interference pattern has a number of equally spaced bright and dark bands. The diffraction pattern has a central bright maximum which is twice as wide as the other maxima. The intensity falls as we go to successive maxima away from the centre, on either side. [1 mark]

(ii) We calculate the interference pattern by superposing two waves originating from the two narrow slits. The diffraction pattern is a superposition of a continuous family of waves originating from each point on a single slit. [1 mark]

(b) (i) $\mu = \dfrac{\sin\left(\dfrac{A + \delta_m}{2}\right)}{\sin\left(\dfrac{A}{2}\right)} = \dfrac{\sin\left(\dfrac{60 + 30}{2}\right)}{\sin\left(\dfrac{60°}{2}\right)} = \sqrt{2}$

[1/½ marks]

Also $\mu = \dfrac{c}{\upsilon} \Rightarrow \upsilon = \dfrac{3 \times 10^8}{\sqrt{2}} m/s$

(ii) At face AC, let the angle of incidence be r_2. For grazing ray, [1/½ marks]

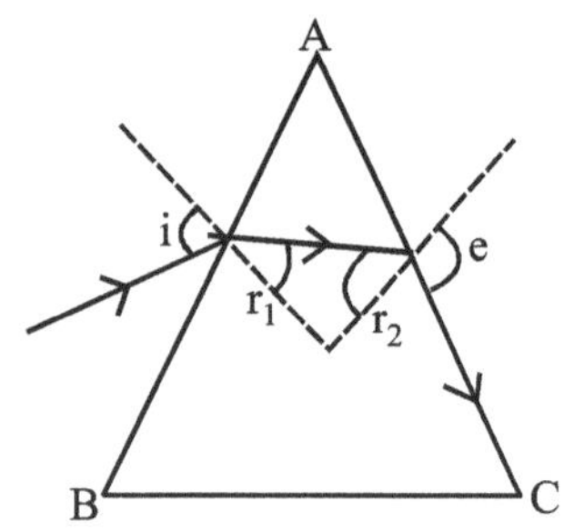

$e = 90°$

$$\Rightarrow \mu = \frac{1}{\sin r_2} \Rightarrow r_2 = \sin^{-1}\left(\frac{1}{\sqrt{2}}\right) = 45°$$

Let angle of refraction at face AB be r_1.
Now $r_1 + r_2 = A$
$\therefore r_1 = A - r_2 = 60° - 45° = 15°$
Let angle of incidence at this face be i

$$\mu = \frac{\sin i}{\sin r_1} \Rightarrow \sqrt{2} = \frac{\sin i}{\sin 15°}$$

$$\therefore i = \sin^{-1}\left(\sqrt{2} \cdot \sin 15°\right) = 21.5°$$

34. (i) When the image is formed at infinity, we can see it with minimum strain in the ciliary muscles of the eye. **[1 mark]**

(ii) The multi-component lenses are used for both objective and the eyepiece to improve image quality by minimising various optical aberrations in lenses. **[1 mark]**

(iii) (a) The compound microscope is used to observe minute nearby objects whereas the telescope is used to observe distant objects. **[1 mark]**
(b) In compound microscope the focal length of the objective is lesser than that of the eyepiece whereas in telescope the focal length of the objective is larger than that of the eyepiece. **[1 mark]**

OR

(iii) (a) The image formed by reflecting type telescope is brighter than that formed by refracting telescope.

[1 mark]

(b) The image formed by the reflecting type telescope is more magnified than that formed by the refracting type telescope. **[1 mark]**

35. (i) LEDs are made up of compound semiconductors and not by the elemental conductor because the band gap in the elemental conductor has a value that can detect the light of a wavelength which lies in the infrared (IR) region.

[1 mark]

(ii) 1.8 eV to 3 eV **[1 mark]**
(iii) LED is reversed biased that is why it is not glowing. **[2 marks]**

OR

(iii) V-I Characteristic curves of pn-junction diode in forward biasing and reverse biasing. **[2 marks]**

All India 2022
CBSE Board Solved Paper
Term-II

Time Allowed : 2 Hours   *Maximum Marks : 35*

General Instructions:

(i) There are **12** questions in all. All questions are compulsory.

(ii) This question paper has three sections : Section A, Section B and Section C.

(iii) Section A contains three questions of two marks each, Section B contains eight questions of three marks each, Section C contains one case study-based question of five marks.

(iv) There is no overall choice. However, an internal choice has been provided in one question of two marks and two questions of three marks. You have to attempt only one of the choices in such questions.

(v) You may use log tables if necessary but use of calculator is not allowed.

1. (a) (i) Distinguish between isotopes and isobars. **2**

    (ii) Two nuclei have different mass numbers A_1 and A_2. Are these nuclei necessarily the isotopes of the same element? Explain.

OR

(b) (i) Name the factors on which photoelectric emission from a surface depends.

    (ii) Define the term 'threshold frequency' for a photosensitive material.

2. Explain the formation of the barrier potential in a p-n junction. **2**

3. Name the extrinsic semiconductors formed when a pure germanium is doped with (i) a trivalent and (ii) pentavalent impurity. Draw the energy band diagrams of extrinsic semiconductors so formed. **2**

4. (a) Write two necessary conditions for total internal reflection.

(b) Two prisms ABC and DBC are arranged as shown in figure.

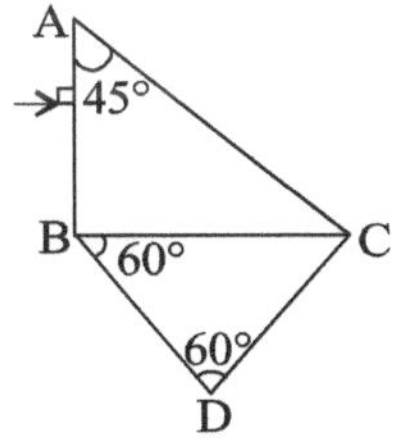

The critical angles for the two prisms with respect to air are 41.1° and 45° respectively. Trace the path of the ray through the combination. **3**

OR

(a) An object is placed in front of a converging lens. Obtain the conditions under which the magnification produced by the lens is (i) negative and (ii) positive.

(b) A point object is placed at O in front of a glass sphere as shown in figure.

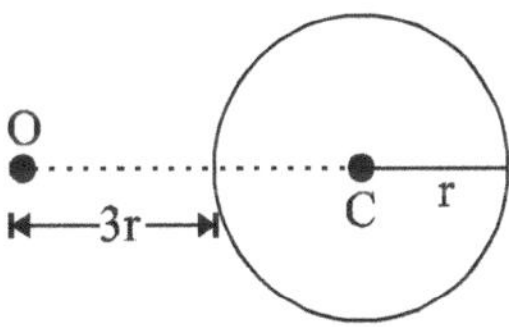

Show the formation of image by the sphere.

5. The work function of a metal is 2.31 eV. Photoelectric emission occurs when light of frequency 6.4×10^{14} Hz is incident on the metal surface. Calculate:

(i) the energy of the incident radiation, (ii) the maximum kinetic energy of the emitted electron and (iii) the stopping potential of the surface. **3**

6. A beam of light consisting of two wavelengths 600 nm and 500 nm is used in a Young's double slit experiment. The slit separation is 1.0 mm and the screen is kept 0.60 m away from the plane of the slits. Calculate:

(i) the distance of the second bright fringe from the central maximum for wavelength 500 nm, and

(ii) the least distance from the central maximum where the bright fringes due to both the wavelengths coincide. **3**

7. Electromagnetic waves of wavelengths λ_1, λ_2 and λ_3 are used in radar systems, in water purifiers and in remote switches of TV, respectively.

    (i) Identify the electromagnetic waves, and

    (ii) Write one source of each of them.   **3**

OR

    (i) State two conditions for two light sources to be coherent.

    (ii) Give two points of difference between an interference pattern due to a double – slit and a diffraction pattern due to a single slit.

8. In a diffraction pattern due to a single slit, how will the angular width of central maximum change, if

    (i) Orange light is used in place of green light,

    (ii) the screen is moved closer to the slit,

    (iii) the slit width is decreased?

Justify your answer in each case.   **3**

9. Briefly explain how emf is generated in a solar cell. Draw its I-V characteristics.   **3**

10. (a) James Chadwick, in 1932, studied the emission of neutral radiations when Beryllium nuclei were bombarded with alpha particles. He concluded that emitted radiations were neutrons and not photons. Explain.

    (b) Two nuclei may have the same radius, even though they contain different number of protons and neutrons. Explain.   **3**

11. (a) The energy of hydrogen atom in an orbit is -1.51 eV. What are kinetic and potential energies of the electron in this orbit?

    (b) The electron in a hydrogen atom is typically found at a distance of about 5.3×10^{-11} m from the nucleus which has a diameter of about 1.0×10^{-15} m. Assuming the hydrogen atom to be a sphere of radius 5.3×10^{-11} m, what fraction of its volume is occupied by the nucleus?   **3**

SECTION - C
CASE STUDY

12. A compound microscope consists of two converging lenses. One of them, of smaller aperture and smaller focal length is called objective and the other of slightly larger aperture and slightly larger focal length is called eye-piece. Both the lenses are fitted in a tube with an arrangement to vary the distance between them. A tiny object is placed in front of the objective at a distance slightly greater than its focal length. The objective produces the image of the object which acts as an object for the eye-piece. The eye piece, in turn produces the final magnified image.

$1 \times 5 = 5$

I. In a compound microscope the images formed by the objective and the eye-piece are respectively

    (a) virtual, real   (b) real, virtual

    (c) virtual, virtual   (d) real, real

II. The magnification due to a compound microscope *does not* depend upon

    (a) the aperture of the objective and the eye-piece

    (b) the focal length of the objective and the eye-piece

    (c) the length of the tube

    (d) the colour of the light used

III. Which of the following is *not correct* in the context of a compound microscope?

    (a) Both the lenses are of short focal lengths.

    (b) The magnifying power increases by decreasing the focal lengths of the two lenses.

    (c) The distance between the two lenses is more than $(f_0 + f_e)$.

    (d) The microscope can be used as a telescope by interchanging the two lenses.

IV. A compound microscope consists of an objective of 10X and an eye-piece of 20X. The magnification due to the microscope would be

    (a) 2   (b) 10

    (c) 30   (d) 200

V. The focal lengths of objective and eye-piece of a compound microscope are 1.2 cm and 3.0 cm respectively. The object is placed at a distance of 1.25 cm from the objective. If the final image is formed at infinity, the magnifying power of the microscope would be

    (a) 100   (b) 150

    (c) 200   (d) 250

Solutions

1. (a) (i) Isotopes are the atomic species of same element differing in mass number(A) but same in atomic number(Z).

Isobars are the atomic species of same element with same mass number(A) but different atomic number(Z). **[1 Mark]**

> **Note**
>
> *Nuclei having different atomic number (Z) and mass number (A) but same number of neutrons N = (A – Z) is called isotones. For examples $_4Be^9$ and $_5B^{10}$; $_6C^{13}$ and $_7N^{14}$, etc.*

(ii) No, because different mass number may be due to different number of protons or neutrons. To be the isotopes of same element, protons number should be same. **[1 Mark]**

OR

(b) (i) The photoelectric emission from a surface depends on the frequency of incident light and nature of surface.

(ii) The minimum cut off frequency below which photoelectric effect doesn't take place is called threshold frequency. **[1 + 1 Mark]**

2. Formation of barrier potential in a P-n junction :

Electrons diffuse from n → p and holes diffuse from p → n side leaving a positively charged donor atom on n–side and negatively charged acceptor atom on p–side. This space charge region on either side is called depletion region. Near the junction this region depletes the movement of free charges. Hence, electric field due to positive space charge on n–side and negative space charge on p–side is created. Due to this electrons and holes now drift in opposite direction in this field and further extend this region.

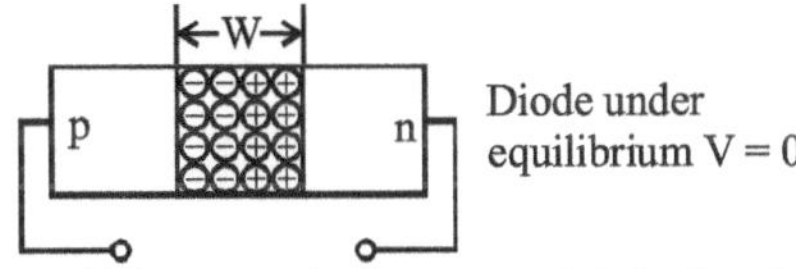

Thus a different polarity potential is developed which prevents movement of electron from n–region to p–region, called **barrier potential** and there is no net current. **[2 Marks]**

3. When pure germanium is doped with a trivalent impurity, p-type semiconductor is formed. When pure germanium is doped with a pentavalent impurity, n-type semicoductor is formed. **[1 Mark]**

Energy band diagram

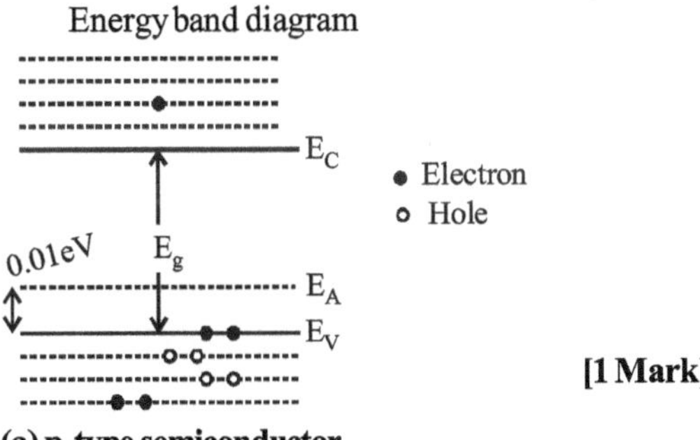

[1 Mark]

(a) p-type semiconductor

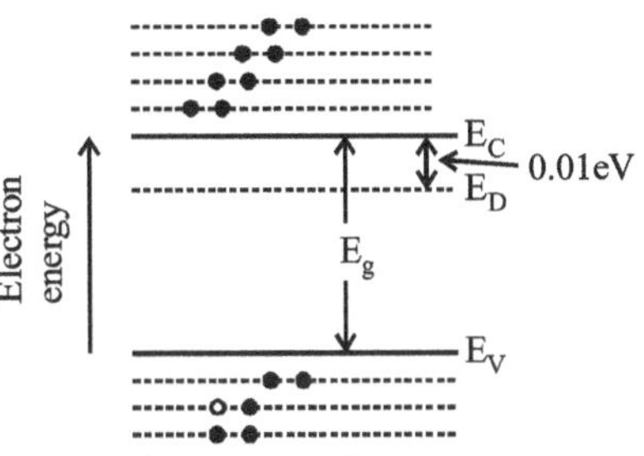

(b) n-type semiconductor

4. (a) Conditions for Total Internal Reflection

(i) The ray of light must travel from denser to rarer medium.

(ii) The angle of incidence must be greater than critical angle **[1 Mark]**

(b) Total internal reflection will take place at points A and B as angle of incidence at both points are greater than critical angle. When ray strikes surface finally at 90° to surface it will emerge out undeviated. **[2 Marks]**

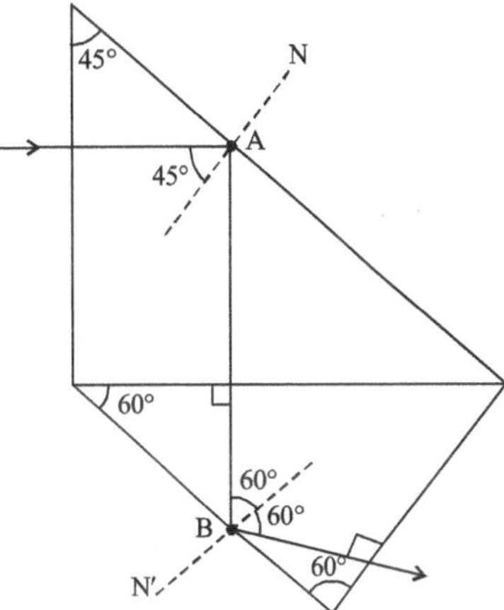

> **Note**
>
> *Brilliance of diamond is due to total internal reflection of light inside them. The critical angle for diamond – air interface $\cong$ 24.4° is very small. By cutting the diamond suitably, multiple total internal reflections can be made to occur.*

OR

(a) When an object is placed between focus (F) and pole (P) of converging lens, the magnification produced by lens is positive. In all other positions of object the magnification produce by converging lens is negative. **[1½ Marks]**

(b) Image formation by the sphere

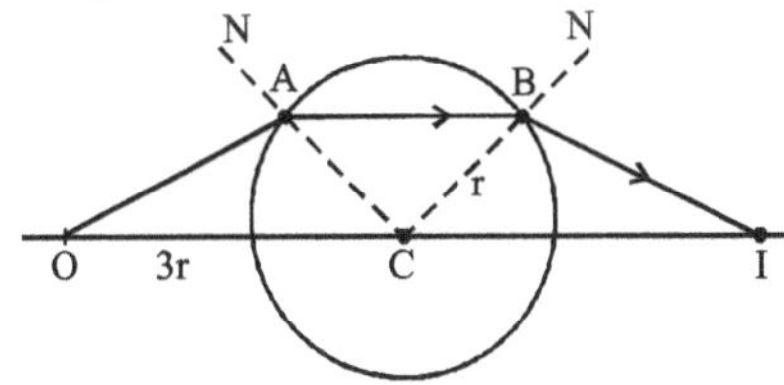

N and N′ are normals at the point of incidences. Rays will Obey laws of refraction at point A refracted ray moves towards N and at point B refracted rays move away from N′. **[1½ Marks]**

5. Given,

Work function of metal, $\phi = 2.31\,eV$

Frequency of incident light, $\nu = 6.4 \times 10^{14}\,Hz$

(a) Energy of incident radiation, $E = h\nu$
$$= 6.63 \times 10^{-34} \times 6.4 \times 10^{14}$$
$$= 42.43 \times 10^{-20}\,J \qquad \textbf{[1 Mark]}$$

(b) Using Einstein's photoelectric equation
$$E = \phi_0 + K.E$$
$$\Rightarrow K.E = E - \phi_0 = \frac{42.43 \times 10^{-20}}{1.6 \times 10^{-19}} - 2.31\,eV$$
$$\Rightarrow K.E = 2.652\,eV - 2.31\,eV$$
$$= 0.34\,eV \qquad \textbf{[1 Mark]}$$

(c) $K.E = eV_0$
where, $V_0 =$ stopping potential
$$\therefore \quad V_0 = \frac{K.E}{e} = \frac{0.34\,eV}{e}$$
$$= 0.34\,V \qquad \textbf{[1 Mark]}$$

Note

Work function or threshold energy is the minimum energy of incident radiation, required to eject the electrons from metallic surface.

6. Given,

Slit separation, $d = 1\,mm = 1 \times 10^{-3}\,m$

Distance of screen from slits, $D = 0.60\,m$

(a) For wavelength, $\lambda_1 = 500\,nm$

Fringe width, $\beta = \dfrac{\lambda D}{d} = \dfrac{500 \times 10^{-9} \times 0.60}{1 \times 10^{-3}}$

$= 300 \times 10^{-6} = 0.3\,nm$

Distance of second bright fringe from central maximum = $2\beta = 2 \times 0.3\,nm = 0.6\,nm$ **[1½ Marks]**

(b) We know that for n^{th} bright fringe
$$x = \frac{n\lambda D}{d}$$

Here, x = common distance from bright fringes by both wavelength

$$x = \frac{n_1 \lambda_1 D}{d} = \frac{n_2 \lambda_2 D}{d}$$
$$\Rightarrow n_1 \lambda_1 = n_2 \lambda_2$$
$$\Rightarrow n_1 \times 600 \times 10^{-9} = n_2 \times 500 \times 10^{-9}$$
$$\Rightarrow 6n_1 = 5n_2 \Rightarrow \frac{n_1}{n_2} = \frac{5}{6}$$

$\therefore$ 5th bright fringe due to wavelength 600 nm coincides with 6 bright fringe due to wavelength 500 nm.

$$\therefore \quad x = \frac{5 \times 600 \times 10^{-9} \times 0.60}{1 \times 10^{-3}}$$

$= 0.18 \times 10^{-2}\,m = 0.18\,cm$ **[1½ Marks]**

7. (i) Electromagnetic wave of wavelength λ_1 is Radio wave. Electromagnetic wave of wavelength λ_2 is ultraviolet rays. Electromagnetic wave of wavelength λ_3 is Infrared waves. **[1½ Marks]**

(ii)

	Wave	Source of Production
λ_1	Radio wave	Produced by rapid acceleration and decelerations of electrons.
λ_2	Ultraviolet rays	Produced by movement of inner shell electrons from one energy level to a lower energy level.
λ_3	Infrared waves	Produced by vibration of atoms and molecules.

[1½ Marks]

OR

(i) Conditions for two light sources to be coherent
(a) Light should be obtained from a single source.
(b) Two sources should give monochromatic light.

[1 Mark]

(ii)

	Diffraction		Interference
1	The diffraction pattern has a central bright maximum which is twice as wide as other maxima.	1	The interference has a number of equally spaced bright and dark bands
2	The diffraction pattern is a superposition of waves originating from each point on a single slit.	2	The interference pattern is due to the superposition of waves emanating from the two narrow slits.

[2 Marks]

Note

Thin layer of oil on water surface and soap bubbles show various colours in white light due to interference of waves reflected from the two surfaces of the film.
In thin films interference takes place between the waves reflected from it's two surfaces and waves refracted through it.

8. We know that angular width of central maximum in diffraction pattern due to single slit is given by

Angular width, $\alpha = \dfrac{2\lambda}{a}$

Here, $\lambda =$ wavelength of light

a = width of slit

(i) Wavelength of orange light is greater than the wavelength of green light. Therefore, if orange light is used, the angular width will increase because angular width $\propto \lambda$.

[1 Mark]

(ii) Decrease of distance between the slit and the screen does not affect the angular width of central maximum.

[1 Mark]

(iii) If slit width (a) is decreased, the angular width will increase as angular width $\propto \dfrac{1}{a}$ **[1 Mark]**

9. The following 3 basic processes occur in generation of emf by a solar cell.

(i) **Generation** of electron hole pair due to light ($hv > E_g$) close to junction. **[½ Mark]**

(ii) **Separation** of electrons and holes due to electric field of depletion region (Electrons reach n–side, holes p–side). **[½ Mark]**

(iii) **Collection** electrons are collected by front contact and holes by back contact (p–side: positive, n–side: negative) giving rise to photovoltage. **[½ Mark]**

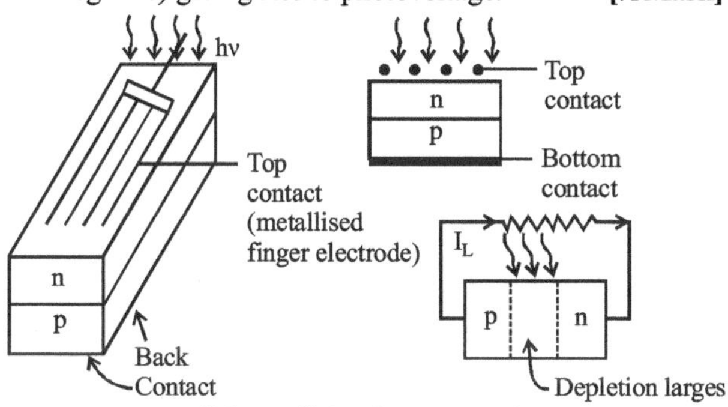

Solar cell (emf generation)

[½ Mark]

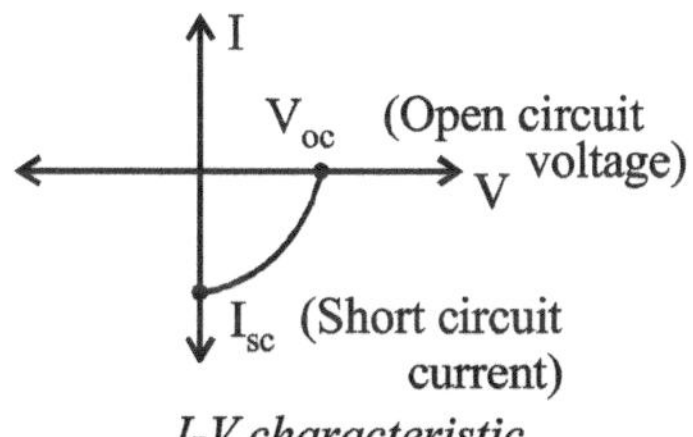

I-V characteristic

[1 Mark]

10. (a) James Chadwick observed emission of neutral radiation when beryllium nuclei were bombarded with alpha particles. He found neutral radiation could knock out protons from light nuclei such as those of helium, carbon and nitrogen. At that time, only neutral radiation was photons. Using principles of conservation of energy and momentum, he showed that if neutral radiation consisted of photons, the energy of photons would be much higher than the energy from bombardment of beryllium nuclei with α particles. It makes him assume that neutral radiation consists of new type of neutral particles called neutrons. Using conservation of energy and momentum, he was able to determine the mass of new particle (neutron) as very nearly the same as mass of proton. **[2 Marks]**

(b) If two nuclei have same sum of number of protons and neutrons, then they will have same mass number (A). Radius of nucleus $\propto A^{1/3}$. **[1 Mark]**
So, they can have the same radii.

11. (a) The energy of hydrogen atom in an orbit, $E = -1.51\,eV$
Kinetic energy of electron $= -E = -(-1.51) = +1.51\ eV$
Potential energy of electron $= -2 \times$ (Kinetic energy of electron)
$= -2 \times 1.51 = -3.02\ eV$ **[½ + ½ Mark]**

(b) Given,

Radius of nucleus, $r = \dfrac{1.0 \times 10^{-15}\,m}{2}$

$= 0.5 \times 10^{-15}\,m$

Volume of nucleus, $V_1 = \dfrac{4}{3}\pi\,(0.5 \times 10^{-15})^3$

Volume of Hydrogen atom, $V_2 = \dfrac{4}{3}\pi\,(5.3 \times 10^{-11})^3$

Fraction of volume occupied by nucleus

$$= \frac{\dfrac{4}{3}\pi\,(0.5 \times 10^{-15})^3}{\dfrac{4}{3}\pi\,(5.3 \times 10^{-11})^3} = \frac{0.125 \times 10^{-45}}{148.87 \times 10^{-33}} = 0.839 \times 10^{-15}$$

$= 0.839 \times 10^{-15}$ **[2 Marks]**

12. **(I)** (b) In compound microscope, the image formed by objective is real and the image formed by eye-piece is virtual. **[1 Mark]**

(II) (a) Magnification due to compound microscope does not depend upon aperture of objective and eye piece. **[1 Mark]**

(III) (c) In compound microscope, two convergent lens are of short focal lengths. The magnifying power increases by decreasing the focal lengths of two lenses.
The distance between objective and eye piece of compound microscope is equal to sum of focal lengths of objective and eye piece i.e., $L = f_o + f_e$. **[1 Mark]**

(IV) (d) Magnifying power of compound microscope (M) = magnifying power of objective × magnifying power of eyepiece
$\Rightarrow$ $M = 10 \times 20 = 200$ **[1 Mark]**

(V) (c) Given,
Focal length of objective lens, $f_o = 1.2$ cm
Focal length of eye-piece, $f_e = 3$ cm
Distance of object from objective, $u_o = 1.25$ cm
Using lens formula for objective
$$\frac{1}{v_o} - \frac{1}{u_o} = \frac{1}{f_o} \Rightarrow \frac{1}{v_o} = \frac{1}{1.2} - \frac{1}{1.25} \Rightarrow v_o = 30\ cm$$

Magnifying power of microscope, $M = \dfrac{v_0}{u_0}\left(\dfrac{D}{f_e}\right)$

$\therefore$ $M = \dfrac{30}{1.25}\left(\dfrac{25}{3}\right) = 200$ **[1 Mark]**

All India 2022
CBSE Board Solved Paper
Term-I

Time Allowed : 1½ Hours   *Maximum Marks : 35*

General Instructions:
  (i)   This question paper contains three sections.
  (ii) Section A has **25** questions. Attempt any **20** questions.
  (iii) Section B has **24** questions. Attempt any **20** questions.
  (iv) Section C has **6** questions. Attempt any **5** questions.
  (v)   All questions carry equal marks.
  (vi) There is no negative marking.

SECTION - A

*This section consists of **25** multiple choice questions with overall choice to attempt any **20** questions. In case more than desirable number of questions are attempted, ONLY first **20** will be considered for evaluation.*

1. A negatively charged object X is repelled by another charged object Y. However an object Z is attracted to object Y. Which of the following is the most possible for the object Z ?
  (a) positively charged only
  (b) negatively charged only
  (c) neutral or positively charged
  (d) neutral or negatively charged

2. In an experiment three microscopic latex spheres are sprayed into a chamber and became charged with charges $+3e$, $+5e$ and $-3e$ respectively. All the three spheres came in contact simultaneously for a moment and got separated. Which one of the following are possible values for the final charge on the spheres ?
  (a) $+5e, -4e, +5e$ (b) $+6e, +6e, -7e$
  (c) $-4e, +3.5e, +5.5e$ (d) $+5e, -8e, +7e$

3. An object has charge of 1 C and gains 5.0×10^{18} electrons. The net charge on the object becomes –
  (a) $-0.80\,C$ (b) $+0.80\,C$ (c) $+1.80\,C$ (d) $+0.20\,C$

4. Kirchhoff's first rule $\Sigma I = 0$ and second rule $\Sigma IR = \Sigma E$ (where the symbols have their usual meanings) are respectively based on
  (a) conservation of momentum and conservation of charge
  (b) conservation of energy and conservation of charge
  (c) conservation of charge, conservation of momentum
  (d) conservation of charge, conservation of energy

5. The electric power consumed by a 220 V–100 W bulb when operated at 110 V is
  (a) 25 W   (b) 30 W
  (c) 35 W   (d) 45 W

6. Which of the following has negative temperature coefficient of radioactivity ?
  (a) metal
  (b) metal and semiconductor
  (c) semiconductor
  (d) metal and alloy

7. Two wires carrying currents I_1 and I_2 lie, one slightly above the other, in a horizontal plane as shown in figure. The region of vertically upward strongest magnetic field is

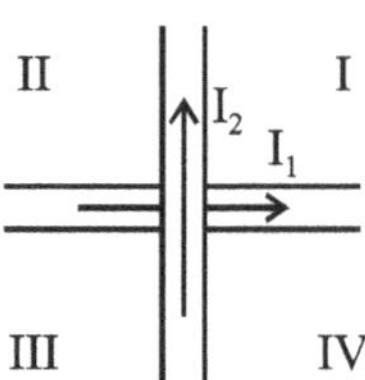

  (a) I   (b) II   (c) III   (d) IV

8. Two parallel conductors carrying current of 4.0 A and 10.0 A are placed 2.5 cm apart in vacuum. The force per unit length between them is –
  (a) $6.4 \times 10^{-5}\,N/m$ (b) $6.4 \times 10^{-2}\,N/m$
  (c) $4.6 \times 10^{-4}\,N/m$ (d) $3.2 \times 10^{-4}\,N/m$

9. If an ammeter is to be used in place of a voltmeter, then we must connect with the ammeter a –
  (a) low resistance in parallel
  (b) low resistance in series
  (c) high resistance in parallel
  (d) high resistance in series

10. The magnetic field at the centre of a current carrying circular loop of radius R, is B_1. The magnetic field at a point on its axis at a distance R from the center of the loop is B_2. Then the ratio (B_1/B_2) is

(a) $2\sqrt{2}$ (b) $\dfrac{1}{2\sqrt{2}}$ (c) $\sqrt{2}$ (d) 2

11. The self-inductance of a solenoid of 600 turns is 108 mW. The self-inductance of a coil having 500 turns with the same length, the same radius and the same medium will be

(a) 95 mH   (b) 90 mH   (c) 85 mH   (d) 75 mH

12. The rms current in a circuit connected to a 50 Hz ac source is 15 A. The value of the current in the circuit $\left(\dfrac{1}{600}\right)$ s after the instant the current is zero, is

(a) $\dfrac{15}{\sqrt{2}}A$ (b) $15\sqrt{2}A$ (c) $\dfrac{\sqrt{2}}{15}A$ (d) 8 A

13. In a circuit the phase difference between the alternating current and the source voltage is $\dfrac{\pi}{2}$. Which of the following cannot be the element(s) of the circuit ?

(a) only C   (b) only L   (c) L and R   (d) L or C

14. The electric potential V at any point (x, y, z) is given by $V = 3x^2$ where x is in metres and V in volts. The electric field at the point $(1\, m, 0, 2m)$ is –

(a) 6 V/m along $-x$-axis   (b) 6 V/m along $+x$-axis
(c) 1.5 V/m along $-x$-axis   (d) 1.5 V/m along $+x$-axis

15. Which of the diagrams correctly represents the electric field between two charged plates if a neutral conductor is placed in between the plates ?

(a) 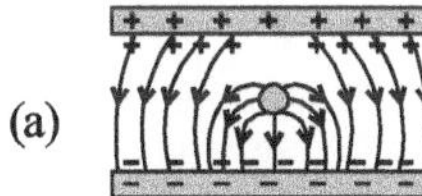   (b) 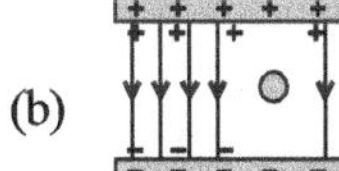

(c) 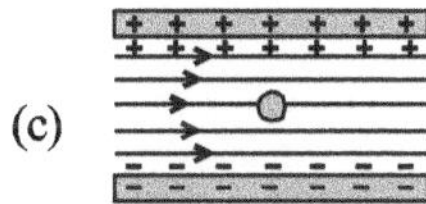   (d) 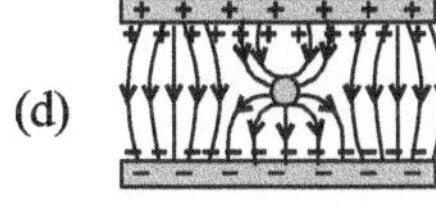

16. A variable capacitor is connected to a 200 V battery. If its capacitance is changed from 2 μF to X μF, the decrease in energy of the capacitor is 2×10^{-2} J. The value of X is

(a) 1 μF   (b) 2 μF
(c) 3 μF   (d) 4 μF

17. A potential difference of 200 V is maintained across a conductor of resistance 10 Ω. The number of electrons passing through it in 1 s is

(a) 1.25×10^{19} (b) 2.5×10^{18}
(c) 1.25×10^{18} (d) 2.5×10^{16}

18. The impedance of a series LCR circuit is –

(a) $R + X_L + X_C$ (b) $\sqrt{\dfrac{1}{X_C^2} + \dfrac{1}{X_L^2} + R^2}$

(c) $\sqrt{X_L^2 - R_C^2 + R^2}$ (d) $\sqrt{R^2 + (X_L - X_C)^2}$

19. When an alternating voltage $E = E_0 \sin \omega t$ is applied to a circuit, a current $I = I_0 \sin\left(\omega t + \dfrac{\pi}{2}\right)$ flows through it. The average power dissipated in the circuit is

(a) $E_{rms} \cdot I_{rms}$ (b) $E_0 I_0$

(c) $\dfrac{E_0 I_0}{\sqrt{2}}$ (d) Zero

20. A current carrying wire kept in a uniform magnetic field, will experience a maximum force when it is
(a) perpendicular to the magnetic field
(b) parallel to the magnetic field
(c) at and angle of 45° to the magnetic field
(d) at and angle of 60° to the magnetic field

21. The voltage across a resistor, an inductor, and a capacitor connected in series to an ac source are 20 V, 15 V and 30 V respectively. The resultant voltage in the circuit is
(a) 5 V   (b) 20 V   (c) 25 V   (d) 65 V

22. In a dc circuit the direction of current inside the battery and outside the battery respectively are
(a) positive to negative terminal and negative to positive terminal
(b) positive to negative terminal and negative to positive terminal
(c) negative to positive terminal and positive to negative terminal
(d) negative to positive terminal and negative to positive terminal

23. The magnitude of electric field due to a point charge 2q, at distance r is E. Then the magnitude of electric field due to a uniformly charged thin spherical shell of radius R with total charge q at a distance $\dfrac{r}{2}$ $(r \gg R)$ will be

(a) $\dfrac{E}{4}$ (b) 0   (c) 2E   (d) 4E

24. The horizontal component of earth's magnetic field at a place is 0.2 G whereas it's total magnetic field is 0.4 G. The angle of dip at the place is
(a) 30°   (b) 45°   (c) 60°   (d) 90°

25. The current in the primary coil of a pair of coils changes from 7 A to 3 A in 0.04 s. The mutual inductance between the two coils is 0.5 H. The induced emf in the secondary coil is –
(a) 50 V   (b) 75 V   (c) 100 V   (d) 220 V

SECTION - B

This section consists of 24 multiple choice questions with overall choice to attempt any 20 questions. In case more than desirable number of questions are attempted, ONLY first 20 will be considered for evaluation.

26. A square sheet of side 'a' is lying parallel to XY plane at $z = a$. The electric field in the region is $\vec{E} = cz^2\hat{k}$. The electric flux through the sheet is

    (a) $a^4 c$ (b) $\dfrac{1}{3}a^3 c$ (c) $\dfrac{1}{3}a^4 c$ (d) 0

27. Three charges q, –q and q_0 are placed as shown in figure. The magnitude of the net force on the charge q_0 at point O is $\left[k = \dfrac{1}{(4\pi\varepsilon_0)}\right]$

    (a) 0

    (b) $\dfrac{2kqq_0}{a^2}$

    (c) $\dfrac{\sqrt{2}kqq_0}{a^2}$ (d) $\dfrac{1}{\sqrt{2}}\dfrac{kqq_0}{a^2}$

28. A + 3.0 nC charge Q is initially at rest at a distance of $r_1 = 10$ cm from a + 5.0 nC charge q fixed at the origin. The charge Q is moved away from q to a new position at $r_2 = 15$ cm. In this process work done by the field is

    (a) 1.29×10^{-5} J   (b) 3.6×10^5 J
    (c) -4.5×10^{-7} J   (d) 4.5×10^{-7} J

29. A car battery is charged by a 12 V supply, and energy stored in it is 7.20×10^5 J. The charge passed through the battery is–

    (a) 6.0×10^4 C   (b) 5.8×10^3 C
    (c) 8.64×10^6 C   (d) 1.6×10^5 C

30. A straight conducting rod of length l and mass m is suspended in a horizontal plane by a pair of flexible strings in a magnetic field of magnitude B. To remove the tension in the supporting string, the magnitude of the current in the wire is

    (a) $\dfrac{mgB}{l}$ (b) $\dfrac{mgl}{B}$ (c) $\dfrac{mg}{lB}$ (d) $\dfrac{lB}{mg}$

31. A constant current is flowing through a solenoid. An iron rod is inserted in the solenoid along its axis. Which of the following quantities will not increase?
    (a) The magnetic field at the centre
    (b) The magnetic flux linked with the solenoid
    (c) The rate of heating
    (d) The self-inductance of the solenoid

32. A circuit is connected to an ac source of variable frequency. As the frequency of the source is increased, the curretn first increases and then decreases. Which of the following combinations of elements is likely to comprise the circuit?
    (a) L, C and R   (b) L and C
    (c) L and R   (d) R and C

33. If n, e, τ and m have their usual meanings, then the resistance of a wire of length l and cross-sectional area A is given by-
    (a) $\dfrac{ne^2 A}{2m\tau l}$ (b) $\dfrac{ml}{ne^2\tau A}$ (c) $\dfrac{m\tau A}{ne^2 l}$ (d) $\dfrac{ne^2\tau A}{2ml}$

34. A proton and an alpha particle move in circular orbits in a uniform magnetic field. Their speeds are in the ratio of 9 : 4. The ratio of radii of their circular orbits $\left(\dfrac{r_p}{r_{alpha}}\right)$ is

    (a) $\dfrac{3}{4}$ (b) $\dfrac{4}{3}$ (c) $\dfrac{8}{9}$ (d) $\dfrac{9}{8}$

35. A coil of area 100 cm^2 is kept at an angle of 30° with a magnetic field of 10^{-1} T. The magnetic field is reduced to zero in 10^{-4} s. the unduced emf in the coil is

    (a) $5\sqrt{3}$ V   (b) $50\sqrt{3}$ V   (c) 5.0 V   (d) 50.0 V

36. A 15 Ω resister an 80 mH inductor and a capacitor of capacitance C are connected in series with a 50 Hz ac source. If the source voltage and current in the circuit are in phase, then the value of capacitance is
    (a) 100 μF   (b) 127 μF   (c) 142 μF   (d) 160 μF

37. Four objects W, X, Y and Z each with charge +q are hold fixed at four points of a square of side d as shown in the figure. Objects X and Z are on the midpoints of the sides of the square. The electrostatic force exerted by object W on object X is F. Then the magnitude of the force exerted by object W on Z is.

    (a) $\dfrac{F}{7}$ (b) $\dfrac{F}{5}$

    (c) $\dfrac{F}{3}$ (d) $\dfrac{F}{2}$

38. Two sources of equal emf are connected in series. This combination is in turn connected to an external resistance R. The internal resistance of two sources are r_1 and r_2 ($r_2 > r_1$). If the potential difference across the source of internal resistance r_2 is zero then R equals to–
    (a) $\dfrac{r_1 + r_2}{r_2 - r_1}$ (b) $r_2 - r_1$ (c) $\dfrac{r_1 r_2}{r_2 - r_1}$ (d) $\dfrac{r_1 - r_2}{r_1 r_2}$

39. Which of following statemetns is correct?
    (a) Magnetic field lines do not form closed loops.
    (b) Magnetic field lines start from north pole and end at south pole of a magnet.
    (c) The tangent at a point on a magnetic field line represents the direction of the magnetic field at that point.
    (d) Two magnetic field lines may intersect each other.

40. The equivalent resistance between A and B of the network shown in figure is
    (a) $3R\,\Omega$ (b) $\left(\dfrac{3}{2}\right)R\,\Omega$

    (c) $2R\,\Omega$ (d) $\left(\dfrac{2}{3}\right)R\,\Omega$

41. A bar magnet has magnetic dipole moment $\vec{M}$. Its initial position is parallel to the direction of uniform magnetic field $\vec{B}$. In this position, the magnitudes of torque and force acting on it respectively are–

(a) 0 and MB   (b) MB and MB

(c) 0 and 0   (d) $|\vec{M} \times \vec{B}|$ and 0

42. Two charges $14\,\mu C$ and $-4\,\mu C$ are placed at $(-12\text{ cm}, 0, 0)$ and $(12\text{ cm}, 0, 0)$ in an external electric field $E = \left(\dfrac{B}{r^2}\right)$, where $B = 1.2 \times 10^6\text{ N/(cm}^2)$ and r is in metres. The electrostatic potential energy of the configuration is

(a) 97.9 J   (b) 102.1 J   (c) 2.1 J   (d) –97.9 J

43. A 300 Ω resistor and a capacitor of $\left(\dfrac{25}{\pi}\right)\,\mu F$ are connected in series to a 200 V – 50 Hz ac source. The current in the circuit is

(a) 0.1 A   (b) 0.4 A   (c) 0.6 A   (d) 0.8 A

44. The core of a transformer is laminated to reduce the effect of

(a) flux leakage   (b) copper loss

(c) hysteresis loss   (d) eddy current

Question No. 45 to 49 are Assertion (A) and Reason (R) type questions. Given below are the two statements labelled as Assertion (A) and Reason (R). Select the most appropriate answer from the options given below :

(a) Both (A) & (R) are true and (R) is the correct explanation of (A)

(b) Both (A) & (R) are true and (R) is not the correct explanation of (A)

(c) (A) is true but (R) is false

(d) (A) is false and (R) is also false

45. Assertion (A) : A negative charge in an electric field moves along the direction of the electric field.

Reason (R) : On a negative charge a force acts in the direction of the electric field.

46. Assertion (A) : The poles of a bar magnet cannot be separated.

Reason (R) : Magnetic monopoles do not exist.

47. Assertion (A) : When radius of a current carrying loop is doubled, its magnetic moment becomes four times.

Reason (R) : The magnetic moment of a current carrying loop is directly proportional to the area of the loop.

48. Assertion (A) : Higher the range, lower is the resistance of an ammeter

Reason (R) : To increase the range of an ammeter additional shunt is added in series to it.

49. Assertion (A) : A step-up trannsformer cannot be used as a step-down transformer.

Reason (R) : A transformer works only in one direction.

*This section consists of **6** multiple choice questions with an overall choice to attempt any **5**. In case more than desirable number of questions are attempted, ONLY first **5** will be considered for evaluation.*

50. Equipotentials at a large distance from a collection of charges whose total sum is not zero are–

(a) spheres   (b) planes

(c) ellipsoids   (d) paraboloids

51. Four charges $-q, -q, +q$ and $+q$ are placed at the corners of a square of side 2 L is shown in figure. The electric potential at point A midway between the two charges $+ q$ and $+q$ is–

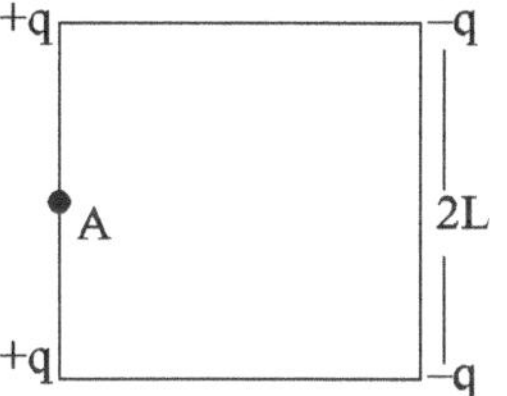

(a) $\dfrac{1}{4\pi\varepsilon_0}\dfrac{2q}{L}\left(1-\dfrac{1}{\sqrt{5}}\right)$ (b) $\dfrac{1}{4\pi\varepsilon_0}\dfrac{2q}{L}\left(1+\dfrac{1}{\sqrt{5}}\right)$

(c) $\dfrac{1}{4\pi\varepsilon_0}\dfrac{q}{2L}\left(1-\dfrac{1}{\sqrt{5}}\right)$ (d) zero

Case Study: (Qs. 52-55)

An experiment was set up with the circuit diagram shown in figure. Given that $R_1 = 10\,\Omega$, $R_2 = R_3 = 5\,\Omega$, $r = 0\,\Omega$ and $E = 5V$

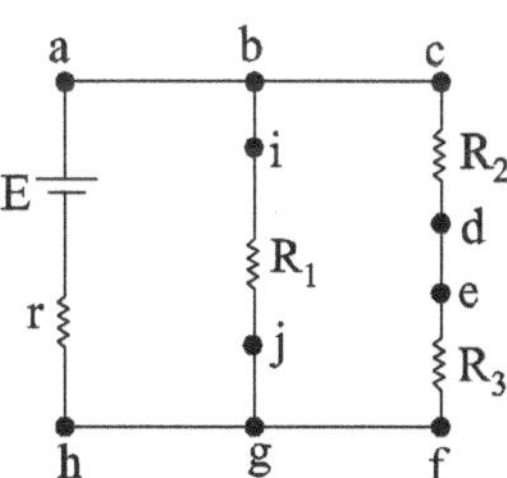

52. The points with the same potential are–

(a) b, c, d   (b) f, h, j   (c) d, e, f   (d) a, b, j

53. The current through branch bg is–

(a) 1 A   (b) $\dfrac{1}{3}$A   (c) $\dfrac{1}{2}$A   (d) $\dfrac{2}{3}$A

54. The power dissipated in R_1 is–

(a) 2 W   (b) 2.5 W   (c) 3 W   (d) 4.5 W

55. The potential difference across R_3 is–

(a) 1.5 V   (b) 2 V   (c) 2.5 V   (d) 3 V

Solutions

1. **(c)** As charged object Y repels negatively charged X so Y must be negatively charged object. And Z is attracted to Y so Z is neutral or positively charged.

2. **(b)** Net charge of three spheres with charges $+3e, +5e, -3e$ $= +5e$.
   Also net charge of $+6e, +6e, -7e = +5e$
   So possible values for the final charge on the spheres are $+6e, +6e, -7e$

3. **(d)** The net charge on the object $= 1C - ne$ $[\because Q = ne]$
   $= 1C - 5 \times 10^{18} \times 1.6 \times 10^{-19}C$
   $= +0.20\,C$

4. **(d)** Kirchhoff's first rule
   $\Sigma I = 0$ and second rule
   $\Sigma IR = V = IR$ are respectively based on conservation of charge and conservation of energy.

5. **(a)** For $220\,V - 100\,W$ bulb
   $$P = \frac{V^2}{R} \Rightarrow R = \frac{V^2}{P} = \frac{(220)^2}{100} = 484\,\Omega$$
   So, electric power consumed when operated at $110\,V$
   $$P = \frac{V^2}{R} = \frac{(110)^2}{484} = 25\,W$$

   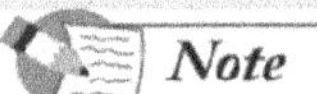
   Note

   If $V_{applied} < V_{rated}$ then % drop in output power of electrical

   device $= \dfrac{P_R - P_{consumed}}{P_R} \times 100$ *($P_R = rated\ power$).*

6. **(c)** Temperature coefficient of resistivity, α $(°C)^{-1}$ of semiconductor is negative.

7. **(b)** In region II magnetic field due to both wires are vertically upwards and add.

8. **(d)** Force per unit length, $\dfrac{F}{l} = \dfrac{\mu_0}{2\pi} \dfrac{i_1 i_2}{r}$
   $$= \frac{4\pi \times 10^{-7} \times 4 \times 10\,N}{2\pi \times 2.5 \times 10^{-2}\,m} = 3.2 \times 10^{-4}\,N/m$$

9. **(d)** Ammeter has low resistance. Large current would flow when used directly across high voltage as voltmeter. High resistance is added in series to reduce current.

10. **(a)** B – magnetic field
    $$B_1 = B\ (center) = \frac{\mu_0 i}{2R}$$
    $$B_2\ (= B\ at\ x = R) = \frac{\mu_0 i R^2}{2(R^2 + x^2)^{3/2}} \quad (Put\ x = R)$$
    $$= \frac{\mu_0 i R^2}{2(2R^2)^{3/2}}$$
    $$= \frac{\mu_0 i}{2 \times 2^{3/2} R} = \frac{\mu_0 i}{2 \times 2\sqrt{2}R} \quad \therefore \frac{B_1}{B_2} = 2\sqrt{2}$$

11. **(d)** Self inductance $L = \dfrac{\mu_0 N^2 A}{l} \Rightarrow L \propto N^2$
    $108\,mH \propto (600)^2$
    new inductance $(L') \propto (500)^2$
    $$\Rightarrow \frac{L'}{108} = \frac{(500)^2}{(600)^2} \Rightarrow L' = \frac{(500)^2}{(600)^2} \times 108$$

$\therefore\ L' = 75\,mH$

Note

Self inductance 'L' does not play any role till there is a constant current flowing in the circuit. It comes in to the picture only when there is a change in current.

12. **(a)** $i = i_0 \sin\omega t$
    $$i = 15\sqrt{2} \sin 2\pi \times 50 \times \frac{1}{600}$$
    $$= 15\sqrt{2} \sin\frac{\pi}{6} = \frac{15\sqrt{2}}{2} = \frac{15}{\sqrt{2}}\,A$$

13. **(c)** In L-R circuit phase difference between current and voltage is different from $90°$. It can be found by impedance triangle.

14. **(a)** Electric field is given by
    $$\bar{E} = \frac{-\partial V}{\partial x}\hat{i} - \frac{\partial V}{\partial y}\hat{j} - \frac{\partial V}{\partial z}\hat{k} = \frac{-\partial 3x^2}{\partial x}\hat{i} = -6x\hat{i}$$
    $$= -6 \times 1\hat{i} = -6\,V/m\hat{i}$$

15. **(d)** Negative charge will appear on the surface of neutral conductor near positive plate and positive charge on surface of conductor near negative plate. Field lines start from positive plate end at $-ve$ charge of ball and start from $+ve$ charge on conductor to $-ve$ plate.

Note

Electric lines of force never intersect the conductor. They are perpendicular and slightly curved near the surface of conductor.

16. **(a)** Energy stored in a capacitor, $E = \dfrac{1}{2}CV^2$
    $\therefore$ Decrease in energy of the capacitor
    $$= \frac{1}{2} \times 2 \times 10^{-6} \times (200)^2 - \frac{1}{2} \times (x \times 10^{-6}) \times (200)^2$$
    $$= (4 - 2x) \times 10^{-2}J = 2 \times 10^{-2}J$$
    $$\Rightarrow \quad 4 - 2x = 2$$
    $$\therefore \quad x = 1\,\mu F$$

17. **(a)** From Ohm's law, current $i = \dfrac{V}{R} = \dfrac{200}{100}A$
    Also, $i = \dfrac{q}{t} = \dfrac{ne}{1s} = 2$
    or, $n \times 1.6 \times 10^{-19} = 2$ $\quad \therefore n = \dfrac{2 \times 10^{19}}{1.6} = 1.25 \times 10^{19}$

18. **(d)** Impedance of the series LCR circuit
    $$= \sqrt{R^2 + (X_L - X_C)^2}$$

19. **(d)** Average power $= E_{rms}\,I_{rms}\cos\phi$
    $$= \frac{E_0}{\sqrt{2}} \frac{I_0}{\sqrt{2}} \cos 90° = 0$$

20. **(a)** Magnetic force $= i\vec{l} \times \vec{B} = i\,lB\sin\theta$
    When $\theta = 90°$ i.e., wire is $\perp$ to $\vec{B}$
    $F_{max} = ilB$

21. **(c)** $V_{resultant} = \sqrt{V_R^2 + (V_L - V_C)^2}$

$\qquad = \sqrt{20^2 + (15 - 30)^2} = 25V$

22. **(c)** In a dc circuit, the direction of current inside the battery is from –ve to +ve terminal and outside the battery it flows from +ve to –ve terminal.

23. **(c)** Electric field due to point charge $\dfrac{K2q}{r^2} = E$

So electric field due to shell outside $\dfrac{Kq}{\left(\dfrac{r}{2}\right)^2} = 2\left(\dfrac{K2q}{r^2}\right) = 2E$

24. **(c)** $B_H = B\cos\delta$

$0.2 = 0.4\cos\delta$

$\Rightarrow \quad \cos\delta = \dfrac{1}{2}$

$\therefore \quad$ Angle of dip $\delta = 60°$

Note

Angle of dip is the angle between the direction of intensity of total magnetic field of earth and a horizontal line in the magnetic meridian.

25. **(a)** Induced $emf = \dfrac{Mdi}{dt}$

$= \dfrac{.5 \times (7 - 3)}{.04} = 50V$

26. **(a)** Electric flux = Electric field × area

$= EA = cz^2\hat{k}.a^2\hat{k}$

$= ca^2\hat{k}.a^2\hat{k} = ca^4$

27. **(c)** Forces due to q is F_q and that due to $-q\ F_{-q}$ are as shown.

Net force $= \sqrt{F_q^2 + F_{-q}^2}$

$= \sqrt{F^2 + F^2} \qquad$ (As $F_{-q} = F_q$)

$= \sqrt{2}F = \dfrac{\sqrt{2}Kqq_0}{a^2} \qquad \left(\because F = \dfrac{Kqq_0}{r^2}\right)$

28. **(d)** Work done by electric field $= \Delta U$

$= \left[\dfrac{Kq_1q_2}{r_1} - \dfrac{Kq_1q_2}{r_2}\right]$

$= K \times 3 \times 10^{-9} \times 5 \times 10^{-9}\left[\dfrac{1}{.01} - \dfrac{1}{.15}\right]$

$= 9 \times 10^9 \times 3 \times 10^{-9} \times 5 \times 10^{-9}[10 - 6.66] = 4.5 \times 10^{-7}J$

29. **(a)** Work done = qV

$\Rightarrow q = \dfrac{\text{Work done}}{V} = \dfrac{W}{V} = \dfrac{7.2 \times 10^5}{12} = 6 \times 10^4 C$

30. **(c)** Magnetic force = weight

$Bil = mg \qquad \therefore$ current $i = \dfrac{mg}{lB}$

Note

Magnetic force does no work when the charged particle is displaced while electric force does work in displacing the charged particle.

31. **(c)** Magnetic field at the centre of solenoid = μni

μ will change due to insertion of iron rod.

Rate of heat will not change as current is constant.

32. **(a)** In LCR circuit current first increases then decreases with increase in frequency.

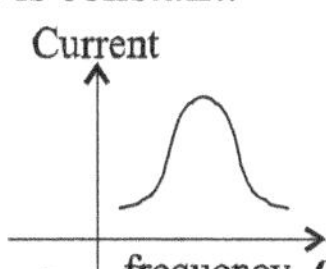

33. **(b)** Current density $J = \sigma E = \dfrac{1}{\rho}E = \dfrac{ne^2\tau}{m}E$

$\therefore \quad \sigma = \dfrac{ne^2\tau}{m}$

Resistance $(R) = \rho\dfrac{l}{A} = \dfrac{1}{\sigma}\dfrac{l}{A}$

Putting value of σ

$R = \dfrac{m}{ne^2\tau}\dfrac{l}{A}$

34. **(d)** Radius of circular path $r = \dfrac{mv}{qB}$

for proton $r_p = \dfrac{m_p v_p}{q_p B}$

for α-particle $r_\alpha = \dfrac{m_\alpha v_\alpha}{q_\alpha B}$

$\dfrac{r_p}{r_\alpha} = \left(\dfrac{m_p}{m_\alpha}\right) \times \left(\dfrac{q_\alpha}{q_p}\right) \times \left(\dfrac{v_p}{v_\alpha}\right) = \dfrac{1}{4} \times \dfrac{2}{1} \times \dfrac{9}{4} = \dfrac{9}{8}$

Note

If a particle enters a magnetic field normally to the magnetic field, then it starts moving in a circular orbit. The point at which, it enters the magnetic field lies on the circumference of the circular path.

35. **(c)** Induced emf, $e = -\dfrac{\Delta\phi}{\Delta t} = \dfrac{\phi_1 - \phi_2}{\Delta t}$

$= \dfrac{B_1 A\cos\theta - B_2 A\cos\theta}{\Delta t}$

$= \dfrac{10^{-1} \times 100 \times 10^{-4} \times \cos 60° - 0 \times 100 \times 10^{-4} \times \cos 60°}{10^{-4}}$

$= 5V$

Note: Area vector makes angle $90° - 30°$ with $\bar{B}$.

36. **(b)** As voltage and current are in phase so circuit is in resonance.

$\therefore \quad \omega^2 = \dfrac{1}{LC} \Rightarrow C = \dfrac{1}{\omega^2 L} = \dfrac{1}{(2\pi \times 50)^2 \times 80 \times 10^{-3}}$

$\Rightarrow \quad C = 1.27 \times 10^{-4} F = 127\ \mu F$

37. **(b)** $F = \dfrac{Kq^2}{(d/2)^2} = \dfrac{4Kq^2}{d^2}$

Let W exerts F' force on Z

$\therefore \quad F' = \dfrac{Kq^2}{\left(\dfrac{\sqrt{5}d}{2}\right)^2} = \left(\dfrac{4}{5}\right)\dfrac{Kq^2}{d^2} = \dfrac{F}{5}$

38. **(b)** From circuit, current $i = \dfrac{2E}{R + r_1 + r_2}$

potential difference across source 2
$= E - ir_2$

$$= E - \frac{2E}{R + r_1 + r_2} \times r_2 = 0$$

$$= \frac{E(R + r_1 + r_2 - 2r_2)}{R + r_1 + r_2} = 0$$

$$\therefore \quad R = r_2 - r_1$$

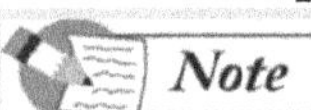

Note

Emf of cell is the potential difference across the terminals of a cell when it is not supplying any current. And potential difference is the voltage across the terminals of a cell when it is supplying current to external resistance.

39. (c) Tangent at a point on magnetic field lines give direction of field. Also it forms closed loop. And two magnetic field lines cannot intersect each other.

40. (c) Resistance which is shorted can be removed from the circuit.

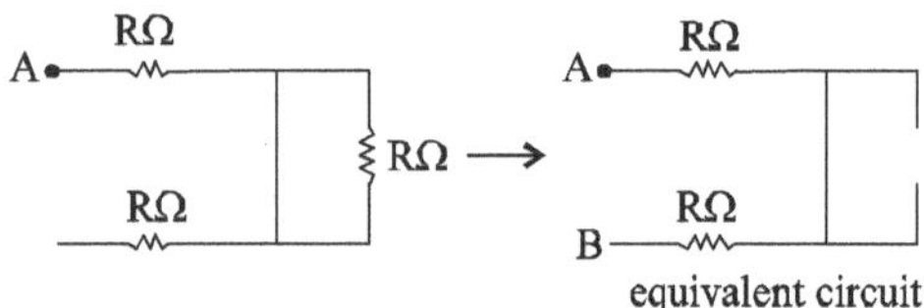

Therefore equivalent resistance $R_{AB} = R + R = 2R\,\Omega$

Note

Decoration of lights in festivals is an example of series grouping whereas all household appliances are connected in parallel grouping.

41. (c) Torque on magnetic dipole $\vec{M}$
$$= \vec{M} \times \vec{B} = MB \sin\theta = MB \sin 0 = 0$$
Force due to field is also zero as forces on both poles are in opposite direction so cancel each other.

42. (a) Electric potential (V)
$$V = -\int_r^\infty \vec{E}.d\vec{r} = -\int_r^\infty \frac{B}{r^2} dr = \frac{B}{r} = \frac{1.2 \times 10^6}{.12m} = 10^7\,V$$
Potential energy of $14\mu C$
$u_1 = 14 \times 10^{-6} \times 10^7\,J = 140\,J$
Potential energy of $-4\mu C$
$u_2 = -4 \times 10^{-6} \times 10^7 = -40\,J$
$$u_3 = \frac{Kq_1q_2}{r} = \frac{9 \times 10^9 \times 14 \times 10^{-6} \times (-4 \times 10^{-6})}{.24m}$$
$$[r = 12 - (-12)\,cm]$$
U (of configuration) $= -2.1\,J$
$= u_1 + u_2 + u_3 = 140 + (-40) + (-2.1) = 97.9\,J$

43. (b) Impedance $Z = \sqrt{R^2 + X_c^2}$
$$X_c = \frac{1}{\omega C} = \frac{1}{2\pi \times 50 \times \dfrac{25}{\pi} \times 10^{-6}} = 400\,\Omega$$
$$\therefore \quad Z = \sqrt{300^2 + 400^2} = 500\,\Omega$$
Current $i = \dfrac{V}{Z} = \dfrac{200}{500} = 0.4\,A$

44. (d) Core of a transformer is laminated mainly to reduce eddy current. It reduces the flux through which eddy current can flow.

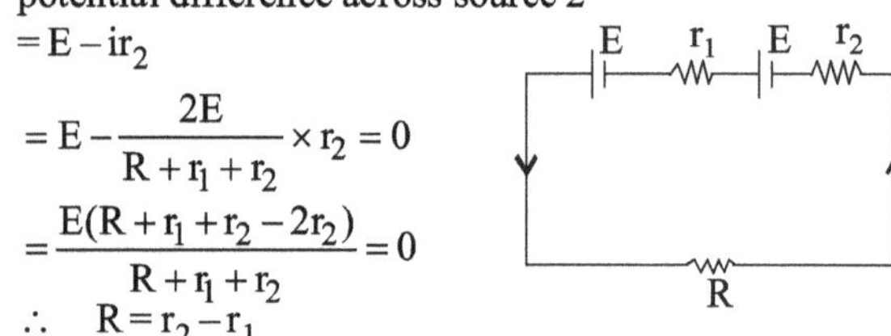

Note

Transformer is a device which raises or lowers the voltage in a.c. circuits through mutual induction. It works on a.c. only and never on d.c. It can increase or decrease either voltage or current but not both simultaneously.

45. (d) –ve charge moves in the opposite direction to the electric field, as it experiences force in the direction opposite to electric field.

46. (a) Magnetic poles always exist in pair, so poles of bar magnet cannot be separated.

47. (a) Magnetic moment is given by $\vec{M} = i\vec{A}$
As radius r gets double area $A = \pi r^2$ becomes 4 times and so does $\vec{M}$. Reason is correct as M is directly proportional to area of loop.

48. (c) Lower shunt resistance will draw more current through it and range of galvanometer and hence ammeter range will increase.
To increase range of ammeter smaller resistance should be added in parallel.

49. (d) A transformer can be used in two direction provided ratings are not exceeded.

50. (a) At large distance collection of charge will act as point charge so, equipotential surface will be a sphere.

51. (a) Potential at point P due to charges at 1, 2, 3, 4 respectively are

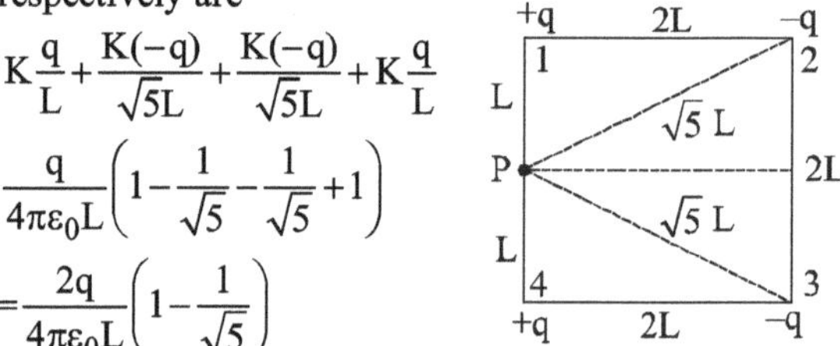

$$K\frac{q}{L} + \frac{K(-q)}{\sqrt{5}L} + \frac{K(-q)}{\sqrt{5}L} + K\frac{q}{L}$$
$$\frac{q}{4\pi\varepsilon_0 L}\left(1 - \frac{1}{\sqrt{5}} - \frac{1}{\sqrt{5}} + 1\right)$$
$$= \frac{2q}{4\pi\varepsilon_0 L}\left(1 - \frac{1}{\sqrt{5}}\right)$$

Note

Potential of a system of point charges at any point P,
$$V = \frac{KQ_1}{r_1} + \frac{KQ_2}{r_2} + \frac{K(-Q_3)}{r_3} + \frac{KQ_4}{r_4}$$
In general, $V = \sum_{i=1}^{x} \frac{KQ_i}{r_i}$

52. (b) f, h, j are at same potential as there is no resistors between them.

53. (c) Current through branch bg
$$i_{bg} = \frac{V_{bg}}{R_{bg}} = \frac{5V}{R_1} = \frac{5}{10} = \frac{1}{2}A$$

54. (b) Power in $R_1 = V_{bg} \times i_{bg} = 5V \times \frac{1}{2}A = 2.5\,W$

55. (c) From given circuit $i_{R_3} = \dfrac{V_{cf}}{R_2 + R_3} = \dfrac{5V}{5 + 5\Omega} = \dfrac{1}{2}A$
$$V_{R_3} = i_{R_3} \times R_3 = \frac{1}{2}A \times 5\Omega = \frac{5}{2}V = 2.5V$$

CBSE TOPPER-2020
Answer Sheet

केन्द्रीय माध्यमिक शिक्षा बोर्ड, दिल्ली
सीनियर स्कूल सर्टिफिकेट परीक्षा (कक्षा बारहवी)
परीक्षार्थी प्रवेश-पत्र के अनुसार भरे

विषय Subject : PHYSICS

विषय कोड Subject Code : 042

परीक्षा का दिन एवं तिथि
Day & Date of the Examination : MONDAY & 02.03.2020

उत्तर देने का माध्यम
Medium of answering the paper : ENGLISH

प्रश्न पत्र के ऊपर लिखे कोड की दर्शाएं Write code No. as written on the top of the question paper :	Code Number	Set Number
	55|2|1	● ② ③ ④

अतिरिक्त उत्तर-पुस्तिका (ओं) की संख्या
No. of supplementary answer -book(s) used — **NO**

बेंचमार्क दिकलांग व्यक्ति : हाँ / नहीं
Person with Benchmark Disabilities : Yes / No — **NO**

विकलांगता का कोड (प्रवेश पत्र के अनुसार)
Code of Disability (As per the admit card) — **NIL**

उप लेखन – लिपिक उपलब्ध करवाया गया : हाँ / नहीं
Whether writer provided : Yes / No — **NO**

यदि दृष्टिहीन हैं तो उपयोग में लाए गये सॉफ्टवेयर का नाम :
If Visually challenged, name of software used — **NIL**

*एक खाने में एक अक्षर लिखें। नाम के प्रत्येक भाग के बीच एक खाना रिक्त छोड़ दें। यदि परीक्षार्थी का नाम 24 अक्षरों से अधिक है, तो केवल नाम के प्रथम 24 अक्षर ही लिखें।

Each letter be written in one box and one box be left blank between each part of the name. In case Candidate's Name exceeds 24 letters, write first 24 letters.

कार्यालय उपयोग के लिए
Space for office use

3

1. (D) R = Q

2. (A) Resistivity.

3. (A) move in a straight line.

4. (B) Ferromagnetic material becomes paramagnetic.

5. (A) electric ~~current~~ field is changing.

6. (A) X-rays.

7. (C) zero as diffusion and drift currents are equal and opposite.

8. (B) Just below the conduction band

9. (A) Binding energy per nucleon increases.

10. (A) neutron converts into a proton emitting antineutrino.

11. If the electric flux entering and leaving a closed surface in air are ϕ_1 and ϕ_2 respectively, the net electric charge enclosed within the surface is $\epsilon_0(\phi_2 - \phi_1)$

12. In Young's double-slit experiment, the path difference between two interfering waves at a point on the screen is $\frac{5\lambda}{2}$, λ being the wavelength of light used. The 3rd dark fringe will lie at this point.

(13) For a higher resolving power of a compound microscope, the wavelength of light used should be <u>smaller</u>.

(14) Unpolarised light passes from a rarer to a denser medium. If the reflected and the refracted rays are mutually perpendicular, the reflected light is linearly polarised <u>perpendicular</u> to the plane of incidence.

(15) Out of red, blue and yellow light, the scattering of <u>blue</u> light is maximum.

(16) Impedance of a capacitor of capacitance $C = \frac{1}{\omega C}$.

$$\omega = 2\pi n.$$

$\therefore$ impedance $= \frac{1}{2\pi n C}$.

(17) A conducting rod of length ℓ is kept parallel to a uniform magnetic field $\vec{B}$ and moved along it with velocity $\vec{v}$. The value of emf induced $= 0$.

CBSE 2019-20

5

(18) Induced emf $= |\varepsilon|$

Rate of change of current $= \dfrac{dI}{dt}$

$\varepsilon = -L\dfrac{dI}{dt} \Rightarrow |\varepsilon| = L\dfrac{dI}{dt}$

The graph is a straight line passing through origin. The slope is equal to inductance L.

(19) Wavelength, $\lambda = \dfrac{hc}{E}$

$\lambda = \dfrac{6.63\times10^{-34} \times 3\times10^{8}}{3.3\times10^{-19}}$ m

$= \dfrac{19.89}{3.3} \times 10^{-7}$ m $\approx 6.03\times10^{-7}$ m

∴ reqd. wavelength $= 6.03\times10^{-7}$ m.

(20) The minimum frequency that an incoming photon must contain so that it can just overcome the work function and start photoelectric effect is called 'threshold frequency' in photoelectric emission.

21. The drift velocity attained by the charge carries in unit electric field is defined as 'mobility' of charge carries in a current-carrying conductor.

$$\therefore \text{mobility } (\mu) = \frac{V_d}{E}$$

We know, drift velocity, $v_d = a\tau$, where τ is relaxation time, and a is acceleration of the charge carrier.

Now, in presence of electric field E, acceleration a of a charged particle of charge e $= \frac{eE}{m}$

$$\therefore v_d = \frac{eE\tau}{m}$$

$$\therefore \frac{v_d}{E} = \frac{e\tau}{m} \Rightarrow \boxed{\mu = \frac{e\tau}{m}}$$

$\therefore \mu$ is charge times relaxation time divided by mass of the particle m.

22. Let, the shunt resistance be of $R\,\Omega$ and it is connected in parallel with ammeter of resistance $0.8\,\Omega$.

In the converted ammeter, $5A$ current can enter.

$\therefore$ ammeter can take upto $1A$, remaining $4A$ flows through shunt.

7

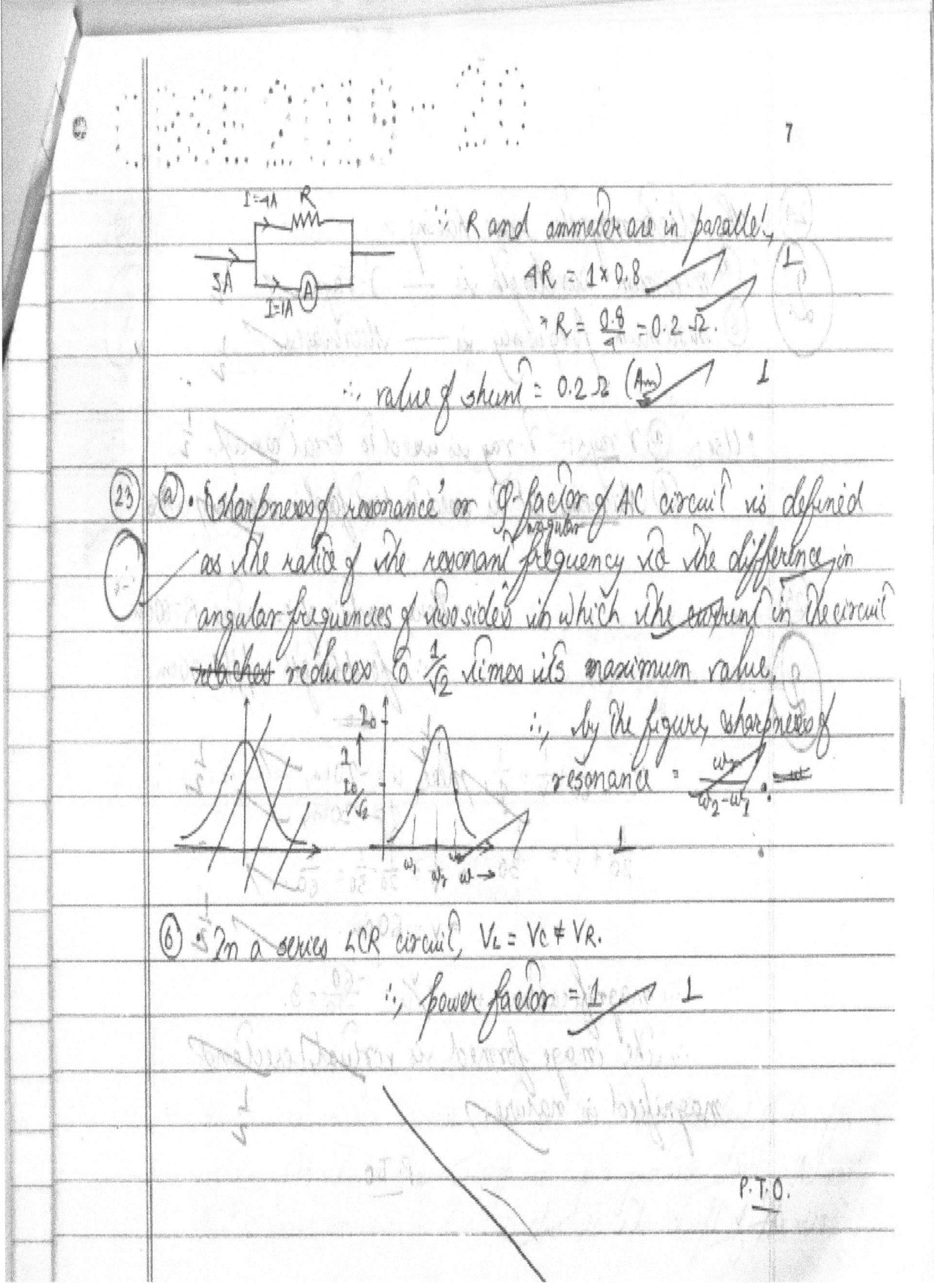

∵ R and ammeter are in parallel,

$4R = 1 \times 0.8$

$\therefore R = \dfrac{0.8}{4} = 0.2\,\Omega$

∴ value of shunt = 0.2 Ω (Ans)

(23) (a) · 'Sharpness of resonance' or 'Q-factor of AC circuit' is defined as the ratio of the resonant frequency to the difference in angular frequencies of two sides in which the current in the circuit reduces to $\frac{1}{\sqrt{2}}$ times its maximum value.

∴ by the figure, sharpness of resonance $= \dfrac{\omega_r}{\omega_2 - \omega_1}$

(b) · In a series LCR circuit, $V_L = V_C \neq V_R$.

∴ power factor = 1

24. The electromagnetic wave having :-

(a) minimum wavelength is — γ-rays.   ½

(b) minimum frequency is — Microwaves.   ½

• Use :- (a) γ-rays :- γ-ray is used to treat cancer. ½

(b) Microwave :- It is used to heat food in microwave ovens.

25. Here, radius of curvature, $R = 60\,cm$

∴ focal length, $|f| = 30\,cm$.

∴ $\dfrac{1}{u} + \dfrac{1}{v} = \dfrac{1}{f}$ here, $u = -20\,cm$,

$f = +30\,cm$,

$\dfrac{1}{-20} + \dfrac{1}{v} = \dfrac{1}{30}$ ⟹ $\dfrac{1}{v} = \dfrac{1}{20} - \dfrac{1}{30} = \dfrac{1}{60}$

⟹ $v = 60\,cm$.   ½

∴ magnification, $m = \dfrac{v}{u} = \dfrac{-60}{-20} = 3$.

∴ the image formed is virtual, erect and magnified in nature.   ½

P.T.O.

6 CBSE 2019-20

9

26. (a) In the Geiger-Marsden scattering experiment, 'b' represents the 'impact parameter', and 'θ' represents the 'scattering angle or angle of deflection'.

(b) (i) Value of b for θ = 0° is the radius of the ~~atom~~ nucleus atom.
(ii) Value of b for θ = 180° is 0.

27. • This is the V-I characteristics of a p-n junction diode.

breakdown voltage
(reverse bias)
Cut off voltage
(Volt)
(forward bias)
(I) mA
(I) µA

•• The current under reverse bias is almost independent of the applied voltage upto the critical voltage in a p-n junction diode. Actually, the current in reverse bias is due to the drift of the minority

10

carriers in presence of the depletion layer electric field. At critical voltage, the minority carriers start moving in the circuit rapidly due to breakdown of the high accelerating potential, but before that, the current remains almost constant because the potential applied is not able to cause rapid movement of charge carriers and also, drift of minority carriers is independent of voltage.

In reverse bias, the depletion layer increases, but this does almost effect to continuous drift of minority carriers due to electric field in depletion layer.

P.T.O.

12

(b) Maximum charge, q, supplied by the battery

$$= C_{eq} \times V$$

$$= \frac{12}{5} \times 7 \ \mu C = \frac{84}{5} \mu C = 16.8 \ \mu C.$$

$\therefore$ charge $= 16.8 \ \mu C.$

(28)

(a) Dipole moment of dipole

$$AB = \vec{p} = p \ \hat{j}.$$

Dipole moment of dipole

$$CD = \vec{p} = p \cos 30^\circ \ \hat{i}$$

$$- p \cos 60^\circ \ \hat{j}$$

$$= p \frac{\sqrt{3}}{2} \ \hat{i} - \frac{p}{2} \ \hat{j}.$$

$\therefore$ net dipole moment $= p \hat{j} + \left(p \frac{\sqrt{3}}{2} \ \hat{i} - \frac{p}{2} \hat{j} \right)$

$(\vec{P})$

$$= p \frac{\sqrt{3}}{2} \ \hat{i} + \frac{p}{2} \ \hat{j}$$

$$\therefore |\vec{P}| = \sqrt{p^2 \frac{3}{4} + \frac{p^2}{4}} = \sqrt{p^2} = p.$$

$\therefore$ magnitude of dipole moment $= p.$

$$\tan\theta = \frac{\frac{p}{2}}{\frac{\sqrt{3}}{2}} = \frac{1}{\sqrt{3}}. \quad \therefore \text{ angle made by it with +ve } x\text{-axis}$$

$$= 30^\circ \ (Ans.)$$

13

Torque acting on a dipole of dipole moment $\vec{p}$ in electric field $\vec{E}$
$$\vec{\tau} = \vec{p} \times \vec{E}$$

For AB, dipole moment $= p\,\hat{j}$.
field $= E\,\hat{i}$.

$\therefore$ Torque, $\vec{\tau}_{AB} = (p\,\hat{j} \times E\,\hat{i}) = pE\,(-\hat{k})$.

For CD, dipole moment $= \left(p\frac{\sqrt{3}}{2}\,\hat{i} - \frac{p}{2}\,\hat{j}\right)$
field $= E\,\hat{i}$.

$\therefore$ Torque, $\vec{\tau}_{CD} = \left(p\frac{\sqrt{3}}{2}\,\hat{i} - \frac{p}{2}\,\hat{j}\right) \times E\,\hat{i}$
$$= pE\frac{\sqrt{3}}{2} \times 0 - \frac{p}{2}E\cdot(-\hat{k}) = \frac{pE}{2}\,\hat{k}.$$

net Torque $= \vec{\tau}_{AB} + \vec{\tau}_{CD} = -\frac{pE}{2}\,\hat{k} = \frac{pE}{2}\,(-\hat{k})$.

$\therefore$ magnitude $= \frac{pE}{2}$.

direction $=$ into the plane of paper $(-\hat{k})$.

29 (a)

Sol. the four resistances R_1, R_2, R_3 and R_4 are connected as shown in the figure and they are connected by battery of emf V. the current

14

distribution is shown in the figure.

In balanced wheatstone bridge, current through galvanometer $= 0$.

$\therefore \; I_g = 0.$

By KVL in loop ABDA, $\;-I_1 R_1 - I_g G + (I - I_1) R_2 = 0, \;\; \text{—(i)}$

$G = $ Resistance of galvanometer.

By KVL in loop BCDB,

$-(I_1 - I_g) R_3 + (I - I_1 + I_g) R_4 + I_g G = 0. \; \text{—(ii)}$

Putting $I_g = 0$ in (i) and (ii).

from (i), $\;-I_1 R_1 + (I - I_1) R_2 = 0$

$\Rightarrow (I - I_1) R_2 = I_1 R_1$

$\Rightarrow \dfrac{R_1}{R_2} = \dfrac{I - I_1}{I_1} \quad \Rightarrow \text{(a)}.$

from (ii), $\;-(I_1) R_3 + (I - I_1) R_4 = 0$

$\Rightarrow (I - I_1) R_4 = I_1 R_3$

$\Rightarrow \dfrac{R_3}{R_4} = \dfrac{I - I_1}{I_1} \quad \Rightarrow \text{(b)}.$

from (a) and (b), $\;\boxed{\dfrac{R_1}{R_2} = \dfrac{R_3}{R_4}}\;$ This is the condition of balance in wheatstone bridge.

P.T.O.

15

① A meter bridge works on the condition of balance in wheatstone bridge.

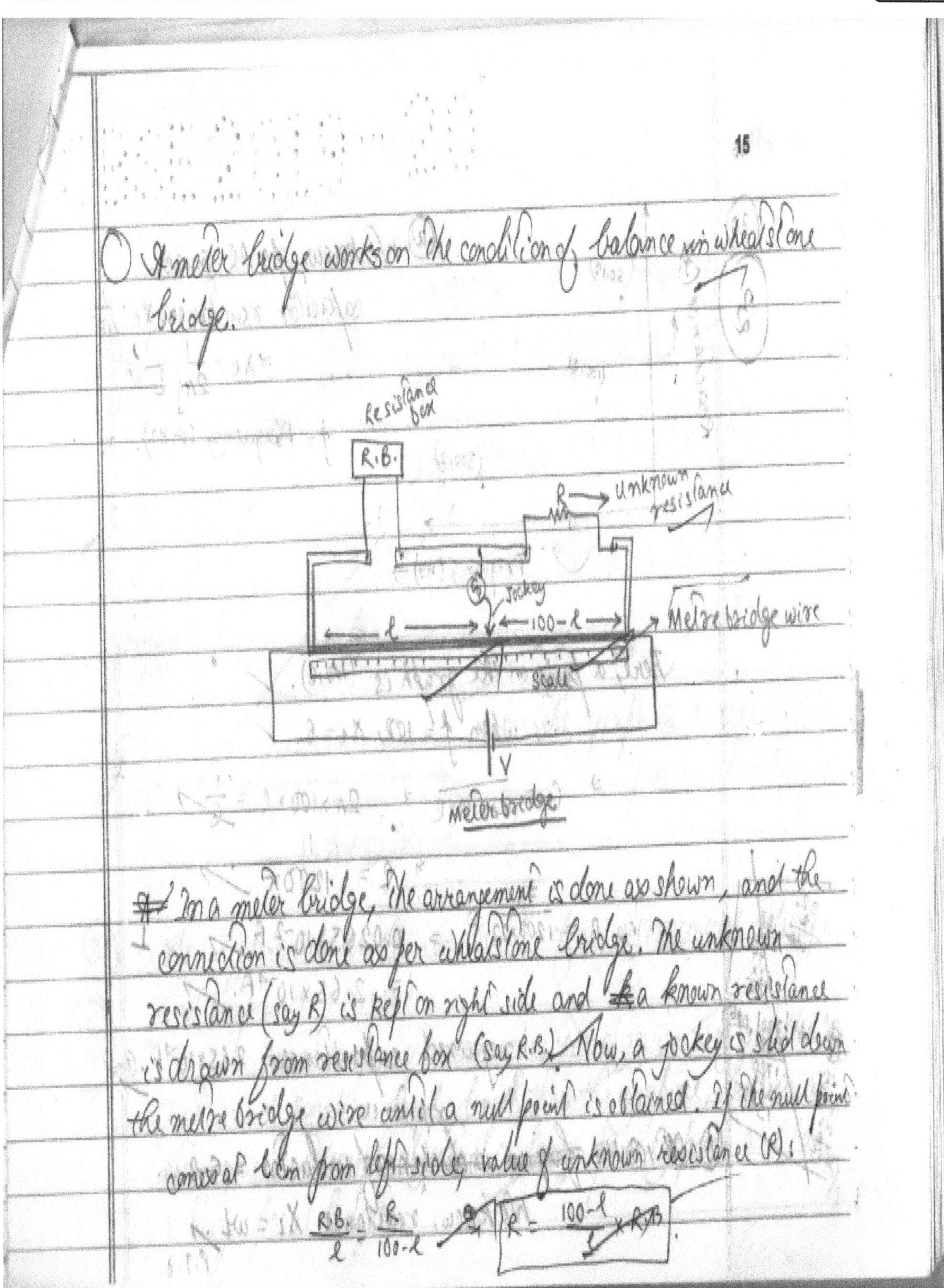

\# In a meter bridge, the arrangement is done as shown, and the connection is done as per wheatstone bridge. The unknown resistance (say R) is kept on right side and a known resistance is drawn from resistance box (say R.B.). Now, a jockey is slid down the metre bridge wire until a null point is obtained. If the null point comes at l cm from left side, value of unknown resistance (R):

$$\frac{R.B.}{l} = \frac{R}{100-l} \implies \boxed{R = \frac{100-l}{l} \times R.B.}$$

16

(30)

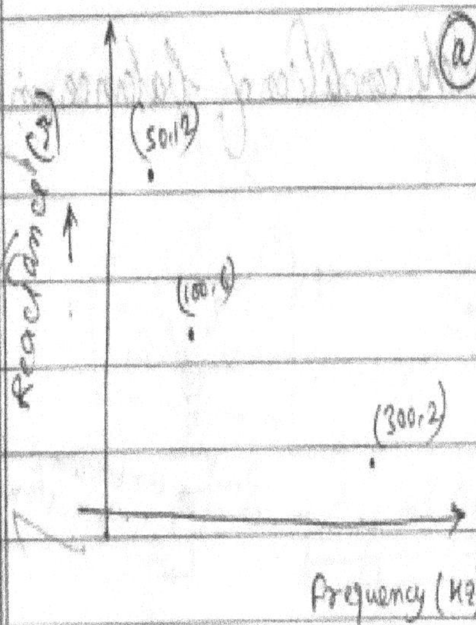

ⓐ We know, for AC source,

capacitor reactance, $X_C = \frac{1}{\omega C}$

$\Rightarrow X_C = \frac{1}{2\pi f C}$,

f = frequency (in Hz).

Here, a point on the graph is (100, 6).

∴, when $f = 100$, $X_C = 6$.

$\Rightarrow 6 = \frac{1}{2\pi \times 100 \times C} \Rightarrow 2\pi \times 100 \times C = \frac{1}{6}$

$\Rightarrow C = \frac{1}{1200\pi}$

∴, $C = \frac{7}{1200 \times 22}$ F $= 0.0265 \times 10^{-2}$ F

$= 2.65 \times 10^{-4}$ F.

∴, required capacitance = 2.65×10^{-4} F. (Ans)

ⓑ ~~At~~ 100 Hz, ~~frequen~~ ~~inductance~~ reactance of inductor = 6 Ω

We know, reactance $X_L = \omega L$,

P.T.O.

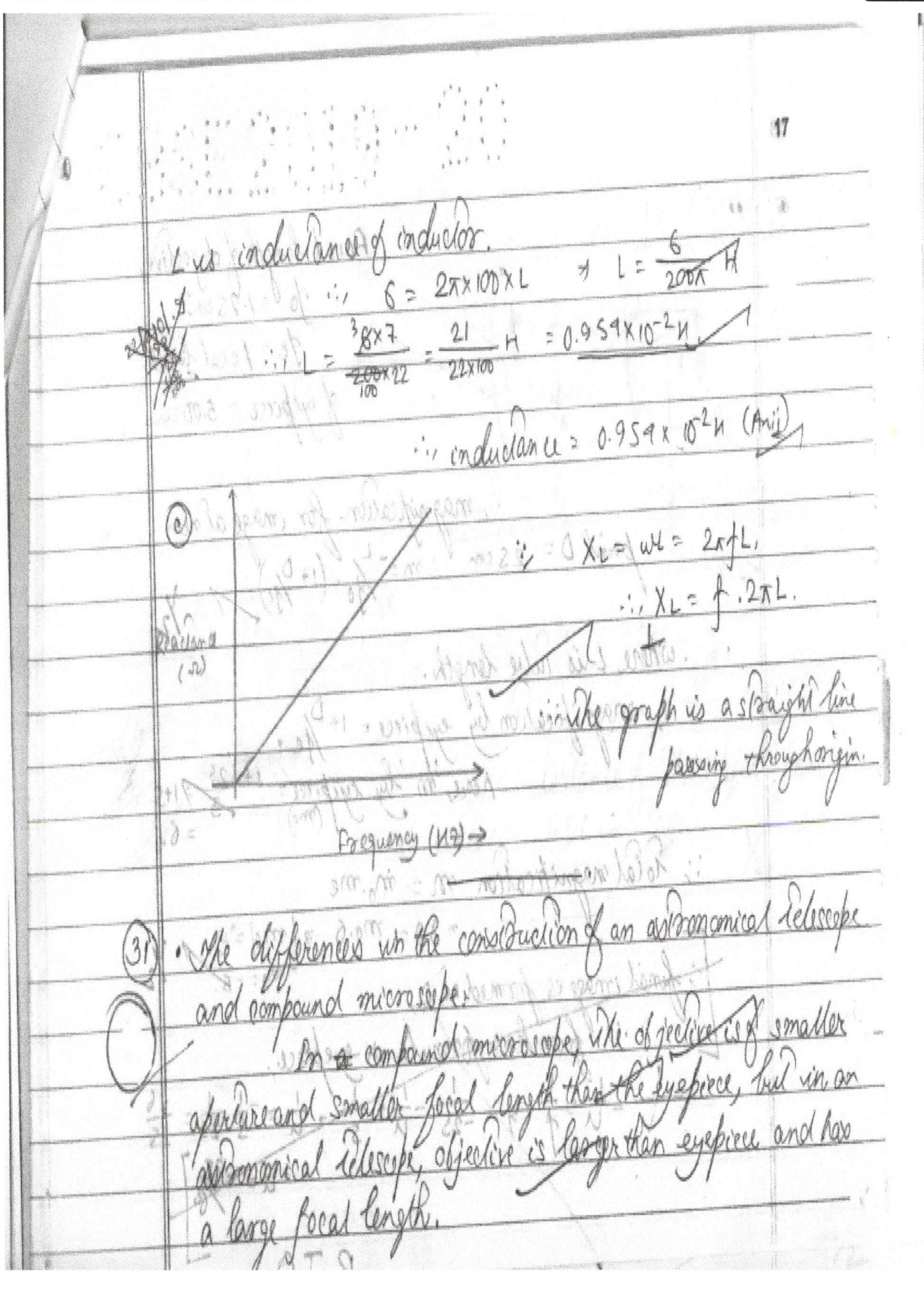

(31) • The differences in the construction of an astronomical telescope and compound microscope.

In a compound microscope, the objective is of smaller aperture and smaller focal length than the eyepiece, but in an astronomical telescope, objective is larger than eyepiece and has a large focal length.

18

Focal length of objective,

$$f_0 = 1.25 \text{ cm},$$

$$f_e = \text{Focal length of eyepiece} = 5.00 \text{ cm}.$$

∴ magnification for image at near point $D = 25$ cm : $m = -\dfrac{L}{f_0} \cdot \left(1 + \dfrac{D}{f_e}\right)$.

where, L is tube length.

∴ magnification by eyepiece $= 1 + \dfrac{D}{f_e}$,

here, m' by eyepiece $(m_e) = 1 + \dfrac{25}{5} = 1 + 5 = 6$.

∴ Total magnification $m = m_0 \cdot m_e$

$$30 = m_0 \cdot 6 \Rightarrow |m_0| = 5$$

$$\Rightarrow m_0 = -5.$$

∵ final image is formed at D,

∴ from lens formula in eyepiece,

$$\frac{1}{v} - \frac{1}{u} = \frac{1}{f} \Rightarrow \frac{1}{-25} - \frac{1}{u} = \frac{1}{5}, \quad \frac{1}{u} = -\frac{1}{5} - \frac{1}{25} = \frac{-6}{25}$$

$$u = -\frac{25}{6}$$

P.T.O.

19

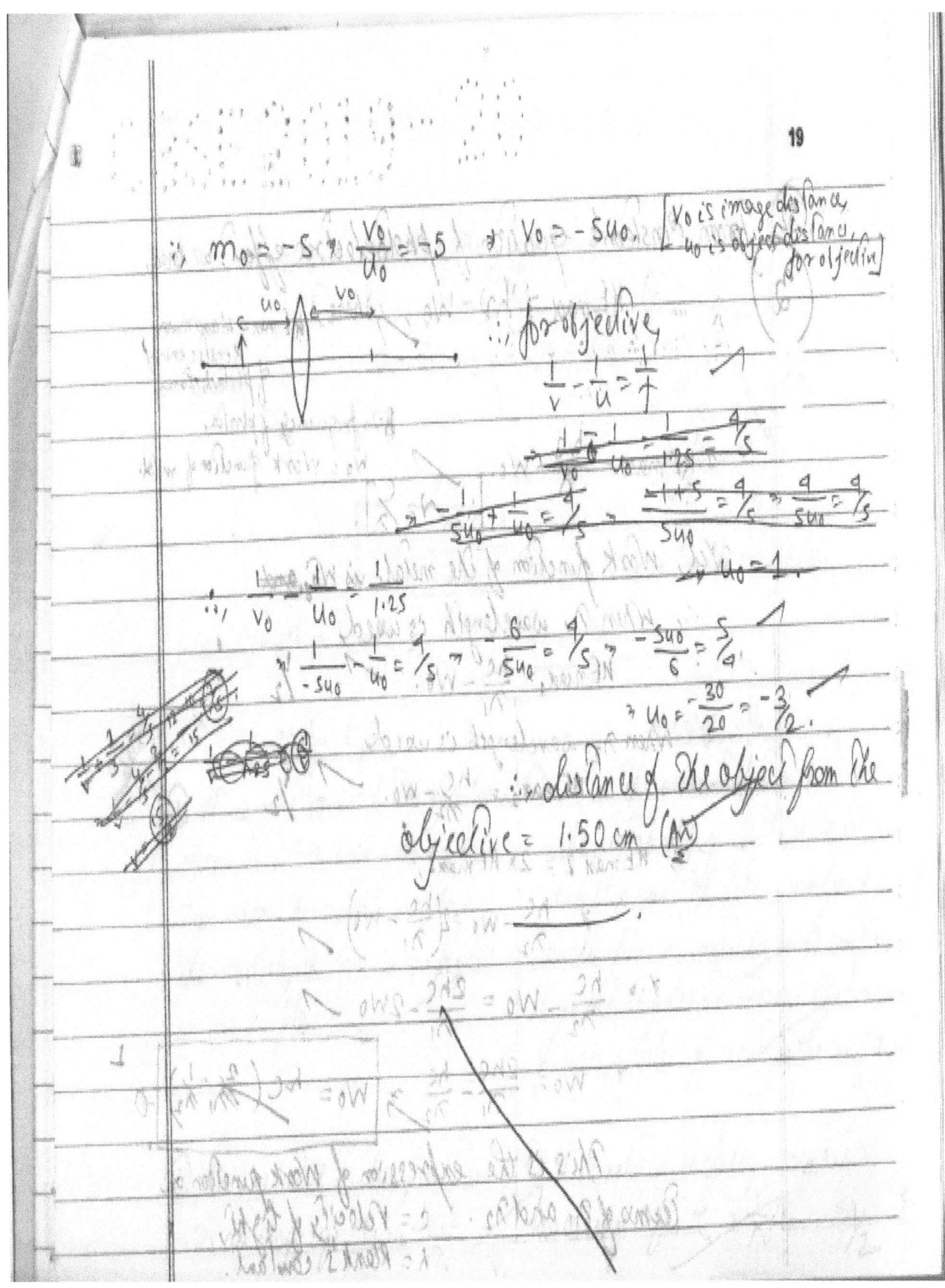
$\therefore m_0 = -5 \Rightarrow \dfrac{v_0}{u_0} = -5 \Rightarrow v_0 = -5u_0$
v_0 is image distance, u_0 is object distance, for objective.

$\therefore$ for objective
$\dfrac{1}{v} - \dfrac{1}{u} = \dfrac{1}{f}$

$\dfrac{1}{v_0} - \dfrac{1}{u_0} = \dfrac{1}{1.25}$

$\dfrac{1}{-5u_0} - \dfrac{1}{u_0} = \dfrac{4}{5} \Rightarrow \dfrac{-6}{5u_0} = \dfrac{4}{5}$

$\Rightarrow u_0 = -\dfrac{30}{20} = -\dfrac{3}{2}$

$\therefore$ distance of the object from the objective = 1·50 cm

32) From Einstein's equation of photoelectric effect, we know,

$$KE_{max} = h\nu - W_0, \quad \text{where,} \quad KE_{max} = \text{Maximum kinetic energy of photoelectrons,}$$

$$\nu = \text{frequency of photon,}$$
$$W_0 = \text{Work function of metal.}$$

$$KE_{max} = \frac{hc}{\lambda} - W_0. \qquad \boxed{\nu = \frac{c}{\lambda}}.$$

Let, Work function of the metal is W_0,

$\therefore$ when λ_1 wavelength is used,

$$KE_{max_1} = \frac{hc}{\lambda_1} - W_0.$$

When λ_2 wavelength is used

$$KE_{max_2} = \frac{hc}{\lambda_2} - W_0.$$

$\therefore KE_{max\,2} = 2 \times KE_{max\,1},$

$$\Rightarrow \frac{hc}{\lambda_2} - W_0 = 2\left(\frac{hc}{\lambda_1} - W_0\right)$$

$$\Rightarrow \frac{hc}{\lambda_2} - W_0 = \frac{2hc}{\lambda_1} - 2W_0$$

$$\Rightarrow W_0 = \frac{2hc}{\lambda_1} - \frac{hc}{\lambda_2} \Rightarrow \boxed{W_0 = hc\left(\frac{2}{\lambda_1} - \frac{1}{\lambda_2}\right)} \text{--}①$$

This is the expression of Work function on terms of λ_1 and λ_2. $c = $ velocity of light,

$$h = \text{Plank's constant.}$$

P.T.O.

21

Let, threshold wavelength be λ_0.

λ_0 is related to W_0 as $W_0 = \dfrac{hc}{\lambda_0}$

$\therefore$ from ①, $\dfrac{hc}{\lambda_0} = hc\left(\dfrac{2}{\lambda_1} - \dfrac{1}{\lambda_2}\right)$

$\Rightarrow \dfrac{1}{\lambda_0} = \dfrac{2}{\lambda_1} - \dfrac{1}{\lambda_2} = \dfrac{2\lambda_2 - \lambda_1}{\lambda_1 \lambda_2}$

$$\boxed{\lambda_0 = \dfrac{\lambda_1 \lambda_2}{2\lambda_2 - \lambda_1}}$$ This is expression of threshold

wavelength in Terms of λ_1 and λ_2 (Ans)

③ ⓐ

Half- life	Average life
ⓘ It is the amount of time of radioactive decay at which half of the nuclei has been decayed and half of the undecayed nuclei are present in the sample.	ⓘ It is the amount of time ratio of the total life of all the radioactive samples and the total number of nuclei present initially in the sample. It actually denotes average life time of each nuclei present in the sample.
ⓘⓘ It is related to decay constant as half-life, $t_{1/2} = \dfrac{\ln 2}{\lambda}$	ⓘⓘ It is related to decay constant as average life, $\tau = \dfrac{1}{\lambda}$

22

(ii) If is less than average life

$$ax \quad t_{1/2} = \frac{\tau}{\ln 2} = \tau \ln 2 = 0.693\,\tau$$

(iii) If is more than average life

$$ax \quad \tau = \frac{t_{1/2}}{\ln 2} = \frac{t_{1/2}}{0.693}$$

(b) Time of decay = Average life or mean life = τ.

Let, initial number of sample be N_0.

We knew, sample present at time t undecayed,

$$N = N_0 e^{-\lambda t}$$

$$\therefore \tau = \frac{1}{\lambda}, \qquad \therefore N = N_0 e^{-\lambda \tau} = N_0 e^{-\tau/\tau} = N_0 e^{-1} = \frac{N_0}{e}$$

$\therefore$ fraction of amount undecayed

$$= \frac{N_0/e}{N_0} = \frac{1}{e} = 0.368$$

$\therefore$ required fraction = 0.368

P.T.O.

(34)
- The function of a solar cell is to convert solar energy (light energy) to electrical energy. 1

" The solar cell is made of a thick (about 300 µm) p-type region and a thin (about 1 µm) n-type region of a p-n junction diode. Solar ~~energy~~ photons of energy (about 1-1·5 eV) are allowed to fall around the depletion region of the diode. It works by three basic processes —

(i) Formation: When photons of appropriate energy range hit the p-n junction depletion region, new electron-hole pairs are generated.

(ii) Separation: On formation, the holes are pushed to p-side and electrons to n-side of the depletion layer by depletion layer electric field acting from n to p.

(iii) Collection: Immediately, the holes are collected by the forward

collector, and electrons of n-side by backward support.
So, p-side becomes positive and n-side becomes
negative.

     Hence, electricity can be generated.

I-V characteristics

short
current
open circuit voltage

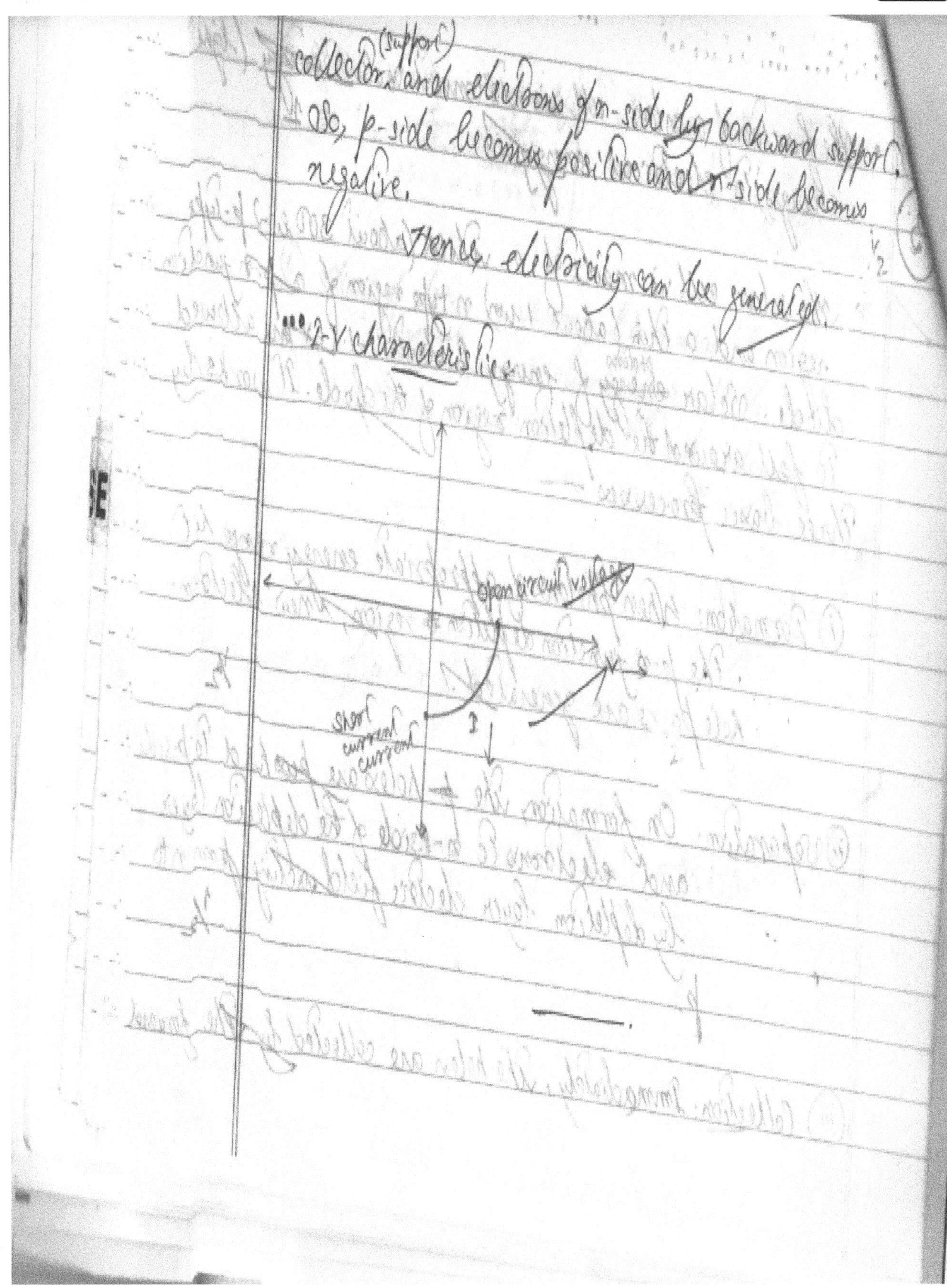

collector (support) and electrons of n-side by backward support.

So, p-side becomes positive and n-side becomes negative.

Hence, electricity can be generated.

I-V characteristics

25. (a) Let, a point charge q is situated in a region. Electric field due to 'q' at a radial distance $r = \dfrac{kq\,\hat{r}}{r^2} = \dfrac{q}{4\pi\varepsilon_0 r^2}$.

Now, consider a uniformly charged spherical shell of radius R, containing charge q.

Let, we take a spherical Gaussian surface of radius $r > R$ & centering at centre of shell, say O.

∴ from symmetry of the figure,
(i) magnitude of $\vec{E}$ throughout the Gaussian surface is constant.
(ii) The angle between $\vec{E}$ and area vector $\vec{S}$ is constant.

Always, $\vec{E} \parallel \vec{S}$

So, using Gauss' law for a sphere of radius r,

$$\oint \vec{E}\cdot \vec{dS} = \frac{q_{in}}{\varepsilon_0}$$

$$\oint E\,ds = \frac{q}{\varepsilon_0} \quad [\because \vec{E}\cdot\vec{dS} = E\,ds\,\cos 0^\circ = E\,ds]$$

$$\Rightarrow E\cdot 4\pi r^2 = \frac{q}{\varepsilon_0} \Rightarrow \boxed{E = \frac{q}{4\pi\varepsilon_0 r^2}}$$

∴ field due to a distance $r = \dfrac{q}{4\pi\varepsilon_0 r^2}$

26

∴ The field at distance r is equal to the field as if whole charge q is placed at the centre.

Now again, taking Gaussian surface of radius $r < R$, inside the shell,

$$\oint \vec{E} \cdot d\vec{S} = \frac{q_{in}}{\epsilon_0}$$

∵ whole charge of shell is at the surface, ∴ $q_{in} = 0$.

$$\Rightarrow \oint \vec{E} \cdot d\vec{S} = 0$$

$$\Rightarrow E \cdot 4\pi r^2 = 0$$

$$\boxed{\vec{E} = 0}$$

graph:

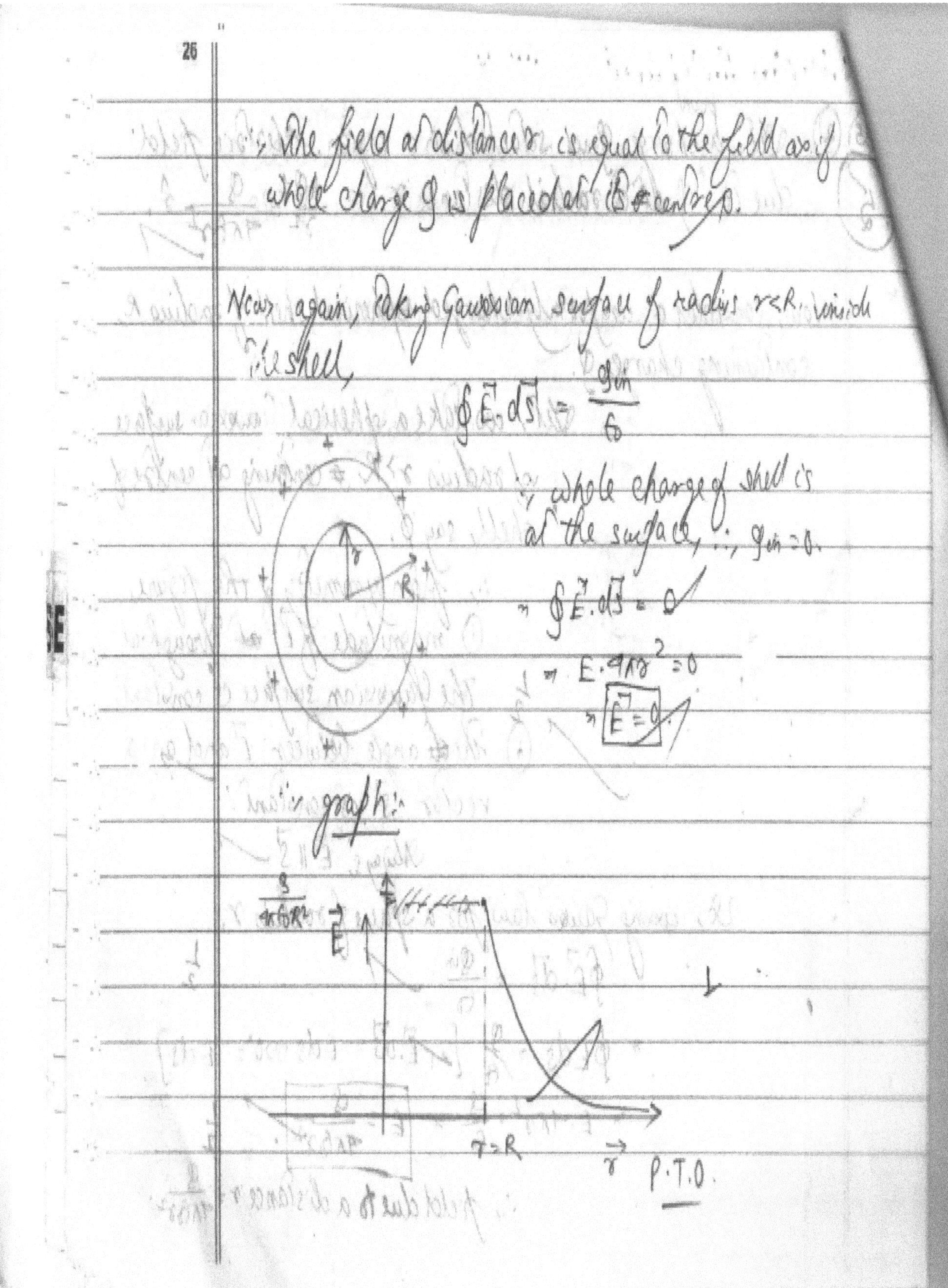

P.T.O.

27

(i)

$+1\mu C \xrightarrow{\quad x \quad} P \qquad\qquad +4\mu C$

$\xleftarrow{\qquad 30\,cm \qquad}$

Sol: The electric field is 0 at distance x cm from $1\mu C$ charge. Let the point be P.

$\therefore$ field at P due to $1\mu C$ charge $= \dfrac{k \times 1\mu C}{x^2}\,\hat{i}$

field at P due to $+4\mu C$ charge $= \dfrac{k \times 4\mu C}{(30-x)^2}(-\hat{i})$

$\therefore$ net field is 0,

$$\dfrac{k \times 1\mu C}{x^2} = \dfrac{k \times 4\mu C}{(30-x)^2}$$

$$\Rightarrow \dfrac{x^2}{(30-x)^2} = \dfrac{1}{4} \Rightarrow \dfrac{x}{30-x} = \pm\dfrac{1}{2}$$

$$\therefore \dfrac{x}{30-x} = \dfrac{1}{2} \qquad\qquad \dfrac{x}{30-x} = -\dfrac{1}{2}$$

$$\Rightarrow 2x = 30-x \qquad\qquad \Rightarrow 2x = x-30$$

$$\Rightarrow x = 10 \qquad\qquad \Rightarrow x = -30.$$

(absurd, since field in same direction)

$\therefore$ the field is 0 at distance 10 cm from $1\mu C$ charge

36) (a)

Sol. A current carrying loop of radius R is carrying current I and placed in y-z plane having centre at O.

We have to find magnetic field at P, a point at a distance x from centre O along x-axis.

∴ Let us take a small segment dl carrying current I.

∴ dB due to this segment at P, by Biot-Savart law,

$$d\vec{B} = \frac{\mu_0 I}{4\pi r^2} \, d\vec{l} \times \hat{r}$$

∴ $d\vec{l}$ and $\hat{r}$ are perpendicular, ∴ $d\vec{l} \times \hat{r} = dl$.

$$|d\vec{B}| = \frac{\mu_0 I \, dl}{4\pi r^2}$$

We see, the magnetic field dB is making angle θ with vertical, where θ is semi-vertical angle of cone formed by P and the loop.

By symmetry, $d\vec{B}\cos\theta$ will be cancelled; hence $d\vec{B}\sin\theta$ is only to be added.

$$\therefore dB\sin\theta = \frac{\mu_0 I \, dl}{4\pi r^2}\sin\alpha$$

But) $\dfrac{x}{r} = \cos\theta \Rightarrow r = x\sec\alpha \Rightarrow r^2 = x^2\sec^2\theta = (R^2 + x^2)$,

$$\therefore d\vec{B} = \frac{\mu_0 I \, dl}{4\pi (R^2+x^2)} \cdot \frac{R}{(R^2+x^2)^{1/2}}$$

Total field $\vec{B} = \int d\vec{B} = \dfrac{\mu_0 I R}{4\pi (R^2+x^2)^{3/2}} \cdot \int dl$

$$= \frac{\mu_0 I R}{2\pi (R^2+x^2)^{3/2}} \cdot 2\pi R$$

$$\boxed{\vec{B} = \frac{\mu_0 I R^2}{2(R^2+x^2)^{3/2}}\,\hat{z}}$$

$\therefore$ This is expression of magnetic field.

earth's magnetic field $= 0.6\times10^{-4}\,T$,

angle of dip $= 30°$,

$I = 5A$

$\therefore$ vertical component $= 0.6\times10^{-4}\times\sin 30°$

$$= 0.3\times10^{-4}\,T.$$

30

The rod carries current from north to south and horizontal component of earth's magnetic field is parallel. So, force due to this component = 0.

The vertical component is pointing downwards, say B. So it will exert force.

$\therefore$ The force on the rod $= |I(\vec{\ell} \times \vec{B})|$

$= |5 \times \ell B \sin 90°|$

$= 5\ell B = 5 \times 2 \times 0.3 \times 10^{-4}\,N$

$= 0.3 \times 10^{-3}\,N$

$\therefore$ magnitude of force $= 0.3 \times 10^{-3}\,N$.

direction according to Fleming's left hand rule:

east to west   (Ans)

(37) (OR), (a) · The locus of all the points on a medium travelling with same frequency and having same phase is called a wavefront.

It propagates along the wave, with the electric and magnetic fields perpendicular mutually and to the direction of wave propagation. It is perpendicular to the ray direction.

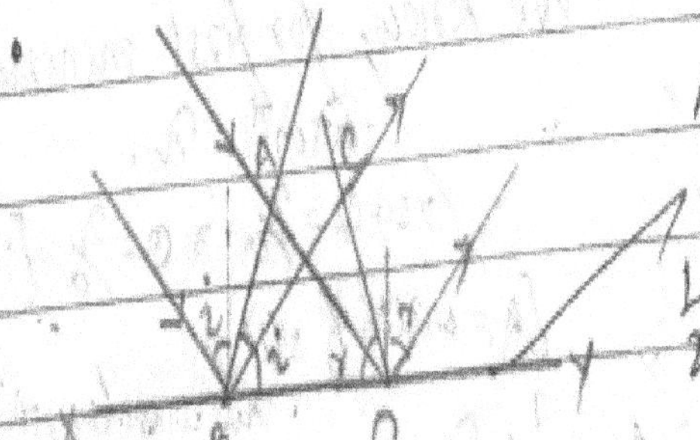

Let, we consider, a plane wavefront AB incident on plane XY at angle of incidence θi. The rays are perpendicular to the wavefront.

By the time ray AO reaches O, Ray from B has travelled a distance C' along.

So, drawing an arc from B and drawing tangent from O on it, it cuts BC at C. ∴, AO = BC [as speed of wave is same]. $\angle ABO = i$, $\angle AOB = r$. r is the angle of reflection.

∴ in △ ABO and △ BCO,
$$AO = BC \quad [\text{from O}]$$
$$BO = BO,$$
$$\angle BAO = \angle BCO \quad [90°].$$

∴, △ ABO ≅ △ BCO.

∴, $\angle ABO = \angle AOB$, ∴ $\boxed{\angle i = \angle r}$.

Hence, law of reflection is proved. In the figure the reflected wavefront is OC.

T.T.

(6) We know, for first minimum,

$$a \sin\theta = \lambda.$$

$$\Rightarrow \sin\theta = \lambda/a \Rightarrow \theta = \lambda/a \quad [\because \theta \text{ is very small}]$$

$$[a = \text{width of slit},$$
$$\lambda = \text{wavelength}].$$

$$\therefore \text{ linear distance} = D\theta = \dfrac{D\lambda}{a}.$$

$$[D \text{ is distance between slit and screen}].$$

Here, $\dfrac{D\lambda}{a} = 2.5 \, mm$

$$\dfrac{1 \times 500 \times 10^{-9}}{a} = 2.5 \times 10^{-3}$$

$$\Rightarrow a = \dfrac{500 \times 10^{-9}}{2.5 \times 10^{-3}} = 200 \times 10^{-6} \Rightarrow 2 \times 10^{-4} \, m$$
$$= 0.2 \, mm$$

$$\therefore \text{ slit width} = 0.2 \, mm \text{ (Ans)}$$

Now, angular distance ~~for a~~ for first secondary maximum:

$$\theta \Rightarrow a \sin\theta = \dfrac{3\lambda}{2} \Rightarrow \theta = \dfrac{3\lambda}{2a}.$$

$$\therefore \text{ linear distance} = \dfrac{3\lambda D}{2a}.$$

$$\therefore \text{ linear distance} = \dfrac{3}{2} \lambda \dfrac{D\lambda}{a} = \dfrac{3}{2} \times 2.5 \, mm$$

$$= 3.75 \, mm$$

$$\therefore \text{ distance} = 3.75 \, mm \text{ (Ans)}$$

1

Sample Paper

LATEST PATTERN

BLUE PRINT

Ch. No.	Chapter Name	Per Unit Marks	Section-A MCQs 1 Mark	Section-B SA 2 Marks	Section-C LA-I 3 Marks	Section-D LA-II 5 Marks	Section-E Case Study 4 Marks	Total Marks
1	Electric Charges and Fields		1 (Q. 16)			1 (Q. 31)	1 (Q. 34)	10
2	Electrostatic Potential and Capacitance	16	2 (Q. 1, 17)					2
3	Current Electricity		1 (Q. 2)		1 (Q. 27)			4
4	Moving Charges and Magnetism		1 (Q. 3)	1 (Q.19)				3
5	Magnetism and Matter		1 (Q. 15)	1 (Q.24)				3
6	Electromagnetic Induction	17		1 (Q. 22)	1 (Q. 26)			5
7	Alternating Current		1 (Q. 4)			1 (Q. 32)		6
8	Electromagnetic Waves		2 (Q. 5, 14)					2
9	Ray optics and Optical Instruments	18	2 (Q. 13,18)	1 (Q. 25)			1 (Q. 35)	8
10	Wave Optics		1 (Q. 6)	1 (Q. 20)		1 (Q. 33)		8
11	Dual Nature of Radiation and Matter		1 (Q. 9)		1 (Q. 28)			4
12	Atoms	12	1 (Q. 8)		1 (Q. 29)			4
13	Nuclei		1 (Q. 7)		1 (Q. 30)			4
14	Semiconductor Electronics: Materials, Devices and Simple Circuits	7	3 (Q. 10, 11, 12)	2 (Q. 21, 23)				7
	Total Marks (Total Questions)		**18 (18)**	**14 (7)**	**15 (5)**	**15 (3)**	**8 (2)**	**70 (35)**

NOTE : The number given inside the bracket denotes question number, ask in the sample paper, while the number given outside the bracket are the number of questions from that particular chapter.

Time Allowed : 3 Hours | **Max. Marks : 70**

General Instructions

1. There are 35 questions in all. All questions are compulsory.
2. This question paper has five sections: Section A, Section B, Section C, Section D and Section E. All the sections are compulsory.
3. Section A contains eighteen MCQ of 1 mark each, Section B contains seven questions of two marks each, Section C contains five questions of three marks each, section D contains three long questions of five marks each and Section E contains two case study based questions of 4 marks each.
4. There is no overall choice. However, an internal choice has been provided in section B, C, D and E. You have to attempt only one of the choices in such questions.
5. Use of calculators is not allowed.

SECTION-A

1. The capacitors of capacity C_1 and C_2 are connected in parallel, then the equivalent capacitance is

   (a) $C_1 + C_2$ (b) $\dfrac{C_1 C_2}{C_1 + C_2}$ (c) $\dfrac{C_1}{C_2}$ (d) $\dfrac{C_2}{C_1}$

2. The powers of two electric bulbs are 100 watt and 200 watt. Both of them are joined with 220 volt. The ratio of resistance of their filament will be

   (a) $4:1$ (b) $1:4$ (c) $1:2$ (d) $2:1$

3. A moving coil galvanometer has N number of turns in a coil of effective area A, it carries a current I. The magnetic field B is radial. The torque acting on the coil is

   (a) $NA^2 B^2 I$ (b) $NABI^2$ (c) $N^2 ABI$ (d) $NABI$

4. The transformer voltage induced in the secondary coil of a transformer is mainly due to
   (a) a varying electric field   (b) a varying magnetic field
   (c) the vibrations of the primary coil   (d) the iron core of the transformer

5. The magnetic field in a travelling electromagnetic wave has a peak value of 20 nT. The peak value of electric field strength is
   (a) 3 V/m   (b) 6 V/m   (c) 9 V/m   (d) 12 V/m

6. If the width of the slit in single slit diffraction experiment is doubled, then the central maximum of diffraction pattern becomes
   (a) broader and brighter   (b) sharper and brighter
   (c) sharper and fainter   (d) broader adn fainter.

7. If the total binding energies of ^2_1H, ^4_2He, $^{56}_{26}Fe$ & $^{235}_{92}U$ nuclei are 2.22, 28.3, 492 and 1786 MeV respectively, identify the most stable nucleus of the following.

   (a) $^{56}_{26}Fe$ (b) ^2_1H (c) $^{235}_{92}U$ (d) ^4_2He

8. The significant result deduced from the Rutherford's scattering experiment is that
   (a) whole of the positive charge is concentrated at the centre of atom
   (b) there are neutrons inside the nucleus
   (c) α-particles are helium nuclei
   (d) electrons are embedded in the atom

9. With reference to the observations in photo-electric effect, identify the correct statements from below:
   A. The square of maximum velocity of photoelectrons varies linearly with frequency of incident light.
   B. The value of saturation current increases on moving the source of light away from the metal surface.
   C. The maximum kinetic energy of photo-electrons decreases on decreasing the power of LED (light emitting diode) source of light.
   D. The immediate emission of photo-electrons out of metal surface can not be explained by particle nature of light/ electromagnetic waves.
   E. Existence of threshold wavelength can not be explained by wave nature of light/electromagnetic waves.
   Choose the correct answer from the options given below:
   (a) A and B only   (b) A and E only   (c) C and E only   (d) D and E only

10. In the energy band diagram of a material shown below, the open circles and filled circles denote holes and electrons respectively. The material is

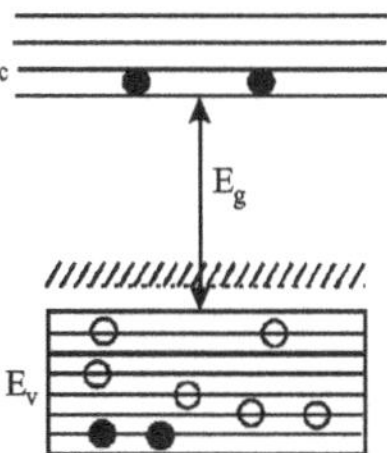

(a) an insulator   (b) a metal   (c) an n-type semiconductor   (d) a p-type semiconductor

11. In the half wave rectifier circuit operating from 50 Hz mains frequency, the fundamental frequency in the ripple would be

(a) 25 Hz   (b) 50 Hz   (c) 70.7 Hz   (d) 100 Hz

12. A pure semiconductor has equal electron and hole concentration of 10^{16} m^{-3}. Doping by indium increases n_h to 5×10^{22} m^{-3}. Then, the value of n_e in the doped semiconductor is

(a) 10^6/m^3 (b) 10^{22}/m^3 (c) 2×10^6/m^3 (d) 2×10^9/m^3

13. The focal length of the objective of a telescope is 60 cm. To obtain a magnification of 20, the focal length of the eye piece should be

(a) 2 cm   (b) 3 cm   (c) 4 cm   (d) 5 cm

14. In electromagnetic spectrum, the frequencies γ-rays, X-rays and ultraviolet rays are denoted by n_1, n_2 and n_3 respectively then

(a) $n_1 > n_2 > n_3$ (b) $n_1 < n_2 < n_3$ (c) $n_1 > n_2 < n_3$ (d) $n_1 < n_2 > n_3$

15. Metals getting magnetised by orientation of atomic magnetic moments in external magnetic field are called

(a) diamagnetic   (b) paramagnetic   (c) ferromagnetic   (d) antimagnetic

For question numbers 16, 17 and 18, two statements are given-one labelled Assertion (A) and the other labelled Reason (R). Select the correct answer to these questions from the codes (a), (b), (c) and (d) as given below.

(a) Both A and R are true and R is the correct explanation of A

(b) Both A and R are true but R is NOT the correct explanation of A

(c) A is true but R is false

(d) A is false and R is also false

16. Assertion (A) : On going away from a point charge or a small electric dipole, electric field decreases at the same rate in both the cases.

Reason (R) : Electric field is inversely proportional to square of distance from the charge or an electric dipole.

17. Assertion (A): When a dielectric slab is gradually inserted between the plates of an isolated parallel-plate capacitor, the energy of the system decreases.

Reason (R): The force between the plates decreases.

18. Assertion (A) : The objective of telescope has small focal length.

Reason (R): If objective and eye lenses of a microscope are interchanged then it can work as telescope.

SECTION-B

19. Derive an expression for the magnetic field at the centre of a circular current carrying coil using Biot – Savart's law.

20. A plane wavefront is incident on

(i) a prism   (ii) a convex lens.

Draw the emergent wavefront in each case.

21. Assuming that the two diodes D_1 and D_2 used in the electric circuit shown in the figure are ideal, find out the value of the current flowing through 2.5Ω resistor.

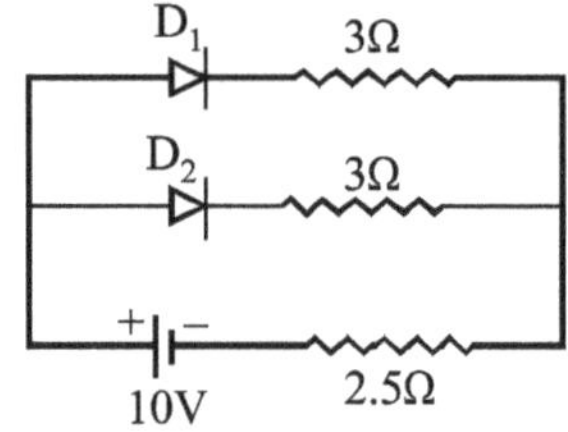

22. A small piece of metal wire is dragged across the gap between the pole piece of a magnet in 0.5 s. The magnetic flux between the pole pieces is known to be 8×10^{-4} Wb. Calculate the induced emf in the wire.
    −ve sign gives the direction of e.m.f.

OR

If the rate of change of current is 2 A/s and induces an e.m.f. of 40 mV in the solenoid, what is the self-inductance of the solenoid?

23. What are the requirements for an element to be a good dopant?

24. A circular coil of N turns and radius R carries a current I. It is unwound and rewound to make another coil of radius R/2, current I remaining the same. Calculate the ratio of the magnetic moments of the new coil and the original coil.

25. Two monochromatic rays of light are incident normally on the face AB of an isosceles right-angled prism ABC. The refractive indices of the glass prism for the two rays '1' and '2' are respectively 1.35 and 1.45. Trace the path of these rays after entering the prism.

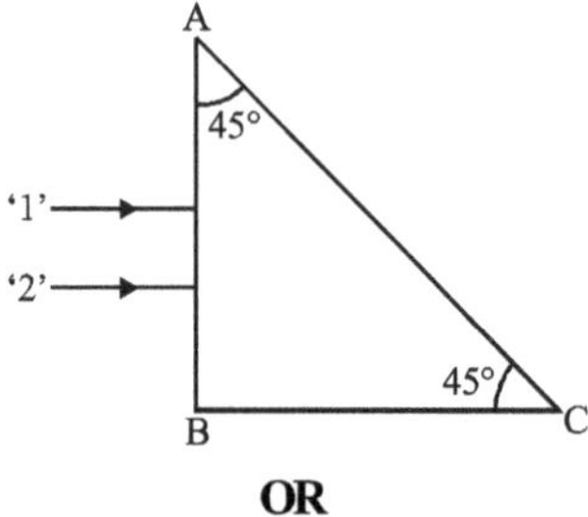

OR

A ray of light passes through an equilateral prism in such a manner that the angle of incidence is equal to angle of emergence and each of these angle is equal to $\frac{3}{4}$ of angle of prism. Find angle of deviation.

SECTION-C

26. Define the term mutual inductance. Write its S.I. unit. Give two factors on which the coefficient of mutual inductance between a pair of coil depends.

27. Define the term resistivity of a conductor. Give its S.I. unit. Show that the resistivity of a conductor is given by $\frac{m}{ne^2\tau}$ where symbols have their usual meanings.

28. Write Einstein's photoelectric equation. Mention the underlying properties of photons on the basis of which this equation is obtained.
    Write two important observations of photoelectric effect which can be explained by Einstein's equation.

OR

A proton and an alpha particle are accelerated through the same potential. Which one of the two has (i) greater value of de–Broglie wavelength associated with it and (ii) less kinetic energy. Give reasons to justify your answer.

29. Show that the radius of the orbit in hydrogen atom varies as n^2, where n is the principal quantum numbers of the atom.

30. How the size of a nuclus is experimentally determined? Write the relation between the radius and mass number of the nucleus. Show that the density of nucleus is independent of its mass number.

OR

(a) In a nuclear reaction :

$$^3_2\text{He} + {}^3_2\text{He} \longrightarrow {}^4_2\text{He} + {}^1_1\text{H} + {}^1_1\text{H} + 12.86\ \text{MeV},$$

though the number of nucleons is conserved on both sides of the reaction, yet the energy is released. How? Explain.

(b) Draw a plot of potential energy between a pair of nucleons as a function of their separation. Mark the regions where potential energy is (i) positive and (ii) negative.

SECTION-D

31. State Gauss theorem in electrostatics and write its mathematical form. Using it, derive an expression for electric field at a point near a thin infinite plane sheet of electric charge. How does this electric field change with a uniformly thick sheet of charge?

OR

(a) An electric dipole of dipole moment $\vec{p}$ consists of point charges $+q$ and $-q$ separated by a distance $2a$ apart. Deduce the expression for the electric field $\vec{E}$ due to the dipole at a distance x from the centre of the dipole on its axial line in terms of the dipole moment $\vec{p}$. Hence show that in the limit $x \gg a$, $\vec{E} \longrightarrow 2\vec{P}/(4\pi\varepsilon_0 x^3)$.

(b) Given the electric field in the region $\vec{E} = 2x\hat{i}$, find the net electric flux through the cube and the charge enclosed by it

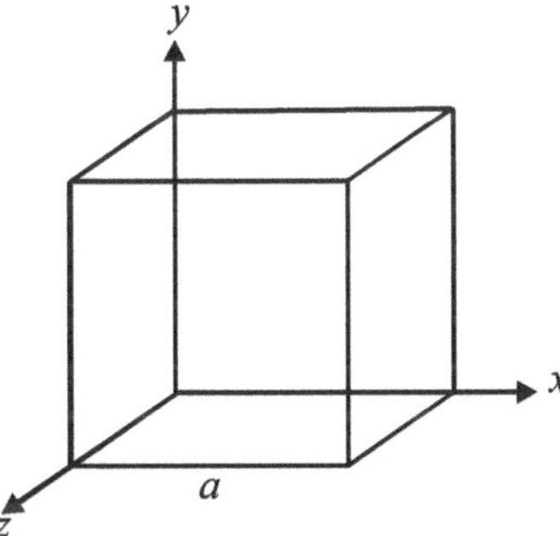

32. A series L-C-R circuit is connected to an AC source having voltage $V = V_m \sin \omega t$. Derive the expression for the instantenous current I and its phase relationship to the applied voltage.
Obtain the condition for resonance to occur.

OR

(a) What do you understand by sharpness of resonance in a series L-C-R circuit? Derive an expression for Q-factor of the circuit.

(b) Three electrical circuits having AC sources of variable frequency are shown in the figures. Initially, the current flowing in each of these is same. If the frequency of the applied AC source is increased, how will the current flowing in these circuits be affected? Give the reason for your answer.

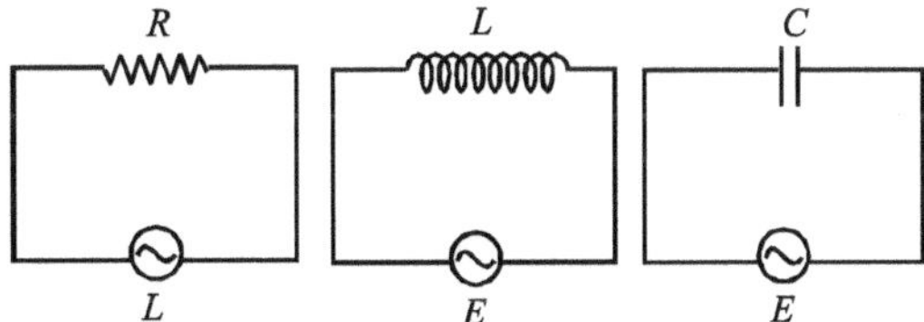

33. (a) Define a wavefront. Using Huygens' principle, verify the laws of reflection at a plane surface.

(b) In a single slit diffraction experiment, the width of the slit is made double the original width. How does this affect the size and intensity of the central diffraction band? Explain.

(c) When a tiny circular obstacle is placed in the path of light from a distant source, a bright spot is seen at the centre of the obstacle. Explain why?

OR

(i) What is the effect on the interference fringes to the Young's double slit experiment when
   (a) the separation between the two slits is decreased?
   (b) the width of the source-slit is increased?

(ii) The intensity at the central maxima in Young's double slit experimental setup is I_0. Show that the intensity at a point where the path difference is $\lambda/3$, is $I_0/4$.

SECTION-E

34. Case Study: Electric Flux & Gauss's Law

Read the following paragraph and answer the questions.

Electric flux over an area in an electric field is the total number of electric lines of force crossing this area.

It is measured by the product of surface area and the corresponding component of electric field normal to the area.

$$\phi = \oint \overline{E} . d\overline{s}$$

It is a scalar quantity. Its SI unit is volt metre (Vm) or Nm^2/C.

(i) Figure shows three point charges, $+2q$, $-q$ and $+3q$. Two charges $+2q$ and $-q$ are enclosed within a surface S. What is the electric flux due to this configuration through the surface S?

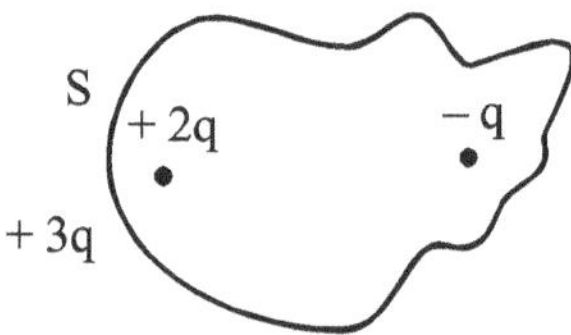

(ii) How does the electric flux due to a point charge enclosed by a spherical Gaussian surface get affected when its radius is increased?

(iii) A charge q is placed at the centre of the open end of a cylindrical vessel. Find the flux of the electric field through the surface of the vessel.

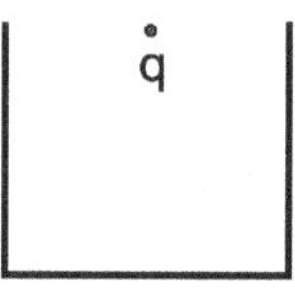

OR

(iii) At the centre of a cubical box $+Q$ charge is placed. Find the value of total flux that is coming out a wall.

35. Case Study: Total internal Reflection

Read the following paragraph and answer the questions.

When light travels from an optically denser medium to a rarer medium at the interface, it is partly reflected back into the same medium and partly refracted to the second medium. This reflection is called the internal reflection.

If the angle of incidence is increased still further, refraction is not possible, and the incident ray is totally reflected. This is called total internal reflection.

(i) When monochromatic light travels from one medium to another, its wavelength changes but frequency remains the same. Explain.

(ii) What is the relation between critical angle and refractive index?

(iii) In total internal reflection when the angle of incidence is equal to the critical angle for the pair of media in contact, what will be angle of refraction ?

OR

(iii) State the criteria for the phenomenon of total internal reflection of light to take place.

2 Sample Paper
LATEST PATTERN

BLUE PRINT

Ch. No.	Chapter Name	Per Unit Marks	Section-A MCQs 1 Mark	Section-B SA 2 Marks	Section-C LA-I 3 Marks	Section-D LA-II 5 Marks	Section-E Case Study 4 Marks	Total Marks
1	Electric Charges and Fields	16			1 (Q. 27)			3
2	Electrostatic Potential and Capacitance		3 (Q. 1, 2, 17)					3
3	Current Electricity		1(Q. 16)			1 (Q. 31)	1 (Q. 34)	10
4	Moving Charges and Magnetism	17	1(Q. 3)			1 (Q.32)		6
5	Magnetism and Matter		1(Q. 5)		1 (Q.26)			4
6	Electromagnetic Induction		1 (Q. 6)	1 (Q. 24)				3
7	Alternating Current		2 (Q. 4, 7)	1 (Q. 19)				4
8	Electromagnetic Waves	18	1 (Q. 8)					1
9	Ray optics and Optical Instruments		1 (Q. 9)	2 (Q. 20, 22)		1 (Q. 33)		10
10	Wave Optics		1 (Q. 18)	1 (Q. 25)			1 (Q. 35)	7
11	Dual Nature of Radiation and Matter	12	1 (Q. 10)		1 (Q. 30)			4
12	Atoms		1 (Q. 12)		1 (Q. 29)			4
13	Nuclei		1 (Q. 11)		1 (Q. 28)			4
14	Semiconductor Electronics: Materials, Devices and Simple Circuits	7	3 (Q. 13, 14, 15)	2 (Q. 21, 23)				7
	Total Marks (Total Questions)		18 (18)	14 (7)	15 (5)	15 (3)	8 (2)	70 (35)

NOTE : The number given inside the bracket denotes question number, ask in the sample paper, while the number given outside the bracket are the number of questions from that particular chapter.

Time Allowed : 3 Hours   **Max. Marks : 70**

General Instructions

1. There are 35 questions in all. All questions are compulsory.
2. This question paper has five sections: Section A, Section B, Section C, Section D and Section E. All the sections are compulsory.
3. Section A contains eighteen MCQ of 1 mark each, Section B contains seven questions of two marks each, Section C contains five questions of three marks each, section D contains three long questions of five marks each and Section E contains two case study based questions of 4 marks each.
4. There is no overall choice. However, an internal choice has been provided in section B, C, D and E. You have to attempt only one of the choices in such questions.
5. Use of calculators is not allowed.

SECTION-A

1. To obtain 3 μF capacity from three capacitors of 2 μF each, they will be arranged.
   (a) all the three in series
   (b) all the three in parallel
   (c) two capacitors in series and the third in parallel with the combination of first two
   (d) two capacitors in parallel and the third in series with the combination of first two

2. The work done in carrying a charge q once around a circle of radius r with a charge Q placed at the centre will be
   (a) $Qq(4\pi\varepsilon_0 r^2)$ (b) $Qq/(4\pi\varepsilon_0 r)$ (c) zero   (d) $Qq^2/(4\pi\varepsilon_0 r)$

3. Two long parallel wires are at a distance of 1 metre. Both of them carry 5 ampere of current. The force of attraction per unit length between the two wires is
   (a) 50×10^{-7} N/m   (b) 2×10^{-8} N/m   (c) 5×10^{-8} N/m   (d) 10^{-7} N/m

4. A transformer is used to light a 100 W and 110 V lamp from a 220 V mains. If the main current is 0.5 amp, the efficiency of the transformer is approximately
   (a) 50%   (b) 90%   (c) 10%   (d) 30%

5. The magnetic susceptibility for diamagnetic materials is
   (a) small and negative   (b) small and positive   (c) large and positive   (d) large and negative

6. Lenz's law is a consequence of the law of conservation of
   (a) charge   (b) mass   (c) energy   (d) momentum

7. Alternating current cannot be measured by D.C. ammeter, because
   (a) A.C. is virtual   (b) A.C. changes its direction
   (c) A.C. cannot pass through D.C. ammeter   (d) average value of A.C for complete cycle is zero

8. The oscillating magnetic field in a plane electromagnetic wave is given by $B_y = 5 \times 10^{-6} \sin 1000\,\pi\,(5x - 4 \times 10^8\,t)$T. The amplitude of electric field will be :
   (a) 15×10^2 Vm^{-1} (b) 5×10^{-6} Vm^{-1} (c) 16×10^{12} Vm^{-1} (d) 4×10^2 Vm^{-1}

9. A concave mirror is used for face viewing has focal length of 0.6m. At whay distance you should hold the mirror from your face to get an upright image with a magnification of 4?
   (a) 0.20 m   (b) 0.25 m   (c) 0.40 m   (d) 0.45 m

10. In a photoelectric experiment, anode potential (V) is plotted against plate current (I)

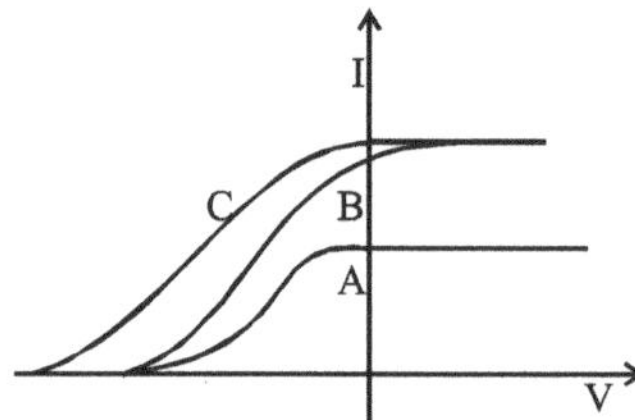

   (a) A and B will have different intensities while B and C will have different frequencies
   (b) B and C will have different intensities while A and C will have different frequencies
   (c) A and B will have different intensities while A and C will have equal frequencies
   (d) A and B will have equal intensities while B and C will have different frequencies

11. The mass number of He is 4 and that for sulphur is 32. The radius of sulphur nuclei is larger than that of helium by

    (a) $\sqrt{8}$ (b) 4   (c) 2   (d) 8

12. Rutherford's atomic model was unstable because
    (a) nuclei will break down   (b) electrons do not remain in orbit
    (c) orbiting electrons radiate energy   (d) electrons are repelled by the nucleus

13. The impurity atoms with which pure silicon may be doped to make it a p-type semiconductor are those of
    (a) phosphorus   (b) boron   (c) antimony   (d) nitrogen

14. When an impurity is doped into an intrinsic semiconductor, the conductivity of the semiconductor
    (a) increases   (b) decreases   (c) remains the same   (d) becomes zero

15. In a reverse biased diode when the applied voltage changes by 1 V, the current is found to change by 0.5 μA. The reverse bias resistance of the diode is
    (a) $2 \times 10^5\,\Omega$ (b) $2 \times 10^6\,\Omega$ (c) $200\,\Omega$ (d) $2\,\Omega$

For question numbers 16, 17 and 18, two statements are given-one labelled Assertion (A) and the other labelled Reason (R). Select the correct answer to these questions from the codes (a), (b), (c) and (d) as given below.
(a) Both A and R are true and R is the correct explanation of A
(b) Both A and R are true but R is NOT the correct explanation of A
(c) A is true but R is false
(d) A is false and R is also false

16. **Assertion (A) :** Bending a wire does not effect electrical resistance.
    Reason (R) : Resistance of wire is proportional to resistivity of material.

17. **Assertion (A) :** The electric potential at any point on the equatorial plane of a dipole is zero.
    Reason (R) : Workdone in rotating a dipole from a direction perpendicular to the field to the given direction is called potential energy of dipole.

18. **Assertion (A) :** In YDSE, if $I_1 = 9I_0$ and $I_2 = 4I_0$ then $\dfrac{I_{max}}{I_{min}} = 25$.

    Reason (R) : In YDSE $I_{max} = \dfrac{1}{2}(\sqrt{I_1} + \sqrt{I_2})^2$ and $I_{min} = \dfrac{1}{2}(\sqrt{I_1} - \sqrt{I_2})^2$.

SECTION-B

19. The graphs (i) and (ii) represent the variation of the opposition offered by the circuit element to the flow of alternating current with frequency of the applied emf. Identify the circuit element corresponding to each graph.

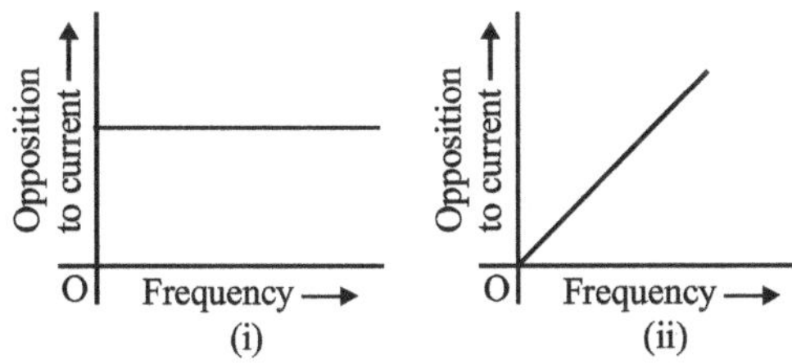

20. A convex lens of focal length 0.5 and concave lens of focal length 1 m are combined. What is the power of the combination of two lenses.

    OR

    The radius of curvature of curved surface of a thin plane - convex lens is 10 cm and the refractive index is 1.5. If the plane surface is silvered what will be the focal length of the lens?

21. What is depletion region? Explain how barrier is created in this region?

22. Draw a labelled ray diagram of refracting type telescope in normal adjustment. Write two main considerations required of an astronomical telescope.

23. The V–I characteristic of silicon diode is shown. Calculate the diode resistance in

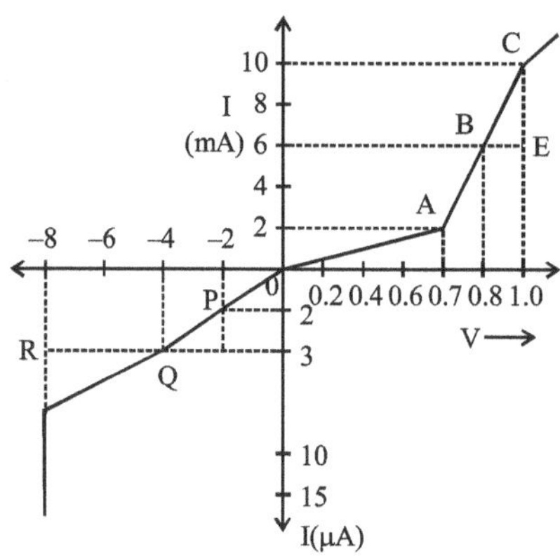

(a) forward bias at V = 0.9 V and   (b) reverse bias at V = – 3.0 V.

24. Predict the polarity of the capacitor in the situation described by adjoining figure. Explain the reason too.

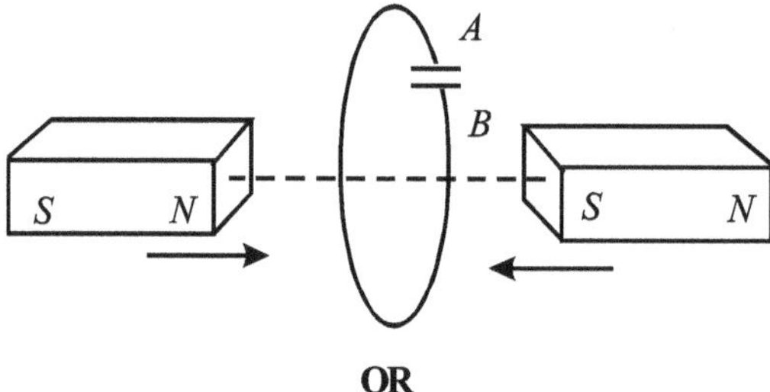

OR

(i) Define mutual induction.

(ii) A pair of adjacent coils has a mutual inductance of 1.5 H. If the current in one coil changes from 0 to 20 A in 0.5 s. what is the change of flux linkage with the other coil?

25. A parallel beam of light of 600 nm falls on a narrow slit and the resulting diffraction pattern is observed on a screen 1.2 m away. It is observed that the first minimum is at a distance of 3 mm from the centre of the screen. Calculate the width of the slit.

SECTION-C

26. Three identical specimens of a magnetic materials, nickel, antimony, aluminium are kept in a non-uniform magnetic field. Draw the modification in the field lined in each case.

27. An electric dipole of length 4 cm, when placed with its axis making an angle of 60° with a uniform electric field, experiences a torque of $4\sqrt{3}$ Nm. Calculate the potential energy of the dipole, if it has charge ± 8 nC.

28. Draw a plot of potential energy of a pair of nucleons, as a function of their separation. Write two important conclusions which you can draw regarding the nature of nuclear forces.

OR

In heavy nuclei, number of neutrons is more than number of protons, why?

29. (a) What is the significance of negative sign in the expression for the energy?

(b) Draw the energy level diagram showing how the line spectra corresponding to Paschen series occur due to transition between energy levels.

OR

(i) In hydrogen atom, an electron undergoes transition from 2nd excited state to the first excited state and then to the ground state. Identify the spectral series to which these transitions belong.

(ii) Find out the wavelengths of the emitted radiations in the two cases.

30. The two lines marked A and B in the given figure, show a plot of de-Broglie wavelength λ

versus, $\dfrac{1}{\sqrt{V}}$, where V is the accelerating potential for two nuclei ^2_1H and ^3_1H .

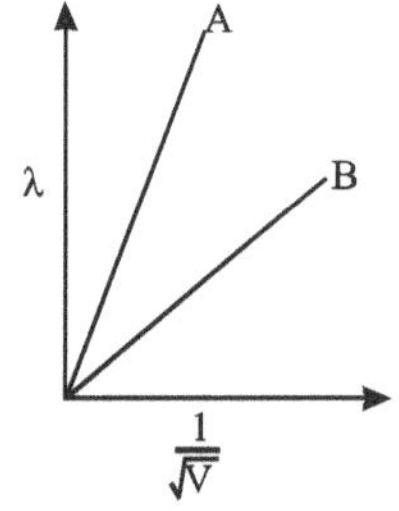

(i) What does the slope of the lines represent?

(ii) Identify, which of the lines corresponded to these nuclei.

SECTION-D

31. (a) State Kirchhoff's rules and explain on what basis they are justified.

(b) Two cells of emfs E_1 and E_2 and internal resistances r_1 and r_2 are connected in parallel. Derive the expression for the (i) emf and (ii) internal resistance of a single equivalent cell which can replace this combination.

OR

What is drift velocity of electrons and relaxation time of free electrons in a metallic conductor carrying a current? Establish a relation between them?

32. State Biot Savart law, expressing it in the vector form. Use it to obtain the expression for the magnetic field at an axial point, distance 'd' from the centre of a circular coil of radius 'a' carrying current 'I'. Also, find the ratio of the magnitudes of the magnetic field of this coil at the centre and at an axial point for which $d = a\sqrt{3}$.

OR

(a) Draw the magnetic field lines due to a current carrying loop.

(b) State using a suitable diagram, the working principle of a moving coil galvanometer. What is the function of radial magnetic field and the soft iron core used in it?

(c) For converting a galvanometer into an ammeter, a shunt resistance of small value is used in parallel, whereas in the case of a voltmeter a resistance of large vlaue is used in series. Explain why?

33. (a) Derive the prism formula, $n_{12} = \dfrac{\sin \dfrac{(A+\delta_m)}{2}}{\sin \dfrac{A}{2}}$

(b) Draw the graph showing the variation of the angle of deviation with angle of incidence, through a prism.

OR

Figure shows a convex spherical surface with centre of curvature C, separating the two media of refractive indices n_1 and n_2. Draw a ray diagram showing the formation of the image of a point object O lying on the principal axis. Derive the relationship between the object and image distance in terms of refractive indices of the media and the radius of curvature R of the surface.

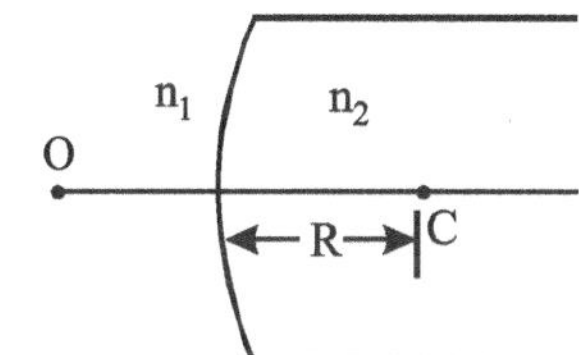

SECTION-E

34. **Case Study: Heating Effect of Current**

Read the following paragraph and answer the questions.

The electric energy consumed in a circuit is defined as *the total work done in maintaining the current in an electric circuit for a given time.*

Electric energy = VIt = Pt = $I^2 Rt$ = $V^2 t / R$

The **S.I. unit** of electric energy is joule (denoted by J)

where 1 joule = 1 watt × 1 second = 1 volt × 1 ampere × 1 sec.

In **household circuits** the electrical appliances are connected in parallel and the electrical energy consumed is measured in kWh

(i) Two 120 V light bulbs, one of 25 W and other of 200 W were connected in series across a 240 V line. One bulb burnt out almost instantaneously. Which one has burnt and why?

(ii) What happens to the power dissipation if the value of electric current passing through a conductor of constant resistance is doubled?

(iii) What is the largest voltage that you can safely put across a resistor marked 196 Ω-1 W?

OR

(iii) A wire of radius r and another wire of radius 2r, both of same material and length are connected in series to each other. The combination is connected across a battery. Find the ratio of the heats produced in the two wires.

35. **Case Study: Young's Double Slit Experiment**

Read the following paragraph and answer the questions.

A student is performing Young's double slit experiment. There are two slits S_1 and S_2. Separation between them is d. There is large screen at a distance $D(D >> d)$ from the slits. The set-up is shown in the following figure. A parallel beam of light is incident upon it. A monochromatic light of wavelength λ is used. The initial phase difference between the two slits which behaves as two coherent sources of light is zero.

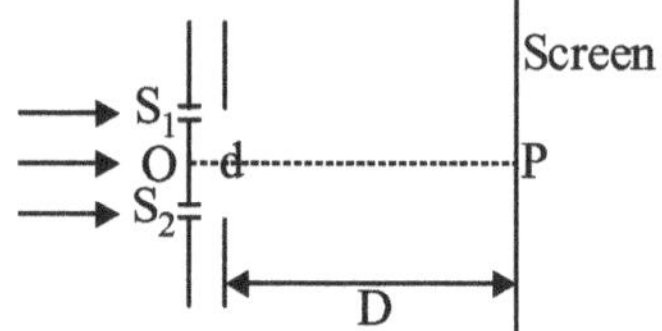

The intensity of light waves on the screen coming out of S_1 and S_2 are same and is I_0. In this situation, the principal maximum is formed at the point P. At the point on screen where principal maximum is formed, phase difference between two interfering waves will be zero.

(i) What will be the effect on interference fringes if red light is replaced by blue light?

(ii) What is the effect on the interference fringes in a Young's double slit experiment when width of the two slits is increased?

(iii) What is the effect on the interference fringes in a Young's double slit experiment when monochromatic source is replaced by a source of white light.

OR

(iii) A double slit arrangement produces fringes for $\lambda = 5890$ Å that are 0.4° apart. What is the angular width if the entire arrangement is immersed in water ? ($\mu_w = 4/3$)

3 Sample Paper
LATEST PATTERN

BLUE PRINT

Ch. No.	Chapter Name	Per Unit Marks	Section-A MCQs 1 Mark	Section-B SA 2 Marks	Section-C LA-I 3 Marks	Section-D LA-II 5 Marks	Section-E Case Study 4 Marks	Total Marks
1	Electric Charges and Fields	16		1 (Q. 21)				2
2	Electrostatic Potential and Capacitance		2 (Q. 1, 16)			1 (Q. 31)	1 (Q. 34)	11
3	Current Electricity				1 (Q. 27)			3
4	Moving Charges and Magnetism	17	1 (Q.3)	1 (Q.23)	1 (Q.26)			6
5	Magnetism and Matter		1 (Q.5)					1
6	Electromagnetic Induction		2 (Q. 2, 6)	1 (Q. 19)				4
7	Alternating Current		1 (Q. 4)			1 (Q. 32)		6
8	Electromagnetic Waves	18	2 (Q. 7, 18)					2
9	Ray optics and Optical Instruments		2 (Q. 8, 9)	1 (Q. 25)				4
10	Wave Optics		1 (Q. 17)	1 (Q. 20)		1 (Q. 33)	1 (Q. 35)	12
11	Dual Nature of Radiation and Matter	12	1 (Q. 10)		1 (Q. 29)			4
12	Atoms		1 (Q. 12)		1 (Q. 28)			4
13	Nuclei		1 (Q. 11)		1 (Q. 30)			4
14	Semiconductor Electronics: Materials, Devices and Simple Circuits	7	3 (Q. 13, 14, 15)	2 (Q. 22, 24)				7
	Total Marks (Total Questions)		18 (18)	14 (7)	15 (5)	15 (3)	8 (2)	70 (35)

NOTE : The number given inside the bracket denotes question number, ask in the sample paper, while the number given outside the bracket are the number of questions from that particular chapter.

Time Allowed : 3 Hours   **Max. Marks : 70**

General Instructions

1. There are 35 questions in all. All questions are compulsory.

2. This question paper has five sections: Section A, Section B, Section C, Section D and Section E. All the sections are compulsory.

3. Section A contains eighteen MCQ of 1 mark each, Section B contains seven questions of two marks each, Section C contains five questions of three marks each, section D contains three long questions of five marks each and Section E contains two case study based questions of 4 marks each.

4. There is no overall choice. However, an internal choice has been provided in section B, C, D and E. You have to attempt only one of the choices in such questions.

5. Use of calculators is not allowed.

SECTION-A

1. A charge Q is enclosed by a Gaussian spherical surface of radius R. If the radius is doubled, then the outward electric flux will
   (a) increase four times   (b) be reduced to half   (c) remain the same   (d) be doubled

2. A magnet is moved towards a coil (i) quickly (ii) slowly, then the induced e.m.f. is
   (a) larger in case (i)   (b) smaller in case (i)
   (c) equal in both the cases   (d) larger or smaller depending upon the radius of the coil

3. If both the number of turns and core length of an inductor is doubled keeping other factors constant, then its self-inductance will be-
   (a) Unaffected   (b) doubled   (c) halved   (d) quadrupled

4. If the susceptibility of dia, para and ferromagnetic materials are χ_d, χ_p, χ_f respectively, then
   (a) $\chi_d < \chi_p < \chi_f$ (b) $\chi_d < \chi_f < \chi_p$ (c) $\chi_f < \chi_d < \chi_p$ (d) $\chi_f < \chi_p < \chi_d$

5. An infinitely long hollow conducting cylinder with radius R carries a uniform current along its surface. Choose the correct representation of magnetic field (B) as a function of radial distance (r) from the axis of cylinder.

(a) 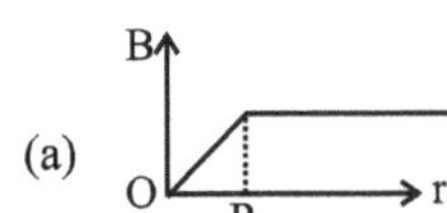   (b) 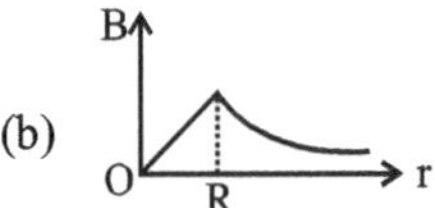   (c) 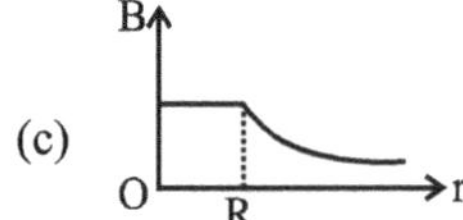   (d) 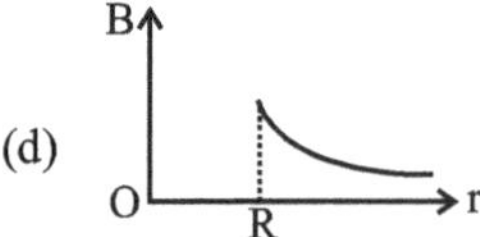

6. A current carrying conductor placed in a magnetic field experiences maximum force when angle between current and magnetic field is
   (a) $3\pi/4$ (b) $\pi/2$ (c) $\pi/4$ (d) zero

7. Select the wrong statement. EM waves
   (a) are transverse in nature.
   (b) travel in free space at a speed of light.
   (c) are produced by accelerating charges.
   (d) travel in all media with same speed.

8. Light travels in two media A and B with speeds 1.8×10^8 ms^{-1} and 2.4×10^8 ms^{-1} respectively. Then the critical angle between them is
   (a) $\sin^{-1}\left(\dfrac{2}{3}\right)$ (b) $\tan^{-1}\left(\dfrac{3}{4}\right)$ (c) $\tan^{-1}\left(\dfrac{2}{3}\right)$ (d) $\sin^{-1}\left(\dfrac{3}{4}\right)$

9. The graph between angle of deviation (δ) and angle of incidence (i) for a triangular prism is represented by

(a) 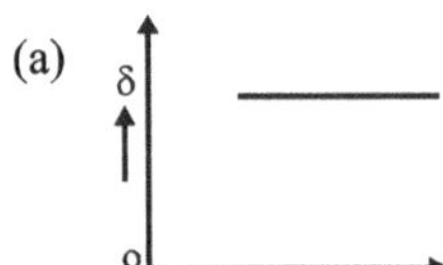   (b) 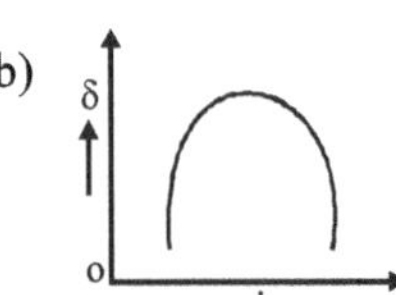   (c) 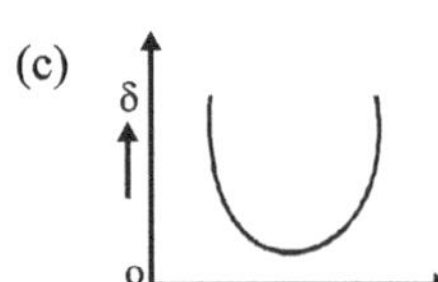   (d) 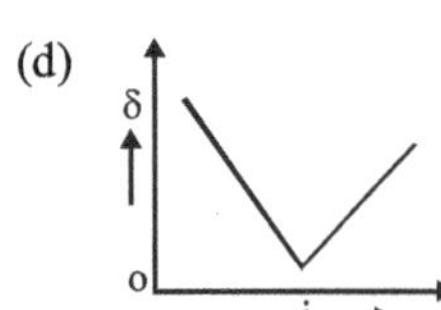

10. If the kinetic energy of a free electron doubles, it's de-Broglie wavelength changes by the factor
    (a) 2   (b) $\dfrac{1}{2}$ (c) $\sqrt{2}$ (d) $\dfrac{1}{\sqrt{2}}$

11. In terms of Bohr radius r_0, the radius of the second Bohr orbit of a hydrogen atom is given by

    (a) $4\,r_0$ (b) $8\,r_0$ (c) $\sqrt{2}\,r_0$ (d) $2\,r_0$

12. M_p denotes the mass of a proton and M_n that of a neutron. A given nucleus, of binding energy B, contains Z protons and N neutrons. The mass M(N, Z) of the nucleus is given by (c is the velocity of light)

    (a) $M(N, Z) = NM_n + ZM_p + B/c^2$ (b) $M(N, Z) = NM_n + ZM_p - Bc^2$

    (c) $M(N, Z) = NM_n + ZM_p + Bc^2$ (d) $M(N, Z) = NM_n + ZM_p - B/c^2$

13. If a small amount of antimony is added to germanium crystal

    (a) it becomes a p–type semiconductor

    (b) the antimony becomes an acceptor atom

    (c) there will be more free electrons than holes in the semiconductor

    (d) its resistance is increased

14. The drift current in a p-n junction is from the

    (a) n-side to the p-side

    (b) p-side to the n-side

    (c) n-side to the p-side if the junction is forward-biased and in the opposite direction if it is reverse biased

    (d) p-side to the n-side if the junction is forward-biased and in the opposite direction if it is reverse-biased

15. If in a p-n junction diode, a square input signal of 10 V is applied as shown

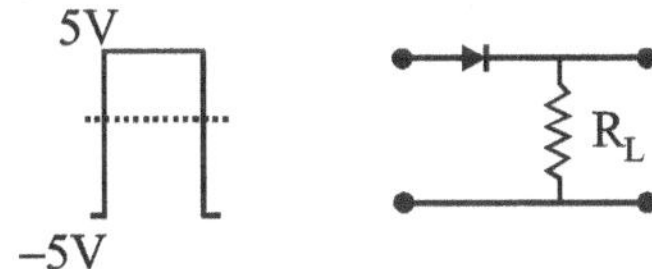

Then the output signal across R_L will be

(a) 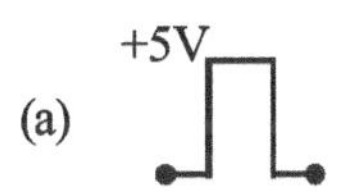

(b) 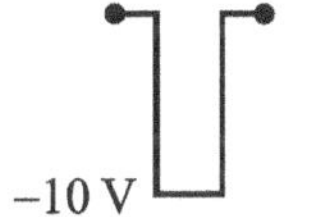

(c)

(d) 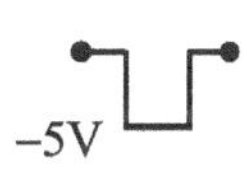

For question numbers 16, 17 and 18, two statements are given-one labelled Assertion (A) and the other labelled Reason (R). Select the correct answer to these questions from the codes (a), (b), (c) and (d) as given below.

(a) Both A and R are true and R is the correct explanation of A

(b) Both A and R are true but R is NOT the correct explanation of A

(c) A is true but R is false

(d) A is false and R is also false

16. **Assertion (A) :** Electric potential and electric potential energy are different quantities.

    Reason (R) : For a system of positive test charge and point charge electric potential energy = electric potential.

17. **Assertion (A) :** Interference pattern is made by using yellow light instead of red light, the fringes becomes narrower.

    Reason (R) : In YDSE, fringe width is given by $\beta = \dfrac{D\lambda}{d}$ and $\lambda_y < \lambda_R$

18. **Assertion (A) :** The velocity of electromagnetic waves depends on electric and magnetic properties of the medium.

    Reason (R) : Velocity of electromagnetic waves in free space is constant.

SECTION-B

19. A 28 turns coil with average diameter of 0.02m is placed perpendicular to a magnetic field of 8000 T. If the magnetic field changes to 3000 T in 4s, what is the magnitude of the induced emf?

20. Answer the following question :

    (i) In what way is diffraction from each slit related to the interference pattern in a double slit experiment?

    (ii) When a tiny circular obstacle is placed in the path of light from a distant source, a bright spot is seen at the centre of the shadow of the obstacle. Explain, why?

21. An electric dipole is held in a uniform electric field.

    (i) Show that no translatory force acts on it.

    (ii) Derive an expression for the torque acting on it.

OR

Two point electric charges of unknown magnitude and sign are placed at a distance 'd' apart. The electric field intensity is zero at a point, not between the charges but on the line joining them. Write two essential conditions for this to happen.

22. What is depletion region? Explain how barrier is created in this region?

23. An electron and a proton moving with a same speed enter the same magnetic field region at right angles to the direction of the field. Show the trajectory followed by the two particles in the magnetic field. Find the ratio of the radii of the circular paths which the particles may describe.

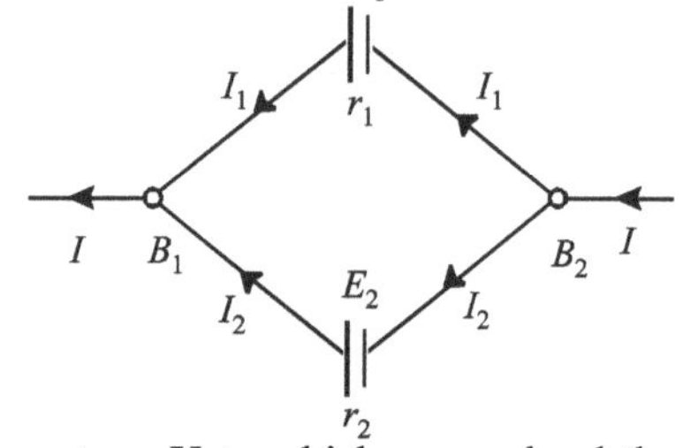

24. How is p – n junction formed ? Explain.

25. Draw the ray diagram showing the formation of image of an object by the compound microscope.

OR

Explain with the help of lens maker's formula. Why does a convex lens behave as -
(i) Converging when immersed in water ($\mu = 1.33$) and
(ii) A diverging lens when immersed in CS_2 solution ($\mu = 1.6$).

SECTION-C

26. (a) Define the current sensitivity of a galvanometer.
    (b) The coil area of a galvanometer is 25×10^{-4} m^2. It consists of 150 turns of a wire and is in a magnetic field of 0.15 T. The restoring torque constant of the suspension fibre is 10^{-6} N m per degree. Assuming the magnetic field to be radial, calculate the maximum current that can be measured by the galvanometer, if the scale can accommodate 30° deflection.

OR

State Biot-Savart law and give the mathematical expression for it.

How does a circular loop carrying current behave as a magnet?

27. Two cells of emf E_1 and E_2 having internal resistances r_1 and r_2 respectively are connected in parallel as shown. Deduce the expressions for the equivalent emf and equivalent internal resistance of a cell which can replace the combination between the points B_1 and B_2.

28. A 12.9 eV beam of electronic is used to bombard gaseous hydrogen at room temperature. Upto which energy level the hydrogen atoms would be excited ?
Calculate the wavelength of the first member of Paschen series and first member of Balmer series.

29. Sketch the graphs showing variation of stopping potential with frequency of incident radiations for two photosensitive materials A and B having threshold frequencies $v_A > v_B$.
(i) In which case is the stopping potential more and why ?
(ii) Does the slope of the graph depend on the nature of the material used ? Explain.

30 . The radius of nucleus of nucleon number 16 is 3×10^{-15} cm. Calculate the radius of nucleus of nucleon number 205.

OR

The Sun is believed to be getting its energy from the fusion of 4 p$^+$ to form a He nucleus and a pair of positrons. Calculate release of energy per fusion in Mev. m(p$^+$) = 1.007825 u. m(e$^+$) = 0.000549 u, m(He) = 4.002603 u, 1 a.m.u = 931.5 MeV.

SECTION-D

31. (i) Show that the effective capacitance, C of a series combination of three capacitors C_1, C_2 and C_3 is given by

$$C = \frac{C_1 C_2 C_3}{\left(C_1 C_2 + C_2 C_3 + C_3 C_1\right)}$$

(ii) A parallel plate capacitor with air has a capacitance of 10 pF. If the distance between the plates is reduced to half and the space between them is filled with a material of dielectric constant 10, find the new capacitance.

OR

(i) A parallel plate capacitor is charged by a battery to a potential. The battery is disconnected and a dielectric slab is inserted to completely fill the space between the plates. How will

    (a) its capacitance,
    (b) electric field between the plates and
    (c) energy stored in the capacitor be affected? Justify your answer giving necessary mathematical expressions for each case.
(ii) Sketch the pattern of electric field lines due to
    (a) a conducting sphere having negative charge on it.
    (b) an electric dipole.

32. Show diagramatically two different arrangements used for winding the primary and secondary coils in a transformer. Assuming the transformer to be an ideal one, write expression for the ratio of it's.
(i) Output voltage to input voltage.
(ii) Output current to input current.
Mention the reasons for energy losses in an actual transformer.

OR

What is impedance? Give its SI unit. Using the phasor diagram or otherwise derive an expression for the impedance of an a.c. circuit containing L, C and R in series. Find the expression for resonant frequency.

33. (a) Using Huygen's construction of secondary wavelets explain how a diffraction pattern is obtained on a screen due to a narrow slit on which a monochromatic beam of light is incident normally.
    (b) Show that the angular width of the first diffraction fringe is half that of the central fringe.
    (c) Explain why the maxima at $\theta = \left(n + \dfrac{1}{2}\right)\dfrac{\lambda}{a}$ become weaker and weaker with increasing n.

OR

Define the term wavefront. State Huygen's principle.

Consider a plane wavefront incident on a thin convex lens. Draw a proper diagram to show how the incident wavefront traverses through the lens and after refraction focusses on the focal point of the lens, giving the shape of the emergent wavefront.

SECTION-E

34. Case Study: Electrostatic Potential
Read the following paragraph and answer the questions.
Electrostatic potential at a point in an electric field is *the minimum work done by an external agent in moving a unit positive charge from infinity or a reference point to that point against the electrical force of the field.*

An equipotential surface is that at every point of which electric potential is same.
(i) Is electrostatic potential necessarily zero at a point where electric field strength is zero.
(ii) Write down the relation between electric field and potential at a point.
(iii) Draw an equipotential surface in a uniform electric field.

OR

(iii) What is an equipotential surface? Show that the electric field is always directed perpendicular to an equipotential surface.

35. Case Study: Interference of Light
Read the following paragraph and answer the questions.
When two coherent sources interact with each other, there will be production of alternate bright and dark fringes on the screen. Young's double-slit experiment demonstrates the idea of making two coherent sources. For better visibility, one has to choose proper amplitude for the sources. The phenomena is good enough to satisfy the conservation of energy principle. The pattern formed in YDSE is of uniform thickness and is nicely placed on a long distance screen.
(i) The light waves from two coherent sources have same intensity $I_1 = I_2 = I_0$. In interference pattern the intensity of light at minima is zero. What will be the intensity of light at maxima ?
(ii) The path difference between two interfering waves at a point on screen is 171.5 times the wavelength. If the path difference is 0.01029 cm. Find the wavelength.
(iii) What is the effect on the interference fringes in a Young's double slit experiment when slits are of unequal width?

OR

(iii) Two beams of light of intensity I_1 and I_2 interfere to give an interference pattern. If the ratio of maximum intensity to that of minimum intensity is 25/9, then find I_1/I_2.

4 Sample Paper

LATEST PATTERN

BLUE PRINT

Ch. No.	Chapter Name	Per Unit Marks	Section-A VSA/A-R/MCQs (Case based) 1 Mark	Section-B SA 2 Marks	Section-C LA-I 3 Marks	Section-D LA-II 5 Marks	Section-E Case Study 4 Marks	Total Marks
1	Electric Charges and Fields	16	1 (Q. 17)	1 (Q. 21)				3
2	Electrostatic Potential and Capacitance		1 (Q. 1)			1 (Q. 31)		6
3	Current Electricity		2 (Q. 7, 8)	1 (Q. 19)	1 (Q. 27)			7
4	Moving Charges and Magnetism	17	3 (Q. 2, 3, 4)				1 (Q. 34)	7
5	Magnetism and Matter			1 (Q.24)				2
6	Electromagnetic Induction					1 (Q. 32)		5
7	Alternating Current				1 (Q. 26)			3
8	Electromagnetic Waves	18	2 (Q. 11, 14)	1 (Q. 22)				4
9	Ray optics and Optical Instruments		3 (Q. 5, 6, 15)	2 (Q. 23, 25)				7
10	Wave Optics		2 (Q. 9, 10)	1 (Q. 20)	1 (Q. 28)			7
11	Dual Nature of Radiation and Matter	12	1 (Q. 12)				1 (Q. 35)	5
12	Atoms		1 (Q. 16)		1 (Q. 29)			4
13	Nuclei				1 (Q. 30)			3
14	Semiconductor Electronics: Materials, Devices and Simple Circuits	7	2 (Q. 13, 18)			1 (Q. 33)		7
	Total Marks (Total Questions)		**18 (18)**	**14 (7)**	**15 (5)**	**15 (3)**	**8 (2)**	**70 (35)**

NOTE : The number given inside the bracket denotes question number, ask in the sample paper, while the number given outside the bracket are the number of questions from that particular chapter.

Time Allowed : 3 Hours   **Max. Marks : 70**

General Instructions

1. There are 35 questions in all. All questions are compulsory.
2. This question paper has five sections: Section A, Section B, Section C, Section D and Section E. All the sections are compulsory.
3. Section A contains eighteen MCQ of 1 mark each, Section B contains seven questions of two marks each, Section C contains five questions of three marks each, section D contains three long questions of five marks each and Section E contains two case study based questions of 4 marks each.
4. There is no overall choice. However, an internal choice has been provided in section B, C, D and E. You have to attempt only one of the choices in such questions.
5. Use of calculators is not allowed.

SECTION-A

1. Which of the following is NOT the property of equipotential surface?
   (a) They do not cross each other.
   (b) The rate of change of potential with distance on them is zero.
   (c) For a uniform electric field they are concentric spheres.
   (d) They can be imaginary spheres.

2. The coil of a moving coil galvanometer is wound over a metal frame in order to
   (a) reduce hysteresis
   (b) increase sensitivity
   (c) increase moment of inertia
   (d) provide electromagnetic damping

3. A current of 10 A is flowing in a wire of length 1.5 m. A force of 15 N acts on it when it is placed in a uniform magnetic field of 2 T. The angle between the magnetic field and the direction of the current is
   (a) 30° (b) 45° (c) 60° (d) 90°

4. The magnetic field due to a current carrying circular loop of radius 3 cm at a point on the axis at a distance of 4 cm from the centre is 54 μT. What will be its value at the centre of loop?
   (a) 125 μT (b) 150 μT (c) 250 μT (d) 75 μT

5. In normal adjustment, for a refracting telescope, the distance between objective and eye piece is 30 cm. The focal length of the objective, when the angular magnification of the telescope is 2, will be:
   (a) 20 cm (b) 30 cm (c) 10 cm (d) 15 cm

6. An object is placed 40 cm from a concave mirror of focal length 20 cm. The image formed is
   (a) real, inverted and same in size
   (b) real, inverted and smaller
   (c) virtual, erect and larger
   (d) virtual, erect and smaller

7. When a current I is set up in a wire of radius r, the drift velocity is v_d. If the same current is set up through a wire of radius 2 r, the drift velocity will be
   (a) $4 v_d$ (b) $2 v_d$ (c) $v_d/2$ (d) $v_d/4$

8. By increasing the temperature, the specific resistance of a conductor and a semiconductor–
   (a) increases for both.
   (b) decreases for both.
   (c) increases for a conductor and decreases for a semiconductor.
   (d) decreases for a conductor and increases for a semiconductor.

9. Two sources of light are said to be coherent, when they give light waves of same
   (a) amplitude and phase
   (b) wavelength and constant phase difference
   (c) intensity and wavelength
   (d) phase and speed

10. Figure shows wavefront P passing through two systems A and B and emerging as Q and then as R. The system A and B could, respectively, be
    (a) a prism and a convergent lens
    (b) a convergent lens and a prism
    (c) a divergent lens and a prism
    (d) a convergent lens and a divergent lens

11. In a plane electromagnetic wave propagating in space has an electric field of amplitude 9×10^3 V/m, then the amplitude of the magnetic field is
    (a) 2.7×10^{12} T   (b) 9.0×10^{-3} T   (c) 3.0×10^{-4} T   (d) 3.0×10^{-5} T

12. For an electron accelerated from rest through a potential V, the de Broglie wavelength associated will be
    (a) $\dfrac{1.772}{\sqrt{V}}$ nm   (b) $\dfrac{1.227}{\sqrt{V}}$ μm   (c) $\dfrac{1.227}{\sqrt{V}}$ nm   (d) $\dfrac{1.772}{\sqrt{V}}$ μm

13. Of the diodes shown in the following diagrams, which one is reverse biased?

    (a) 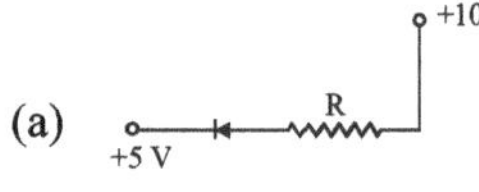   (b) 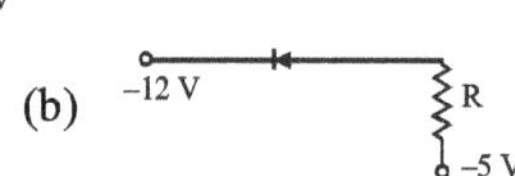   (c) 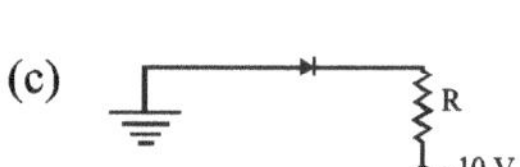   (d) 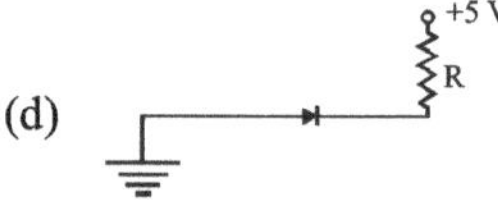

14. If E and B represent electric and magnetic field vectors of the electromagnetic wave, the direction of propagation of electromagnetic wave is along
    (a) E   (b) B   (c) B × E   (d) E × B

15. A prism has a refracting angle of 60°. When placed in the position of minimum deviation, it produces a deviation of 30°. The angle of incidence is
    (a) 30°   (b) 45°   (c) 15°   (d) 60°

For question numbers 16, 17 and 18, two statements are given-one labelled Assertion (A) and the other labelled Reason (R). Select the correct answer to these questions from the codes (a), (b), (c) and (d) as given below.
(a) Both A and R are true and R is the correct explanation of A
(b) Both A and R are true but R is NOT the correct explanation of A
(c) A is true but R is false
(d) A is false and R is also false

16. **Assertion (A) :** Balmer series lies in the visible region of electromagnetic spectrum.

    Reason (R) : $\dfrac{1}{\lambda} = R\left[\dfrac{1}{2^2} - \dfrac{1}{n^2}\right]$ where $n = 3, 4, 5$.

17. **Assertion (A) :** The property that the force with which two charges attract or repel each other are not affected by the presence of a third charge, is known as superposition of charges.
    Reason (R) : Force on any charge due to a number of other charge is the vector sum of all the forces on that charge due to other charges, taken one at a time.

18. **Assertion (A) :** In semiconductors, thermal collisions are respossible for taking a valence electron to the conduction band.
    Reason (R) : The number of conduction electrons go on increasing with time as thermal collisions continuously take place.

SECTION-B

19. The plot of the variation of potential difference across a combination of three identical cells in series, versus current is shown below. What is the emf and internal resistance of each cell ?

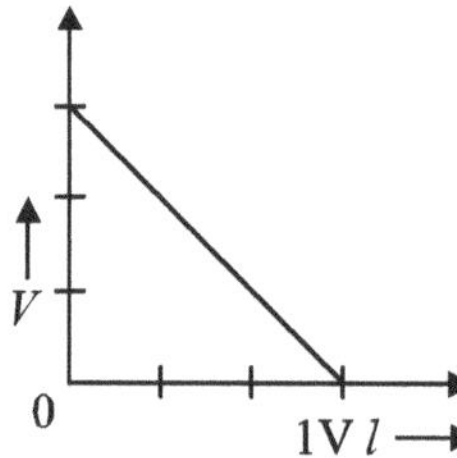

20. Draw the graphs showing intensity pattern in young's double slit experiment and diffraction due to a single slit.

    OR

    Two narrow slits are illuminated by a single monochromatic source. Name the pattern obtained on the screen. One of the slits is now completely covered, what is the name of the pattern obtained now on the screen?

21. Two point charges $3\,\mu$C and $-3\,\mu$C are located 20 cm apart in vacuum.
    (a) Calculate the electric field at the mid point O of the line AB, joining the charges.
    (b) What is the force experienced by a negative test charge of magnitude 1.5×10^{-9} C placed at this point?

22. Name the constituent radiation of electromagnetic spectrum which is used for
(i) aircraft navigation   (ii) studying the crystal structure
Write the frequency range for each.

23. An equiconvex lens of focal length 15 cm is cut into two equal halves in thickness. What is the focal length of each half?

OR

A convex lens of focal length 30 cm is placed coaxially in contact with a concave lens of focal length 40 cm. Determine the power of the combination. Will the system be converging or diverging in nature?

24. Compare the magnetic field of a bar magnet and a solenoid.

25. The velocity of light in air is 3×10^8 ms^{-1} and in a liquid is 2.5×10^8 ms^{-1}. If the ray of light passes from liquid to air, calculate the value of critical angle.

SECTION-C

26. An inductor L of inductance X_L is connected in series with a bulb B and an ac source. How would brightness of the bulb change when (i) number of turn in the inductor is reduced, (ii) an iron rod is inserted in the inductor and (iii) a capacitor of reactance $X_C = X_L$ is inserted in series in the circuit. Justify your answer in each case.

27. Two heating elements of resistances R_1 and R_2 when operated at a constant supply of voltage V, consume powers P_1 and P_2, respectively. Deduce the expressions for the power of their combination when they are, in turn, connected in
(i) series and   (ii) parallel across their same voltage supply.

OR

Use Kirchhoff's rules to determine the value of the current I_1 flowing in the circuit shown in the figure.

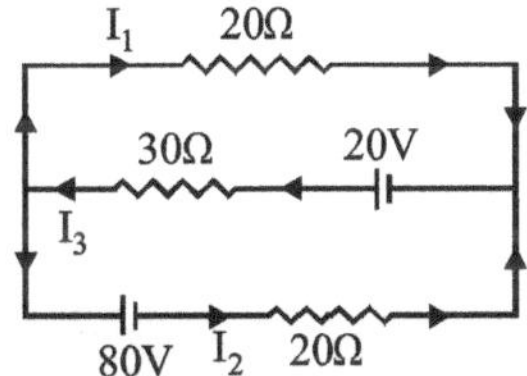

28. Explain the formation of secondary minima in the diffraction pattern due to a single slit.

29. Using Rutherford model of the atom, derive the expression for the total energy of the electron in hydrogen atom. What is the significance of total negative energy possessed by the electron?

OR

Using Bohr's postulates of the atomic model, derive the expression for radius of nth electron orbit. Hence obtain the expression for Bohr's radius.

30. If both the no. of p^+ and no. of n^0 s are conserved in each nuclear reaction, in what way is mass converted into energy or vice versa?

SECTION-D

31. Derive the relation $C = \dfrac{\varepsilon_0 A}{d}$ for the capacitance of a parallel plate capacitor, where symbols have their usual meanings. A parallel plate capacitor is charged to a potential difference 'V' and disconnected from the supply. If the distance between the plates is doubled, explain how does (i) electric field and (ii) energy stored in the capacitor change?

OR

A capacitor is charged to potential V_1. The power supply is then disconnected and the capacitor is then connected in parallel to another capacitor of potential V_2.
(a) Derive an expression for the common potential of the combination of capacitor.
(b) Show that the total energy of combination is less than the sum of the energy stored in them before they are connected.

32. (i) State Faraday's law of electromagnetic induction.
(ii) In the diagram given, a coil B is connected to low voltage bulb L and placed parallel to another coil 'A' as shown. Explain the following observations.
(a) Bulb lights and

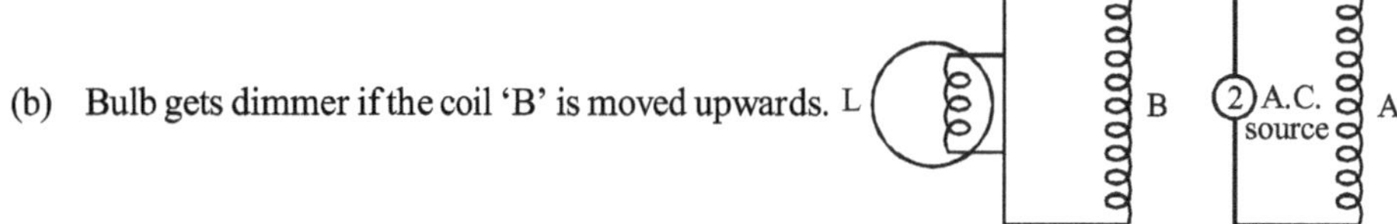

(b) Bulb gets dimmer if the coil 'B' is moved upwards.

OR

(a) Describe a simple experiment (or activity) to show that the polarity of emf induced in a coil is always such that it tends to produce a current which opposes the change of magnetic flux that produces it.

(b) The current flowing through an inductor of self inductance L is continuously increasing. Plot a graph showing the variation of
    (i)   Magnetic flux versus the current
    (ii) Induced emf versus dI/dt
    (iii) Magnetic potential energy stored versus the current.

33. Explain the different types of materials on the basis of their energy gaps.

OR

Explain the effect of doping on energy bands of a semiconductor.

SECTION-E

34. Case Study: Torque on a Coil

Read the following paragraph and answer the questions.

A rigid circular loop has a radius of 0.20 m and is in the x-y plane. A clockwise current I is carried by the loop, as shown. The magnitude of the magnetic moment of the loop is 0.75 A-m^2. A uniform external magnetic field, B = 0.20 T in the positive x-direction, is present

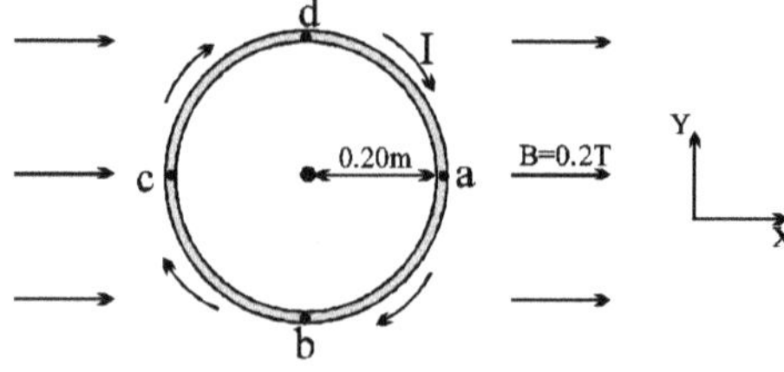

    (i)   Find the magnitude of the magnetic torque exerted on the loop

    (ii) In figure, an external torque changes the orientation of loop from one of lowest potential energy to one of highest potential energy. Find the work done by the external torque.

    (iii) Current I is flowing in a coil of area A and number of turns is N, then find the magnetic moment of the coil.

OR

    (iii) A circular loop of area 0.02 m^2 carrying a current of 10A, is held with its plane perpendicular to a magnetic field induction 0.2 T. Calculate the torque acting on the loop is.

35. Case Study: Photoelectric Effect

Read the following paragraph and answer the questions.

Read the following paragraph and answer the questions.

A physicist wishes to eject electrons by shining light on a metal surface. The light source emits light of wavelength of 450 nm. The table lists the only available metals and their work functions.

Metal	W_0 (eV)
Barium	2.5
Lithium	2.3
Tantalum	4.2
Tungsten	4.5

    (i)   Which metal(s) can be used to produce electrons by the photoelectric effect from given source of light ?

    (ii) In a photoelectric effect experiment, for radiation with frequency υ_0 with $h\upsilon_0$ = 8eV, electrons are emitted with energy 2 eV. What is the energy of the electrons emitted for incoming radiation of frequency 1.25 υ_0?

    (iii) Light of frequency 1.5 times the threshold frequency is incident on a photosensitive material. What will be the photoelectric current if the frequency is halved and intensity is doubled?

OR

    (iii) Find the momentum of photon whose frequency is f.

5 Sample Paper
LATEST PATTERN

BLUE PRINT

Ch. No.	Chapter Name	Per Unit Marks	Section-A MCQs 1 Mark	Section-B SA 2 Marks	Section-C LA-I 3 Marks	Section-D LA-II 5 Marks	Section-E Case Study 4 Marks	Total Marks
1	Electric Charges and Fields	16	3 (Q. 1, 3, 16)			1 (Q. 31)		8
2	Electrostatic Potential and Capacitance		1 (Q. 4)	1 (Q. 21)				3
3	Current Electricity		2 (Q. 5, 6)		1 (Q. 27)			5
4	Moving Charges and Magnetism	17	1 (Q. 2)			1 (Q. 32)		6
5	Magnetism and Matter		1 (Q. 7)					1
6	Electromagnetic Induction		2 (Q. 8, 9)	1 (Q. 22)			1 (Q. 35)	8
7	Alternating Current			1 (Q. 19)				2
8	Electromagnetic Waves	18	1 (Q. 10)					1
9	Ray optics and Optical Instruments		3 (Q.11, 12, 18)	1 (Q. 25)	1 (Q. 29)			8
10	Wave Optics			2 (Q. 20, 23)		1 (Q. 33)		9
11	Dual Nature of Radiation and Matter	12			1 (Q. 28)			3
12	Atoms						1 (Q. 34)	4
13	Nuclei		3 (Q. 13, 14, 17)	1 (Q. 24)				5
14	Semiconductor Electronics: Materials, Devices and Simple Circuits	7	1 (Q. 15)		2 (Q. 26, 30)			7
	Total Marks (Total Questions)		18 (18)	14 (7)	15 (5)	15 (3)	8 (2)	70 (35)

NOTE : The number given inside the bracket denotes question number, ask in the sample paper, while the number given outside the bracket are the number of questions from that particular chapter.

Time Allowed : 3 Hours   **Max. Marks : 70**

General Instructions

1. There are 35 questions in all. All questions are compulsory.
2. This question paper has five sections: Section A, Section B, Section C, Section D and Section E. All the sections are compulsory.
3. Section A contains eighteen MCQ of 1 mark each, Section B contains seven questions of two marks each, Section C contains five questions of three marks each, section D contains three long questions of five marks each and Section E contains two case study based questions of 4 marks each.
4. There is no overall choice. However, an internal choice has been provided in section B, C, D and E. You have to attempt only one of the choices in such questions.
5. Use of calculators is not allowed.

SECTION-A

1. The force between two small charged spheres having charges of 1×10^{-7} C and 2×10^{-7} C placed 20 cm apart in air is
   (a) 4.5×10^{-2} N   (b) 4.5×10^{-3} N   (c) 5.4×10^{-2} N   (d) 5.4×10^{-3} N

2. The coil of a moving coil galvanometer is wound over a metal frame in order to
   (a) reduce hysteresis   (b) increase sensitivity
   (c) increase moment of inertia   (d) provide electromagnetic damping

3. Two point charges $+8q$ and $-2q$ are located at $x = 0$ and $x = L$ respectively. The point on x axis at which net electric field is zero due to these charges is
   (a) 8L   (b) 4L   (c) 2 L   (d) L

4. The total charge on the system of capacitors $C_1 = 1\ \mu F$, $C_2 = 2\ \mu F$, $C_3 = 4\ \mu F$ and $C_4 = 3\ \mu F$ connected in parallel is : (Assume a battery of 20 V is connected to the combination)
   (a) $200\ \mu C$ (b) $200\ C$ (c) $10\ \mu C$ (d) $10\ C$

5. Two wires A and B of the same material, having radii in the ratio 1 : 2 and carry currents in the ratio 4 : 1. The ratio of drift speed of electrons in A and B is
   (a) 16 : 1   (b) 1 : 16   (c) 1 : 4   (d) 4 : 1

6. The figure below shows currents in a part of electric circuit. The current i is
   (a) 1.7 amp
   (b) 3.7 amp
   (c) 1.3 amp
   (d) 1 amp

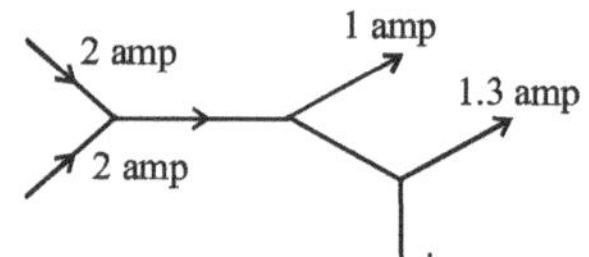

7. When the temperature of a magnetic material decreases, the magnetization
   (a) decreases in a diamagnetic material   (b) decreases in a paramagnetic material
   (c) decreases in a ferromagnetic material   (d) remains the same in a diamagnetic material

8. Two different wire loops are concentric and lie in the same plane. The current in the outer loop (I) is clockwise and increases with time. The induced current in the inner loop
   (a) is clockwise
   (b) is zero
   (c) is counter clockwise
   (d) has a direction that depends on the ratio of the loop radii.

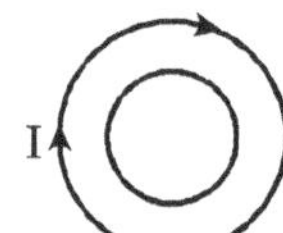

9. When the current in a coil changes from 2 amp. to 4 amp. in 0.05 sec., an e.m.f. of 8 volt is induced in the coil. The coefficient of self inductance of the coil is
   (a) 0.1 henry   (b) 0.2 henry   (c) 0.4 henry   (d) 0.8 henry

10. Which is the correct ascending order of wavelengths?
    (a) $\lambda_{visible} < \lambda_{X-ray} < \lambda_{gamma-ray} < \lambda_{microwave}$ (b) $\lambda_{gamma-ray} < \lambda_{X-ray} < \lambda_{visible} < \lambda_{microwave}$
    (c) $\lambda_{X-ray} < \lambda_{gamma-ray} < \lambda_{visible} < \lambda_{microwave}$ (d) $\lambda_{microwave} < \lambda_{visible} < \lambda_{gamma-ray} < \lambda_{X-ray}$

11. An electromagnetic radiation of frequency n, wavelength λ, travelling with velocity v in air, enters a glass slab of refractive index μ. The frequency, wavelength and velocity of light in the glass slab will be respectively

(a) $\dfrac{n}{\mu}, \dfrac{\lambda}{\mu}$ and $\dfrac{v}{\mu}$ (b) $n, \dfrac{\lambda}{\mu}$ and $\dfrac{v}{\mu}$ (c) $n, 2\lambda$ and $\dfrac{v}{\mu}$ (d) $\dfrac{2n}{\mu}, \dfrac{\lambda}{\mu}$ and v

12. Two thin lenses are in contact and the focal length of the combination is 80 cm. If the focal length of one lens is 20 cm, then the power of the other lens will be
(a) 1.66 D   (b) 4.00 D   (c) –100 D   (d) –3.75 D

13. When the number of nucleons in nuclei increases, the binding energy per nucleon
    (a) increases continuously with mass number
    (b) decreases continuously with mass number
    (c) remains constant with mass number
    (d) first increases and then decreases with increase of mass number

14. The nuclei of which one of the following pairs of nuclei are isotones?
    (a) $_{34}Se^{74}$, $_{31}Ga^{71}$ (b) $_{38}Sr^{84}$, $_{38}Sr^{86}$ (c) $_{42}Mo^{92}$, $_{40}Zr^{92}$ (d) $_{20}Ca^{40}$, $_{16}S^{32}$

15. In _______ semiconductor, the fermi level lies in the energy gap, very close to conduction band.
    (a) *p*-type   (b) *n*-type   (c) intrinsie   (d) None of these

For question numbers 16, 17 and 18, two statements are given-one labelled Assertion (A) and the other labelled Reason (R). Select the correct answer to these questions from the codes (a), (b), (c) and (d) as given below.
(a) Both A and R are true and R is the correct explanation of A
(b) Both A and R are true but R is NOT the correct explanation of A
(c) A is true but R is false
(d) A is false and R is also false

16. **Assertion (A)** : When a conductor is placed in an external electrostatic field, the net electric field inside the conductor becomes zero after a small instant of time.
    Reason (R) : It is not possible to set up an electric field inside a conductor.

17. **Assertion (A)** : Density of all the nuclei is same.
    Reason (R) : Radius of nucleus is directly proportional to the cube root of mass numbers.

18. **Assertion (A)** : Critical angle is minimum for violet colour.

    Reason (R) : Because critical angle $\theta_c = \sin^{-1}\left(\dfrac{1}{\mu}\right)$ and $\mu \propto \dfrac{1}{\lambda}$.

SECTION-B

19. In an ideal transformer, the number of turns in the primary and secondary are 200 and 1000 respectively. If the power input to the primary is 10 kW at 200 V, calculate (i) output voltage and (ii) current in primary.

20. How will the interference pattern in Young's double slit experiment get affected, when
    (i) distance between the slits S_1 and S_2 reduced and
    (ii) the entire setup is immersed in water? Justify your answer in each case.

21. (i) Depict the equipotential surfaces for a system of two identical positive point charges placed a distance d apart.
    (ii) Write the expression for the potential energy of a system of two point charges q_1 and q_2 brought from infinity to the points with positions r_1 and r_2 respectively in presence of external electric field E.
    OR
    A test charge, q is moved without acceleration from A to C along the path from A to B and then from B to C in electric field E as shown in the figure. (i) Calculate the potential difference between A and C. (ii) At which point (of the two) is the electric potential more and why?

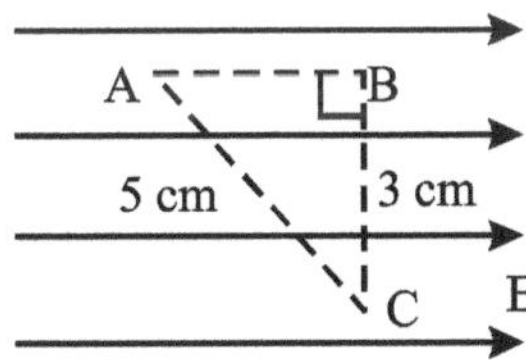

22. (i) Define mutual induction.
    (ii) A pair of adjacent coils has a mutual inductance of 1.5 H. If the current in one coil changes from 0 to 20 A in 0.5 s. what is the change of flux linkage with the other coil?

23. Laser light of wavelength 630 nm incident on a pair of slits produces an interference pattern in which the bright fringes are separated by 7.2 mm. Calculate the wavelength of another source of laser light which produce interference fringes separated by 8.1 mm using same pair of slits.

24. (a) In a typical nuclear reaction, e.g.

$$_1^2 H +_1^2 H \longrightarrow _2^3 He + n + 3.27 \text{ MeV}$$

    although number of nucleons is conserved, yet energy is released. How? Explain.

    (b) Show that nuclear density in a given nucleus is independent of mass number A.

25. A telescope consists of an objective of focal length 75 cm and an eyepiece of focal length 5 cm. Calculate the minimum and maximum magnifying power of the telescope.

OR

A container is filled with two different liquids which do not mix. The liquid of refractive index 1.6 is 40 cm deep and the liquid of refractive index 1.5 is 30 cm deep. What is the apparent depth of the vessel when viewed normally?

SECTION-C

26. Compare n-type and p-type semiconductors.

27. A cell of emf 'E' and internal resistance 'r' is connected across a variable resistor 'R'. Plot a graph showing variation of terminal voltage 'V' of the cell versus the current 'I'. Using the plot, show how the emf of the cell and its internal resistance can be determined.

28. A deuteron and an alpha particle are accelerated with the same accelerating potential.
    Which one of the two has
    (a) greater value of de-Broglie wavelength, associated with it and
    (b) less kinetic energy? Explain.

OR

    (i) Monochromatic light of frequency 5.0×10^{14} Hz is produced by a laser. The power emitted is 3.0×10^{-3} W. Estimate the number of photons emitted per second on an average by the source.
    (ii) Draw a plot showing the variation of photoelectric current versus the intensity of incident rediation on a given photosensitive surface.

29. An equiconvex lens of refractive index μ_1 focal length 'f' and radius of curvature 'R' is immersed in a liquid of refractive index μ_2. For (i) $\mu_2 > \mu_1$, and (ii) $\mu_2 < \mu_1$, draw the ray diagrams in the two cases when a beam of light coming parallel to the principal axis is incident on the lens. Also find the focal length of the lens in terms of the original focal length and the refractive index of the glass of the lens and that of the medium.

30. Why do we say that an intrinsic semiconductor is like an insulator at 0 K?

OR

Describe full wave rectification by diode.

SECTION-D

31. (a) "The outward electric flux due to charge + Q is independent of the shape and size of the surface which encloses it." Give two reasons to justify this statement.

    (b) Two large parallel plane sheets have uniform charge densities $+ \sigma$ and $- \sigma$. Determine the electric field (i) between the sheets, and (ii) outside the sheets.

OR

    (a) Define electric dipole moment. Is it a scalar or a vector? Derive the expression for the electric field of a dipole at a point on the equatorial plane of the dipole.

    (b) Draw the equipotential surfaces due to an electric dipole. Locate the points where the potential due to the dipole is zero.

32. Describe the motion of a charged particle in a uniform magnetic field. Obtain an expression for the radius of the path of the charged particle moving perpendicular to uniform magnetic field. Show that the time taken to complete one revolution by the particle is independent of its speed.

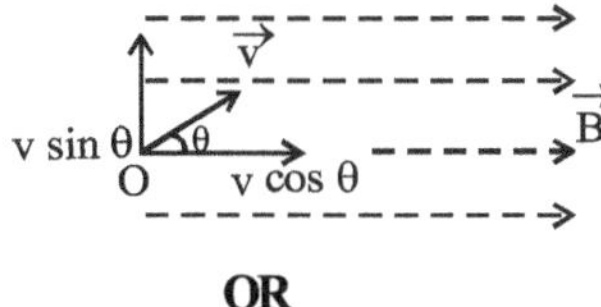

OR

Two infinitely long straight parallel wires, '1' and '2', carrying steady currents I_1 and I_2 in the same direction are separated by a distance d. Obtain the expression for the magnetic field $\vec{B}$ due to the wire '1' acting on wire '2'. Hence find out, with the help of a suitable diagram, the magnitude and direction of this force per unit length on wire '2' due to wire '1'. How does the nature of this force changes if the currents are in opposite direction? Use this expression to define the S.I. unit of current.

33. (a) What is the phenomenon of diffraction?

(b) Why is the intensity maximum at the central maximum on the diffraction pattern?

(c) At what positions, secondary maxima and minima are obtained and, why is the intensity of light at secondary maxima less than that of central maximum in the diffraction pattern.

OR

(i) In a single narrow slit (illuminated by a monochromatic source) diffraction experiment, deduce the conditions for the central maximum and secondary maxima and minima observed in the diffraction pattern. Also explain why the secondary maxima go on becoming weaker in intensity as the order increases.

(ii) Answer the following questions

    (a) How does the width of the slit affect the size of the central diffraction band?

    (b) When a tiny circular obstacle is placed in the path of light from a distant source, why is a bright spot seen at the centre of the shadow of the obstacle?

SECTION-E

34. Case Study: Energy Levels and the Line Spectra of Hydrogen Atom

Read the following paragraph and answer the questions.

The energy levels of a hypothetical one electron atom as shown below.

$n = \infty$	0 eV
$n = 5$	−0.80 eV
$n = 4$	−1.45 eV
$n = 3$	−3.08 eV
$n = 2$	−5.30 eV
$n = 1$	−15.6 eV

(i) Find the ionization potential of the atom.

(ii) Find the short wavelength limit of the series terminating at $n = 2$.

(iii) Find the excitation potential for the state $n = 3$.

OR

(iii) Find the wave number of the photon emitted for the transition $n = 3$ to $n = 1$.

35. Case Study: Electromagnetic Induction

Read the following paragraph and answer the questions.

When the magnet with its N-pole facing the coil is moved towards the coil, the galvanometer shows some deflection while the magnet is in motion showing that an electric current is produced in the coil even though no conventional source of e.m.f. is in the circuit. The current is called the induced current and the e.m.f. responsible for it is called the **induced e.m.f.**

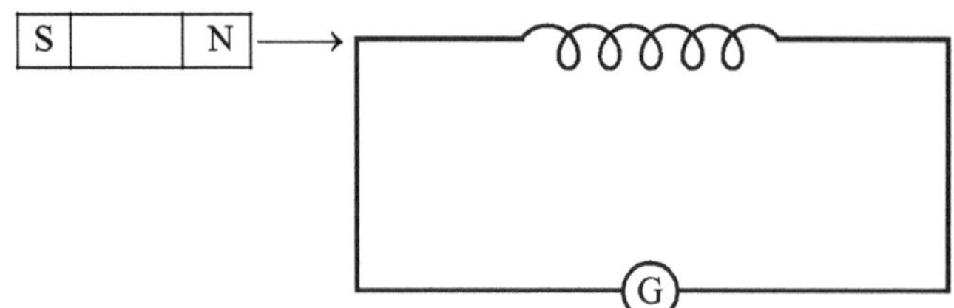

(i) In which direction will the current be induced in the closed loop if the magnet is moved as shown in the figure.

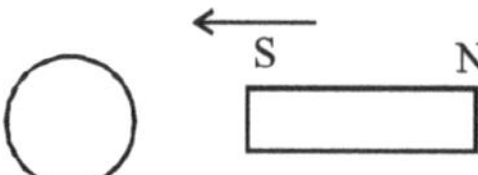

(ii) A magnet is moved in the direction indicated by an arrow between two coils AB and CD as shown in the figure. Find the direction of current in each coil.

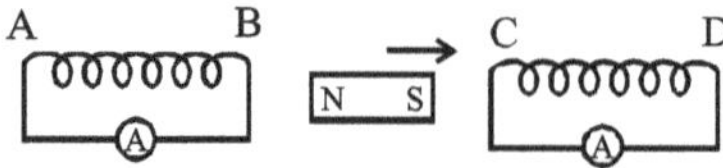

(iii) The following figure shows a horizontal solenoid 'PQ' connected to a battery 'B' and switch 'S'. A copper ring 'R' is placed on a frictionless track, the axis of the ring being along the axis of the solenoid. What would happen to the ring as the switch 'S' is closed?

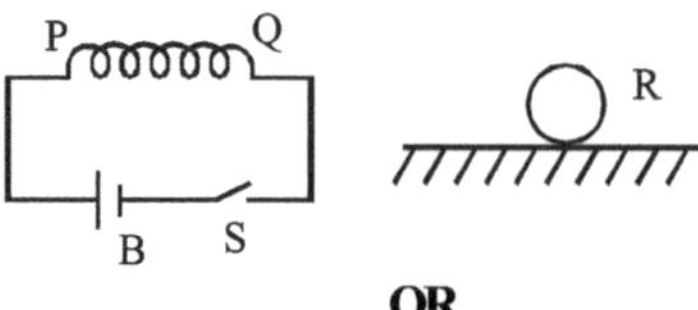

OR

(iii) A bar magnet falls from a height 'h' through a metal ring. Will its acceleration be equal to g? Give reason for your answer.

6 Sample Paper

LATEST PATTERN

BLUE PRINT

Ch. No.	Chapter Name	Per Unit Marks	Section-A MCQs 1 Mark	Section-B SA 2 Marks	Section-C LA-I 3 Marks	Section-D LA-II 5 Marks	Section-E Case Study 4 Marks	Total Marks
1	Electric Charges and Fields	16	1 (Q. 4)	1 (Q. 21)	1 (Q. 28)			6
2	Electrostatic Potential and Capacitance		2 (Q. 1, 7)			1 (Q. 31)		7
3	Current Electricity				1 (Q. 27)			3
4	Moving Charges and Magnetism	17	4 (Q. 2, 3, 5, 6)	1 (Q. 19)				6
5	Magnetism and Matter		1 (Q.15)					1
6	Electromagnetic Induction			1 (Q.23)	1 (Q.26)			5
7	Alternating Current		1 (Q. 16)				1 (Q. 34)	5
8	Electromagnetic Waves	18	1 (Q. 17)	1 (Q. 22)				3
9	Ray optics and Optical Instruments		4 (Q. 8, 11, 14, 18)	1 (Q. 25)				6
10	Wave Optics		2 (Q. 9, 10)	1 (Q. 24)		1 (Q. 33)		9
11	Dual Nature of Radiation and Matter	12				1 (Q. 32)		5
12	Atoms		1 (Q. 12)		1 (Q. 29)			4
13	Nuclei				1 (Q. 30)			3
14	Semiconductor Electronics: Materials, Devices and Simple Circuits	7	1 (Q. 13)	1 (Q. 20)			1 (Q. 35)	7
	Total Marks (Total Questions)		18 (18)	14 (7)	15 (5)	15 (3)	8 (2)	70 (35)

NOTE : The number given inside the bracket denotes question number, ask in the sample paper, while the number given outside the bracket are the number of questions from that particular chapter.

Time Allowed : 3 Hours   **Max. Marks : 70**

General Instructions

1. There are 35 questions in all. All questions are compulsory.
2. This question paper has five sections: Section A, Section B, Section C, Section D and Section E. All the sections are compulsory.
3. Section A contains eighteen MCQ of 1 mark each, Section B contains seven questions of two marks each, Section C contains five questions of three marks each, section D contains three long questions of five marks each and Section E contains two case study based questions of 4 marks each.
4. There is no overall choice. However, an internal choice has been provided in section B, C, D and E. You have to attempt only one of the choices in such questions.
5. Use of calculators is not allowed.

SECTION-A

1. Three capacitors each of 4 μF are to be connected in such a way that the effective capacitance is 6μF. This can be done by connecting them :
   (a) all in series   (b) all in parallel   (c) two in parallel and one in series
   (d) two in series and one in parallel

2. A charged particle of mass m and charge q travels on a circular path of radius r that is perpendicular to a magnetic field B. The time taken by the particle to complete one revolution is

   (a) $\dfrac{2\pi q^2 B}{m}$ (b) $\dfrac{2\pi m q}{B}$ (c) $\dfrac{2\pi m}{qB}$ (d) $\dfrac{2\pi q B}{m}$

3. Two thin, long, parallel wires, separated by a distance 'd' carry a current of 'i' A in the same direction. They will
   (a) repel each other with a force of $\mu_0 i^2/(2\pi d)$ (b) attract each other with a force of $\mu_0 i^2/(2\pi d)$
   (c) repel each other with a force of $\mu_0 i^2/(2\pi d^2)$ (d) attract each other with a force of $\mu_0 i^2/(2\pi d^2)$

4. Which statement is true for Gauss law-
   (a) All the charges whether inside or outside the gaussian surface contribute to the electric flux.
   (b) Electric flux depends upon the geometry of the gaussian surface.
   (c) Gauss theorem can be applied to non-uniform electric field.
   (d) The electric field over the gaussian surface remains continuous and uniform at every point.

5. The current sensitivity of a galvanometer is defined as
   (a) the current flowing through the galvanometer when a unit voltage is applied across its terminals.
   (b) current per unit deflection.
   (c) deflection per unit current.
   (d) dflection per unit current when a unit voltage is applied across its terminals

6. A circular coil of wire consisting of 100 turns each of radius 9 cm carries a current of 0.4 A. The magnitude of manetic field at the centre of the coil is
   (a) 2.4×10^{-4} T   (b) 3.5×10^{-4} T   (c) 2.79×10^{-4} T   (d) 3×10^{-4} T

7. Which of the following figure shows the correct equipotential surfaces of a system of two positive charges?

(a) 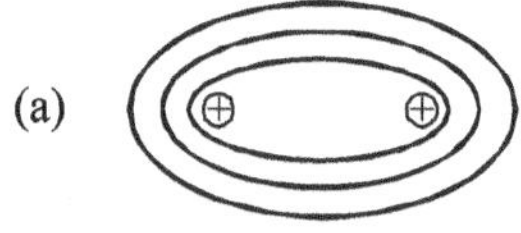   (b) 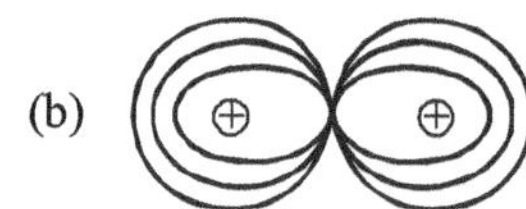

(c) 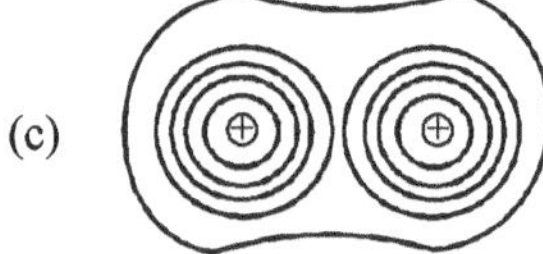   (d) 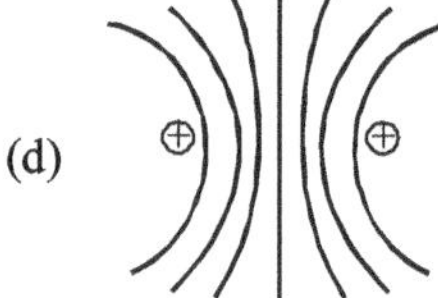

8. Light travels in two media M_1 and M_2 with speeds 1.5×10^8 ms^{-1} and 2.0×10^8 ms^{-1} respectively. The critical angle between them is:

   (a) $\tan^{-1}\left(\dfrac{3}{\sqrt{7}}\right)$ (b) $\tan^{-1}\left(\dfrac{2}{3}\right)$ (c) $\cos^{-1}\left(\dfrac{3}{4}\right)$ (d) $\sin^{-1}\left(\dfrac{2}{3}\right)$

9. The phenomenon of diffraction can be treated as interference phenomenon if the number of coherent sources is
   (a) one
   (b) two
   (c) zero
   (d) infinity

10. A wavefront AB passing through a system C emerges as DE. The system C could be
    (a) a slit
    (b) a biprism
    (c) a prism
    (d) a glass slab

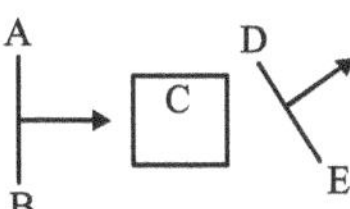

11. A double convex lens of focal length 6 cm is made of glass of refractive index 1.5. The radius of curvature of one surface is double that of other surface. The value of small radius of curvature is
    (a) 6 cm
    (b) 4.5 cm
    (c) 9 cm
    (d) 4 cm

12. Which of the following series in the spectrum of hydrogen atom lies in the visible region of the electromagnetic spectrum?
    (a) Paschen series
    (b) Balmer series
    (c) Lyman series
    (d) Brackett series

13. For a p-type semiconductor, which of the following statements is **true**?
    (a) Electrons are the majority carriers and trivalent atoms are the dopants.
    (b) Holes are the majority carriers and trivalent atoms are the dopants.
    (c) Holes are the majority carriers and pentavalent atoms are the dopants.
    (d) Electrons are the majority carriers and pentavalent atoms are the dopants.

14. If the focal length of objective lens is increased then magnifying power of :
    (a) microscope will increase but that of telescope decrease.
    (b) microscope and telescope both will increase.
    (c) microscope and telescope both will decrease
    (d) microscope will decrease but that of telescope increase.

15. Magnetic permeability is maximum for
    (a) diamagnetic substance
    (b) paramagnetic substance
    (c) ferromagnetic substance
    (d) All of the above

For question numbers 16, 17 and 18, two statements are given-one labelled Assertion (A) and the other labelled Reason (R). Select the correct answer to these questions from the codes (a), (b), (c) and (d) as given below.

(a) Both A and R are true and R is the correct explanation of A
(b) Both A and R are true but R is NOT the correct explanation of A
(c) A is true but R is false
(d) A is false and R is also false

16. **Assertion (A) :** The alternating current lags behind the e.m.f by a phase angle of $\pi/2$, when current flows through an inductor.
    Reason (R) : The inductive reactance increases as the frequency of ac source decreases.

17. **Assertion (A) :** The basic difference between various types of electromagnetic waves lies in their wavelength or frequencies.
    Reason (R) : Electromagnetic waves travel through vacuum with the same speed.

18. **Assertion (A) :** If P_1 and P_2 be the powers of two thin lenses located coaxially in a medium of refractive index μ at a distance d, then the power P of the combination is
    $$P = P_1 + P_2 - P_1 P_2 d/\mu$$
    Reason (R) : Because for above given system equivalent focal length is given by $F = \dfrac{f_1 f_2}{f_1 + f_2 - d/\mu}$ and $P = \dfrac{1}{F}$.

SECTION-B

19. A coil of 200 turns has a cross-sectional area 900 mm². It carries a current of 2A. The plane of the coil is perpendicular to a uniform magnetic field of 0.5 T. Calculate (i) the magnetic moment of the coil and (ii) the torque acting on the coil.

20. Distinguish between 'intrinsic' and 'extrinsic' semiconductors.

21. Two identical plane metallic surfaces A and B are kept parallel to each other in air, separated by a distance of 1 cm as shown in the figure. A is given a positive potential of 10 V and the outer surface of B is earthed.
    (i) What is the magnitude and direction of the uniform electric field between Y and Z?
    (ii) What is the workdone in moving a charge of 20 μC from X to Y?

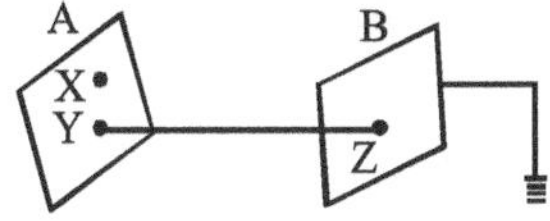

22. Give two characteristics of electromagnetic waves. Write the expression for velocity of electromagnetic waves in terms of permittivity and permeability of the medium.

OR

Identify the part of the electromagnetic spectrum which is
(i) suitable for radar systems used in air craft navigation.
(ii) adjacent to low frequency end of the electromagnetic spectrum.
(iii) produced in nuclear reactions.
(iv) produced by bombarding a metal target by high speed electrons.

23. State Lenz's law.
A metallic rod held horizontally along east-west direction, is allowed to fall under gravity. Will there be an emf induced at its ends? Justify your answer.

OR

Current in a circuit falls steadily from 2.0 A to 0.0 A in 10 ms. If an average emf of 200 V is induced, calculate the self-inductance of the circuit.

24. Answer the following questions :

(a) In a double slit experiment using light of wavelength 600 nm, the angular width of the fringe formed on a distant screen is 0.1°. Find the spacing between the two slits.

(b) Light of wavelength 5000 Å propagating in air gets partly reflected from the surface of water. How will the wavelengths and frequencies of the reflected and refracted light be affected?

25. A prism of refractive index $\sqrt{2}$ has a refracting angle of 60°. At what angle a ray must be incident on it so that it suffers minimum deviation.

SECTION-C

26. Two concentric circular coils, one of small radius r and the other of large radius R, such that R >> r, are placed coaxially with centres coinciding. Obtain the mutual inductance of the arrangement.

OR

Derive the formula for the self inductance of a long solenoid.

27. What is the emf of a cell ? State the factors on which its value depends. Derive a relation between emf E, contact potential V, internal resistance r of a cell and external resistance R. Proove that emf is more than potential difference.

28. An electric dipole consists of the two particles, having the opposite charges $+2 \times 10^{-6}$ C and -2×10^{-6} C and separated by a distance of 10^{-2} m. What is the electric dipole moment of the dipole? Calculate the electric field at a point P on the axis of dipole at a distance of 1 m from it's mid point. Also, calculate the electric field at a point P on the equator of dipole at a distance of 1 m from its mid point.

29. In a Geiger-Marsden experiment, calculate the distance of closest approach to the nucleus of Z = 80, when an α-particle of 8 MeV energy impinges on it before it comes to momentarily rest and reverses its direction.
How will the distance of closest approach be affected when the kinetic energy of the α-particle is doubled?

OR

Show that the electron revolving around the nucleus in a radius 'r' with orbital speed 'v' has magnetic moment $evr/2$. Hence, using Bohr's postulate of the quantization of angular momentum obtain the expression for the magnetic moment of hydrogen atom in its ground state.

30. Assuming that p^+ and n^0 have equal masses, calculate how many times nuclear matter is denser than water. Take m(nucleon) $= 1.67 \times 10^{-27}$ kg and $R_0 = 1.2 \times 10^{-15}$ m.

SECTION-D

31. (a) Obtain the expression for the potential due to an electric dipole of dipole moment p at a point 'x' on the axial line.
(b) Two identical capacitors of plate dimensions : $l \times b$ and plate separation d have dielectric slabs filled in between the space of the plates as shown in the figures.

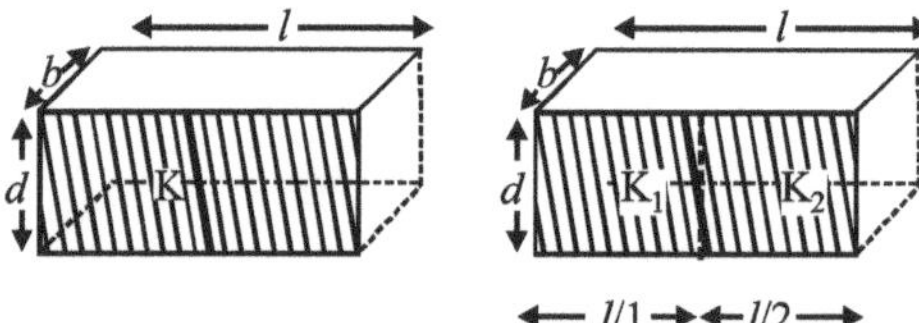

Obtain the relation between the dielectric constants K, K_1 and K_2.

OR

A parallel plate capacitor with air as dielectric is charged by a d.c. source to a potential V. Without disconnecting the capacitor from the source, air is replaced by another dielectric medium of dielectric constant 10. State with reason, how does
(i)   electric field between the plates and
(ii) energy stored in the capacitor change.

32. (a) Why photoelectric effect cannot be explain on the basis of wave nature of light? Give reasons.
    (b) Write the basic features of photon picture of electromagnetic radiation on which Einstein's photoelectric equation is based.

OR

Write Einstein's photoelectric equation and mention which important features in photoelectric effect can be explained with the help of this equation.

The maximum kinetic energy of the photoelectrons gets doubled when the wavelength of light incident on the surface changes from λ_1 to λ_2. Derive the expressions for the threshold wavelength λ_0 and work function for the metal surface.

33. (a) Write the necessary conditions to obtain sustained interference fringes.
    (b) In Young's double slit experiment, plot a graph showing the variation of fringe width versus the distance of the screen from the plane of the slits keeping other parameters same. What information can one obtain from the slope of the curve?
    (c) What is the effect on the fringe width if the distance between the slits is reduced keeping other parameters same?

OR

(a) Write two characteristics features distinguishing the diffraction pattern from the interference fringes obtained in Young's double slit experiment.
(b) Two wavelengths of sodium light 590 nm and 596 nm are used, in turn, to study the diffraction taking place due to a single slit of aperture 1×10^{-4} m. The distance between the slit and the screen is 1.8 m. Calculate the separation between the position of the first maxima of the diffraction pattern obtained in the two cases.

SECTION-E

34. **Case Study: Series LCR Circuit and Resonance**

    Read the following paragraph and answer the questions.

    In a series LCR circuit with an ideal ac source of peak voltage $E_0 = 50$V, frequency $v = \dfrac{50}{\pi}$ Hz and R = 300Ω. The average electric field energy stored in the capacitor and average magnetic energy stored in the coil are 25 mJ and 5 mJ respectively. The value of RMS current in the circuit is 0.1 A. Then find :
    (i)   Find the capacitance (C) of the capacitor.
    (ii) Find the inductance (L) of inductor.
    (iii) Find the sum of rms potential difference across each of the three elements.

    OR

    (iii) In a series combination of R, L and C to an A.C. source at resonance, if R = 20 ohm, then find the impedance Z of the combination.

35. **Case Study: P-N Junction Diode and its Characteristics**

    Read the following paragraph and answer the questions.
    A Si diode (p-n junction) is connected to a resistor and a biasing battery of variable voltage V_B. Assume that the diode requires a minimum current of 1 mA to be above the knee point 0.7 V of its V-I characteristic curve. Also assume that the voltage V across the diode is independent of current above the knee (cut-off) point

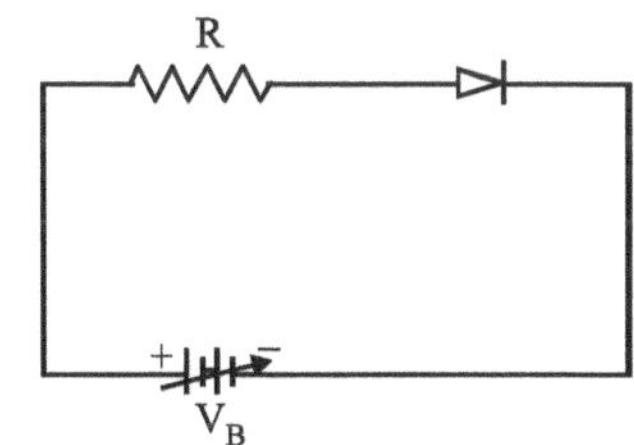

    (i)   If $V_B = 5$V, then find the maximum value of R so that the voltage V is above the knee point voltage.
    (ii) If $V_B = 5$V, then find the value of R in order to establish a current of 5 mA in the circuit.
    (iii) If $V_B = 6$V and 5mA current flows through the circuit, then calculate the power dissipated in R.

    OR

    (iii) A semiconductor device is connected in a series circuit with a battery and a resistance. A current is found to pass through the circuit. If the polarity of the battery is reversed, the current drops to almost zero. Name the device.

7 Sample Paper

LATEST PATTERN

BLUE PRINT

Ch. No.	Chapter Name	Per Unit Marks	Section-A MCQs 1 Mark	Section-B SA 2 Marks	Section-C LA-I 3 Marks	Section-D LA-II 5 Marks	Section-E Case Study 4 Marks	Total Marks
1	Electric Charges and Fields		1 (Q. 1)			1 (Q. 31)		6
2	Electrostatic Potential and Capacitance	16	1 (Q. 2)	1 (Q. 20)				3
3	Current Electricity				1 (Q. 27)		1 (Q. 34)	7
4	Moving Charges and Magnetism		4 (Q. 3, 5, 6, 18)					4
5	Magnetism and Matter		1 (Q. 4)					1
6	Electromagnetic Induction	17			1 (Q.26)		1 (Q. 35)	7
7	Alternating Current					1 (Q. 32)		5
8	Electromagnetic Waves			1 (Q. 25)				2
9	Ray optics and Optical Instruments	18	3 (Q. 7, 10, 13)	2 (Q. 22, 24)				7
10	Wave Optics		2 (Q. 14, 15)	1 (Q. 19)		1 (Q. 33)		9
11	Dual Nature of Radiation and Matter		2 (Q. 8, 16)		1 (Q. 28)			5
12	Atoms	12	1 (Q. 17)		1 (Q. 29)			4
13	Nuclei		3 (Q. 9, 11, 12)					3
14	Semiconductor Electronics: Materials, Devices and Simple Circuits	7		2 (Q. 21, 23)	1 (Q. 30)			7
	Total Marks (Total Questions)		18 (18)	14 (7)	15 (5)	15 (3)	8 (2)	70 (35)

NOTE : The number given inside the bracket denotes question number, ask in the sample paper, while the number given outside the bracket are the number of questions from that particular chapter.

Time Allowed : 3 Hours   **Max. Marks : 70**

General Instructions

1. There are 35 questions in all. All questions are compulsory.
2. This question paper has five sections: Section A, Section B, Section C, Section D and Section E. All the sections are compulsory.
3. Section A contains eighteen MCQ of 1 mark each, Section B contains seven questions of two marks each, Section C contains five questions of three marks each, section D contains three long questions of five marks each and Section E contains two case study based questions of 4 marks each.
4. There is no overall choice. However, an internal choice has been provided in section B, C, D and E. You have to attempt only one of the choices in such questions.
5. Use of calculators is not allowed.

SECTION-A

1. If E_a be the electric field strength of a short dipole at a point on its axial line and E_e that on the equatorial line at the same distance, then
   (a) $E_e = 2E_a$ (b) $E_a = 2E_e$ (c) $E_a = E_e$ (d) None of these

2. A unit charge moves on an equipotential surface from a point A to point B, then
   (a) $V_A - V_B = +ve$ (b) $V_A - V_B = 0$ (c) $V_A - V_B = -ve$ (d) it is stationary

3. A charged particle enters into a magnetic field with a velocity vector making an angle of 30° with respect to the direction of magnetic field. The path of the particle is
   (a) circular   (b) helical   (c) elliptical   (d) straight line

4. The ratio of intensity of magnetisation and magnetising field is called
   (a) permeability   (b) magnetic intensity
   (c) magnetic intensity   (d) magnetic susceptibility

5. The deflection in a moving coil galvanometer is
   (a) directly proportional to the torsional constant
   (b) directly proportional to the number of turns in the coil
   (c) inversely proportional to the area of the coil
   (d) inversely proportional to the current flowin g

6. Three wires A, B and C are situated at the same distance. A current of 1A, 2A, 3A flows through these wires in the same direction. Then the resultant force on B is directed
   (a) Towards A
   (b) Towards C
   (c) Perpendicular to the plane of paper and outward
   (d) Perpendicular to the plane of paper and inward

7. The focal length of the objective of a telescope is 60 cm. To obtain a magnification of 20, the focal length of the eye piece should be
   (a) 2 cm   (b) 3 cm   (c) 4 cm   (d) 5 cm

8. A steel ball of mass m is moving with a kinetic energy K. The de-Broglie wavelength associated with the ball is
   (a) $\dfrac{h}{2mK}$ (b) $\sqrt{\dfrac{h}{2mK}}$ (c) $\dfrac{h}{\sqrt{2mK}}$ (d) None of these

9. Nucleus of an atom whose atomic mass is 24 consists of
   (a) 11 electrons, 11 protons and 13 neutrons   (b) 11 electrons, 13 protons and 11 neutrons
   (c) 11 protons and 13 neutrons   (d) 11 protons and 13 electrons

10. A lens made of glass whose index of refraction is 1.60 has a focal length of + 20 cm in air. Its focal length in water, whose refractive index is 1.33, will be
    (a) three times longer than in air   (b) two times longer than in air
    (c) same as in air   (d) None of these

11. The radius of germanium (Ge) nuclide is measured to be twice the radius of $^{9}_{4}\text{Be}$. The number of nucleons in Ge are
    (a) 74   (b) 75   (c) 72   (d) 73

12. Two nucleons are at a separation of 1 fermi. The net force between them is F_1 if both are neutrons, F_2 if both are protons and F_3 if one is proton and the other is a neutron. Then
    (a) $F_1 > F_2 > F_3$ (b) $F_1 = F_3 > F_2$ (c) $F_2 > F_1 > F_3$ (d) $F_1 = F_2 > F_3$

13. You are asked to design a shaving mirror assuming that a person keeps it 10 cm from his face and views the magnified image of the face at the closest comfortable distance of 25 cm. The radius of curvature of the mirror would then be :
    (a) 60 cm   (b) –24 cm   (c) – 60 cm   (d) 24 cm

14. Two beams of light of intensity I_1 and I_2 interfere to give an interference pattern. If the ratio of maximum intensity to that of minimum intensity is 25/9, then I_1/I_2 is
    (a) 5/3   (b) 4   (c) 81/625   (d) 16

15. Consider the diffraction pattern obtained from the sunlight incident on a pinhole of diameter 0.1 μm. If the diameter of the pinhole is slightly increased, it will affect the diffraction pattern such that
    (a) Its size decreases, and intensity decreases   (b) Its size increases, and intensity increases
    (c) Its size increases, but intensity decreases   (d) Its size decreases, but intensity increases

For question numbers 16, 17 and 18 two statements are given-one labelled Assertion (A) and the other labelled Reason (R). Select the correct answer to these questions from the codes (a), (b), (c) and (d) as given below.
(a) Both A and R are true and R is the correct explanation of A
(b) Both A and R are true but R is NOT the correct explanation of A
(c) A is true but R is false
(d) A is false and R is also false

16. **Assertion (A) :** In photoelectric effect on increasing the intensity of light, kinetic energy of electrons increased but photoelectric current remains unchanged.
    Reason (R) : The photoelectric current depends on frequency of light.

17. **Assertion (A) :** Bohr had to postulate that the electrons in stationary orbits around the nucleus do not radiate.
    Reason (R) : According to classical physics all moving electrons radiate.

18. **Assertion (A):** Magnetic moment of an atom is due to both the orbital motion and spin motion of every electron.
    Reason (R) : A charged particle produces magnetic field.

SECTION-B

19. Give two points of difference between interference and diffraction.

20. A parallel plate capacitor with air between its plates having plate area of 6×10^{-3} m^2 and separation between them 3 mm is connected to a 100 V supply. Explain what would happen when a 3 mm thick mica sheet of dielectric constant 6 is inserted between the plates
    (a) while voltage supply remains constant and
    (b) while voltage supply is disconnected.

21. (a) In the following diagram, is the junction diode forward biased or reverse biased?

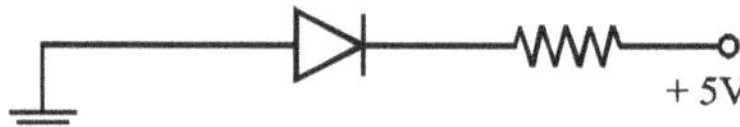

    (b) Draw the circuit diagram of a full wave rectifier and state how it works.
    OR
    What happens to the width of depletion layer of a p-n junction when it is
    (i) forward biased?   (ii) reverse biased?

22. A small bulb (assumed to be a point source) is placed at the bottom of a tank containing water to a depth of 60 cm. Find out the area of the surface of water through which light from the bulb, can emerge. Take the value of the refractive index of water to be 4/3.

23. Consider the half wave rectifier in fig. Assume diode to be a silicon diode with a threshold voltage of 0.7 V. Draw the output if the input is a sine wave with an amplitude of 2 V.

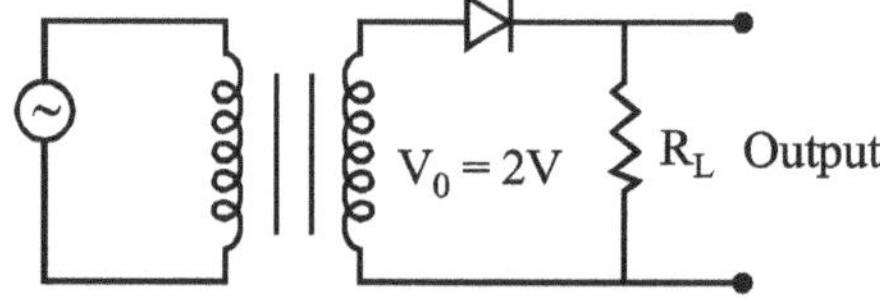

24. A ray of light passes through an equilateral glass prism such that the angle of incidence is equal to the angle of emergence and each of these angles is equal to 3/4 of angle of prism. Find the angle of deviation.

OR

Calculate the speed of light in a medium whose critical angle is 45°. Does critical angle for a given pair of media depend on the wavelength of incident light? Give reason.

25. A plane electromagnetic wave travels along Z-direction. What can you say about directions of electric and magnetic field vector ? If the frequency of the wave is 30 MHz, what is its wavelength?

SECTION-C

26. Define the term 'mutual inductance' between the two coils.

Obtain the expression for mutual inductance of a pair of long coaxial solenoids each of length l and radii r_1 and r_2 ($r_2 \gg r_1$). Total number of turns in the two solenoids are N_1 and N_2, respectively.

OR

A vertical metallic pole falls down through the plane of the magnetic meridian. Will any e.m.f. be produced between its ends? Give reason for your answer.

27. Define relaxation time of the free electrons drifting in a conductor. How is it related to the drift velocity of free electrons? Use this relation to deduce the expression for the electrical resistivity of the material.

28. A student performs an experiment on photoelectric effect, using two materials A and B. A plot of V_{stop} vs ν is given in Fig.

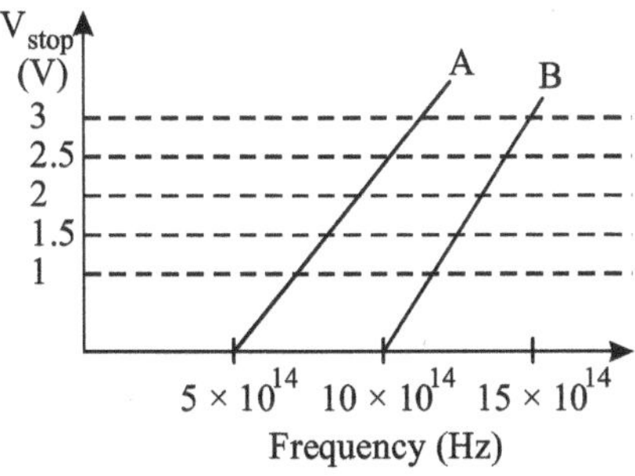

   (i)   Which material A or B has a higher work function?
   (ii) Given the electric charge of an electron $= 1.6 \times 10^{-19}$ C, find the value of h obtained from the experiment for both A and B. Comment on whether it is consistent with Einstein's theory:

29. Using postulates of Bohr's theory of hydrogen atom, show that
   (i)   radii of orbits increases as n^2, and

   (ii) the total energy of electron increases as $\dfrac{1}{n^2}$, where n is the principal quantum numbers of the atom.

OR

State the basic assumption of the Rutherford model of the atom. Explain in brief why this model cannot account for the stability of an atom?

30. Write any two distinguishing features between conductors, semiconductors and insulators on the basis of energy band diagrams.

SECTION-D

31. State Guass's law in electrostatics. A cube which each side a is kept is an electric field. given by E = Cx. (as is shown in the figure where, C is a positive dimensional constant.
Find out :

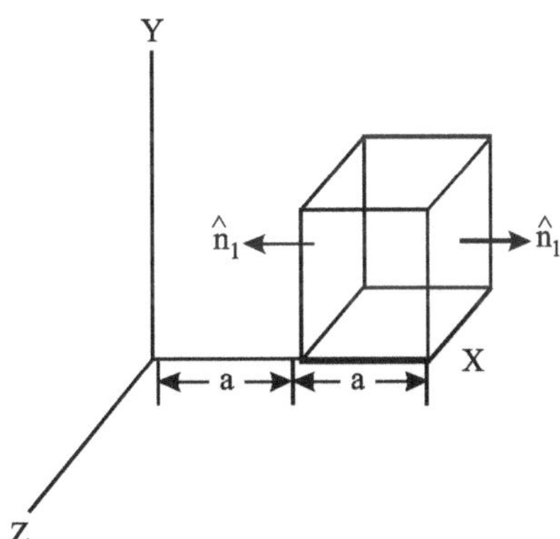

(i)   The electric flux through the cube, and
(ii)   The net charge inside the cube.

OR

A hollow cylindrical box of length 0.5 m and area of cross-section 20 cm^2 is placed in a three dimensional coordinate system as shown in the figure. The electric field in the region is given by $\vec{E} = 20x\,\hat{i}$, where E is NC^{-1} and x is in metres. Find :

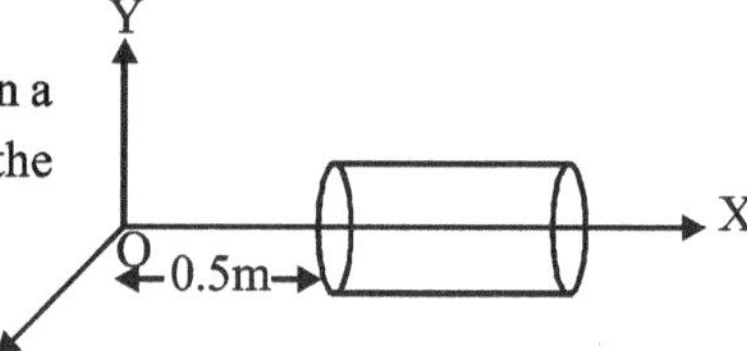

(i)   Net flux through the cylinder
(ii)   Charge enclosed in the cylinder

32. A series LCR circuit is connected across an a.c. source of variable angular frequency 'ω'. Plot a graph showing variation of current 'i' as a function of 'ω' for two resistances R_1 and R_2 $(R_1 > R_2)$.
Answer the following questions using this graph.
(a)   In which case is the resonance sharper and why?
(b)   In which case is the power dissipation more and why?

OR

In a series LCR circuit connected to an ac source of variable frequency and voltage v = v$_m$ sin ωt, draw a plot showing the variation of current (I) with angular frequency (ω) for two different values of resistance R_1 and R_2 $(R_1 > R_2)$. Write the condition under which the phenomenon of resonance occurs. For which value of the resistance out of the two curves, a sharper resonance is produced? Define Q-factor of the circuit and give its significance.

33. In Young's double slit experiment, the two slits 0.15 mm apart are illuminated by monochromatic light of wavelength 450 nm. The screen is 1.0 m away from the slits.
(i)   Find the distance of the second
     (a)   bright fringe,
     (b)   dark fringe from the central maximum.
(ii)   How will the fringe pattern change if the screen is moved away from the slits?

OR

(a)   Use Huygens' principle to show the propagation of a plane wavefront from a denser medium to a rarer medium. Hence find the ratio of the speeds of wavefronts in the two media.

SECTION-E

34. Case Study: Drift Velocity

Read the following paragraph and answer the questions.
The motion of free electrons in a conductor are continuous and random. They collide with positive metal ions and change direction during each collision. So thermal velocities are randomly distributed and average velocity is zero.
When a potential difference is applied across the ends of a conductor, electrons are drifted towards the positive terminal of the field, this velocity is called drift velocity (v$_d$).
(i)   How does the drift velocity of electrons in a metallic conductor vary with increase in temperature?
(ii)   If the length of a wire conductor is doubled by stretching it, keeping the potential difference across it constant, by what factor does the drift speed of electrons change?
(iii)   If p.d. V applied acorss a conductor is increased to 2V, how will the drift velocity of the electrons change?

OR

(iii)   Derive a relation between the current flowing through a conductor and drift velocity.

35. Case Study: Self Induction

Read the following paragraph and answer the questions.
Self Induction is a property of a coil due to which the coil opposes any change in the strength of current flowing through it by inducing an e.m.f. in itself. Whenever the key in the circuit is closed or opened, the current in the circuit increases or decreases. The variation of current causes a variation in magnetic flux linked with the circuit ($\therefore \phi \propto \beta \propto i$) hence, an induced emf is developed in the circuit.
(i)   How does the self-inductance of an air core coil change, when (i) the number of turns in the coil is decreased and (ii) an iron rod is introduced in the coil.
(ii)   If the number of turns in the solenoid is doubled, keeping other factors constant, how does the self-inductance of the coil change?
(iii)   If the rate of change of current is 2 A/s and induces an e.m.f. of 40 mV in the solenoid, what is the self-inductance of the solenoid?

OR

(iii)   If the self inductance of an iron core inductor increases from 0.01 mH to 10 mH on introducing the iron core into it, what is the relative permeability of the core material used?

8 Sample Paper

BLUE PRINT

Ch. No.	Chapter Name	Per Unit Marks	Section-A MCQs 1 Mark	Section-B SA 2 Marks	Section-C LA-I 3 Marks	Section-D LA-II 5 Marks	Section-E Case Study 4 Marks	Total Marks
1	Electric Charges and Fields	16	1 (Q. 16)					1
2	Electrostatic Potential and Capacitance			2 (Q. 20, 23)				4
3	Current Electricity				2 (Q. 26, 27)	1 (Q. 31)		11
4	Moving Charges and Magnetism	17	2 (Q. 1, 4)	1 (Q. 19)			1 (Q. 35)	8
5	Magnetism and Matter		1 (Q.2)					1
6	Electromagnetic Induction					1 (Q. 32)		5
7	Alternating Current		1 (Q. 3)	1 (Q. 25)				3
8	Electromagnetic Waves	18	2 (Q. 5, 8)					2
9	Ray optics and Optical Instruments		1 (Q. 6)	1 (Q. 24)		1 (Q. 33)		8
10	Wave Optics		5 (Q. 7, 9, 10, 17, 18)		1 (Q. 28)			8
11	Dual Nature of Radiation and Matter	12	1 (Q. 11)				1 (Q. 34)	5
12	Atoms				1 (Q. 29)			3
13	Nuclei		2 (Q. 12, 13)	1 (Q. 21)				4
14	Semiconductor Electronics: Materials, Devices and Simple Circuits	7	2 (Q. 14, 15)	1 (Q. 22)	1 (Q. 30)			7
	Total Marks (Total Questions)		18 (18)	14 (7)	15 (5)	15 (3)	8 (2)	70 (35)

NOTE : The number given inside the bracket denotes question number, ask in the sample paper, while the number given outside the bracket are the number of questions from that particular chapter.

Time Allowed : 3 Hours | **Max. Marks : 70**

General Instructions

1. There are 35 questions in all. All questions are compulsory.
2. This question paper has five sections: Section A, Section B, Section C, Section D and Section E. All the sections are compulsory.
3. Section A contains eighteen MCQ of 1 mark each, Section B contains seven questions of two marks each, Section C contains five questions of three marks each, section D contains three long questions of five marks each and Section E contains two case study based questions of 4 marks each.
4. There is no overall choice. However, an internal choice has been provided in section B, C, D and E. You have to attempt only one of the choices in such questions.
5. Use of calculators is not allowed.

SECTION-A

1. A particle of mass m and charge q enters a magnetic field B perpendicularly with a velocity v. The radius of the circular path described by it will be
   (a) Bq/mv (b) mq/Bv (c) mB/qv (d) mv/Bq

2. The magnetic susceptibility is negative for :
   (a) diamagnetic material only
   (b) paramagnetic material only
   (c) ferromagnetic material only
   (d) paramagnetic and ferromagnetic materials

3. If wattless current flows in the AC circuit, then the circuit is
   (a) Purely Resistive circuit
   (b) Purely Inductive circuit
   (c) LCR series circuit
   (d) RC series circuit only

4. Magnetic field at the centre of a circular coil of radius r, through which a current I flows is
   (a) directly proportional to r
   (b) inverseley proportional to I
   (c) directly proportional to I
   (d) directly proprotional to I^2

5. Which of the following electromagnetic waves has the longest wavelength?
   (a) uv-rays (b) Visible light (c) Radio waves (d) Microwaves

6. The magnifying power of a telescope is 9. When it is adjusted for parallel rays, the distance between the objective and the eye piece is found to be 20 cm. The focal length of lenses are
   (a) 18 cm, 2 cm (b) 11 cm, 9 cm (c) 10 cm, 10 cm (d) 15 cm, 5 cm

7. A plane wave passes through a convex lens. The geometrical shape of the wavefront that emerges is
   (a) plane
   (b) diverging spherical
   (c) converging spherical
   (d) None of these

8. The ratio of contributions made by the electric field and magnetic field components to the intensity of an electromagnetic wave is: (c = speed of electromagnetic waves)
   (a) $1:1$ (b) $1:c$ (c) $1:c^2$ (d) $c:1$

9. Wavefront is the locus of all points, where the particles of the medium vibrate with the same
   (a) phase (b) amplitude (c) frequency (d) period

10. Two coherent monochromatic light beams of intensities I and 4I are superposed. The maximum and minimum possible intensities in the resulting beam are
    (a) $5I$ and I (b) $5I$ and $3I$ (c) $9I$ and I (d) $9I$ and $3I$

11. A proton and α-particle are accelerated through the same potential difference. The ratio of their de-Broglie wavelength will be
    (a) $1:1$ (b) $1:2$ (c) $2:1$ (d) $2\sqrt{2}:1$

12. If radius of the $^{27}_{13}\text{Al}$ nucleus is estimated to be 3.6 fermi then the radius of $^{125}_{52}\text{Te}$ nucleus be nearly
    (a) 8 fermi (b) 6 fermi (c) 5 fermi (d) 4 fermi

13. The mass defect in a particular nuclear reaction is 0.3 grams. The amount of energy liberated in kilowatt hour is (Velocity of light = 3×10^8 m/s)
    (a) 1.5×10^6 (b) 2.5×10^6 (c) 3×10^6 (d) 7.5×10^6

14. Which one of the following represents forward bias diode?

(a) $-4V$ —▷|— R ·W· $-3V$

(b) $-2V$ —▷|— R ·W· $+2V$

(c) $3V$ —▷|— R ·W· $5V$

(d) $0V$ —▷|— R ·W· $-2V$

15. In half wave rectification, if the input frequency is 60 Hz, then the output frequency is would be:

(a) 30 Hz   (b) 60 Hz   (c) 120 Hz   (d) Zero

For question numbers 16, 17 and 18, two statements are given-one labelled Assertion (A) and the other labelled Reason (R). Select the correct answer to these questions from the codes (a), (b), (c) and (d) as given below.

(a) Both A and R are true and R is the correct explanation of A

(b) Both A and R are true but R is NOT the correct explanation of A

(c) A is true but R is false

(d) A is false and R is also false

16. Assertion (A) : Four point charges q_1, q_2, q_3 and q_4 are as shown in figure. The flux over the shown Gaussian surface depends only on charges q_1 and q_2.

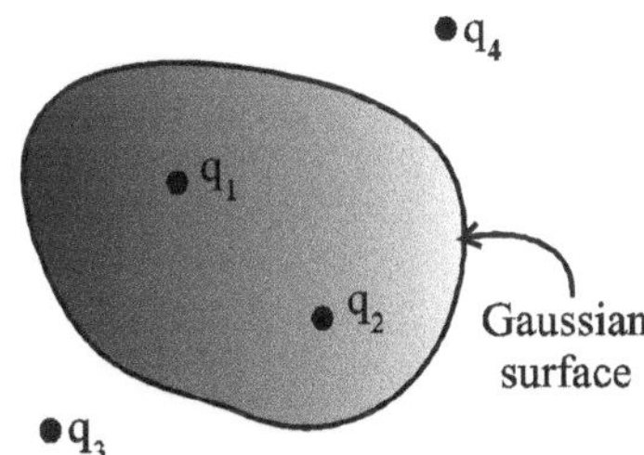

Reason (R) : Electric field at all points on Gaussian surface depends only on charges q_1 and q_2.

17. Assertion (A) : Diffraction takes place for all types of waves mechanical or non-mechanical, transverse or longitudinal.

Reason (R) : Diffraction's effect are perceptible only if wavelength of wave is comparable to dimensions of diffracting device.

18. Assertion (A) : In Young's double slit experiment if wavelength of incident monochromatic light is just doubled, number of bright fringe on the screen will increase.

Reason (R) : Maximum number of bright fringe on the screen is inversely proportional to the wavelength of light used.

SECTION-B

19. A circular coil of closely wound N turns and radius, r carries a current, I. Write the expression for the following

(i) the magnetic field at its centre.

(ii) the magnetic moment of this coil.

20. An infinite number of the identical capacitors, each of the capacitance 1 μF, are connected, as shown. Then, what is the equivalent capacitance between the points A and B?

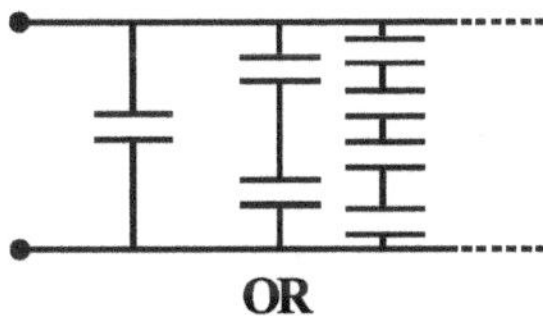

OR

A slab of material of dielectric constant K has the same area as that of the plates of a parallel plate capacitor but has the thickness 2d/3, where d is the separation between the plates. Find out the expression for its capacitance when the slab is inserted between the plates of the capacitor.

21. The three stable isotopes of neon: $_{10}^{20}\text{Ne}$, $_{10}^{21}\text{Ne}$ and $_{10}^{22}\text{Ne}$ have respective abundances of 90.51%, 0.27% and 9.22%. The atomic masses of the three isotopes are 19.99 u, 20.99 u and 21.99 u, respectively. Obtain the average atomic mass of neon.

22. A full wave rectifier uses two diodes, the internal resistance of each diode may be assumed constant at 30 Ω. The transformer r.m.s. secondary voltage from centre tap to each end of the secondary is 50V and load resistance is 970 Ω. Find (i) the mean load current (ii) the r.m.s. value of load current.

23. Derive an expression for the potential at a point due to a short dipole. Hence show what will be the potential at an axial and an equatorial point.

OR

An electric dipole is free to move in a uniform electric field. Explain its motion when it is placed (i) parallel to the field and (ii) perpendicular to the field.

24. (a) Write the necessary conditions for the phenomenon of total internal reflection to occur.
(b) Write the relation between the refractive index and critical angle for a given pair of optical media.

25. When an alternating voltage of 220 V is applied across a device X, a current of 0.5 A flows through the circuit and is in phase with the applied voltage. When the same voltage is applied across another device Y, the same current again flows through the circuit but it leads the applied voltage by $\pi/2$ radian.
(a) Name the devices X and Y.
(b) Calculate the current flowing in the circuit when same voltage is applied across the series combination of X and Y.

SECTION-C

26. Two cells of e.m.f's 1.5V and 2V having internal resistances 2 Ω and 1 Ω respectively, have their negative terminals joined by a wire of 6 Ω and positive terminals joined by a wire of 6 Ω and positive terminals by a wire of 4 Ω resistance. A third resistance wire of 8 Ω connects middle points of these wires. Draw the circuit diagram. Using Kirchhoff's law, find the potential difference at the end of this third wire.

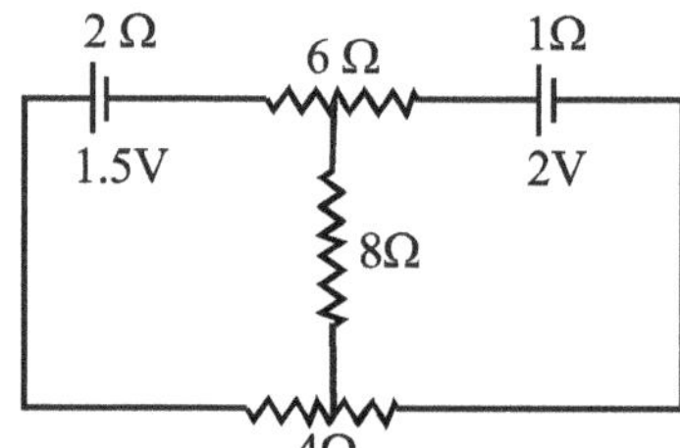

27. Two identical cells of e.m.f 1.5V each joined in parallel provide supply to an external circuit consisting of two resistance of 17 Ω each joined in parallel. A very high resistance voltmeter reads the terminal voltage of cells to be 1.4 V. Calculate the internal resistance of each cell.

OR

Two cells of e.m.f 6V and 12 V and internal resistances 1 Ω and 2 Ω respectively are connected in parallel so as to send current in the same direction through an external resistance of 15 Ω.
(i) Draw the circuit diagram.
(ii) Using Kirchhoff's laws calculate
(a) Current through each branch of the circuit
(b) Potential difference across the 15 Ω resistance.

28. What is the effect on the interference pattern observed in a Young's double slit experiment when
(i) monochromatic light is replaced by white light?
(ii) source is moved closer to the double-slit plane?
(iii) the widths of two slits are increased?

29. The ground state energy of hydrogen atom is –13.6 eV. If an electron makes a transition from an energy level –0.85 eV to –1.51 eV, calculate the wavelength of the spectral line emitted. To which series of hydrogen spectrum does this wavelength belong?

30. In an intrinsic semiconductor, explain how current flow takes place.

OR

A specimen of Si is to be doped by 1 ppm of pentavalent As. If Si has 5×10^{28} atoms /m^3, calculate the number of electrons and holes.

SECTION-D

31. Define resistivity of material. State its S. I units and discuss its variation with temperature in case of (i) metals (ii) semiconductors and (iii) insulators.

OR

(i) State Kirchhoff's rules.
(ii) A battery of 10V and negligible internal resistance is connected across the diagonally opposite corners of a cubical network consisting of 12 resistors each of 1 Ω resistance. Use Kirchhoff's rules to determine.

(a) the equivalent resistance of the network and

(b) the total current in the network.

32. (a) Write an expression of magnetic moment associated with a current (I) carrying circular coil of radius r having N turns.

(b) Consider the above mentioned coil placed in YZ plane with its centre at the origin. Derive expression for the value of magnetic field due to it at point $(x, 0, 0)$.

OR

(a) Define current sensitivity of a galvanometer. Write its expression.

(b) A galvanometer has resistance G and shows full scale deflection for current I_g.

    (i) How can it be converted into an ammeter to measure current upto I_0 $(I_0 > I_g)$?

    (ii) What is the effective resistance of this ammeter?

33. A biconvex lens with its two faces of equal radius of cuivature R is made of a transparent medium of refractive index μ_1. It is kept in contact with a medium of refractive index μ_2 as shown in the figure.

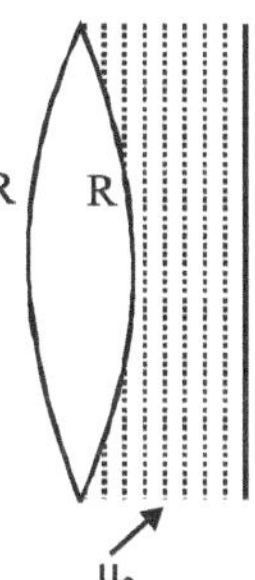

(a) Find the equivalent focal length of the combination.

(b) Obtain the condition when this combination acts as a diverging lens.

(c) Draw the ray diagram for the case $\mu_1 > (\mu_2 + 1) / 2$, when the object is kept far away from the lens. Point out the nature of the image formed by the system.

OR

(i) Draw a ray diagram to show refraction of a ray of monochromatic light passing through a glass prism. Deduce the expression for the refractive index of glass in terms of angle of prism and angle of minimum deviation.

(ii) Explain briefly how the phenomenon of total internal reflection is used in fibre optics.

SECTION-E

34. Case Study: Photoelectric Effect

Read the following paragraph and answer the questions.

When a high frequency electromagnetic radiation is incident on a metallic surface, electrons are emitted from the surface. Energy of emitted photoelectrons depends only on the frequency of incident electromagnetic radiation and the number of emitted electrons depends only on the intensity of incident light.

Einstein's photoelectric equation $[K_{max} = h\nu - \phi]$ correctly explains the PE, where υ = frequency of incident light and ϕ = work function.

(i) Light of wavelength 3300 is incident on two metals A and B, whose work functions are 4 eV and 2 eV, respectively. Which metal will emit photoelectrons?

(ii) For photoelectric effect in a metal, the graph of the stopping potential V_0 (in volt) versus frequency υ (in hertz) of the incident radiation is shown in fig. Find work function of the metal (in eV).

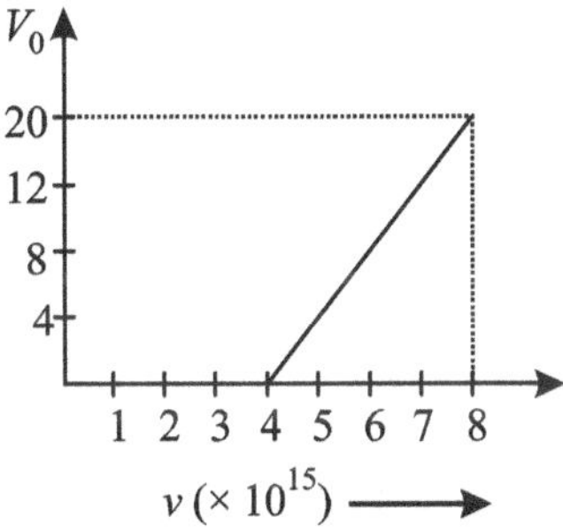

(iii) Find the slope of the graph shown in fig. [here h is the Planck's constant and e is the charge of an electron]

OR

(iii) Name the factor on which the magnitude of saturation photoelectric current depends.

35. Case Study: Motion of Charged Particle in Magnetic Field

Read the following paragraph and answer the questions.

A particle of mass m and charge q, moving with velocity V enters Region II normal to the boundary as shown in the figure. Region II has a uniform magnetic field B perpendicular to the plane of the paper. The length of the Region II is l.

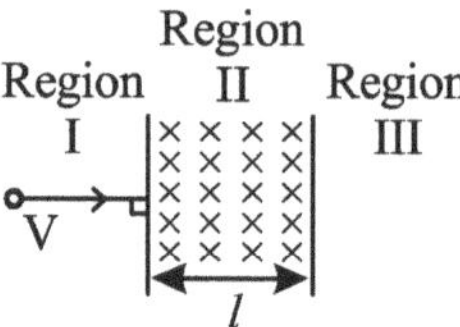

(i) Find the velocity when path length of the particle in Region II is maximum.

(ii) If the direction of the initial velocity of the charged particle is neither along nor perpendicular to that of the magnetic field, then what will be the nature of orbit?

(iii) A charged particle moves with velocity $\vec{V}$ in a uniform magnetic field $\vec{B}$. Find the magnetic force experienced by the particle.

OR

(iii) The force $\vec{F}$ experienced by a particle of charge q moving with velocity $\vec{v}$ in a magnetic field $\vec{B}$ is given by $\vec{F} = q(\vec{v} \times \vec{B})$. Which pair of vectors is always at right angles to each other?

9 Sample Paper

LATEST PATTERN

BLUE PRINT

Ch. No.	Chapter Name	Per Unit Marks	Section-A MCQs 1 Mark	Section-B SA 2 Marks	Section-C LA-I 3 Marks	Section-D LA-II 5 Marks	Section-E Case Study 4 Marks	Total Marks
1	Electric Charges and Fields	16						
2	Electrostatic Potential and Capacitance			2 (Q. 21, 24)		1 (Q. 31)		9
3	Current Electricity		2 (Q. 1, 5)	1 (Q. 22)	1 (Q. 27)			7
4	Moving Charges and Magnetism	17	2 (Q. 4, 7)	1 (Q. 19)	1 (Q. 26)			7
5	Magnetism and Matter		1 (Q. 2)					1
6	Electromagnetic Induction					1 (Q. 32)		5
7	Alternating Current						1 (Q. 34)	4
8	Electromagnetic Waves	18	3 (Q. 3, 6, 18)	1 (Q. 25)				5
9	Ray optics and Optical Instruments					1 (Q. 33)	1 (Q. 35)	9
10	Wave Optics		2 (Q. 8, 17)	1 (Q. 20)				4
11	Dual Nature of Radiation and Matter	12			1 (Q. 28)			3
12	Atoms		1 (Q. 9)		1 (Q. 29)			4
13	Nuclei		2 (Q. 10, 11)		1 (Q. 30)			5
14	Semiconductor Electronics: Materials, Devices and Simple Circuits	7	5 (Q. 12, 13, 14, 15, 16)	1 (Q. 23)				7
	Total Marks (Total Questions)		18 (18)	14 (7)	15 (5)	15 (3)	8 (2)	70 (35)

NOTE : The number given inside the bracket denotes question number, ask in the sample paper, while the number given outside the bracket are the number of questions from that particular chapter.

Time Allowed : 3 Hours | **Max. Marks : 70**

General Instructions

1. There are 35 questions in all. All questions are compulsory.
2. This question paper has five sections: Section A, Section B, Section C, Section D and Section E. All the sections are compulsory.
3. Section A contains eighteen MCQ of 1 mark each, Section B contains seven questions of two marks each, Section C contains five questions of three marks each, section D contains three long questions of five marks each and Section E contains two case study based questions of 4 marks each.
4. There is no overall choice. However, an internal choice has been provided in section B, C, D and E. You have to attempt only one of the choices in such questions.
5. Use of calculators is not allowed.

SECTION-A

1. A 25 W and 100 W bulb are joined in series and connected to the mains. Which bulb will glow brighter?
   (a) 25 W bulb
   (b) 100 W bulb
   (c) Both bulb will glow brighter
   (d) None will glow brighter

2. Relative permittivity and permeability of a material are ε_r and μ_r, respectively. Which of the following values of these quantities are allowed for a diamagnetic material?
   (a) $\varepsilon_r = 1.5, \mu_r = 0.5$
   (b) $\varepsilon_r = 0.5, \mu_r = 0.5$
   (c) $\varepsilon_r = 1.5, \mu_r = 1.5$
   (d) $\varepsilon_r = 0.5, \mu_r = 1.5$

3. An em wave is propagating in a medium with a velocity $\vec{V} = V\hat{i}$. The instantaneous oscillating electric field of this em wave is along $+y$ axis. Then the direction of oscillating magnetic field of the em wave will be along
   (a) $-z$ direction
   (b) $+z$ direction
   (c) $-x$ direction
   (d) $-y$ direction

4. A long straight wire of radius a carries a steady current I. The current is uniformly distributed over its cross-section. The ratio of the magnetic fields B and B', at radial distances $\dfrac{a}{2}$ and 2a respectively, from the axis of the wire is :
   (a) 1/4
   (b) 1/2
   (c) 1
   (d) 4

5. The resistance of a metal increases with increasing temperature because
   (a) the collisions of the conducting electrons with the electrons increase
   (b) the collisions of the conducting electrons with the lattice consisting of the ions of the metal increase
   (c) the number of conduction electrons decreases
   (d) the number of conduction electrons increases

6. When light propagates through a material medium of relative permittivity $\in_r$ and relative permeability μ_r, the velocity of light, v is given by: (c-velocity of light in vacuum)
   (a) $v = \sqrt{\dfrac{\mu_r}{\in_r}}$
   (b) $v = \sqrt{\dfrac{\in_r}{\mu_r}}$
   (c) $v = \dfrac{c}{\sqrt{\in_r \mu_r}}$
   (d) $v = c$

7. Current sensitivity of a moving coil galvanometer is 5 div/mA and its voltage sensitivity (angular deflection per unit voltage applied) is 20 div/V. The resistance of the galvanometer is
   (a) $40\,\Omega$
   (b) $25\,\Omega$
   (c) $500\,\Omega$
   (d) $250\,\Omega$

8. In Young's double slit expt. the distance between two sources is 0.1 mm. The distance of the screen from the source is 20 cm. Wavelength of light used is 5460 Å. The angular position of the first dark fringe is
   (a) $0.08°$
   (b) $0.16°$
   (c) $0.20°$
   (d) $0.32°$

9. The energy of a hydrogen atom in the ground state is $-13.6\,eV$. The energy of a He^+ ion in the first excited state will be
   (a) $-13.6\,eV$
   (b) $-27.2\,eV$
   (c) $-54.4\,eV$
   (d) $-6.8\,eV$

10. A certain mass of Hydrogen is changed to Helium by the process of fusion. The mass defect in fusion reaction is 0.02866 a.m.u. The energy liberated per a.m.u. is
    (Given : 1 a.m.u = 931 MeV)
    (a) 26.7 MeV
    (b) 6.675 MeV
    (c) 13.35 MeV
    (d) 2.67 MeV

11. Binding energy per nucleon plot against the mass number for stable nuclei is shown in the figure. Which curve is correct?
(a) A

(b) B

(c) C

(d) D

12. If the two ends of a p-n junction are joined by a wire
(a) there will not be a steady current in the circuit
(b) there will be a steady current from the n-side to the p-side
(c) there will be a steady current from the p-side to the n-side
(d) there may or may not be a current depending upon the resistance of the connecting wire

13. Pure Si at 500K has equal number of electron (n_e) and hole (n_h) concentrations of 1.5×10^{16} m^{-3}. Doping by indium increases n_h to 4.5×10^{22} m^{-3}. The doped semiconductor is of
(a) n–type with electron concentration
$n_e = 5 \times 10^{22}$ m^{-3}
(b) p–type with electron concentration
$n_e = 2.5 \times 10^{10}$ m^{-3}
(c) n–type with electron concentration
$n_e = 2.5 \times 10^{23}$ m^{-3}
(d) p–type having electron concentration
$n_e = 5 \times 10^9$ m^{-3}

14. A p-type semiconductor is
(a) positively charged   (b) negatively charged   (c) uncharged
(d) uncharged at 0K but charged at higher temperatures

15. In a p-type semiconductor the acceptor level is situated 60 meV above the valence band. The maximum wavelength of light required to produce a hole will be
(a) 0.207×10^{-5} m   (b) 2.07×10^{-5} m   (c) 20.7×10^{-5} m   (d) 2075×10^{-5} m

For question numbers 16, 17 and 18 two statements are given-one labelled Assertion (A) and the other labelled Reason (R). Select the correct answer to these questions from the codes (a), (b), (c) and (d) as given below.
(a) Both A and R are true and R is the correct explanation of A
(b) Both A and R are true but R is NOT the correct explanation of A
(c) A is true but R is false
(d) A is false and R is also false

16. **Assertion (A) :** When two semi conductor of p and n type are brought in contact, they form p-n junction which act like a rectifier.
Reason (R) : A rectifier is used to convent alternating current into direct current.

17. **Assertion (A) :** In YDSE, if $I_1 = 9I_0$ and $I_2 = 4I_0$ then $\dfrac{I_{max}}{I_{min}} = 25$.

Reason (R) : In YDSE $I_{max} = (\sqrt{I_1} + \sqrt{I_2})^2$ and $I_{min} = (\sqrt{I_1} - \sqrt{I_2})^2$.

18. **Assertion (A) :** Ultraviolet radiations of higher frequency waves are dangerous to human being.
Reason (R) : Ultraviolet radiation are absorbed by the atmosphere.

SECTION-B

19. Define the S.I. unit of magnetic field. "A charge moving at right angles to a uniform magnetic field does not undergo change in kinetic energy." – Why?

20. Write the distinguishing features between a diffraction pattern due to a single slit and the interference fringes produced in Young's double slit experiment.

21. Calculate the equivalent capacitance of the combination between the points P and Q as shown in figure.

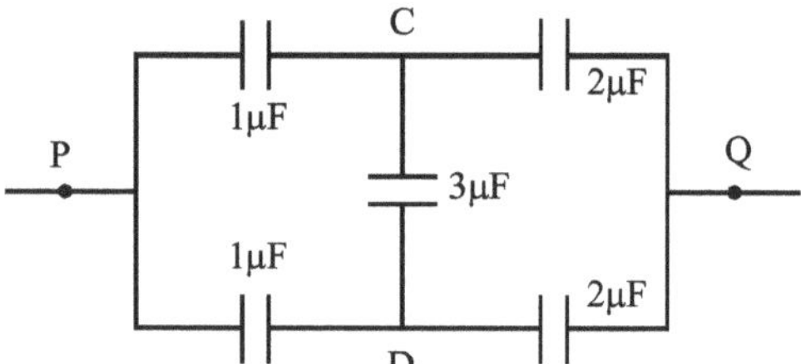

22. Deduce ohm's law using the concept of drift velocity.

23. The acceptor levels in p–type semiconductor are 57 meV above the valence band. Determine the maximum wavelength which can create a hole.

24. Two uniformly large parallel thin plates having charge densities $+\sigma$ and $-\sigma$ are kept in the X-Z plane at a distance d apart. Sketch an equipotential surface due to electric field between the plates. If a particle of mass m and charge $-q$ remains stationary between the plates. What is the magnitude and direction of this field?

OR

Two point charges Q and q are placed at a distance of x and x/2 respectively from a third point charge 4q, all charges are on the same straight line. Calculate the magnitude and nature of charge Q, such that the net force experienced by the charge q is zero.

25. When can a charge act as a source of electromagnetic waves? How are the directions of electric and magnetic field vectors, in an electromagnetic wave related to each other and to the direction of propagation of the wave?

Which physical quantity, if any, has the same value for waves belonging to the different parts of electromagnetic spectrum?

OR

What do electromagnetic waves consist of ? Explain on what factors does its velocity in vacuum depend.

SECTION-C

26. Derive an expression for the force on a current carrying conductor placed in a magnetic field.

27. A cell of emf 'E' and internal resistance 'r' is connected across a variable load resistor R. Draw the plots of the terminal voltage V versus (i) R and (ii) the current I.

28. A proton and an α-particle have the same de-Broglie wavelength. Determine the ratio of (i) their accelerating potentials (ii) their speeds.

OR

(i) Monochromatic light of frequency 6.0×10^{14} Hz is produced by a laser. The power emitted is 2.0×10^{-3} W. Estimate the number of photons emitted per second on an average by the source.

(ii) Draw a plot showing the variation of photoelectric current versus the intensity of incident radiation on a given photosensitive surface.

29. Using Bohr's postulates, derive the expression for the frequency of radiation emitted when electron in hydrogen atom undergoes transition from higher energy state (quantum number n_i) to the lower state, (n_f).

When electron in hydrogen atom jumps from energy state $n_i = 4$ to $n_f = 3, 2, 1$. Identify the spectral series to which the emission lines belong.

OR

What do you understand by energy level diagram? Discuss the various series of hydrogen spectrum with its help.

30. From the relation $R = R_0 A^{1/3}$, where R_0 is a constant and A is the mass number of a nucleus, show that the nuclear matter density is nearly constant (i.e. independent of A).

SECTION-D

31. Using Gauss's law obtain the expression for the electric field due to uniformly charged spherical shell of radius R at a point outside the shell. Draw a graph showing the variation of electric field with r, for $r > R$ and $r < R$.

OR

(a) Derive the expression for the capacitance of a parallel plate capacitor having plate area A and plate separation d.

(b) Two charged spherical conductors of radii R_1 and R_2 when connected by a conducting wire acquire charges q_1 and q_2 respectively. Find the ratio of their surface charge densities in terms of their radii.

32. (i) State Faraday's laws of electromagnetic induction. Express it mathematically.

(ii) The given figure shows an inductor L and resistor R connected in parallel to a battery B through a switch S. The resistance of R is same as that of the coil that makes L. Two identical bulbs, P and Q are put in each arm of the circuit as shown in the figure. When S is closed, which of the two bulbs will light up earlier? Justify your answer.

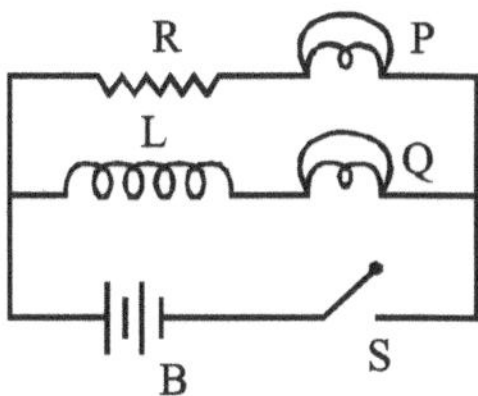

OR

What do you mean by mutual inductance of two nearby coils? Find an expression for mutual inductance of a solenoid.

33. Define magnifying power of a telescope. Write its expression.

A small telescope has an objective lens of focal length 150 cm and an eyepiece of focal length 5 cm. If this telescope is used to view a 100 m high tower 3 km away, find the height of the final image when it is formed 25 cm away from the eyepiece.

OR

A ray of light passes through an equilateral prism in such a way that the angle of incidence is equal to the angle of emergence and each of these angles is 3/4th the angle of the prism. Determine the (i) angle of deviation and (ii) the refractive index of the prism.

SECTION-E

34. Case Study: Transformers
Read the following paragraph and answer the questions.
A thermal power plant produces electric power of 600 kW at 4000 V, which is to be transported to a place 20 km away from the power plant for consumers' usage. It can be transported either directly with a cable of large current carrying capacity or by using a combination of step-up and step-down transformers at the two ends. The drawback of the direct transmission is the large energy dissipation. In the method using transformers, the dissipation is much smaller. In this method , a step-up transformer is used at the plant side so that the current is reduced to a smaller value. At the consumers' end, a step-down transformer is used to supply power to the consumers at the specified lower voltage. It is reasonable to assume that the power cable is purely resistive and the transformers are ideal with power factor unity. All the currents and voltages mentioned are rms values.

(i) How can the flux leakage in a transformer be reduced?

(ii) What is the cause of hysteresis loss in a transformer?

(iii) Why can't transformer be used to step up or step down dc voltage?

OR

(iii) In a transformer $\dfrac{V_S}{V_P} = \dfrac{N_S}{N_P}$. What are the assumption made in obtaining the relation?

35. Case Study: Combination of thin lenses in contact
Read the following paragraph and answer the questions.
Combination of lenses helps to obtain diverging or converging lenses of desired magnification. It also enhances sharpness of the image. The total magnification m of the combination is a product of magnification (m_1, m_2, m_3,...) of individual lenses $m = m_1 m_2 m_3 \ldots$ System of combination of lenses is commonly used in designing lenses for cameras, microscopes, telescopes and other optical instruments.

(i) Two identical thin plano-convex glass lenses (refractive index 1.5) each having radius of curvature of 20 cm are placed with their convex surfaces in contact at the centre. The intervening space is filled with oil of refractive index 1.7. Find the focal length of the combination.

(ii) The given lens is broken into four parts rearranged as shown. If the initial focal length is f, then after rearrangment. What is the equivalent focal length?

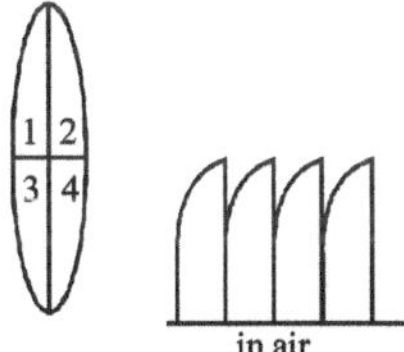

(iii) The power of a lens (biconvex) is 1.25 m^{-1} in particular medium. Refractive index of the lens is 1.5 and radii of curvature are 20 cm and 40 cm respectively. Find the refractive index of surrounding medium.

OR

(iii) A biconvex lens has radii of curvature, 20 cm each, if the refractive index of the material of the lens is 1.5. Find the power of the lens.

10 Sample Paper

BLUE PRINT

Ch. No.	Chapter Name	Per Unit Marks	Section-A MCQs 1 Mark	Section-B SA 2 Marks	Section-C LA-I 3 Marks	Section-D LA-II 5 Marks	Section-E Case Study 4 Marks	Total Marks
1	Electric Charges and Fields	16	2 (Q. 1, 2)		1 (Q. 29)			5
2	Electrostatic Potential and Capacitance		2 (Q. 3, 17)	1 (Q. 20)				4
3	Current Electricity		2 (Q. 4, 5)	1 (Q. 19)	1 (Q. 27)			7
4	Moving Charges and Magnetism	17	2 (Q. 6, 7)			1 (Q. 31)		7
5	Magnetism and Matter		1 (Q. 8)					1
6	Electromagnetic Induction		1 (Q. 18)		1 (Q.26)			4
7	Alternating Current		2 (Q. 9, 16)		1 (Q.28)			5
8	Electromagnetic Waves	18	1 (Q. 11)	1 (Q. 21)				3
9	Ray optics and Optical Instruments		3 (Q.12, 13, 14)	2 (Q. 22, 25)				7
10	Wave Optics		1 (Q. 15)	1 (Q. 23)		1 (Q. 33)		8
11	Dual Nature of Radiation and Matter	12				1 (Q. 32)		5
12	Atoms						1 (Q. 34)	4
13	Nuclei				1 (Q. 30)			3
14	Semiconductor Electronics: Materials, Devices and Simple Circuits	7	1 (Q.10)	1 (Q. 24)			1 (Q. 35)	7
	Total Marks (Total Questions)		18 (18)	14 (7)	15 (5)	15 (3)	8 (2)	70 (35)

NOTE : The number given inside the bracket denotes question number, ask in the sample paper, while the number given outside the bracket are the number of questions from that particular chapter.

Time Allowed : 3 Hours   **Max. Marks : 70**

General Instructions

1. There are 35 questions in all. All questions are compulsory.
2. This question paper has five sections: Section A, Section B, Section C, Section D and Section E. All the sections are compulsory.
3. Section A contains eighteen MCQ of 1 mark each, Section B contains seven questions of two marks each, Section C contains five questions of three marks each, section D contains three long questions of five marks each and Section E contains two case study based questions of 4 marks each.
4. There is no overall choice. However, an internal choice has been provided in section B, C, D and E. You have to attempt only one of the choices in such questions.
5. Use of calculators is not allowed.

SECTION-A

1. Two point charges placed in a medium of dielectric constant 5 are at a distance r between them, experience an electrostatic force 'F'. The electrostatic force between them in vacuum at the same distance r will be-
   (a) 5F   (b) F   (c) F/2   (d) F/5

2. When an electric dipole $\vec{P}$ is placed in a uniform electric field $\vec{E}$ then at what angle between $\vec{P}$ and $\vec{E}$ the value of torque will be maximum?
   (a) 90°   (b) 0°   (c) 180°   (d) 45°

3. From a point charge, there is a fixed point A. At A, there is an electric field of 500 V/m and potential difference of 3000 V. Distance between point charge and A will be
   (a) 6m   (b) 12m   (c) 16m   (d) 24m

4. Resistance of conductor is doubled keeping the potential difference across it constant. The rate of generation of heat will
   (a) become one fourth   (b) be halved
   (c) be doubled   (d) become four times

5. A wire of a certain material is stretched slowly by ten per cent. Its new resistance and specific resistance become respectively:
   (a) 1.2 times, 1.3 times   (b) 1.21 times, same
   (c) both remain the same   (d) 1.1 times, 1.1 times

6. A coil of one turn is made of a wire of certain length and then from the same length a coil of two turns is made. If the same current is passed in both the cases, then the ratio of the magnetic inductions at their centres will be
   (a) 2 : 1   (b) 1.4   (c) 4 : 1   (d) 1 : 2

7. A wire X of length 50 cm carrying a current of 2 A is placed parallel to a long wire Y of length 5 m. The wire Y carries a current of 3 A. The distance between two wires is 5 cm and currents flow in the same direction. The force acting on the wire Y is :

   (a) 1.2×10^{-5} N directed towards wire X.

   (b) 1.2×10^{-4} N directed away from wire X.

   (c) 1.2×10^{-4} N directed towards wire X.

   (d) 2.4×10^{-5} N directed towards wire X.

8. Among which of the following the magnetic susceptibility does not depend on the temperature?
   (a) Dia-magnetism   (b) Para-magnetism   (c) Ferro-magnetism   (d) Ferrite

9. An alternating voltage $V = V_0 \sin \omega t$ is applied across a circuit. As a result, a current $I = I_0 \sin (\omega t - \pi/2)$ flows in it. The power consumed per cycle is
   (a) zero   (b) $0.5\, V_0 I_0$ (c) $0.707\, V_0 I_0$ (d) $1.414\, V_0 I_0$

10. A d.c. battery of V volt is connected to a series combination of a resistor R and an ideal diode D as shown in the figure below. The potential difference across R will be

(a)   2V when diode is forward biased

(b)   zero when diode is forward biased

(c)   V when diode is reverse biased

(d)   V when diode is forward biased

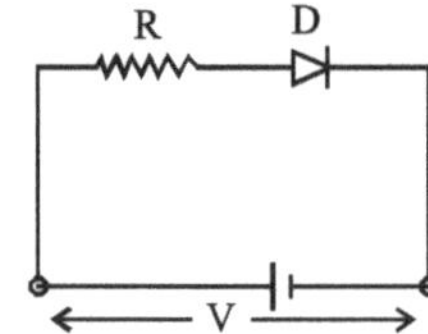

11. The electromagnetic waves

(a) travel with the speed of sound

(b) travel with the same speed in all media

(c) travel in free space with the speed of light

(d) do not travel through a medium

12. Magnifying power of an objective of a compound microscope is 8. If the magnifying power of microscope is 32 then magnifying power of eye piece is

(a) 7   (b)   5   (c)   4   (d)   3

13. A ray of light travelling inside a rectangular glass block of refractive index $\sqrt{2}$ is incident on the glass-air surface at an angle of incidence of $45°$. The refractive index of air is one. Under these conditions the ray will

(a) emerge into the air without any deviation

(b) be reflected back into the glass

(c) be absorbed

(d) emerge into the air with an angle of refraction equal to $90°$

14. Which of the following is incorrect statement?

(a) the magnification produced by a convex mirror is always less than one

(b) a virtual, erect, same-sized image can be obtained using a plane mirror

(c) a virtual, erect, magnifield image can be formed using a concave mirror

(d) a real, inverted, same-sized image can be formed using a convex mirror

15. A slit of width a is illuminated by red light of wavelength 6500 Å. If the first minimum falls at $\theta = 30°$, the value of a is

(a) 6.5×10^{-4} mm   (b)   1.3 micron   (c)   3250 Å   (d) 2.6×10^{-4} cm

For question numbers 16, 17 and 18, two statements are given-one labelled Assertion (A) and the other labelled Reason (R). Select the correct answer to these questions from the codes (a), (b), (c) and (d) as given below.

(a)   Both A and R are true and R is the correct explanation of A

(b)   Both A and R are true but R is NOT the correct explanation of A

(c)   A is true but R is false

(d)   A is false and R is also false

16. Assertion (A) : A capacitor blocks direct current in the steady state.

Reason (R) : The capacitive reactance of the capacitor is inversely proportional to frequency f of the source of emf.

17. Assertion (A) : For a charged particle moving from point P to point Q, the net work done by an electrostatic field on the particle is independent of the path connecting point P to point Q.

Reason (R) : The net work done by a conservative force on an object moving along a closed loop is zero.

18. Assertion (A) : Lenz's law violates the principle of conservation of energy.

Reason (R) : Induced emf always opposes the change in magnetic flux responsible for its production.

SECTION-B

19. Consider n cells connected in series in a row and m such rows connected in parallel. Obtain an expression for the maximum current from such a combination.

OR

Draw a graph showing the variation of resistivity with temperature for nichrome. Which property of nichrome is used to make standard resistance coils ?

20. Figure shows two identical capacitors C_1 and C_2, each of 2 μF capacitance, connected to a battery of 5V. Initially switch 'S' is closed. After some time S is left open and dielectric slabs of dielectric constant $K = 5$ are inserted to fill completely the space between the plates of the two capacitors. How will the (i) charge and (ii) potential difference between the plates of the capacitors be affected after the slabs are inserted?

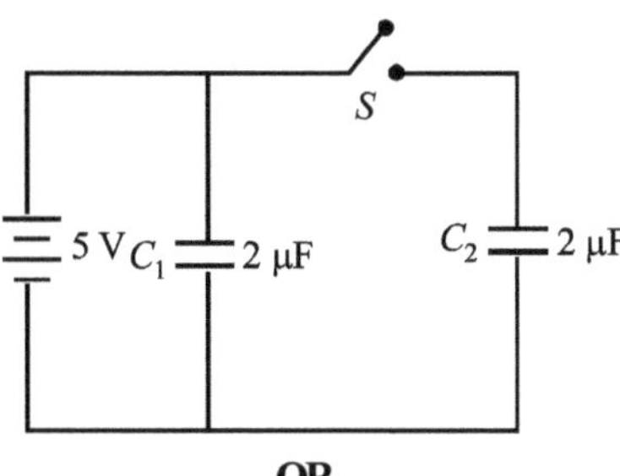

OR

Net capacitance of three identical capacitors in series is $1\ \mu F$. What will be their net capacitance if connected in parallel? Find the ratio of energy stored in the two configurations if they are both connected to the same source.

21. Identify the part of the electromagnetic specturm which is :
    (a) suitable for radar system used in aircraft navigation.
    (b) produced by bombarding a metal target by high speed electrons.

22. Derive the relation, $\delta = \left(n_{12} - 1\right) A$.

23. What is the shape of the wavefront in each of the following cases;
    (a) Light diverging from a point source.
    (b) Light emerging out of a convex lens when a point source is placed at its focus.
    (c) The portion of the wavefront of light from a distant star intercepted by the Earth.

24. A student wants to use two p-n junction diodes to convert alternating current into direct current. Draw the labelled circuit diagram she would use and explain how it works.

OR

In an intrinsic semiconductor, explain how current flow takes place.

25. A convex lens of focal length 20 cm and a concave lens of focal length 5 cm are kept along the same axis with a separation 'd' between them. What is the value of d, if a parallel beam of light incident on convex lens, leaves the concave lens as a parallel beam?

SECTION-C

26. Derive the formula for the self-inductance of a long solenoid.

27. A battery of emf E and internal resistance r when connected across an external resistance of 12 ohm produces a current of 0.5 A. When connected across a resistance of 25 ohm it produces a current of 0.25 A. Determine the (i) emf and (ii) internal resistance of the cell.

OR

Write a relation between current and drift velocity of electrons in a conductor. Use this relation to explain how the resistance of a conductor changes with the rise in temperature.

28. Derive an expression for the root mean square value (R.M.S.) of an alternating current.

OR

Derive an expression for the a.c. across a resistance R connected to an alternating source of e.m.f. $E = E_0 \sin \omega\, t$. Explain the variations of e.m.f. and current graphically and with a phasor diagram.

29. A point charge $+10\ \mu C$ is at a distance 5 cm directly above the centre of a square of side 10 cm, as shown in Fig. What is the magnitude of the electric flux through the square? (Hint: Think of the square as one face of a cube with edge 10 cm.)

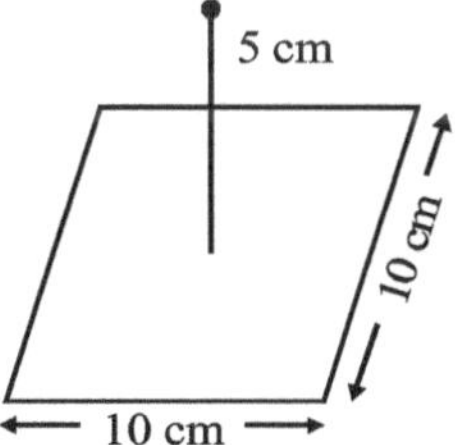

30. (a) Two stable isotopes of lithium ^6_3Li and ^7_3Li have respective abundances of 7.5% and 92.5%. These isotopes have masses 6.01512 u and 7.01600 u respectively. Find the atomic mass of lithium.

(b) Boron has two stable isotopes, $^{10}_5\text{B}$ and $^{11}_5\text{B}$. Their respective masses are 10.01294 u and 11.00931u, and the atomic mass of boron is 10.811 u. Find the abundances of $^{10}_5\text{B}$ and $^{11}_5\text{B}$.

SECTION-D

31. Derive an expression for the torque on a rectangular coil of area A, carrying a current I placed in a magnetic field B. The angle between the direction of B and the vector perpendicular to the plane of the coil is α.

OR

Deduce an expression for the frequency of revolution of a charged particle in a magnetic field and show that it is independent of velocity or energy of the particle.

32. Define the terms 'cut-off voltage' and 'threshold frequency' in relation to the phenomenon of photoelectric effect.
Using Einstein's photoelectric equation show how the cut-off voltage and threshold frequency for a given photosensitive material can be determined with the help of a suitable plot/graph.

OR

A proton and a deuteron are accelerated through the same accelerating potential. Which one of the two has

(a) greater value of de-Broglie wavelength associated with it, and

(b) less momentum?

Give reasons to justify your answer.

33. (a) In Young's double-slit experiment, monochromatic light of wavelength λ, the intensity of light at a point on the screen where path difference is λ is K units. What is the intensity of light at a point where path difference is $\dfrac{\lambda}{3}$?

(b) In double-slit experiment using light of wavelength 600 nm, the angular width of a fringe formed on a distant screen is 0.1°. What is the spacing between the two slits?

OR

A beam of light consisting of two wavelengths, 650 nm and 520 nm is used to obtain interference fringes in a Young's double-slit experiment.

(a) Find the distance of the third bright fringe on the screen from the central maximum for wavelength 650 nm.

(b) What is the least distance from the central maximum where the bright fringes due to both wavelengths coincide?

SECTION-E

34. Case Study: Energy Levels of Hydrogen Atom
Read the following paragraph and answer the questions.
In a mixture of H-He$^+$ gas (He$^+$ is singly ionized He atom), H atoms and He$^+$ ions are excited to their respective first excited states. Subsequently, H atoms transfer their total excitation energy to He$^+$ ions (by collisions). Assume that the Bohr model of atom is exactly valid.

(i) Find the quantum number n of the state finally populated in He$^+$ ions.

(ii) Find the wavelength of light emitted in the visible region by He$^+$ ions after collisions with H atoms.

(iii) Find the ratio of the kinetic energy of the n = 2 electron for the H atom to that of He$^+$ ion.

OR

(iii) In a hydrogen atom following the Bohr's postulates the product of linear momentum and angular momentum is proportional to $(n)^x$ where 'n' is the orbit number. Find the value of 'x'.

35. Case Study: Energy Band Theory of Solids
Read the following paragraph and answer the questions.
Doping changes the fermi energy of a semiconductor. Consider silicon, with a gap of 1.11 eV between the top of the valence bond and the bottom of the conduction band. At 300K the Fermi level of the pure material is nearly at the midpoint of the gap.

Suppose that silicon is doped with donor atoms, each of which has a state 0.15 eV below the bottom of the silicon conduction band, and suppose further that doping raises the Fermi level to 0.11 eV below the bottom of that band.

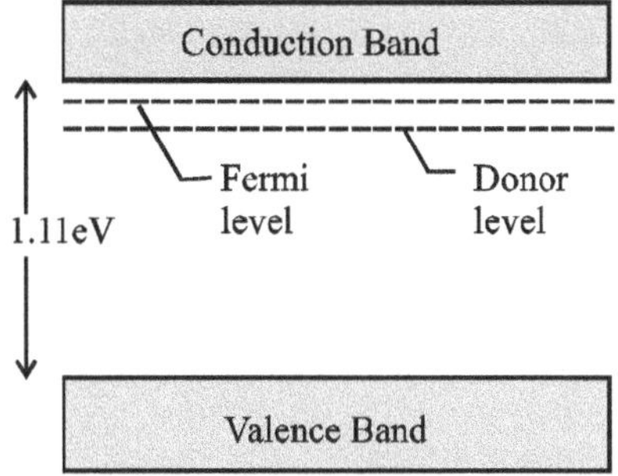

(i) What is the ratio of number of conduction electrons to the number of holes in intrinsic semiconductor?

(ii) Name the impurity which is added to a pure silicon to make it a p-type semiconductor.

(iii) How does the conductance of a semiconducting material change when an impurity is doped into an intrinsic semiconductor

OR

(iii) In full wave rectification, if the input frequency is 60 Hz, then find the output frequency.

SOLUTIONS

SAMPLE PAPER-1

1. (a) In parallel grouping of capacitors
$$C_{eq} = C_1 + C_2 + \ldots\ldots\ldots C_n \qquad \text{(1 mark)}$$

2. (d) As $R = \dfrac{1}{\text{Power}}$ $\qquad \therefore R_1 : R_2 = 2 : 1$ (1 mark)

3. (d) $\tau = MB \sin\theta \Rightarrow \tau_{max} = NIAB$, $(\theta = 90°)$ (1 mark)

4. (b) Voltage induced in the secondary coil of a transformer is mainly due to a varying magnetic field. (1 mark)

5. (b) From question,
$$B_0 = 20\,nT = 20 \times 10^{-9}\,T$$
$$\vec{E}_0 = \vec{B}_0 \times \vec{C}$$
$$|\vec{E}_0| = |\vec{B}_0| \cdot |\vec{C}| = 20 \times 10^{-9} \times 3 \times 10^8 = 6\,V/m. \qquad \text{(1 mark)}$$
($\because$ velocity of light in vacuum $C = 3 \times 10^8\,ms^{-1}$)

6. (b) Width of central maximum in diffraction pattern due to single slit $= \dfrac{2\lambda D}{d}$ where λ is the wavelength, D is the distance between screen and slit and a is the slit width. As the slit width a increases, width of central maximum becomes sharper or narrower. As same energy is distributed over a smaller area. Therefore central maximum becomes brigther. (1 mark)

7. (a) $\text{B.E}_H = \dfrac{2.22}{2} = 1.11$
$$\text{B.E}_{He} = \dfrac{28.3}{4} = 7.08$$
$$\text{B.E}_{Fe} = \dfrac{492}{56} = 8.78 = \text{maximum}$$
$$\text{B.E}_U = \dfrac{1786}{235} = 7.6$$
$^{56}_{26}\text{Fe}$ is most stable as it has maximum binding energy per nucleon. (1 mark)

8. (a) The significant result deduced from the Rutherford's scattering is that whole of the positive charge is concentrated at the centre of atom i.e. nucleus. (1 mark)

9. (d) Intensity $\propto 1/(\text{distance})^2$; No. of photoelectrons emitted is proportional to intensity of incident light. (1 mark)

10. (d) For a p-type semiconductor, the acceptor energy level, as shown in the diagram, is slightly above the top E_v of the volume band. With very small supply of energy an electron from the valence band can jump to the level E_A and ionise acceptor negatively. (1 mark)

11. (b) In half wave rectifier, we get the output only in one half cycle of input a.c. therefore, the frequency of the ripple of the output is same as that of input a.c. i.e., 50 Hz. (1 mark)

12. (d) Here, $n_i = 10^{16}\,m^{-3}$, $n_h = 5 \times 10^{22}\,m^{-3}$
As $n_e n_h = n_i^2$
$$\therefore n_e = \dfrac{n_i^2}{n_h} = \dfrac{(10^{16}\,m^{-3})^2}{5 \times 10^{22}\,m^{-3}} = 2 \times 10^9\,m^{-3} \qquad \text{(1 mark)}$$

13. (b) In normal adjustment,
$$M = \dfrac{f_0}{f_e} = 20,\ f_e = \dfrac{f_0}{20} = \dfrac{60}{20} = 3\ \text{cm} \qquad \text{(1 mark)}$$

14. (a) From electromagnetic spectrum, frequencies of γ-rays is greater than frequency of X-rays. Frequency of X-rays is greater than frequency of ultraviolet rays. (1 mark)

15. (b) Paramagnetic (1 mark)

16. (d) A is false but R is also false (1 mark)

17. (c) A is true but R is false (1 mark)

18. (d) A is false but R is also false (1 mark)

19. From Biot – Savart's law, the magnetic field due to an element of length $2l$ of the current carrying conductor is
$$dB = \dfrac{\mu_0}{4\pi}\dfrac{Id\ell \sin\theta}{r^2} \qquad \text{(½ mark)}$$
Here $\theta = 90°$ ($\because$ $d\ell$ is tangential, angle between the radius and the tangent is 90°)

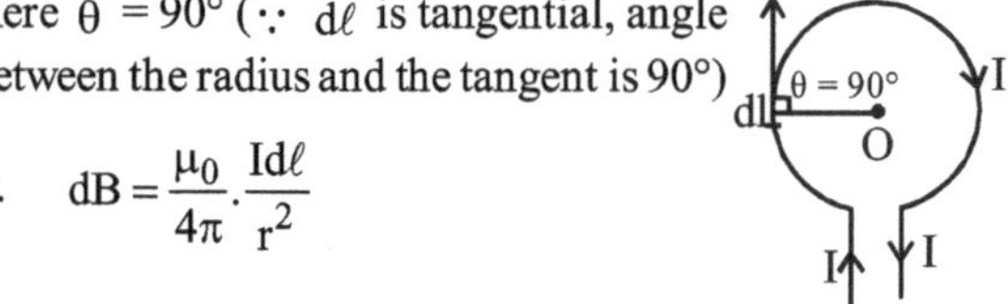

$$\therefore\quad dB = \dfrac{\mu_0}{4\pi}.\dfrac{Id\ell}{r^2}$$
$\therefore$ Total magnetic field at the centre O due to the whole circular coil
$$= B = \int dB = \dfrac{\mu_0 I}{4\pi r^2}\int d\ell = \dfrac{\mu_0 I}{4\pi r^2}.2\pi r = \dfrac{\mu_0 I}{2r}$$
For a coil of n number of turns, $B = \dfrac{\mu_0 nI}{2r}$ (1½ marks)
It is perpendicular to the plane of the coil and directed inwards.

20. Refraction of a plane wave form by
(i) A thin prism.

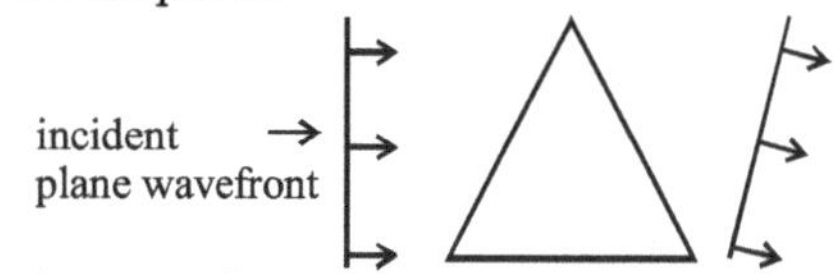

(ii) A convex lens

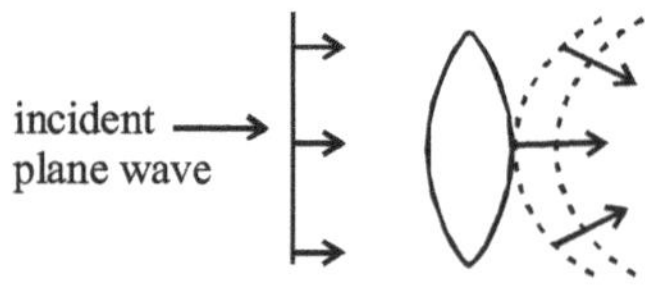

(1 + 1 = 2 marks)

21. Diodes D_1 and D_2 are ideal, therefore, they do not offer any resistance. Hence the two 3 ohm resistors are in parallel, hence,
$$R_p = 3 \times 3/3 + 3 = 9/6 = 1.5\,\Omega$$
Now, R_p and 2.5 ohm resistors are in series, hence, net resistance
$$R = R_p + 2.5 = 1.5 + 2.5 = 4.0\Omega$$
Hence, current through the circuit and through 2.5 Ω resistors
$$I = V/R = 10/4 = 2.5\ A \qquad \text{(2 marks)}$$

22. Induced emf $= e = -\dfrac{d\phi}{dt} = -\dfrac{8 \times 10^{-4}}{0.5}$

$$= -1.6 \times 10^{-3}\,V = -1.6\,mV$$

–ve sign gives the direction of e.m.f. (2 marks)

OR

Iuduced e.m.f. $= e = -L\dfrac{di}{dt}$

$$\therefore \quad L = \left|\dfrac{e}{di/dt}\right| = \dfrac{40 \times 10^{-3}}{2}$$

$$= 20 \times 10^{-3}\,H = 20\,mH.$$ (2 marks)

23. The impurity atoms should be such that (i) it doesn't distort the original pure semiconductor lattice, (ii) it occupies only a few of the original semiconductor atom sites in the crystal and (iii) size of the dopant and semiconductor atom should be same. (2 marks)

24. Length of the wire is same in both cases

$$\therefore \quad N_1 \times (2\pi R) = N_2 \times 2\pi \left(\dfrac{R}{2}\right)$$

So, $N_2 = 2N_1$

Now, the ratio of magnetic moments is given by

$$\dfrac{M_1}{M_2} = \dfrac{N_1 I A_1}{N_2 I A_2} = \dfrac{N_1 \times \pi R_1^2}{N_2 \times \pi R_2^2}$$

$$\dfrac{M_1}{M_2} = \left(\dfrac{N_1}{2N_1}\right) \times \left(\dfrac{R}{R/2}\right) = \dfrac{1}{2} \times 4 = 2$$

$$M_1 : M_2 = 2 : 1$$ (2 marks)

25. Critical angle of ray 1:

$\sin(c_1) = 1/\mu_1 = 1/1.35 \Rightarrow c_1 = \sin^{-1}(1/1.35) = 47.73°$

Similarly, critical angle of ray 2:

$\sin(c_2) = 1/\mu_2 = 1/1.45 \Rightarrow c_2 = \sin^{-1}(1/1.45) = 43.6°$

Both the rays will fall on the side AC with angle of incidence (i) equal to 45°.

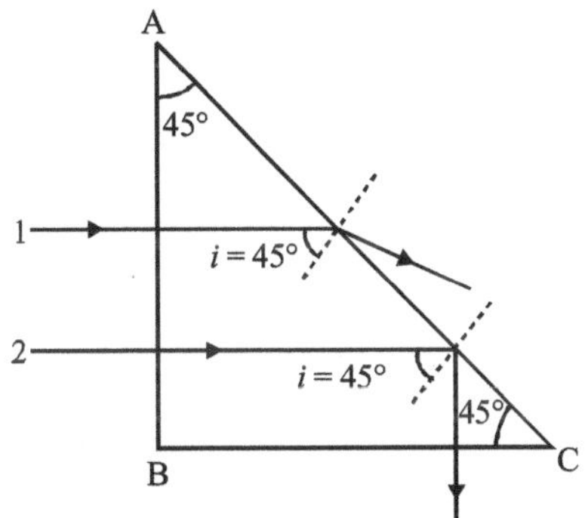

(2 marks)

Critical angle of ray 1 is greater than that of i. Hence, it will emerge from the prism, as shown in the figure. Critical angle of ray 2 is less than that of i. Hence, it will be internally reflected.

OR

Here, $i = e = \dfrac{3}{4}A, A = 60°$; $\delta = i + e - A$

$$= 2 \times \dfrac{3}{4}A - A = \dfrac{2A}{4} = \dfrac{1}{2} \times 60° = 30°$$ (2 marks)

26. Coefficient of mutual inductance between a pair of coils is numerically equal to the amount of magnetic flux linked with one coil when unit current flows through the other coil. Its S.I. unit is Henry.

It depends on size, shape, number of turns and nature of material of two coils. It also depends on the relative placement of the two coils. (1+1+1 = 3 marks)

27. Specific resistance of a material is defined as the resistance of unit length and unit cross-sectional area of the conductor. S.I. unit is ohm - m.

$$R = \dfrac{m\ell}{ne^2 A\tau} = \left(\dfrac{m}{ne^2\tau}\right)\dfrac{\ell}{A}$$ (1+½ marks)

Also $R = \dfrac{\rho\ell}{A}$ (1 + ½ marks)

28. Einstein's photoelectric equation

$$h\nu = h\nu_0 + \dfrac{1}{2}mv^2 \qquad h\nu = h\nu_0 + eV_s,$$

where v is the velocity of the ejected electrons and V_s is the stopping potential.

This equation is based on the following properties of photons:

(i) A photon is a packet of energy. It frequency and h plank's constant.

(ii) When a photon is incident on a photoelectric material, it is completely absorbed by the electron. The energy of the photon is used in ejecting electron and the balance if any is used up in imparting kinetic energy to the electron.

Two important observation which can be explained by the equation :

(i) The photoelectric emission takes place only if the incident light has a frequency greater than the threshold frequency ν_0. If $\nu < \nu_0$, then $\dfrac{1}{2}mv^2$ will be –ve, which is not possible. Hence, electron will not be emited. (1 + 1 + 1 = 3 marks)

(ii) When the frequency of the incident light increases, then $\dfrac{1}{2}mv^2$ i.e., kinetic energy of electron increases because work function $= h\nu_0$ is fixed. With increase in frequency more and more energy is available to the electron ejected and hence stopping potential also increases.

OR

(i) de–Broglie wavelength of a charged particle is given by $\lambda \propto \dfrac{1}{\sqrt{mq}}$

If m_p and e are mass and charge of a proton respectively, and m_α and $2e$ are mass and charge of an alpha particle respectively, then,

$$\dfrac{\lambda_p}{\lambda_\alpha} = \sqrt{\dfrac{m_\alpha q_\alpha}{m_p q_p}} = \sqrt{\dfrac{(4m_p)(2e)}{(m_p)(e)}} = 2\sqrt{2}$$ (1½ marks)

$$\lambda_p = 2\sqrt{2}$$

Thus, de-broglie wavelength associated with proton is $2\sqrt{2}$ times of the de-broglie wavelength of alpha particle.

(ii) For same accelerating potential K.E. $\propto$ q
Charge of an alpha particle is more as compared to a proton. So, it will have a greater value of K.E.
Hence, proton will have lesser kinetic energy.

(1½ marks)

29. Electron revolves in a stable orbit, the centripetal force is provided by electrostatic force of attraction acting on it, due to positive charges in the nucleus.
Hence,

$$\frac{mv_n^2}{r_n} = \frac{1}{4\pi\varepsilon_0}\cdot\frac{e^2}{r_n^2}$$

$$\Rightarrow v_n^2 = \frac{e^2}{4\pi\varepsilon_0 mr_n} \qquad ...(i)$$

(1 mark)

and from Bohr's quantum condition, we have

$$mv_nr_n = \frac{nh}{2\pi} \text{ or } v_n = \frac{nh}{2\pi mr_n} \qquad ...(ii)$$

(1 mark)

Squaring Eq (ii) and then equating it with Eq. (i), we get

$$\frac{n^2h^2}{4\pi^2 m^2 r_n^2} = \frac{e^2}{4\pi\varepsilon_0 mr_n}$$

(1 mark)

$$\Rightarrow r_n = \frac{n^2h^2}{4\pi^2 m^2} \times \frac{4\pi\varepsilon_0 m}{e^2} = \frac{\varepsilon_0 h^2}{\pi me^2}.n^2$$

30. The size of the nucleus is experimentally determined using Rutherford's α-scattering experiment and the distance of closed approach and impact parameter.
The relation between radius and mass number of nucleus is,

$$R = R_0 A^{1/3}, \text{ where } R_0 = 1.2 \text{ fm}$$

Nuclear density,

$$\rho = \frac{\text{Mass of nucleus}}{\text{Volume of nucleus}} = \frac{mA}{\frac{4}{3}\pi(R_0 A^{1/3})^3}$$

$$\rho = \frac{mA}{\frac{4}{3}\pi R_0^3 A} \quad \text{or} \quad \rho = \frac{m}{\frac{4}{3}\pi R_0^3}$$

(1 + 1 + 1 = 3 marks)

It is clear that ρ does not depend on mass number.

OR

(a) In the nuclear reaction

$$_2^3\text{He} + _2^3\text{He} \longrightarrow _2^4\text{He} + _1^1\text{H} + _1^1\text{H} + 12.86 \text{ MeV}$$

Number of nucleons on left side
= number of nucleons on right side
$3 + 3 = 4 + 1 + 1 = 6$. Thus, total number of nucleons is conserved. The energy is being released because sum of the masses of $_2^3\text{He}$ and $_2^3\text{He}$ is more than the sum of the masses of $_2\text{He}^4$, $_1\text{H}^1$ and $_1\text{H}^1$ i.e., products. Thus there is some mass defect Δm. (1½ marks)

According to Einstein's mass energy relation

$$\Delta E = \Delta mc^2$$

Hence in nuclear reaction though the number of nucleons is conserved, the energy is released.

(b) Plot of potential energy between a pair of nucleons as a function of their separation :

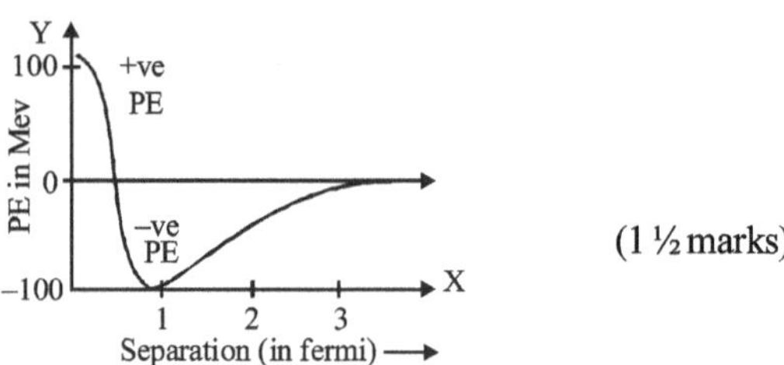

(1 ½ marks)

31. Gauss's theorem:– The surface integral of electrostatic field $(\vec{E})$ produced by any source over any closed surface S in vacuum, or the total electric flux over the closed surface in vacuum is $\dfrac{1}{\varepsilon_0}$ times the total charge (Q) contained inside S.

$$\phi_E = \oint \vec{E}.d\vec{S} = \frac{Q}{\varepsilon_0}$$

(1 mark)

Electric field intensity due to a thin infinite sheet of charge:

Let σ be the surface density of charge and P be a point at a distance r from the sheet where $\vec{E}$ has to be calculated. $\vec{E}$ on either side is perpendicular to the sheet.

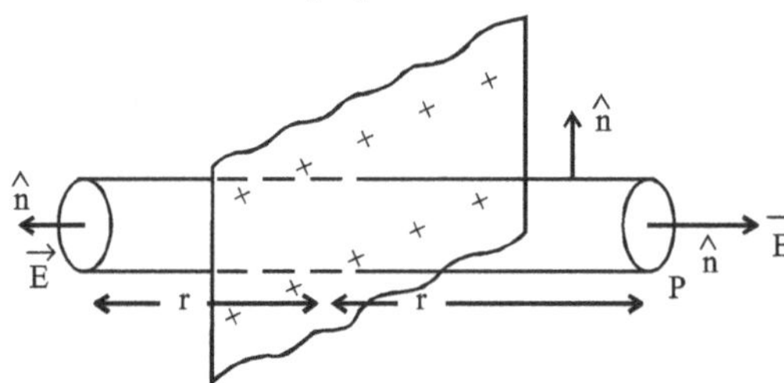

Imagine a cylinder of cross-sectional area ds around P and length 2r, piercing through the sheet. At the two edges, $\vec{E} \parallel \hat{n}$ (or $\vec{dS}$). At the curved surfaces $\vec{E} \perp \hat{n}$ (or $\vec{dS}$). So, there is no contribution to electric flux from the curved surfaces of the cylinder.

Electric flux over the edges $= 2\vec{E}.\vec{dS} = 2EdS$

Total charge enclosed by the cylinder $= \sigma dS$

By Gauss's theorem, $2EdS = \dfrac{q}{\varepsilon_0} = \dfrac{\sigma dS}{\varepsilon_0}$

$$\therefore E = \frac{\sigma}{2\varepsilon_0}.$$

If the infinite plane sheet has uniform thickness, the surface density of charge is same on both the surfaces of the sheet.
Electric field intensity at any point P due to each surface $= E_1 = E_2 = \sigma/2\varepsilon_0$

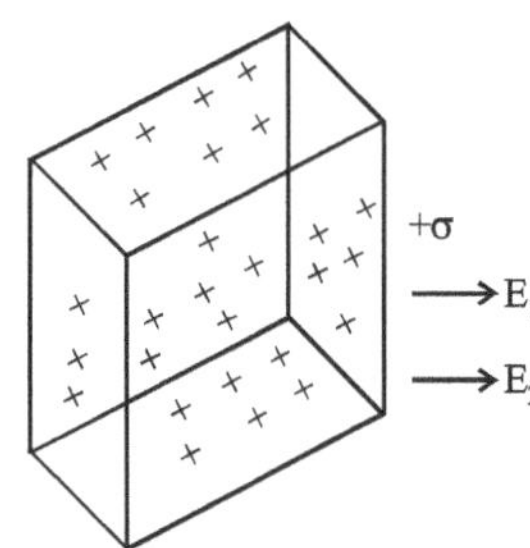

$\therefore$ By superposition principle, total electric field intensity

$$= E = E_1 + E_2 = \frac{\sigma}{2\varepsilon_0} + \frac{\sigma}{2\varepsilon_0} = \frac{\sigma}{\varepsilon_0}.$$

(2 marks)

OR

(a) We have to calculate the field intensity (E) at a point P on the axial line of the dipole and at a distance OP = x from the centre O of the dipole.

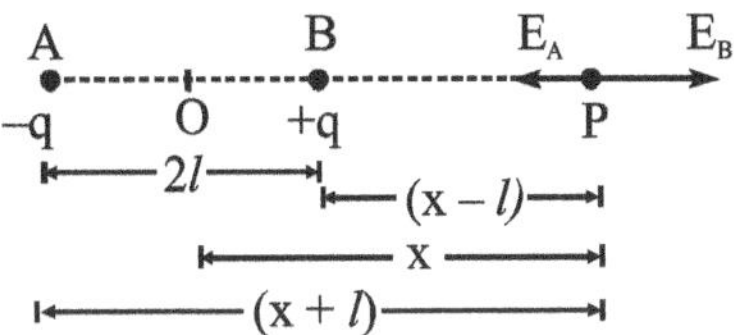

Electric field on axial line of an electric dipole
Resultant electric field intensity at the point P is

$$E_p = E_A + E_B$$

The vectors E_A and E_B are collinear and opposite.

$$\therefore \quad E_p = E_B - E_A$$

Here, $E_A = \dfrac{1}{4\pi\varepsilon_0} \cdot \dfrac{q}{(x+l)^2} \Rightarrow E_B = \dfrac{1}{4\pi\varepsilon_0} \cdot \dfrac{q}{(x-l)^2}$

$$\therefore E_p = \dfrac{1}{4\pi\varepsilon_0}\left[\dfrac{q}{(x-l)^2} - \dfrac{q}{(x+l)^2}\right] = \dfrac{1}{4\pi\varepsilon_0}\dfrac{4qlx}{(x^2-l^2)^2}$$

Hence, $E_p = \dfrac{1}{4\pi\varepsilon_0}\dfrac{4px}{(x^2-l^2)^2}$ **(2½ marks)**

If dipole is short, $2l << x$, then $E_p = \dfrac{2px}{4\pi\varepsilon_0 x^3}$

(b) The electric field has only x component, for faces normal to x direction, the angle between E and Δs is $\pm\dfrac{\pi}{2}$. Therefore, the flux is separately zero for each face of the cube except the two shaded ones.

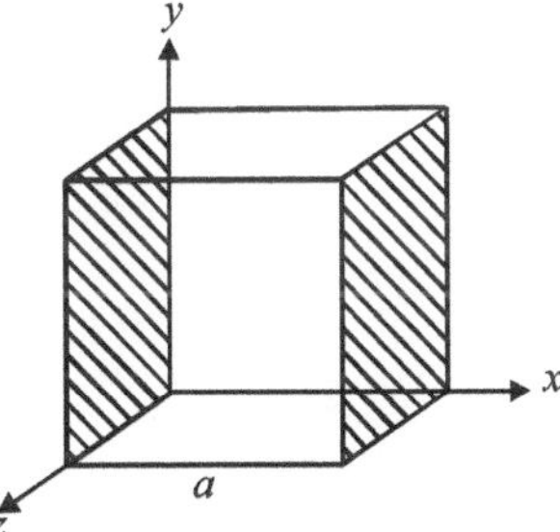

The magnitude of the electric field at the left face is E_L = 0 (As x = 0 at the left face)
The magnitude of the electric field at the right face is E_R = 2a (As $x = a$ at the right face)
Their corresponding fluxes are

$$\phi_L = \vec{E}_L \cdot \Delta\vec{S} = 0$$

$$\phi_R = \vec{E}_L \cdot \Delta\vec{S} = E_R\Delta S \cos\theta = E_R\Delta S \ (\because \theta = 0°)$$
$$\Rightarrow \phi_R = E_R a^2$$

Net flux (ϕ) through the cube $= \phi_L + \phi_R = 0 + E_R a^2 = E_R \, a^2$

$$\phi = 2a(a^2) = 2a^3$$

From, Gauss's law

$$\phi = \dfrac{q}{\varepsilon_0} \Rightarrow q = \phi\varepsilon_0$$ **(2½ marks)**

$$\therefore q = 2a^3\varepsilon_0$$

32. Phase difference between voltage and current,

$$\tan\phi = \dfrac{X_L - X_C}{R} \quad .....\text{(i)}$$

and, $I_0 = \dfrac{V_0}{2} = \dfrac{V_0}{\sqrt{(X_L - X_C)^2 + R^2}}$

$\therefore$ Expression of AC, $I = I_0 \sin(\omega t = \phi)$ **(2 marks)**

Condition for resonance
Inductive reactance must be equal to capacitive reactance
i.e., $X_L = X_C$
As, $X_L = X_C$ **(1 mark)**

$$\Rightarrow \omega_0 L = \dfrac{1}{\omega_0 C} \Rightarrow \omega_0^2 = \dfrac{1}{LC}$$

$$\omega_0 = \dfrac{1}{\sqrt{LC}}$$

where, ω_0 = resonant angular frequency.
Impedance becomes minimum and equal to ohmic resistance
i.e., $Z = Z_{minimum} = R$
AC becomes maximum,

$$\therefore I_{max} = \dfrac{V_{max}}{Z_{min}} = \dfrac{V_{max}}{R}$$ **(2 marks)**

Voltage and current arrives in same phase.

OR

(a)

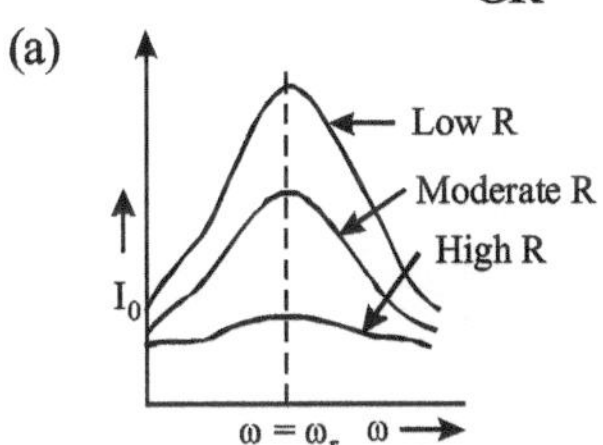

The sharpness of resonance in series L-C-R circuit refers how quick fall of alternating current in circuit takes place when frequency of alternating voltage shifts away from resonant frequency. It is measured by quality factor (Q-factor) of circuit.
The Q-factor of series resonant circuit is defined as the ratio of the voltage developed across the capacitance or inductance at resonance to the impressed voltage which is the voltage applied.

i.e., quality factor (Q) = $\dfrac{\text{voltage across L or C}}{\text{applied voltage}}$

$$Q = \dfrac{(\omega_r L)I}{RI}$$

$[\because$ applied voltage = voltage across $R]$

or $Q = \dfrac{\omega_r L}{R}$ or $Q = \dfrac{(1/\omega_r IC)I}{RI} = \dfrac{1}{RC\omega_r}$

$$\therefore Q = \dfrac{L}{RC \cdot \dfrac{1}{\sqrt{LC}}} \quad \left[\text{using } \omega_r = \dfrac{1}{\sqrt{LC}}\right]$$

$$= \dfrac{1}{R}\sqrt{\dfrac{L}{C}}$$

or $\quad Q = \dfrac{1\sqrt{LC}}{RC} = \dfrac{1}{R}\sqrt{\dfrac{L}{C}} \quad \left[\text{using } \omega_r = \dfrac{1}{\sqrt{LC}}\right]$

Thus, $Q = \dfrac{1}{R}\sqrt{\dfrac{L}{C}}$ (2 marks)

This is required expression.

(b) Let initially I_r current is flowing in all the three circuits. If frequency of applied AC source is increased then, the change in current will occur in following manner:

Circuit containing resistance R only There will not be any effect in the current, on changing the frequency of AC source.

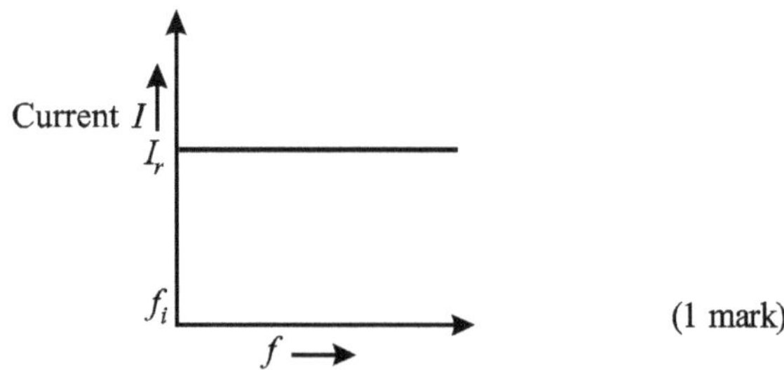

(1 mark)

where, f_i = initial frequency of AC source.

There is no effect on current with the increase in frequency.

AC circuit containing inductance only With the increase of frequency of AC source, inductive reactance increase as

$I = \dfrac{V_{\text{rms}}}{X_L} = \dfrac{V_{\text{rms}}}{2\pi f L}$

For given circuit,

$I \propto \dfrac{1}{f}$

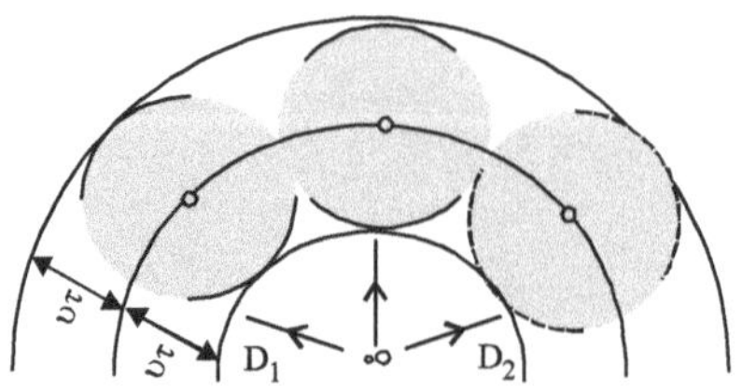

(1 mark)

Current decreases with the increase of frequency.

AC circuits containing capacitor only

$X_C = \dfrac{1}{\omega C} = \dfrac{1}{2\pi f C}$

Current, $I = \dfrac{V_{\text{rms}}}{X_C} = \dfrac{V_{\text{rms}}}{\left(\dfrac{1}{2\pi f C}\right)}$

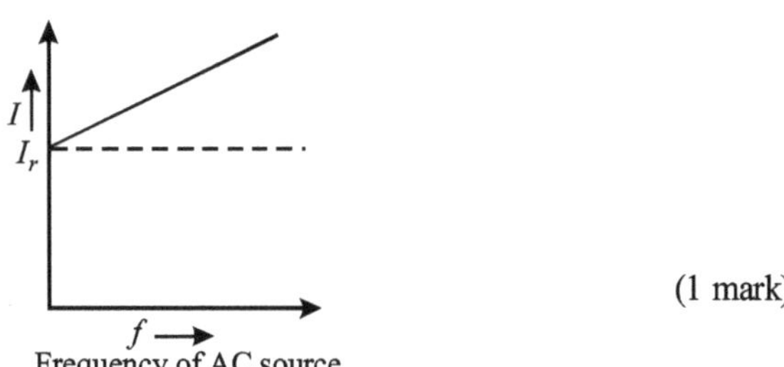

(1 mark)

$I = 2\pi f C V_{\text{rms}}$

For given circuit, $I \propto f$

Current increases with the increase of frequency.

33. (a)   A **wavefront** is defined as the continuous locus of all the particles of a medium, which are vibrating in the same phase or it is a surface of constant phase.   (½ mark)

Huygens' principle:

(1)   Every points on the given wavefront (called primary wavefront) acts as a fresh source of new disturbance (secondary wavelets), which travel in all directions with the velocity of light in the medium.

(2)   A surface touching these secondary wavelets, tangentially in the forward direction at any instant gives the new wavefront at that instant. This is called secondary wavefront.   (1 mark)

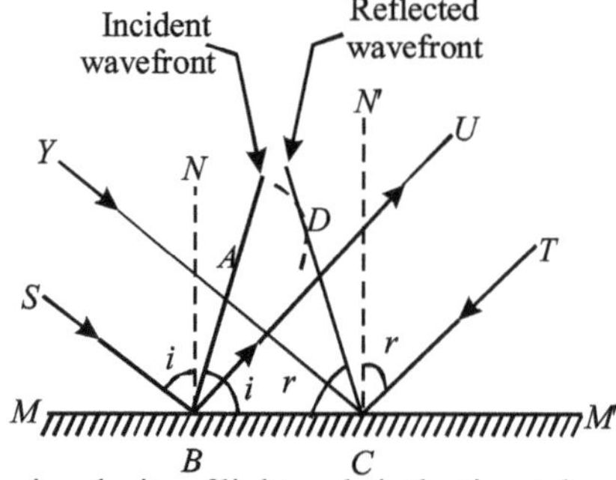

The above model has one shortcoming: we also have a backwave which is shown as D_1D_2 in figure. Huygens argued that the amplitude of the secondary wavelets is maximum in the forward direction and zero in the backward direction, by making this assumption, Huygens could explain the absence of the backwave.

Let a plane wavefront AB is incident on the plane mirror MM'. As per Huygen's wave theory, every point on wavefront again behaves like a light source and emits secondary wavelets. In the time taken by the wave to reach from A to C, the secondary wavelets from B gets spread over a hemisphere of radius.

where, c is velocity of light and t is the time taken by wave in going from A to C. The tangent plane CD drawn from the point C over this hemisphere of radius ct gives new reflected wavefront CD corresponding to incident wavefront AB.

Let i and r be angles of incidence and reflection respectively.

Now, in $\triangle ABC$ and $\triangle DCB$

$\angle BAC = \angle CDB$	[each 90°, ray $\perp$ wavefront]
$BC = BC$	(common)
$AC = DB$	[From Eq. (i)]
$\Rightarrow \quad \triangle ABC \cong \triangle DCB$	(RHS congruence)
$\Rightarrow \quad \angle ABC = \angle DCB$	
or $\quad i = r$	

$$\left[\because SB \perp AB \Rightarrow \angle NBA = 90° - i \; and \; BN \perp BC \atop \Rightarrow \angle ABC = i\right]$$

Similarly, $\angle N'CT = \angle DCB = r$

$\Rightarrow$ Angle of incidence = Angle of reflection

Also, incident ray, reflected ray and normal meet at one point on a plane.

Thus, laws of reflection are verified using Huygen's principle. (2 marks)

(b) As the number of point sources increases, their contribution towards intensity also increases. Intensity varies as square of the slit width. Thus, when the width of the slit is made double the original width, intensity will get four times of its original value.

Width of central maximum is given by, $\beta = \dfrac{2D\lambda}{b}$

So, with the increase in size of slit, the width of central maxima decreases. Hence, double the size of the slit would results as half the width of the central maxima. (1 mark)

(c) The waves diffracted from the edge of the circular obstacle interfere constructively at the centre of the shadow producing a bright spot. (½ mark)

OR

(i) (a) From the fringe width expression,

$$\beta = \dfrac{\lambda D}{d}$$

With the decrease in separation between two slits, the fringe-width d increases. (1 mark)

(b) For interference fringes to be seen,

$$\dfrac{s}{S} < \dfrac{\lambda}{d}$$

Condition should be satisfied

where, s = size of the source,

S = distance of the source from the plane of two slits.

As the source-slit-width increase, fringe pattern gets less and less sharp.

When the source-slit is so wide, the above condition does not satisfied and the interference pattern disappears. (1 mark)

(ii) Intensity at a point is given by,

$I = 4I' \cos^2 \phi/2$ (1 mark)

where, ϕ = phase difference,

I' = intensity produced by each one of the individual sources.

At central maxima, $\phi = 0$, the intensity at the central maxima,

$I = I_0 = 4I'$

or $\quad I' = \dfrac{I_0}{4}$ .... (i)

As, path difference $= \dfrac{\lambda}{3}$

Phase difference,

$\phi' = \dfrac{2\pi}{\lambda} \times$ path difference $= \dfrac{2\pi}{\lambda} \times \dfrac{\lambda}{3} = \dfrac{2\pi}{3}$ (1 mark)

Now, intensity at the point,

$I'' = 4I'\cos^2 \dfrac{1}{2}\left(\dfrac{2\pi}{3}\right) = 4I'\cos^2 \dfrac{\pi}{3} = 4I' \times \dfrac{1}{4} = I'$ (1 mark)

or $\quad I'' = \dfrac{I_0}{4}$ [From eq. (i)]

34. (i) By Gauss's theorem

Electric flux through the closed surface S is

$$\phi_s = \dfrac{\Sigma q}{\varepsilon_0} = \dfrac{+2q - q}{\varepsilon_0} = \dfrac{q}{\varepsilon_0}$$ (1 mark)

(ii) According to Gauss's law, flux through a closed surface is given by $\phi = \dfrac{q}{\varepsilon_0}$

Here, q is the charge enclosed by the Gaussian surface. Since, on increasing the radius of the Gaussian surface, charge through the spherical Gaussian surface will not be affected when its radius is increased. (1 mark)

(iii) The flux is zero according to Gauss' Law because it is a open surface which enclosed a charge q. (2 marks)

OR

(iii) According to Gauss' Law

$$\oint E.ds = \dfrac{Q_{enclosed \; by \; closed \; surface}}{\varepsilon_o} = flux$$

so total flux = Q/ε_o

Since cube has six face, so flux coming out through one wall or one face is $Q/6\varepsilon_o$. (2 marks)

35. (i) Because refractive index for a given pair of media is independent of frequency of light. (1 mark)

(ii) Refractive index, $\mu = \dfrac{1}{\sin C}$ (1 mark)

(iii) For total internal reflection when $i = i_c$, then

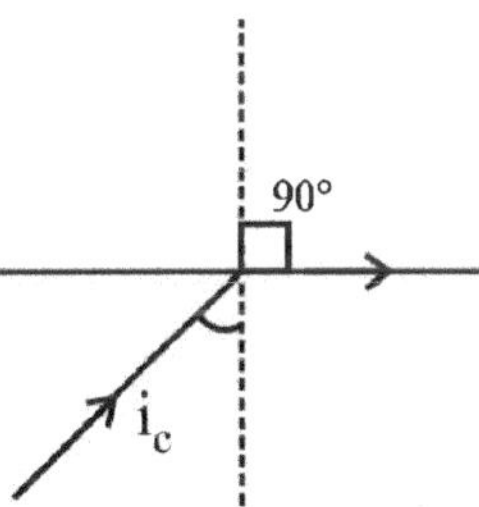

refracted ray grazes with the surface. That means the angle of refraction $r = 90°$. (2 marks)

OR

(iii) Criteria for total internal reflection of light are.

(a) Light must travel from a denser to a rarer medium. (1 mark)

(b) Angle of incidence must be greater than the critical angle. (1 mark)

1. **(c)** $C = \dfrac{2 \times 2}{2 + 2} + 2 = 3\ \mu F$ (1 mark)

2. **(c)** The potential at any point of circular path will be same. (1 mark)

3. **(a)** $F = \dfrac{\mu_0}{4\pi} \times \dfrac{2 i_1 i_2}{r}$

$= 50 \times 10^{-7}$ N/m. Here F is force per unit length. (1 mark)

4. **(b)** Efficiency of the transformer

$\eta = \dfrac{P_{output}}{P_{input}} \times 100 = \dfrac{100}{220 \times 0.5} \times 100 = 90.9\%$ (1 mark)

5. **(a)** Small and negative (1 mark)

6. **(c)** Lenz's law is a consequence of the law of conservation of energy. (1 mark)

7. **(d)** Alternating current cannot be measured by D.C. ammeter because average value of A.C. for complete cycle is zero. (1 mark)

8. **(d)** Compare with $B_y = B_0 \sin (kx - \omega t)$

$\omega = 4 \times 10^8$, $K = 5$

Here, $B_0 = 5 \times 10^{-6}$

$\omega = 4 \times 10^8$, $K = 5$

$v =$ Speed of wave $= \dfrac{4 \times 10^8}{5} = 8 \times 10^7 \quad \left[\because v = \dfrac{\omega}{k}\right]$

$E_0 = vB_0 = 40 \times 10^1 = 4 \times 10^2$ V/m (1 mark)

9. **(d)** $M = 4 = -\dfrac{V}{4} \Rightarrow V = -4u$

Using mirror formula $\dfrac{1}{V} + \dfrac{1}{4} = \dfrac{1}{F} \Rightarrow \dfrac{1}{-4u} + \dfrac{1}{4} = \dfrac{-1}{0.6}$

$\Rightarrow \dfrac{1 - 40}{-44} = \dfrac{-1}{0.6} \Rightarrow 4 = -0.45$ m (1 mark)

10. **(a)** From the graph it is clear that A and B have the same stopping potential and therefore the same frequency. Also B and C have the same intensity. (1 mark)

11. **(c)** $\dfrac{R_s}{R_{He}} = \left(\dfrac{A_s}{A_{He}}\right)^{1/3} = \left(\dfrac{32}{4}\right)^{1/3} = 2$ (1 mark)

12. **(b)** Rutherford's atomic model was unstable because electrons do not remain in orbit. (1 mark)

13. **(b)** To make a p-type semiconductor, pure silicon is doped with trivalent impurity like boron. (1 mark)

14. **(a)** On adding impurity. Conductivity of the semiconductor increases. (1 mark)

15. **(b)** Reverse resistance

$= \dfrac{\Delta V}{\Delta I} = \dfrac{1}{0.5 \times 10^{-6}} = 2 \times 10^6\ \Omega$ (1 mark)

16. **(a)** Resistance, $R = \rho \dfrac{l}{A}$

Here, ρ = resistivity

l = length

A = area of cross-section

Bending a wire does not change length (l) or area of cross-section (A). Hence, resistance remains same. (1 mark)

17. **(b)** At any point on equitorial plane of dipole,

$V = 0$ (1 mark)

18. **(c)** $I_{max} = (\sqrt{I_1} + \sqrt{I_2})^2$

$I_{min} = (\sqrt{I_1} - \sqrt{I_2})^2$ (1 mark)

19. **(i)** From graph (i), it is clear that resistance (opposition to current) is not changing with frequency, i.e., resistance does not depend on frequency of applied source, so the circuit element here is pure resistance (R).

From graph (ii), it is clear that resistance increases linearly with frequency, so the circuit element here is an inductor.

Inductive resistance $X_L = 2\pi f L \Rightarrow X_L \propto f$

$(1 + 1\ \text{mark})$

20. Given : $f_1 = 0.5\ m_1$, $f_2 = -1m$

Power of combination

$p = p_1 + p_2 = \dfrac{1}{f_1} + \dfrac{1}{f_2} = \dfrac{1}{0.5} + \dfrac{1}{(-1)} = 2 - 1 = 1\ D$

(2 marks)

OR

For plano-convex lens, $R_1 = \infty$; $R_2 = -10$ cm. $\mu = 1.5$

$\therefore \dfrac{1}{f} = (\mu - 1)\left(\dfrac{1}{R_1} - \dfrac{1}{R_2}\right) = (1.5 - 1)\left(\dfrac{1}{\infty} - \dfrac{1}{-10}\right)$

$= 0.5 \times \dfrac{1}{10} = \dfrac{5}{100} = \dfrac{1}{20} \quad \therefore f = 20\text{cm}$

Since the plane surface is silvered therfore the focal length

$= \dfrac{f}{2} = \dfrac{20}{2} = 10\text{cm}$ (2 marks)

21. Electrons diffuse from $n \to p$ and holes diffuse from $p \to n$ side leaving a positively charged donor atom on n–side and negatively charged acceptor atom on p–side. This space charge region on either side is called depletion region. Near the junction this region depletes the movement of free charges. Hence, electric field due to positive space charge on n–side and negative space charge on p–side is created. Due to this electrons and holes now drift in opposite direction in this field and further extend this region.

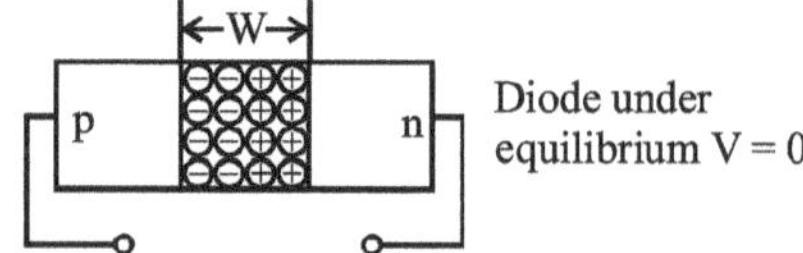

Thus a different polarity potential is developed which prevents movement of electron from n–region to p–region, called **barrier potential** and there is no net current.

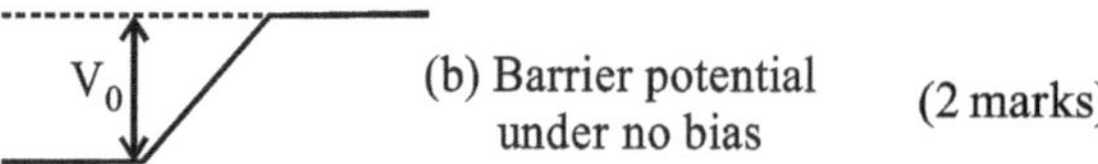

(b) Barrier potential under no bias (2 marks)

22. The labelled ray diagram of refracting type teloscope in normal adjustment is as shown :

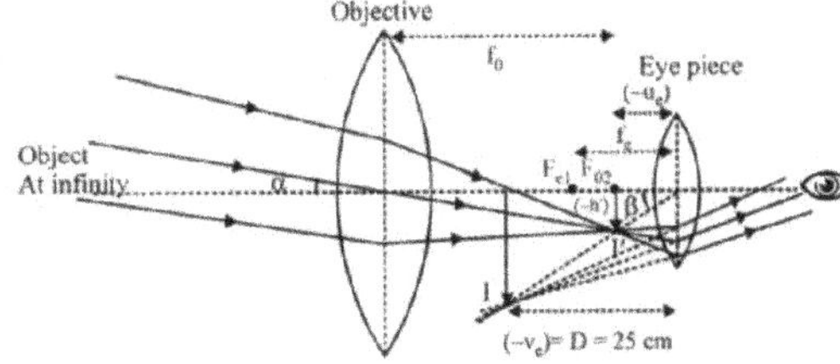

(1 mark)

The two considerations are (i) Objective should be of large focal length and apearture (ii) Eyepiece should be of small focal length and aperture. (½ + ½ mark)

23. (a) In forward bias, $V = +0.9V$

$$\Delta V = BE = 1.0 - 0.8 = 0.2 \text{ V}$$
$$\Delta I = CE = 10 - 6 = 4 \text{ mA}$$

∴ Forward resistance,

$$R_f = \frac{\Delta V}{\Delta I} = \frac{0.2}{4 \times 10^{-3}} = 50\Omega.$$ (1 mark)

(b) Reverse characteristics, $V = -3$ V

$$\Delta V = -2 - (-4) = 2 \text{ V}$$
$$\Delta I = 3 - 2 = 1 \,\mu A$$

∴ Reverse resistance,

$$R_r = \frac{\Delta V}{\Delta I} = \frac{2V}{1 \times 10^{-6}} = 2 \times 10^{6}\Omega.$$ (1 mark)

24. Induced current is in anticlockwise when seen from left hand side and its direction is in clockwise when seen from right hand side.

Therefore B is as negative plate while A is as (+) ve plate. (1 + 1 mark)

OR

(i) Mutual induction: It is the phenomenon in which a change of current in one coil induces an emf in another coil placed near it. The coil in which the current changes is called the primary coil and the coil in which the emf is induced is called the secondary coil. (1 mark)

(ii) As we know, $e = -M\dfrac{dI}{dt}$

$$e = -1.5 \times \frac{20 - 0}{0.5} = -60V$$

So, the flux linked with the other coil is given by

$$\Delta\phi = e \times \Delta t = -60 \times 0.5 = -30 \text{ Wb}$$ (1 mark)

25. Given : $\lambda = 600$ nm $= 600 \times 10^{-9}$ m, D = 1.2 m, $\beta = 3 \times 10^{-3}$ m, d = ?

Distance of the first minimum

$$\beta = \frac{\lambda D}{d} \Rightarrow d = \frac{\lambda D}{\beta} = \frac{600 \times 10^{-9} \times 1.2}{3 \times 10^{-3}} = 2.4 \times 10^{-4} \text{ m}$$ (2 marks)

26. Nickel is a ferromagnetic substance so field lines

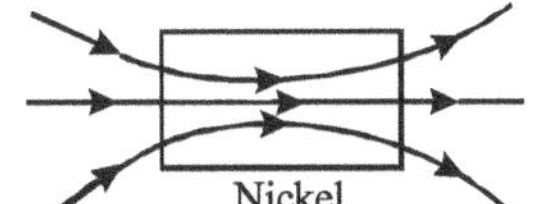

Antimony is a diamagnetic substance so field lines

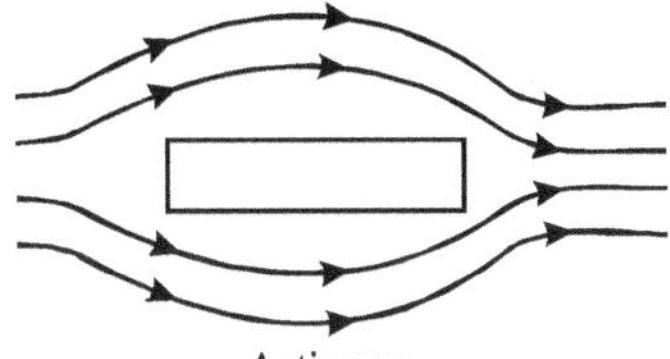

Aluminium is a paramagnetic substance so field lines

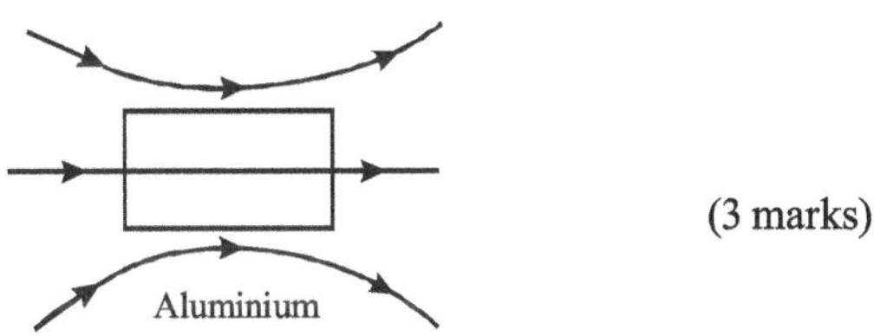

(3 marks)

27. Torque on a dipole which is placed in an uniform electric field (E) is given by,

$$\tau = PE \sin\theta = (ql) E \sin\theta \qquad \text{...(1)}$$

Here, l is the length of the dipole, Q is the charge and E is the electric field. (1½ marks)

Potential energy,

$$U = -PE \cos\theta = -(ql) E \cos\theta \qquad \text{...(2)}$$

Dividing (2) by (1), $\dfrac{\tau}{U} = \dfrac{ql E \sin\theta}{-ql E \cos\theta} = -\tan\theta$

$$\Rightarrow U = \frac{-\tau}{\tan\theta} \Rightarrow U = \frac{-\tau}{\tan 60°} \Rightarrow U = \frac{-4\sqrt{3}}{\sqrt{3}}$$

$$\Rightarrow U = -4J$$ (1½ marks)

28. Graph between the potential energy of a pair of nucleons as a function of their separation.

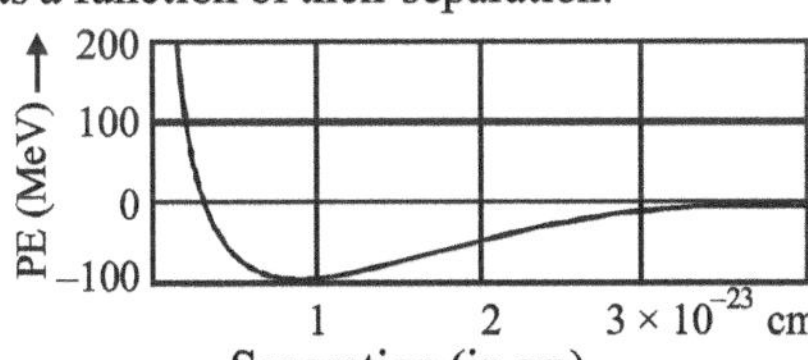

(2 marks)

The conclusions drawn from the graph are

(i) Nuclear force is a short range force.

(ii) Nuclear force is of attractive nature for separation between the nuclei greater than 1 fm and of repulsive nature when separation in less than 1 fm. (1 mark)

OR

If number of protons is large, coulomb's repulsion would be large hence nucleus would split. To hold the nucleons inside the nucleus no. of neutrons is large to increase nuclear force which is a short range force and acts between neighbours only. (3 marks)

29. (a) The negative sign in the expression for the energy signify that the electron is bound to the nucleus and is not free. (1 mark)

(b) Energy level diagram for the Paschen series

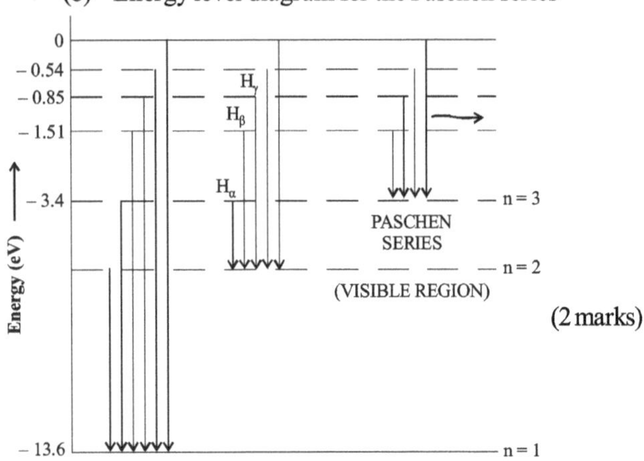

(2 marks)

The Paschen series of the hydrogen atom is produced when transitions take place from higher orbits to the third orbit.

i.e., $n_1 = 3$ and $n_2 = 4, 5, 6, \ldots\ldots$ so on.

OR

(i) An electron undergoes transition from 2nd excited state to the first excited state is Balmer series and then to the ground state is Lyman series. (1 mark)

(ii) The wavelength of the emitted radiations in the two cases.

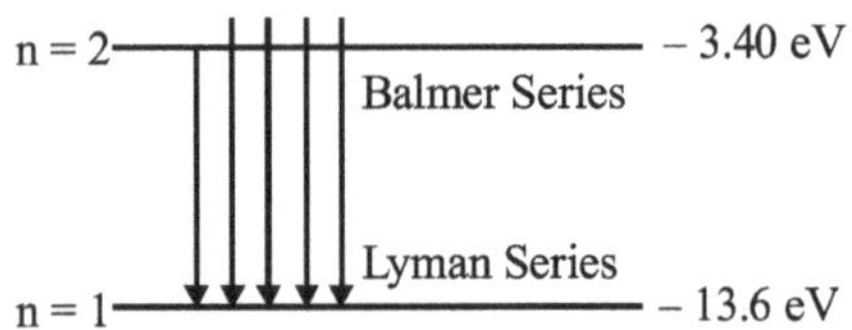

For $n_2 \xrightarrow{\lambda} n_1$

$$\Delta E = (-3.40 + 13.6) = 10.20 \, \text{eV}$$

$$\lambda = \frac{12.43 \times 10^{-7}}{10.2} = 1.218 \times 10^{-7} \, \text{m}$$

$$\lambda = 1218 \, \text{Å}$$

(2 marks)

30. ∵ de-Broglie wavelength of accelerating charge particle is given by

$$\lambda = \frac{h}{\sqrt{2mqV}} \Rightarrow k\sqrt{V} = \frac{h}{\sqrt{2mq}} = \text{constant}$$ (1 mark)

(i) The slope of the line represent $\dfrac{h}{\sqrt{2mq}}$ (1 mark)

(ii) $_1H^2$ and $_1H^3$ carry same charge (as they have same atomic number)

$$\therefore \quad \lambda\sqrt{V} = \frac{1}{\sqrt{m}}$$ (1 mark)

The lighter mass i.e., $_1H^2$ is represented by line of greater slope i.e., A and similarly $_1H^3$ by line B.

31. (a) Kirchhoff's first rule (Junction rule): The algebraic sum of the currents meeting at a point in an electrical circuit is always zero.

$$\sum I = 0$$

This law is justified on the basis of law of conservation of charge.

Kirchhoff's second law (Loop rule): In a closed loop, the algebraic sum of the emfs is equal to the algebraic sum of the products of the resistances and the current flowing through them.

$$\sum \varepsilon + \sum I R = 0$$ (2 marks)

This law is justified on the basis of law of conservation of energy.

(b)

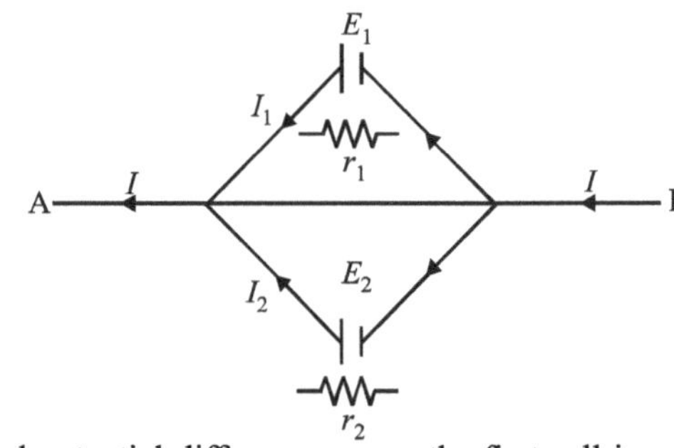

Terminal potential difference across the first cell is

$$V = E_1 - I_1 r_1 \Rightarrow I_1 = \frac{E_1 - V}{r_1}$$

For the second cell, terminal potential difference will be equal to that across the first cell. So, $V = E_2 - I_2 r_2$

$$\Rightarrow \quad I_2 = \frac{E_2 - V}{r_2}$$

Let E be effective emf and r is effective internal resistance. Let I be the current flowing through the cell. $I = I_1 + I_2$

$$\Rightarrow \quad I = \frac{E_1 - V}{r_1} + \frac{E_2 - V}{r_2}$$

$$\Rightarrow \quad I = \frac{r_2(E_1 - V) + r_1(E_2 - V)}{r_1 r_2}$$

$$\Rightarrow \quad I r_1 r_2 = E_1 r_2 + E_2 r_1 - (r_1 + r_2)V$$

$$\Rightarrow \quad V = \frac{E_1 r_2 + E_2 r_1}{r_1 + r_2} - \frac{I r_1 r_2}{r_1 + r_2}$$

Comparing the equation with $V = E - Ir$, we get

Emf, $E = \dfrac{E_1 r_2 + E_2 r_1}{r_1 + r_2}$

Internal resistance, $r = \dfrac{r_1 r_2}{r_1 + r_2}$ (3 marks)

OR

Drift velocity is defined as the average velocity with which the free electrons get drifted towards the positive end of the conductor under the influence of an external electric field.

Relaxation time is the average time that has elapsed since each electron suffered its last collision with the atoms or ions of conductor.

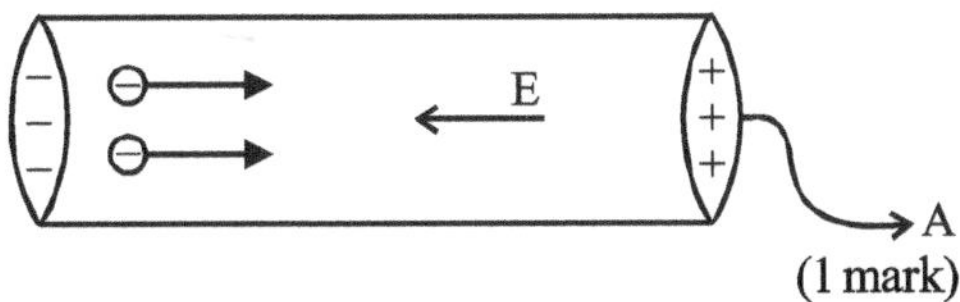

(1 mark)

Consider a metalic conductor of length l, and V be the potential difference applied across the ends. Then the magnitude of electric field,

$$E = \frac{V}{\ell}.$$

Since the charge on electron is $-e$, each electron experiences a force,

$$\vec{F} = -e\vec{E} \qquad \text{......(i)}$$

If m is the mass of an electric, the acceleration of each electron is,

$$\vec{a} = \frac{-e\vec{E}}{m} \qquad \text{......(ii)}$$

Due to this acceleration, apart from its thermal velocity, acquires additional velocity compenent in a direction opposite to the direction of electric field. At any instant of time, the velocity acquired by electron having thermal velocity u_1 will be $\vec{v}_1 = \vec{u}_1 + \vec{a}\,\tau_1$ and so on.

Where τ_1 is the time elapsed after it's last collision.

$\therefore$ The average velocity of all the electrons in the conductor (i.e., the drift velocity)

$$\vec{v}_d = \frac{\vec{v}_1 + \vec{v}_2 + ... + \vec{v}_n}{n} = \frac{\vec{a}(\tau_1 + \tau_2 + ... + \tau_n)}{n}$$ (Since the average thermal velocity of electrons is zero).

$$= \vec{a}\,\tau \text{ where } \tau = \frac{\tau_1 + \tau_2 + ... + \tau_n}{n} \text{ is the relaxation}$$

time. (3 marks)

Putting the value of $\vec{a}$ from (2) drift velocity speed

$$\vec{v}_d = \frac{e\vec{E}\tau}{m}.$$

$\therefore$ Average drift speed $v_d = \dfrac{eE\tau}{m}$ (1 mark)

32. **Biot-Savart's law:–** The strength of magnetic field or magnetic flux density at a point P (dB) due to current element dl depends on,

(i) $dB \propto I$

(ii) $dB \propto dl$

(iii) $dB \propto \sin\theta$

(iv) $dB \propto \dfrac{1}{r^2}$,

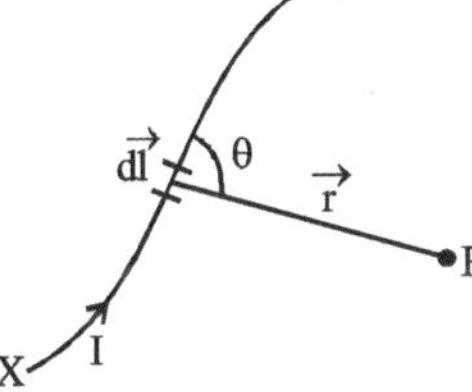

Combining, $dB \propto \dfrac{Idl\sin\theta}{r^2} \Rightarrow dB = k\dfrac{Idl\sin\theta}{r^2}$

[k = Proportionality constant]

In S.I. units, $k = \dfrac{\mu_0}{4\pi}$ where μ_0 is called permeability of free space.

$$\mu_0 = 4\pi \times 10^{-7} \text{ TA}^{-1}\text{m}$$

$\therefore \quad dB = \dfrac{\mu_0}{4\pi}\dfrac{Idl\sin\theta}{r^2}$ and, $d\vec{B} = \dfrac{\mu_0}{4\pi}I\dfrac{(\vec{dl} \times \vec{r})}{r^3}$ (2 marks)

$d\vec{B}$ is perpendicular to the plane containing $\vec{d\ell}$ and $\vec{r}$ and is directed inwards.

Let there be a circular loop of wire whose centre O and radius a located in the YZ plane and carrying a steady current I. We have to calculate the magnetic field at an axial point P at a distance 'd' from the centre of the loop.

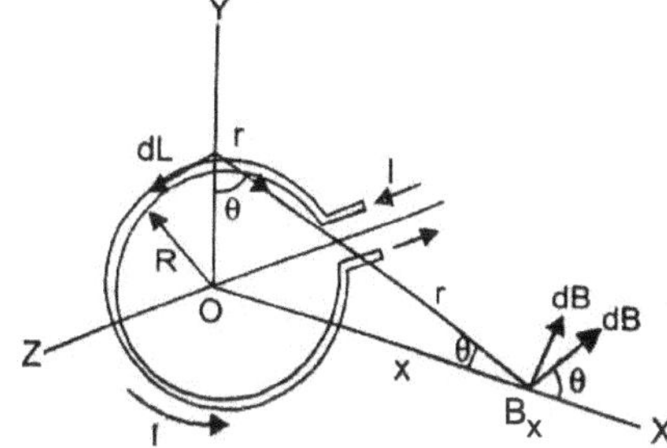

From the figure it is clear that any lement dL is perpendicular to $\hat{r}$, furthermore all the elements around the loop are at the same distance r from P, where $r^2 = d^2 + a^2$.

Now from Biot Savart's law the magnetic field at point P due to the current element dL

$$dB = \frac{\mu_0}{4\pi}\frac{I|\vec{dL} \times \hat{r}|}{r^2} = \frac{\mu_0}{4\pi}\frac{IdL}{(d^2 + a^2)} \qquad ...(i)$$

The direction of the magnetic field dB due to the element dL is perpendicular to the plane formed by $\hat{r}$ and dL as shown in figure above. The vector dB can be resolved into components dB_x aong the X axis and dBy which is perpendicular to the X-axis when the components perpendicular to the X-axis are assumed over the whole loop, the result is zero. That is, by symmetry any element on one side of the loop will set up a perpendicular component that cancels the component set up by an element diametrically opposite it. Therefore, it is obvious that the resultant magnetic field at P will be along the X-axis. This result can be obtained by integrating the component $dB_x = dB\cos\theta$. Therefore,

$$B = \oint dB\cos\theta = \frac{\mu_0 I}{4\pi}\oint\frac{dL\cos\theta}{d^2 + a^2} \qquad ...(ii)$$

where the integral is to be taken over the entire loop since θ, x are constants for all elements of the loop and since

$$\cos\theta = \frac{a}{\sqrt{d^2 + a^2}}, \text{ therefore,}$$

$$B = \frac{\mu_0 Ia}{4\pi(d^2 + a^2)^{3/2}}\oint dL = \frac{\mu_0 Ia^2}{2(d^2 + a^2)^{3/2}}$$

$$B_C = \frac{\mu_0 I}{2a}$$

And magnetic field on the axial line, when $d = a\sqrt{3}$

$$B_d = \frac{\mu_0 Ia^2}{2(3a^2 + a^2)^{3/2}} = \frac{\mu_0 Ia^2}{16a^3} = \frac{\mu_0 I}{16a} \qquad ...(iv)$$

From (iii) and (iv)

$$\frac{B_c}{B_d} = \frac{\dfrac{\mu_0 I}{2a}}{\dfrac{\mu_0 I}{16a}} = 8 \qquad \text{(3 marks)}$$

OR

(a) The magnetic field due to a current carrying loop :

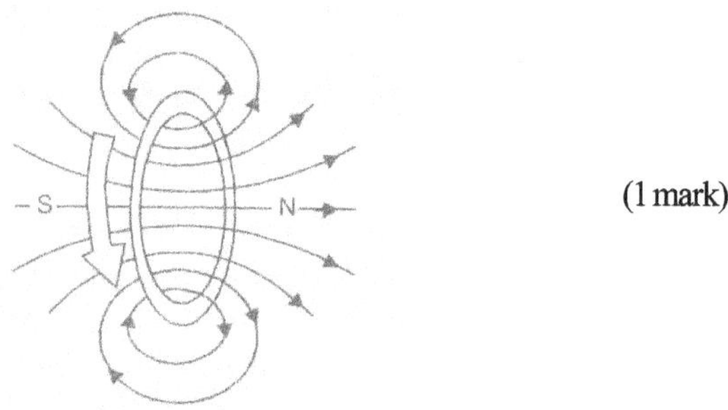

(1 mark)

(b)   The labelled diagram of a moving coil galvanometer :

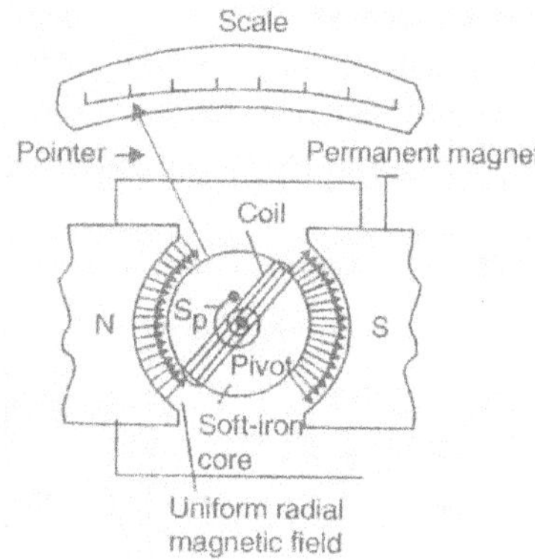

Working principle : When a current carrying coil is placed in a magnetic field, it experience a torque, which tends to rotate it.

Function of radial magnetic field : It ensures that the plane of the coil remains parallel to the magnetic field.

Function of sof iron core : It ensures that the magnetic field is strong and remains on the coil. **(2 marks)**

(c)   An ammeter is an instrument for measuring current therefore, its resistance has to be kept low as it is connected in series. Hence shunt of low resistance is joined in parallel to convert a galvanometer into an ammeter.

A voltmeter is a high resistance device. It is connected in parallel. Therefore its resistance is kept high such that the current in the main circuit is not affected. Hence a high resistance is joined in parallel to convert a galvanometer into a voltmeter. **(2 marks)**

33.   Consider a triangular prism ABC. The angles of incidence and refraction at the first face AB are i and r_1, while the angle of incidence at the second face AC is r_2 and the angle of emergence e. The angle between the emergent ray and the direction of the incident ray is called the angle of deviation, δ.

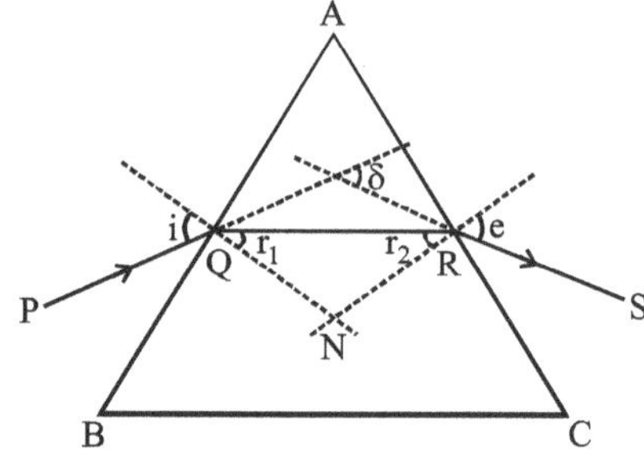

From the Quadrilateral AQNR, $\qquad \angle A + \angle QNR = 180°$

From the triangle QNR, $r_1 + r_2 + \angle QNR = 180°$

Comparing these two equations,

$$r_1 + r_2 = A \qquad \qquad \text{...(i)}$$

The total deviation,

$$\delta = (i - r_1) + (e - r_2)$$

ie., $\delta = i + e - A \qquad \qquad \text{...(ii)}$

(since $r_1 + r_2 = A$)

Thus the angle of deviation depends on the angle of incidence.

$\therefore \quad \delta = \delta_m, i = e \Rightarrow r_1 = r_2.$

equation (i) gives,

$$2r = A \text{ or } r = \frac{A}{2} \qquad \qquad \text{...(iii)}$$

Also equation (ii) gives,

$$\delta_m = 2i - A \quad \text{ or } \quad i = \frac{(A + \delta_m)}{2} \qquad \text{...(iv)}$$

The refractive index of the prism is

$$n_{21} = \frac{n_2}{n_1} = \frac{\sin\left[\left(\dfrac{A + \delta_m}{2}\right)\right]}{\sin\left[\dfrac{A}{2}\right]} \qquad \text{...(v)}$$

For a small angled prism D_m is also very small.

$$\text{So,} \quad n_{21} = \frac{\sin\left[\left(\dfrac{A + \delta_m}{2}\right)\right]}{\sin\left[\dfrac{A}{2}\right]} \qquad \text{(3 marks)}$$

(b)   A graph between angle of deviation and angle of incidence is shown below.

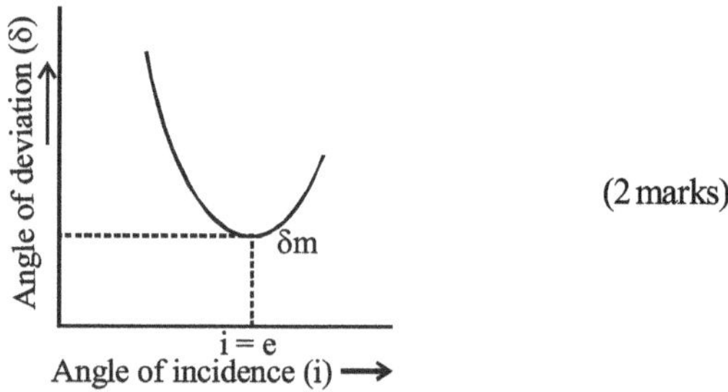

(2 marks)

From the graph we can see that at the minimum deviation δ_m, the refracted ray inside the prism becomes parallel to its base.

OR

From figure,

$PC = +R$

$PI = +v$

$PO = -u$

Let, $NM = h$

The convex spherical refracting surface forms the image of object O and I. The radius of curvature is R

In $\triangle NCO$, $\ i = \gamma + \alpha$ ...(i)

In $\triangle NCI$, $\ \gamma = r + \beta$

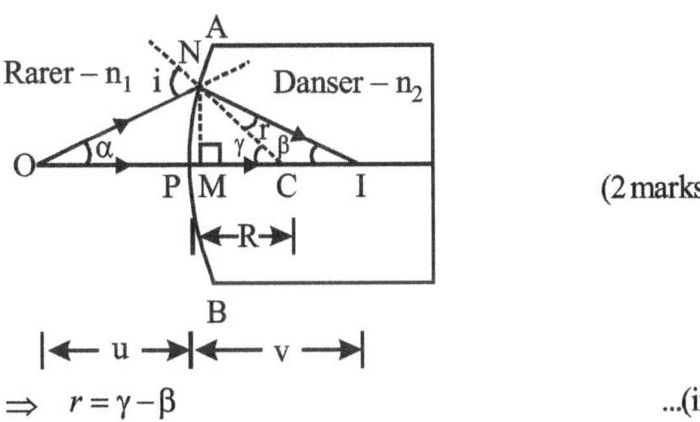

(2 marks)

$\Rightarrow\ r = \gamma - \beta$ ...(ii)

For small angles α, β and γ, we have

$$\alpha \simeq \tan\alpha = \frac{MN}{MO} = \frac{MN}{PO} = \frac{+h}{-u}$$
$$\beta \simeq \tan\beta = \frac{MN}{MI} = \frac{MN}{PI} = \frac{h}{-v}$$
$$\gamma \simeq \tan\gamma = \frac{MN}{MC} = \frac{MN}{PC} = \frac{h}{+R}$$

    ...(iii)

Assuming M is very close to P.

By Snell's law, $\dfrac{n_2}{n_1} = \mu = \dfrac{\sin i}{\sin r}$

For small i and r,

$\dfrac{n_2}{n_1} = \dfrac{i}{r}$ or $rn_2 = in_1$ $\ n_2(\gamma - \beta) = (\alpha - \gamma)n_1$

[From Eqs. (i) and (ii)]

$$(n_2 - n_1)\gamma = n_1\alpha + n_2\beta$$

$$(n_2 - n_1)\left(\frac{h}{R}\right) = n_1\left(\frac{h}{-u}\right) + n_2\left(\frac{h}{v}\right) \quad \text{[From Eq. (iii)]}$$

$\Rightarrow\ \dfrac{n_2}{v} - \dfrac{n_1}{u} = \dfrac{n_2 - n_1}{R}$ (3 marks)

34. (i) As $P = \dfrac{V^2}{R}$.

$\therefore$ 25 W bulb has more resistance. Same current flows through both of them. So the 25 W bulb will develop more heat and burns out instantaneously.   (1 mark)

(ii) $\because P = I^2R$, If I is doubled, it becomes 4 times.   (1 mark)

(iii) $V^2 = PR \Rightarrow V = \sqrt{196 \times 1} = 14$ volt.   (2 marks)

OR

(iii) $H = I^2 Rt$. Here $R_1 = \rho\dfrac{\ell}{\pi r^2}$ and $R_2 = \rho\dfrac{\ell}{\pi(2r)^2}$.

That is, $R_1 = 4R_2$. Hence, $\dfrac{H_1}{H_2} = 4$.   (2 marks)

35. (i) As $\beta = \dfrac{D\lambda}{d}$ i.e. $\beta \propto \lambda$ $\because \lambda_b < \lambda_r$

Therefore fringe width is reduced and fringes come closer.   (1 mark)

(ii) Fringe width, $\beta = \dfrac{D\lambda}{d}$

Here, D = distance between screen to slits

d = distance between slits

When slit width (d) increases, fringe width will decrease.   (1 mark)

(iii) Coloured fringes are formed at screen.   (2 marks)

OR

(iii) Let θ be the angular width in water. We know angular width $= \dfrac{\lambda}{d}$

$\Rightarrow$ Angular width $\propto \lambda$ (1 mark)

$$\frac{\theta}{0.4°} = \frac{\lambda_w}{\lambda_a} \quad \text{...... (i)}$$

Now, $_a\mu_w = \dfrac{\lambda_a}{\lambda_w} \Rightarrow \dfrac{\lambda_a}{\lambda_w} = \dfrac{4}{3}$

Hence from eq. (1), we have

$$\frac{\theta}{0.4°} = \frac{3}{4} \Rightarrow \theta = 0.3° \quad \text{(1 mark)}$$

1. **(c)** By Gauss's theorem, $\phi = \dfrac{Q_{in}}{\epsilon_0}$

Thus, the net flux depends only on the charge enclosed by the surface. Hence, there will be no effect on the net flux if the radius of the surface is doubled. (1 mark)

2. **(a)** When the magnet is moved quickly, the rate of change of flux is larger. This implies larger emf is induced.

(1 mark)

3. **(b)** $L = \mu_0 \dfrac{N^2}{l} A$

$L' = \mu_0 \dfrac{(2N)^2}{2l} A$

$\sin C = \dfrac{1}{\mu} = \dfrac{V_1}{V_2} = 2\mu_0 \dfrac{N^2}{l} A = 2L$ (1 mark)

4. **(a)** $\chi_d < \chi_p < \chi_f$ (1 mark)

For diamagnetic substance χ_d is small negative (10^{-5})

For paramagnetic substances χ_p is small and positive (10^{-3} to 10^{-5})

For ferromagnetic substanes χ_f is very large (10^3 to 10^5)

5. **(d)** $\vec{B} = O,\ r < R$

$= \dfrac{\mu_0 I}{2r},\ r \geq R$

So, $B = 0,\ r < R$

$\propto \dfrac{1}{2},\ r \geq R$. Therefore graph will be as such (1 mark)

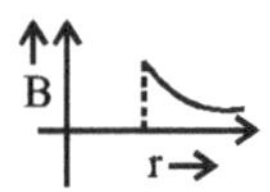

6. **(b)** $F = iBl \sin\theta$. This is maximum when $\sin\theta = 1$ (1 mark) or $\theta = \pi/2$.

7. **(d)** The speed of EM-waves depends on the properties of the medium. (1 mark)

8. **(d)** $\sin C = \dfrac{1}{\mu} = \dfrac{v_1}{v_2} \Rightarrow C = \sin^{-1}\left(\dfrac{v_1}{v_2}\right) = \sin^{-1}\left(\dfrac{3}{4}\right)$

(1 mark)

9. **(c)** For the prism as the angle of incidence (i) increases, the angle of deviation (δ) first decreases goes to minimum value and then increases. (1 mark)

10. **(d)** de-Broglie wavelength,

$\lambda = \dfrac{h}{p} = \dfrac{h}{\sqrt{2.m.(K.E)}} \quad \therefore \quad \lambda \propto \dfrac{1}{\sqrt{K.E}}$

If K.E is doubled, λ becomes $\dfrac{\lambda}{\sqrt{2}}$ (1 mark)

11. **(a)** As $r \propto n^2$, therefore, radius of 2nd Bohr's orbit $= 4\,r_0$

(1 mark)

12. **(d)** Mass defect $= \dfrac{B.E}{c^2}$ (1 mark)

Mass of nucleus = Mass of proton
+ mass of neutron − mass defect

13. **(c)** When small amount of antimony (pentavalent) is added to germanium crystal then crystal becomes n-type semi conductor. Therefore, there will be more free electrons than holes in the semiconductor. (1 mark)

14. **(a)** The drift current in p-n junction is from the n-side to the p-side. (1 mark)

15. **(a)** The current will flow through R_L when the diode is forward biased. (1 mark)

16. **(c)** Electrostatic potential = electrostatic potential energy per unit charge (1 mark)

17. **(a)** Fringe width, $\beta \propto \lambda$ (1 mark)

18. **(b)** Velocity of electromagnetic wave is a medium

$V_{medium} = \dfrac{1}{\sqrt{\mu\varepsilon}}$ (1 mark)

19. Given, $n = 28$, $dB = 8000 - 3000 = 5000$ T, $dt = 4$s

$d = 0.02$ m., $A = \dfrac{\pi d^2}{4} = \dfrac{22}{7} \times \dfrac{(0.02)^2}{4}$

$e = \dfrac{d\phi}{dt} = \dfrac{d}{dt}(nBA) = nA\dfrac{dB}{dt}$

$e = 28 \times \dfrac{22}{7} \times \dfrac{(0.02)^2}{4} \times \dfrac{5000}{4} = 11$ volt. (2 marks)

20. (i) The intensity of interference fringes in a double slit experiment is modulated by the diffraction pattern of each slit.

(ii) The waves diffracted from the edge of the circular obstacle interfere constructively at the centre of the shadow producing a bright spot. (1 + 1 mark)

21.

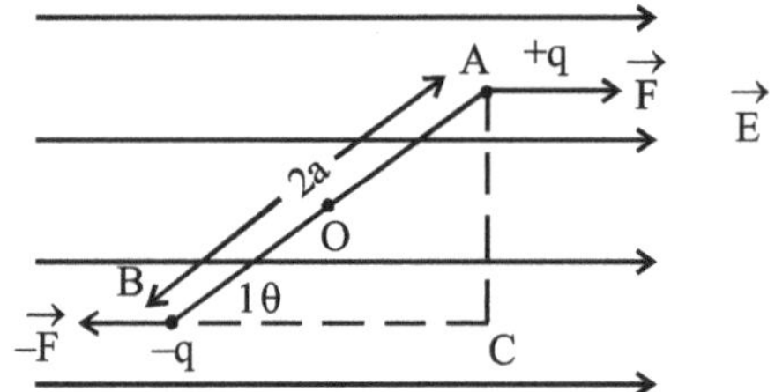

(i) Let the dipole AB is held in the uniform electric field $\vec{E}$ at an angle θ.

Force on $+q = q\vec{E}$ along $\vec{E}$.

and force on $-q = -q\vec{E}$ opposite to $\vec{E}$.

$\therefore$ Net force on the dipole $= q\vec{E} - q\vec{E} = 0$ (1 mark)

(ii) Two equal and parallel forces from a couple which will rotate the dipole in clockwise direction and tends to align it along the direction of the field.

$\therefore$ Torque = force × perpendicular distance between the forces

$\tau = F \times AC = qE \times AB \sin\theta$

$\quad = qE \times 2a \sin\theta$

$\tau = pE \sin\theta,$

$\quad$ where $p = q \times 2a$

$\therefore\ \vec{\tau} = \vec{p} \times \vec{E}$

(1 mark)

OR

(a) The two charges are of opposite sign so that force will be attractive in nature.

(b) The two charges have different magnitudes – the charge of smaller magnitude will be nearer to the point where the total field intensity is zero.   (1 + 1 mark)

22. Electrons diffuse from n → p and holes diffuse from p → n side leaving a positively charged donor atom on n–side and negatively charged acceptor atom on p–side. This space charge region on either side is called depletion region. Near the junction this region depletes the movement of free charges. Hence, electric field due to positive space charge on n–side and negative space charge on p–side is created. Due to this electrons and holes now drift in opposite direction in this field and further extend this region.

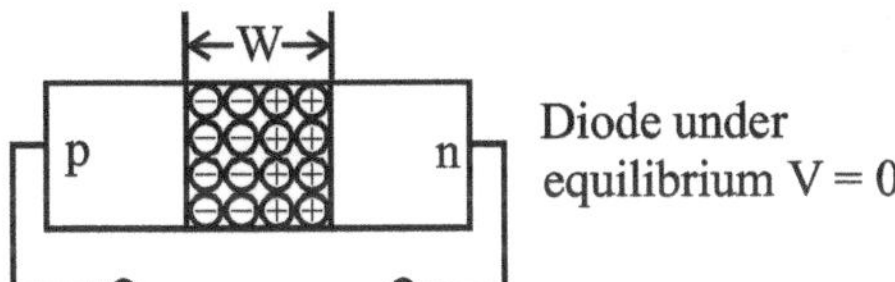

Diode under equilibrium V = 0

Thus a different polarity potential is developed which prevents movement of electron from n–region to p–region, called **barrier potential** and there is no net current.

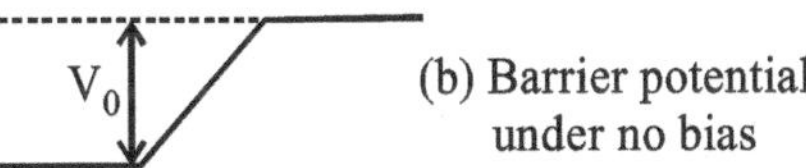

(b) Barrier potential under no bias

          (1 + 1 mark)

23. When a charged particle enters the magnetic field at right angle, then the particle experiences a magnetic force due to which it follows a circular path.

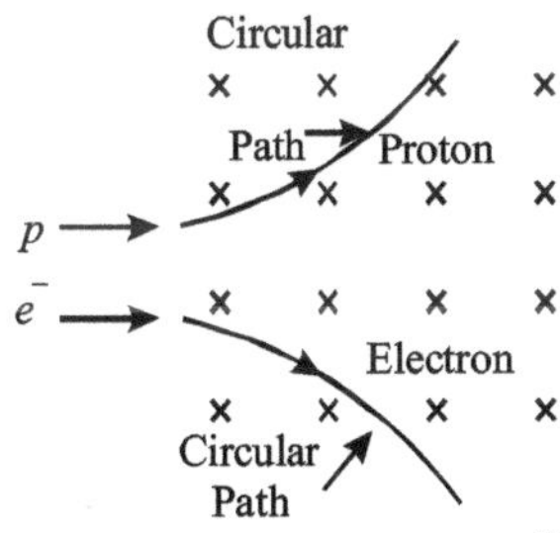

Radius of the circular path, $r = \dfrac{mv}{qB}$

For same speed v, and same charge

Magnetic field $r \propto m$

∵ As, $m_e < m_p$

⇒ therefore, $r_e < r_p$ (2 marks)

The curvature of path of Proton is much more and in opposite direction of the curvature of path of electron.

24. When p– and n– type semiconductors are joined in thin wafer form they form a junction. In p– type semiconductor concentration of holes is more and on n – side electrons are in majority, hence due to this gradient both electrons and holes diffuse to the other side leaving behind ionised donor and acceptor atoms which are immobile.

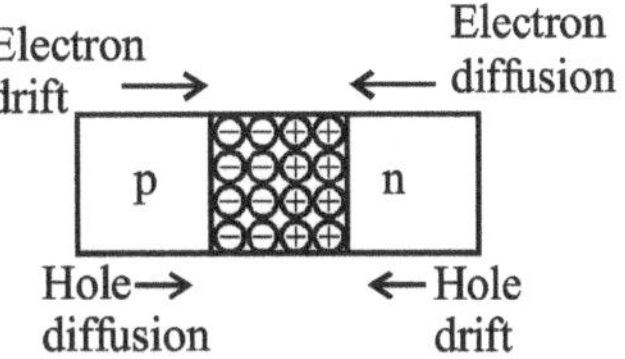

As charges diffuse a layer of negative charges (acceptor) is found on p–side and positive charges (donor) on n–side near the junction. This is depletion layer and creates an electric field due to which electrons on p– side move to n–side. This is called drift current. Thus space charge region of either side extends, forming p–n junction.   (2 marks)

25.

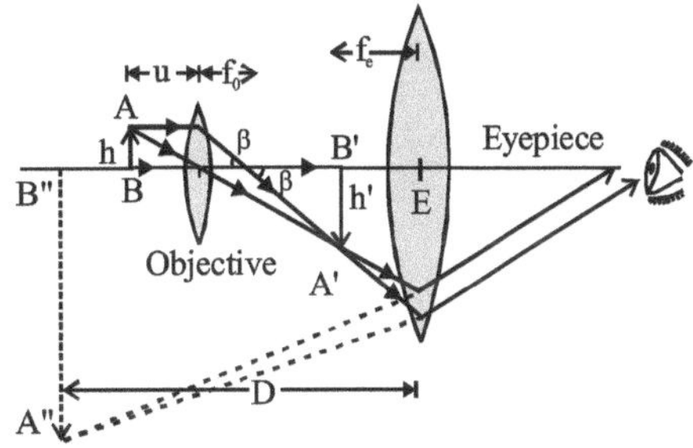

          (2 marks)

OR

As $\dfrac{1}{f} = \left(\dfrac{\mu_2}{\mu_1} - 1\right)\left(\dfrac{1}{R_1} - \dfrac{1}{R_2}\right)$

for lens material $\mu_2 = 1.5$

(i) If the convex lens is immersed in water ($\mu = 1.33$) its focal length will be positive hence it behaves as converging lens.

(ii) If the convex lens is immersed CS_2 solution ($\mu = 1.6$) its focal length will be negative hence it behaves as diverging lens.   (1 + 1 mark)

26. (a) The current sensitivity of a galvanometer is defined as the deflection per unit current.   (1 mark)

(b) Given :

$A = 25 \times 10^{-4}\,m^2$, $n = 150$

$B = 0.15\,T$, $C = 10^{-6}\,Nm$

$\theta = 30°$ $I = ?$

From the expression

$I = \dfrac{c\theta}{nBA}$

$= \dfrac{10^{-6} \times 30}{150 \times 0.15 \times 25 \times 10^{-4}} = 5.3\,mA$ (2 marks)

OR

Biot-Savart law : For the magnetic field $\vec{dB}$ at a point P associated with a current element of length $\vec{d\ell}$ of a wire carrying a steady current I.

$dB \propto I$

$dB \propto d\ell$

$dB \propto \dfrac{1}{r^2}$

$dB \propto \sin\theta$

Combining all these

$dB \propto \dfrac{Id\ell \sin\theta}{r^2}$

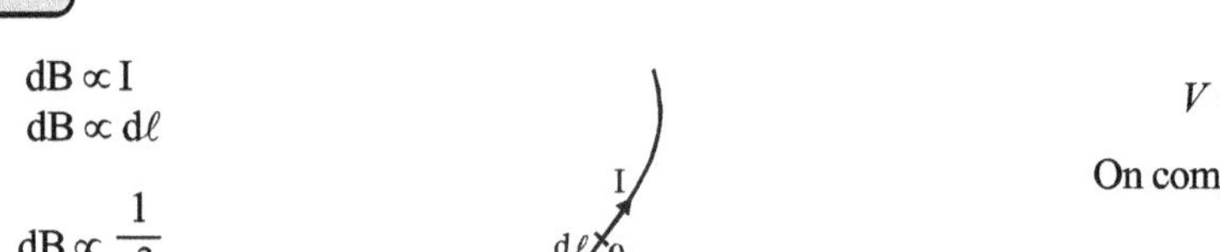

or, $dB = \dfrac{\mu_0}{4\pi} \times \dfrac{I\,d\ell\,\sin\theta}{r^2}$ (1½ marks)

μ_0 is called **permeability of free space**

As current carrying loop has the magnetic field lines around it, thus it behaves as a magnet with two mutually opposite poles.

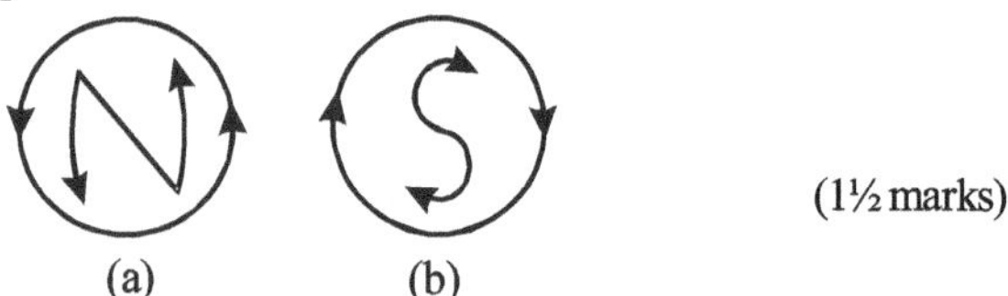

(1½ marks)

    (a)   (b)

The anticlockwise flow of current behaves like a north pole where clockwise flow as south pole. Hence, loop behaves as a magnet.

27. By Kirchhoff's current rule

$I = I_1 + I_2$

Across cell E_1, potential difference (V)

$V = V_{B_2} - V_{B_1} = E_1 - I_1 r_1$

Across cell E_2, potential difference (V)

$V = V_{B_2} - V_{B_1} = E_2 - I_2 r_2$

On solving above equations we get,

$I_1 = \dfrac{E_1 - v}{r_1}$ and $I_2 = \dfrac{E_2 - v}{r_2}$

$\therefore \quad I = \left(\dfrac{E_1 - V}{r_1}\right) + \left(\dfrac{E_2 - V}{r_2}\right)$

$\Rightarrow \quad I = \left(\dfrac{E_1}{r_1} + \dfrac{E_2}{r_2}\right) - V\left(\dfrac{1}{r_1} + \dfrac{1}{r_2}\right)$

$V\left(\dfrac{r_1 + r_2}{r_1 r_2}\right) = \left(\dfrac{E_1 r_2 + E_2 r_1}{r_1 r_2}\right) - I$

$V = \left(\dfrac{E_1 r_2 + E_2 r_1}{r_1 + r_2}\right) - I\left(\dfrac{r_1 r_2}{r_1 + r_2}\right)$

Let equivalent emf and equivalent internal resistance of combination are E_{eq} and r_{eq}, then potential difference across combination is given

$V = E_{eq} - I r_{eq}$

On comparing we get,

$E_{eq} = \dfrac{E_1 r_2 + E_2 r_1}{r_1 + r_2}$ and $r_{eq} = \dfrac{r_1 r_2}{r_1 + r_2}$ (3 marks)

28. Energy of the electron in the nth state of an atom is given

as, $E_n = \dfrac{-13.6 Z^2}{n^2} \text{eV}$ (1 mark)

Here, z is the atomic number of the atom.

For hydrogen atom, $z = 1$

Energy required to excite an atom from initial state (n_i) to final state (n_f)

$= -\dfrac{13.6}{n_f^2} + \dfrac{13.6}{n_i^2}\text{eV}$

This energy must be equal to or less than the energy of the incident electron beam.

$\therefore \; -\dfrac{13.6}{n_f^2} + \dfrac{13.6}{n_i^2} = 12.9$

Energy of the electron in the ground state $= \dfrac{13.6}{1^2} = -13.6\text{ eV}$

$\therefore \; -\dfrac{13.6}{n_f^2} + 13.6 = 12.9 \Rightarrow 13.6 - 12.9 = \dfrac{13.6}{n_f^2}$

$n_f^2 = \dfrac{13.6}{0.7} = 19.43 \Rightarrow n_f = 4.4$

State cannot be a fraction number.

$\therefore \; n_f = 4$

Hence, the hydrogen atom would be excited up to 4th energy level.   (1 mark)

Rydberg's formula for the spectrum of the hydrogen atom is given by,

$\dfrac{1}{\lambda} = R\left[\dfrac{1}{n_1^2} - \dfrac{1}{n_2^2}\right]$

Here, λ is the wavelength.

Rydberg's constant, $R = 1.097 \times 10^7 \text{m}^{-1}$

For the first member of the Paschen series:

$n_1 = 3 \quad ; \quad n_2 = 4$

$\dfrac{1}{\lambda} = 1.097 \times 10^7 \left[\dfrac{1}{3^2} - \dfrac{1}{4^2}\right]$ or $\quad \lambda = 18761\text{ Å}$

For the first member of Balmer series:

$n_1 = 2$
$n_2 = 3$

$\dfrac{1}{\lambda} = 1.097 \times 10^7 \left[\dfrac{1}{2^2} - \dfrac{1}{3^2}\right] \quad \lambda = 6563\text{ Å}$ (1 mark)

29. Graph between stopping potential and the frequency of the incident radiation.

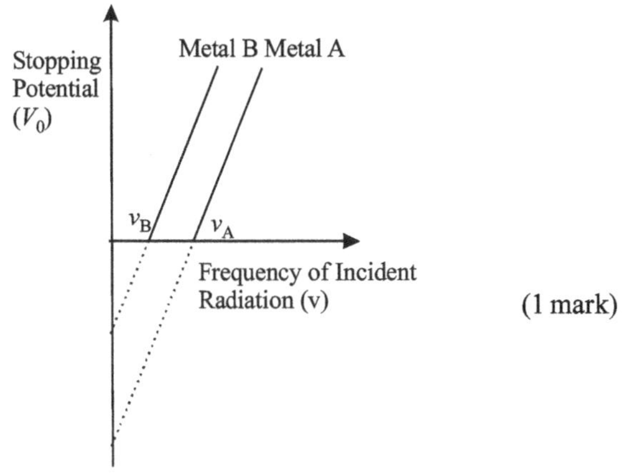

(1 mark)

From the graph,

(i) The stopping potential is inversely proportional to the threshold frequency. Hence the stopping potential is higher for metal B. (1 mark)

(ii) The slope of the graph does not depend on the nature of the material used

As we know,

$$K_{max} = hv - \phi_0 = eV_0$$

Dividing the whole equation by e, we get

$$\frac{hv}{e} - \frac{\phi_0}{e} = V_0$$

From the above equation, the slope of the graph is $\dfrac{h}{e}$ (on comparing with the straight line equation). Thus, we see that the slope is independent of the nature of the photoelectric material. (1 mark)

30. Using, $\dfrac{R_2}{R_1} = \left(\dfrac{A_2}{A_1}\right)^{1/3}$ where $A_1 = 16$, (1 mark)

$A_2 = 205$, $R_1 = 3 \times 10^{-15}$.

$$\therefore \quad R_2 = R_1 \left(\frac{205}{16}\right)^{1/3} = R_1(12.8)^{1/3} = 3 \times 10^{-15}(12.8)^{1/3}$$

Solving $R_2 = 3 \times 10^{-15} \times 2.35 = 7.05 \times 10^{-15}$ m. (2 marks)

OR

$$4\,^{1}_{1}H \longrightarrow \,^{4}_{2}He + 2(\,^{0}_{+1}e) + Q$$ (1 mark)

$\Delta m = 4 \times 1.007825 - 4.002603 - 2 \times 0.000549$
$\quad = 0.0276$ u.

E fusion $= 0.0276 \times 931.5 = 25.7$ MeV (2 marks)

31. (i)

$C_1 \qquad C_2 \qquad C_3$

$+\ \ -$

In series combination of capacitors, same charge lie on each capcitor for any value of capacitances. Also, potential difference across the combination is equal to the algebraic sum of potential differences across each capacitor i.e.,

$$V = V_1 + V_2 + V_3$$

As, $q = C_1 V_1 \qquad \therefore V_1 = \dfrac{q}{C_1}$

Similarly, $V_2 = \dfrac{q}{C_2}$ $V_3 = \dfrac{q}{C_3}$ (½ mark)

$\therefore$ Total potential difference

$$V = \frac{q}{C_1} + \frac{q}{C_2} + \frac{q}{C_3} \Rightarrow \frac{1}{C} = \frac{1}{C_1} + \frac{1}{C_2} + \frac{1}{C_3}$$

or, $C = \dfrac{C_1 C_2 C_3}{C_1 C_2 + C_2 C_3 + C_3 C_1}$ (2½ marks)

(ii) Here $C_1 = \dfrac{\varepsilon_0 A}{d} = 10$ pF, $C_2 = \dfrac{k\,\varepsilon_0 A}{d/2}$

$= 10 \times 10 \times 2\,\text{pF} = 200\,\text{pF}$.

OR

(i) On introduction of dieletric slab in isolated charged capacitor.

(a) The capacitance (C') becomes K times of original capacitor as

i.e. $C' = \dfrac{K\varepsilon_0 A}{d}$ (1 mark)

(b) Charge remain conserved in the phenomenon.

$\phi = \phi'$

$$CV = C'V' \Rightarrow V' = \frac{CV}{C'} = \frac{CV}{KC}$$

or, $V' = \dfrac{V}{K}$

Potential difference decreases and become $\dfrac{1}{K}$ times of original value. (1 mark)

(c) Energy stored initially

$$U = \frac{q^2}{2C}$$

Energy stored later,

$$U' = \frac{q^2}{2(KC)} \quad [\because C' = KC]$$

$$\Rightarrow U' = \frac{1}{K}\left(\frac{q^2}{2C}\right) \Rightarrow U' = \frac{1}{K}(U)$$

The energy stored in capacitor decrease and become $\dfrac{1}{K}$ times of original energy. (1 mark)

(ii) (a) Electric field lines due to a conducting sphere are shown in the figure.

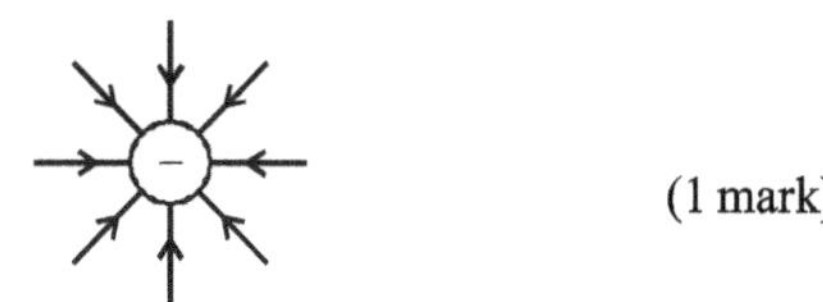

(1 mark)

(b) Electric field lines due to an electric dipole are shown

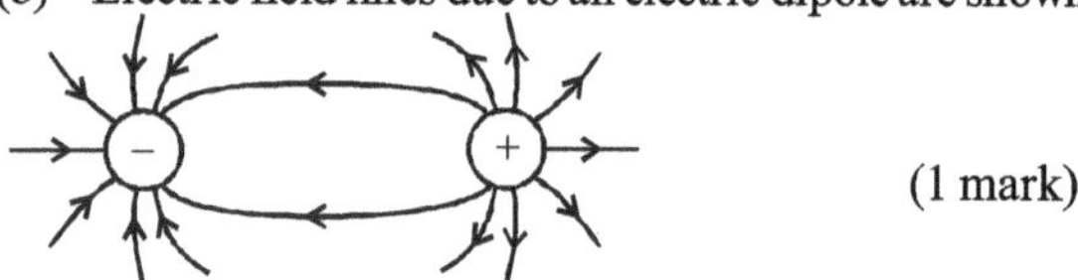

(1 mark)

32. The first arrangement is when two coils on top of each other.

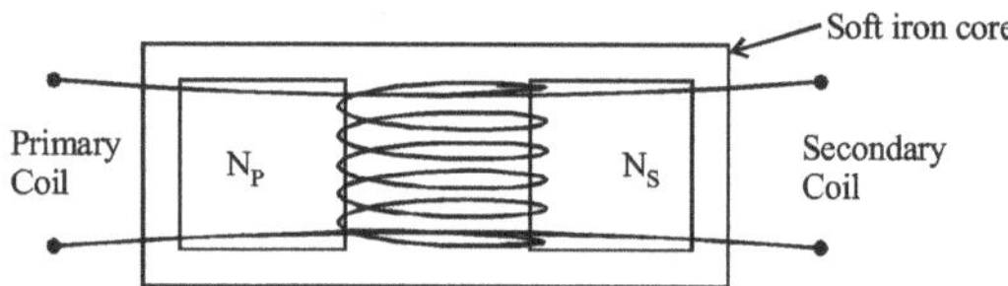

The second arrangement is where two coils are wound on separate limbs of the core.

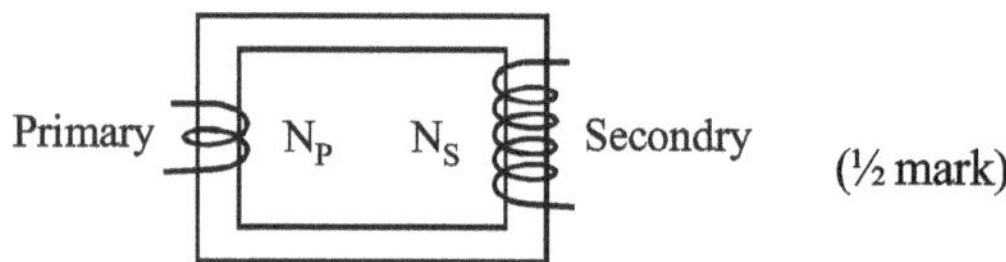

(½ mark)

Ratio of output voltage to input voltage, $\dfrac{E_S}{E_P} = \dfrac{N_S}{N_P}$

(1 mark)

Ratio of output current to input current, $\dfrac{I_S}{I_P} = \dfrac{N_P}{N_S}$

(1 mark)

Energy losses in a transformer

(i) **Copper loss:** Energy is lost as heat from the copper coils due to joule heating in the conducting wires.

(ii) **Iron loss:** Energy is lost as heat from the iron core of the transformer due to eddy current produced in the core. It can be minimised by the laminated core.

(iii) **Leakage of magnetic flux:** Due to this loss, magnetic flux linked with the primary will not be equal to that linked with secondary.

(iv) **Hysteresis loss:** Loss of heat energy due to repeated magnetisation and demagnetisation of the iron core.

(v) **Magnetostriction:** Humming noise of a transformer.

(2½ marks)

OR

The obstruction posed by a circuit to the flow of a.c. is called its impedance (Z).

$$Z = \frac{V}{I} = \frac{\text{rms applied voltage}}{\text{rms current}}$$

(1 mark)

It's S.I. unit is ohm.

Series LCR circuit :

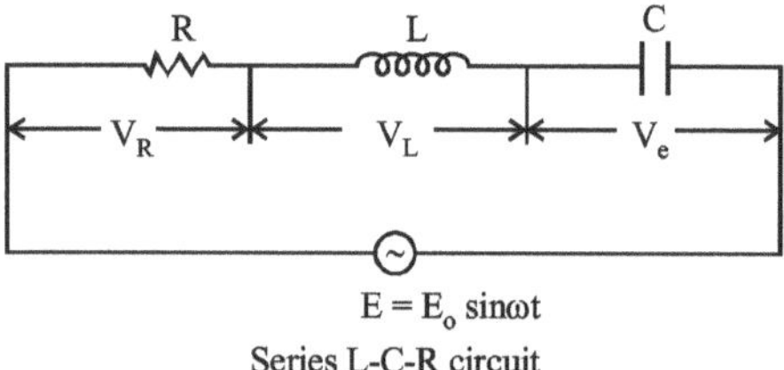

Series L-C-R circuit

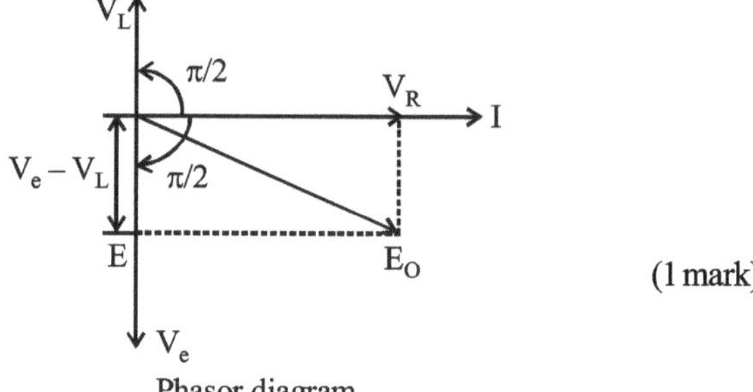

(1 mark)

Phasor diagram

Consider a resistance (R), inductance (L) and capacitance (C) are connected in series and an alternating source of voltage $E = E_0 \sin \omega t$ is applied across it. Since they are connected in series, the current I flowing through all of them is same.

Let the voltage across the resistance R is V_R, voltage across inductance L is V_L and voltage across capacitance C is V_C. Since the current and the voltage across the resistor are in phase so they are represented by a phasor in the same direction. The voltage (V_L) across the inductor leads current by an angle $\pi/2$ while the voltage (V_C) across the capacitor lags behind the current by $\pi/2$. V_L and V_C are in opposite direction, so their resultant potential difference $= V_C - V_L$ (where $V_C > V_L$).

So the phasors V_R and $(V_C - V_L)$ are perpendicular to each other. The resultant of them is equal to E, the applied instantaneous voltage.

$$\therefore \quad E^2 = V_R^2 + (V_C - V_L)^2$$

$$\Rightarrow \quad E = \sqrt{V_R^2 + (V_C - V_L)^2}$$

But $V_R = IR$, $V_C = X_C I$ and $V_L = X_L I$

where $X_C = \dfrac{1}{\omega C}$ and $X_L = \omega L$.

$$\therefore \quad E = \sqrt{I^2 R^2 + (IX_C - IX_L)^2}$$

$$= I\sqrt{R^2 + (X_C - X_L)^2}$$

(2 marks)

$$\Rightarrow \quad Z = \sqrt{R^2 + \left(\frac{1}{\omega C} - \omega L\right)^2}$$

The phase difference between voltage and current I can be given by the phase angle φ,

where, $\tan \varphi = \dfrac{X_C - X_L}{R}$

For resonance, $X_C - X_L = 0 \quad \therefore \varphi = 0$

Also, $\dfrac{1}{\omega C} = \omega L \Rightarrow \omega^2 = \dfrac{1}{LC}$

$$\therefore \quad \text{Resonant frequency} = \omega_r = \frac{1}{\sqrt{LC}}$$

(1 mark)

33. (a) A parallel beam of light with a plane wavefront WW' is made to fall on a single slit AB. As width of the slit AB = d is of the order of wavelength of light, therefore diffraction occurs on passing through the slit.

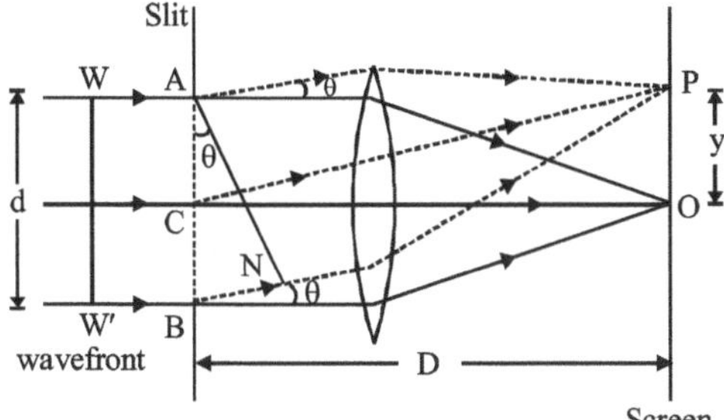

Diffraction of light at single slit

The wavelets from the single wavefront reach the centre O on the screen in same phase and hence interfere constructively to give central maximum (bright fringe). The diffraction pattern obtained on the screen consists of a central bright band, having alternate dark and weak bright band of decreasing intensity on both sides.

Consider a point P on the screen at which wavelets travelling in a direction, making angle θ with CO, are brought to focus by the lens. The wavelets from points A and B will have a path difference equal to BN.

From the right angled Δ ANB, we have

BN = AB sin θ or BN = d sin θ (1 mark)

To establish the condition for secondary minima, the slit is divide into 2, 4, 6, ... equal parts such that corresponding wavelets from successive regions interfere with path difference of $\lambda/2$.

or for nth secondary minimum, the slit can be divided into 2n equal parts.

Hence, for nth secondary minimum, path difference = $d \sin \theta_n = n\lambda$

or $\sin \theta_n = \dfrac{n\lambda}{d}$ (n = 1, 2, 3, ...)   (1 mark)

To establish the condition for secondary maxima, the slit is divided into 3, 5, 7, ... equal parts such that corresponding wavelets from alternate regions interfere with path difference of $\lambda/2$.

or for nth secondary maximum, the slit can be divided into (2n + 1) equal parts.

Hence, for nth secondary maximum,

$$d \sin \theta_n = (2n+1)\dfrac{\lambda}{2} \quad (n = 1, 2, 3, ...)$$

or $\sin \theta_n = (2n+1)\dfrac{\lambda}{2d}$ (1 mark)

Hence, the diffraction pattern can be graphically shown as below. The point O corresponds to the position of point with path difference, d sin θ = λ, 2λ, ... are secondary minima. The above conditions for diffraction maxima and minima are exactly reverse of mathematical conditions for interference maxima and minima.

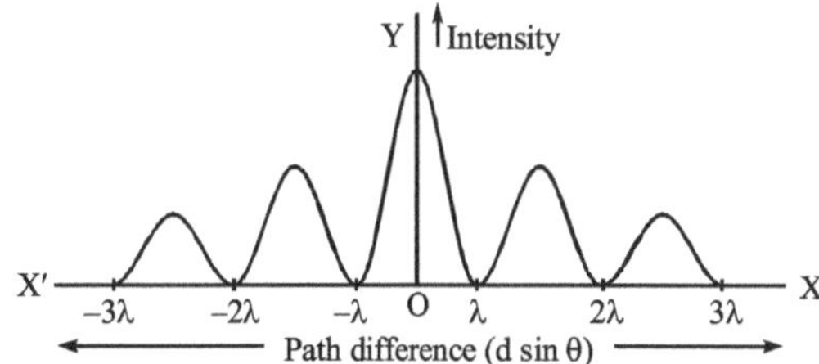

(b) For central bright fringe,

$$\theta = 0°$$

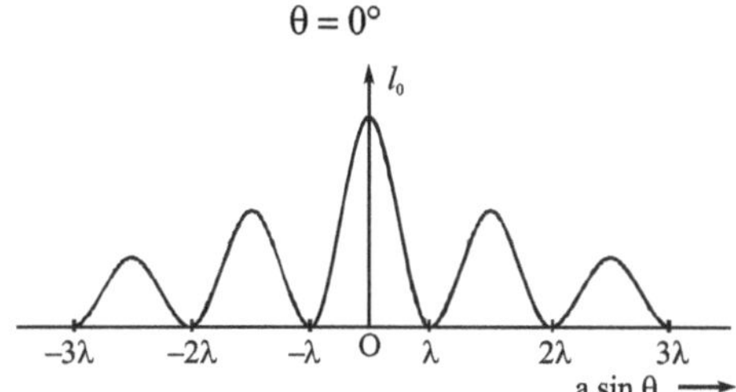

For first dark fringe,

$$a \sin \theta = \pm\lambda \quad \text{or} \quad \sin \theta = \pm\dfrac{\lambda}{a}$$

If θ is small, then $\sin \theta \approx \theta$

So, $\quad \theta = \pm\dfrac{\lambda}{a}$

So, the half angular width of central maximum is

$$\theta \approx \sin \theta = \dfrac{\lambda}{a} \quad \text{(1 mark)}$$

(c) On increasing the value of n, the part of slit contributing to the maximum decreases. Hence, the maxima becomes weaker.   (1 mark)

OR

Wavefront is defined as the locus of all the points in space that reach a particular distance by a propagating wave at the same instant.   (1 mark)

Huygens Principle is based on the following assumptions:

Each point on the primary wavefront acts as a source of secondary wavelets, sending out disturbances in all directions in a similar manner as the original source of light does.

The new position of the wavefront at any instant (called secondary wavefront) is the envelope of the secondary wavelets at that instant.   (2 marks)

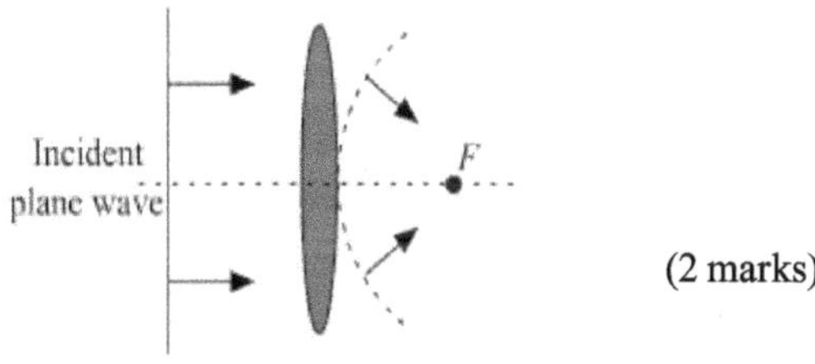

Spherical wavefront

   (2 marks)

34. (i) No, it is not necessary.

$$\because \quad E = -\frac{dV}{dr}$$

$\therefore$ If V is constant, E will be zero.

Ex: The electric field inside a hollow spherical conductor is zero but potential is not zero. *(1 mark)*

(ii) Electric field, $E = -\dfrac{dV}{dr}$

i.e. electric field at a point is the negative of the electric potential gradient at that point. *(1 mark)*

(iii) It is a plane surface perpendicular to the electric field. *(2 marks)*

OR

(iii) An equipotential surface is that at every point of which electric potential is same. Consider two points A and B on the equipotential surface.

By definition, potential difference between two points A and B = work done in carrying a unit positive charge from A to B.

$$\Rightarrow \quad V_A - V_B = W_{AB} = \vec{E}.\vec{\ell}$$

But $V_A = V_B$ $\qquad \therefore \vec{E}.\vec{\ell} = 0$

$$\Rightarrow \quad Edl \cos\theta = 0 \Rightarrow \cos\theta = 0 \Rightarrow \theta = 90°$$

$$\therefore \quad \vec{E} \perp d\vec{\ell}$$

$\therefore$ Electric field $(\vec{E})$ is directed perpendicular to the equipotential surface. *(2 marks)*

35. (i) Maximum intensity in interference pattern

$$I_{max} = \left(\sqrt{I_1} + \sqrt{I_2}\right)^2 = \left(2\sqrt{I_0}\right)^2 = 4I_0.$$ *(1 mark)*

(ii) Path difference $= 171.5\lambda = \dfrac{343}{2}\lambda$

$=$ odd multiple of half wavelength .

It means dark fringe is observed.

According to question, $0.01029 = \dfrac{343}{2}\lambda$

$$\Rightarrow \lambda = \frac{0.01029 \times 2}{343} = 6 \times 10^{-5} \text{ cm}$$

$$\Rightarrow \lambda = 6000 \text{ Å}.$$ *(1 mark)*

(iii) When slits are of unequal width, then intensity of sources S_1 and S_2 is not equal. So, position of minimum intensity will not be completely dark. *(2 marks)*

OR

(iii) $\dfrac{I_{max}}{I_{min}} = \dfrac{25}{9}$ or $\left(\dfrac{a_1 + a_2}{a_1 - a_2}\right)^2 = \dfrac{25}{9}$

where a denotes amplitude.

$\dfrac{a_1 + a_2}{a_1 - a_2} = \dfrac{5}{3}$ or $5a_1 - 5a_2 = 3a_1 + 3a_2$

or, $5a_1 - 5a_2 = 3a_1 + 3a_2$ or $2a_1 = 8a_2$

or, $\dfrac{a_1}{a_2} = 4$ or $\left(\dfrac{a_1}{a_2}\right)^2 = 16 = \dfrac{I_1}{I_2}.$ *(2 marks)*

1. **(c)** As all other statements are correct. In uniform electric field equipotential surfaces are never concentric spheres but are planes $\perp$ to Electric field lines. (1 mark)

2. **(d)** The coil of a moving coil galvanometer is wound over metallic frame to provide electromagnetic damping so it becomes dead beat galvanometer. (1 mark)

3. **(a)** $F = IIB \sin\theta$ or $\sin\theta = \dfrac{F}{IIB}$

$$\sin\theta = \frac{15}{10 \times 1.5 \times 2} = \frac{1}{2} \text{ or } \theta = 30°$$ (1 mark)

4. **(c)** $B = \dfrac{\mu_0 i\, a^2}{2(x^2 + a^2)^{3/2}}$

$$B' = \frac{\mu_0 i}{2a} = \frac{\mu_0 i\, a^2}{2a(x^2 + a^2)^{3/2}}\left(\frac{(x^2 + a^2)^{3/2}}{a^2}\right)$$

$$B' = \frac{B.(x^2 + a^2)^{3/2}}{a^3}$$

Put $x = 4$ & $a = 3 \Rightarrow B' = \dfrac{54(5^3)}{3 \times 3 \times 3} = 250\mu T$ (1 mark)

5. **(a)** $\because f_0 + f_e = 30$

And magnification, $m = \dfrac{f_0}{f_e}$

$$2 = \frac{f_0}{f_e} \Rightarrow f_0 = 2f_e \Rightarrow f_0 + \frac{f_0}{2} = 30 \therefore f_0 = 20 \text{ cm}$$ (1 mark)

6. **(a)** Real, inverted and same in size because object is at the centre of curvature of the mirror. (1 mark)

7. **(d)** $I = nAe v_d$ or $v_d \propto 1/\pi r^2$ (1 mark)

8. **(c)** Specific resistance of a conductor increases and for a semiconductor decreases with increase in temperature because for a conductor, temperature coefficient of resistivity $\alpha = +$ve and for a semiconductar, $\alpha = -$ve (1 mark)

9. **(b)** For coherent sources λ is same and phase is also same or phase diff. is constant. (1 mark)

10. **(b)** P to Q: convergence increasing; Q to R : direction changing. (1 mark)

11. **(d)** $B_0 = \dfrac{E_0}{c} = \dfrac{9 \times 10^3}{3 \times 10^8} = 3 \times 10^{-5} T.$ (1 mark)

12. **(c)** $\lambda = \dfrac{1.227}{\sqrt{V}}$ nm , as $\lambda = \dfrac{h}{p} = \dfrac{h}{\sqrt{2meV}}$

Substituting the numerical values of h, m and e we get the result. (1 mark)

13. **(d)** Positive terminal is at lower potential (0V) and negative terminal is at higher potential 5V. (1 mark)

14. **(d)** The direction of propagation of electromagnetic wave is perpendicular to both electric field E and magnetic field B, *i.e.*, in the direction of E × B by right thumb rule. The diagram given below

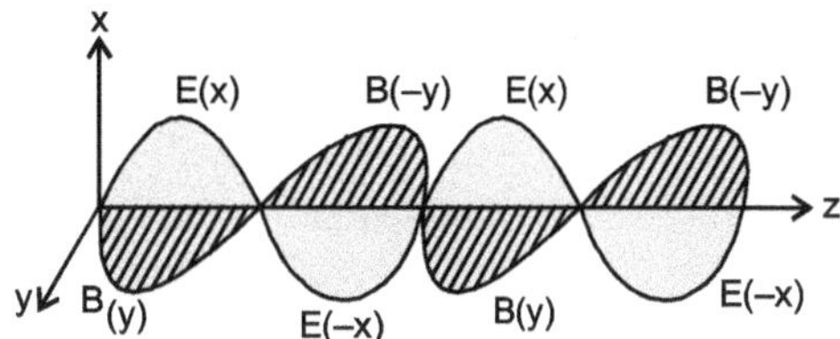

So, electromagnetic wave is along the z-direction which is give the cross product of E and B direction is perpendicular to E and B from $\vec{E}$ to $\vec{B}$. *i.e.*, $(E \times B)$ in z-direction. (1 mark)

15. **(b)** $i = \dfrac{A + \delta_m}{2} = \dfrac{60 + 30}{2} = 45°$ (1 mark)

16. **(a)** For Balmer series $\dfrac{1}{\lambda} = R\left[\dfrac{1}{2^2} - \dfrac{1}{n^2}\right]$ where , $n = 3, 4, 5$ (1 mark)

17. **(b)** The individual force are unaffected due to presence of other charges. This is the principal of superposition of charges. Force on any charge due to a number of other charges is the vector sum of all the forces on that charge due to the other charges, taken one at a time. (1 mark)

18. **(c)** Thermal collisions are responsible for taking a valence electron to the conduction band. (1 mark)

19. According to the definition of the terminal potential difference,

$V = E - Ir$

E is the EMF and r is the total internal resistance of the circuit.

$I = 0 \Rightarrow V = E$

From the graph we can see

$E = 6 V$

As there are three cells we can write,

$E = 3 \times e \Rightarrow e = 2 V$

And, when, $V = 0$

$$\Rightarrow E = Ir \Rightarrow r = \frac{E}{I} = \frac{6}{1} = 6\Omega$$ (1+1 marks)

As per the question the cells are connected in series, so

$r' = \dfrac{r}{3} = 2\Omega$

20. **(i)** 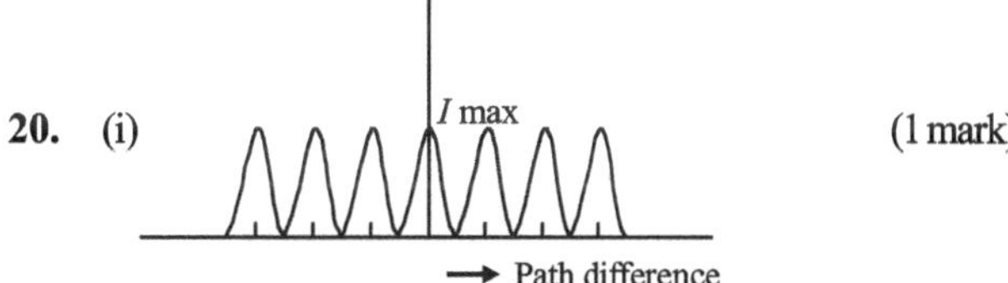

(1 mark)

(ii)

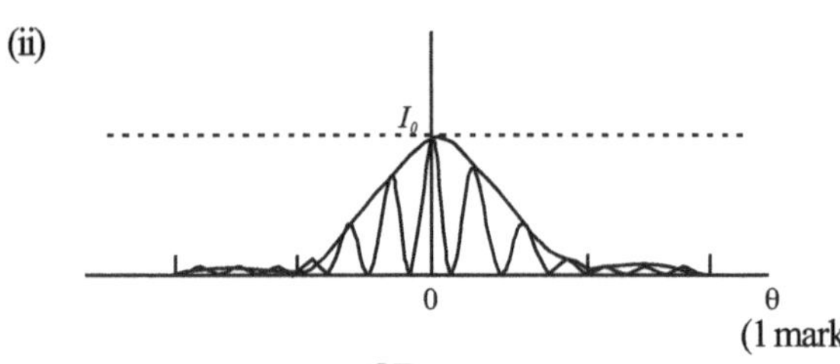

(1 mark)

OR

When two narrow slits are illuminated by a single monochromatic source, the pattern obtained on the screen is interference pattern which consists of alternate bright and dark fringes.

When one of the slits is covered, there is a diffraction pattern on the screen. (2 marks)

21. (a) $+3\mu C$ ... $-3\mu C$

A ... O ... B

←—— 20 cm ——→

Electric field at 'O' due to $+3\mu C$ at

$$A\ E_A = \frac{1}{4\pi \in_0}\frac{q_A}{AO^2} = \frac{9\times 10^9 \times 3\times 10^{-6}}{(10\times 10^{-2})^2}$$

$$= 27\times 10^5 \ N/C \ \text{along AO}.$$

Electric field at 'O' due to $-3\mu C$ at B,

$$E_B = \frac{1}{4\pi \in_0}\frac{q_B}{BO^2} = \frac{9\times 10^9 \times 3\times 10^{-6}}{(10\times 10^{-2})^2}$$

$$= 27\times 10^5 \ N/C \ \text{along OB}.$$

Total field at O = 54 × 10⁵ N/C towards right. (1½ marks)

(b) Force on test charge

$F = q\,E = 1.5 \times 10^{-9} \times 54 \times 10^5 = 8.1 \times 10^{-3}\,N$

The force is attractive acting along OA. (½ mark)

22. (i) Microwaves are used for aircraft navigation, their frequency range is 10^9 Hz to 10^{12} Hz.

(ii) X-rays are used to study crystal structure, their frequency range is 10^{18} Hz to 10^{20} Hz. (1 + 1 = 2 marks)

23. As $\dfrac{1}{f} = (\mu-1)\left(\dfrac{1}{R_1} - \dfrac{1}{R_2}\right)$ f = 15 cm

$$\frac{1}{15} = (\mu-1)\left(\frac{1}{R} + \frac{1}{R}\right)\ R_1 = R$$

$R_2 = -R$

$$\frac{1}{15} = (\mu-1)\frac{2}{R} \Rightarrow \frac{\mu-1}{R} = \frac{1}{30}$$

When the lens is cut into two equal halves

$R_1 = R, R_2 = \infty$

$$\therefore \frac{1}{f'} = (\mu-1)\left(\frac{1}{R} - \frac{1}{\infty}\right) \Rightarrow (\mu-1)\times\frac{1}{R}$$

$$\Rightarrow \frac{1}{f'} = \frac{1}{30}$$ (2 marks)

$\therefore$ f' = 30 cm.

OR

Focal length of convex lens, $f_1 = 30$ cm

focal length of concave lens, $f_2 = -40$ cm

As we know power of the lens

$$P = \frac{1}{f\,(\text{in metre})}$$

Power of the convex lens

$$P_1 = \frac{100}{f_1} = \frac{100}{30} = \frac{10}{3} = 3.33\,D$$

Power of the concave lens

$$P_2 = \frac{-100}{40} = -2.5\,D$$

$\therefore$ Power of the combination

$P = P_1 + P_2 = 3.33\,D - 2.5\,D = 0.83\,D$

Since the power of combination is +ve, hence system, is converging in nature. (2 marks)

24. The North and South poles of a bar magnet are fixed, so the direction of magnetic field of a bar magnet is fixed. The poles of a solenoid can be reverse by reversing the direction of current through it. So the direction of magnetic field of a solenoid can be changed. (2 marks)

25. Given : $c = 3 \times 10^8$ ms⁻¹, $v = 2.5 \times 10^8$ ms⁻¹.

$$\mu = \frac{c}{v} = \frac{3\times 10^8}{2.5\times 10^8} = 1.2$$

As, $\sin c = \dfrac{1}{\mu} = \dfrac{1}{1.2} = 0.8333$

$\sin c \approx \sin 57° \quad \therefore \quad c = 57°$ (2 marks)

OR

Given : $A = 60°$. $\delta_m = 45°$.

for minimum deviation, $r_1 = r_2$

As, $r_1 + r_2 = A°$

$\therefore 2r_1 = 60° \quad \therefore \quad r_1 = 30°$ (2 marks)

26. (i) When the number of turns in the inductor is reduced, the self inductance of coil decreases; so impedance of circuit reduces and so current increases. Thus the brightness of the bulb increases.

(ii) If soft iron rod is inserted in the inductor, then the inductance L increases. Therefore, the current through the bulb will decrease, decreasing the brightness of the bulb.

(iii) When capacitor of reactance $X_C = X_L$ is introduced the net reactance of circuit becomes zero, so impedance of circuit decreases. Therefore Z = R, so current in the circuit increases, hence brightness of bulb increases. Thus brightness of bulb increases in both cases.

(1 + 1 + 1 = 3 marks)

27. Resistance of two heating elements are:

$$P_1 = \frac{V^2}{R_1} \Rightarrow R_1 = \frac{V^2}{P_1} \ \text{and}\ P_2 = \frac{V^2}{R_2},\ R_2 = \frac{V^2}{P_2}$$

(i) In series combination

$$R_S = R_1 + R_2 = \frac{V^2}{P_1} + \frac{V^2}{P_2} = V^2\left(\frac{P_1 + P_2}{P_1\,P_2}\right)$$

$$\therefore P_S = \frac{V^2}{R_s} = \frac{V^2}{V^2\left(\dfrac{P_1 + P_2}{P_1 P_2}\right)} = \frac{P_1 P_2}{P_1 + P_2}$$

(ii) In parallel combination

$$\frac{1}{R_p} = \frac{1}{R_1} + \frac{1}{R_2} = \frac{1}{\dfrac{V^2}{P_1}} + \frac{1}{\dfrac{V^2}{P_2}} = \frac{P_1}{V^2} + \frac{P_2}{V^2}$$

$$\frac{1}{R_p} = \frac{1}{V^2}(P_1 + P_2)$$

power consumption in parallel combination

$$P_p = \frac{V^2}{R_p} = V^2\left[\frac{1}{V^2}(P_1 + P_2)\right] = P_1 + P_2 \quad (1\tfrac{1}{2} + 1\tfrac{1}{2} = 3\text{ marks})$$

OR

From Kirchoff's Ist rule or junction rule

For junction f,

$I_1 + I_2 = I_3$

or, $I_1 = I_3 - I_2$ ... (i)

From kirchoff's 2nd rule or loop rule

In loop 'abcfa'

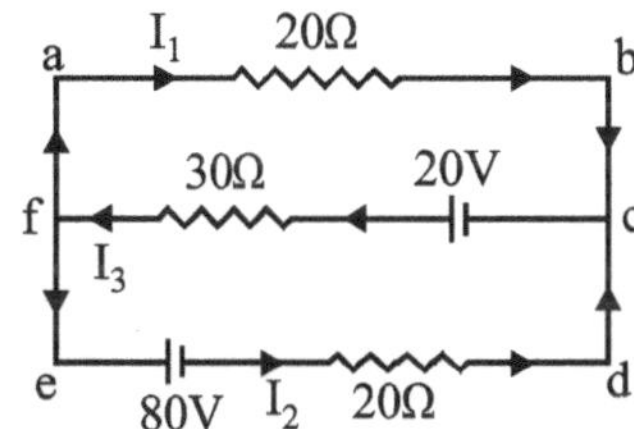

$-20I_1 + 20 - 30I_3 = 0$

or, $2I_1 + 3I_3 = 2$ ... (ii)

In loop 'fcdef,'

$30I_3 - 20 + 20I_2 - 80 = 0$

or, $3I_3 + 2I_2 = 10$ ... (iii)

Substituting equation (i) in (ii)

$2(I_3 - I_2) + 3I_3 = 2$

or, $5I_3 - 2I_2 = 2$ ...(iv)

Adding equations (iii) and (iv)

$8I_3 = 12$

or, $I_3 = 3/2$ A

Substituting in equation (iii) and solving

$I_2 = 11/4$A

Substituting for I_3 and I_2 in equation (i)

$I_1 = 3/2 - 11/4 = -5/4$ A (3 marks)

28. The positions of secondary minima are at $\theta = \dfrac{n\lambda}{a}$. Consider first the angle θ where the path difference is λ, then $\theta = \dfrac{\lambda}{a}$. Now divide the slit into two equal halves each of size $\dfrac{a}{2}$. Therefore, the path difference between the waves arising from the two halves of the slit will be $\dfrac{\lambda}{2}$. As

a result the waves reaching at any point on the screen will have a phase difference of 180° and hence cancel each other. Therefore, the intensity fall to zero and a minimum is produced. (3 marks)

29. If, F_c – centripetal force required to keep a revolving electron in orbit

F_e – electrostatic force of attraction between the revolving electron and the nucleus then, for a dynamically stable orbit in a hydrogen atom, where $Z = 1$,

$F_c = F_e$

$$\frac{mv^2}{r} = \frac{(e)(e)}{4\pi\varepsilon_0 r^2} \qquad \text{...(i)}$$

$$r = \frac{e^2}{4\pi\varepsilon_0 mv^2} \qquad \text{...(ii)}$$

K.E. of electron in the orbit, $K = \dfrac{1}{2}mv^2$

From equation (i), $K = \dfrac{e^2}{8\pi\varepsilon_0 r}$

Potential energy of electron in orbit,

$$U = \frac{(e)(-e)}{4\pi\varepsilon_0 r} = \frac{-e^2}{4\pi\varepsilon_0 r}$$

Negative sign indicates that revolving electron is bound to the positive nucleus.

$\therefore$ Total energy of electron in hydrogen atom

$$E = k + U = \frac{e^2}{8\pi\varepsilon_0 r} - \frac{e^2}{4\pi\varepsilon_0 r} \; ; \; \boxed{E = -\frac{e^2}{8\pi\varepsilon_0 r}} \quad (2\text{ marks})$$

Therefore, total energy of electrons in orbit of hydrogen atom is negative. Hence, the electron bound to the nucleus i.e., the electron is not free to leave the orbit around the nucleus. (1 mark)

OR

According to the postulates of Bohr's atomic model, the electrons revolve around the nucleus only in those orbits for which the angular momentum is the integral multiple of $h/2\pi$. Where h is plank's constant.

$\therefore L = nh/2\pi$

Angular momentum is given by $L = mvr$

According to Bohr's postulate,

$$L_n = mv_n r_n = \frac{nh}{2\pi} \qquad \text{...(i)}$$

$$v_n = \frac{nh}{2\pi m r_n} \quad [\text{from equation (i)}]$$

From, Bohr's postulate of atomic model

$$\frac{mv_n^2}{r_n} = \frac{Kze^2}{r_n^2} \; : r_n = \frac{Kze^2}{mv_n^2}$$

Putting the value of v_n and $z = 1$ (for hydrogen atom).

$$r_n = \frac{n^2 h^2}{4\pi^2 mKe^2} \qquad (3\text{ marks})$$

This is the expression for Bohr's radius. This shows $r \propto n^2$.

30. As n^0 no. and p^+ no. are conserved, the rest mass of n^0 and p^+ is same but total binding energy is not same on either side of nuclear reaction. This diference appears in form of energy released or absorbed in the nuclear reaction. Since B. E contributes to mass thus we say that difference in masses of nuclei on two sides of the reactio gets converted into energy. This is mass-energy interconversion. (3 marks)

31. Let Q = Total charge on each plate of the capacitor, A = Area of each plate

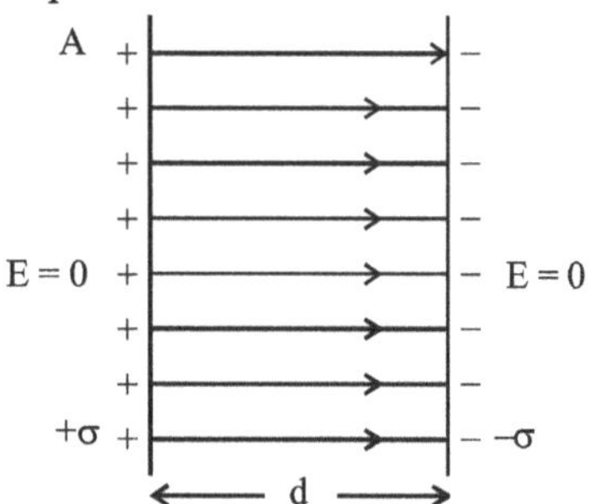

$\therefore$ Surface charge density $\sigma = \dfrac{Q}{A}$

$\because$ E is uniform between the plates

$\therefore$ $E = \dfrac{\sigma}{\varepsilon_0} = \dfrac{Q}{\varepsilon_0 A}$

$\therefore$ $C = \dfrac{Q}{V} = \dfrac{Q}{Ed}$ $(\because V = Ed)$

or, $C = \dfrac{Q}{\dfrac{Qd}{\varepsilon_0 A}} = \dfrac{\varepsilon_0 A}{d}$ (3 marks)

When the capacitor is charged to a potential V, the charge stored in the capacitor Q = CV. Now capacitor is disconnected from the source and distance between the plates is doubled.

(i) Capacitance $= C = \dfrac{Q}{V} = \dfrac{Q}{Ed}$

$\therefore$ New capacitance $C' = \dfrac{Q}{2Ed} = \dfrac{C}{2}$

$\therefore$ Capacitance becomes half. (1 mark)

(ii) Energy $= \dfrac{Q^2}{2C'} = \dfrac{Q^2}{2C/2} = 2\dfrac{Q^2}{2C} = 2E.$

$\therefore$ Energy becomes double. (1 mark)

OR

(a) Let C_1 and C_2 are the capacitances, q_1 and q_2 are the charges, V_1 and V_2 are potential of the capacitors respectively.

$\therefore$ $q_1 = C_1 V_1$ and $q_2 = C_2 V_2$

Before sharing, total charge $= q_1 + q_2$

$= C_1 V_1 + C_2 V_2$

When the capacitors are joined by a wire, charge will flow from higher to lower potential till both the potentials are equal. This equal potential is called common potential (V)

If q'_1 and q'_2 are charges on C_1 and C_2 after redistribution of charges, then

$q'_1 = C_1 V$ and $q'_2 = C_2 V$

$\because$ Total charge after connecting them together remains same as before.

$q = q'_1 + q'_2 = C_1 V + C_2 V = (C_1 + C_2)V$

$\therefore$ $(C_1 + C_2) V = C_1 V_1 + C_2 V_2$

$V = \dfrac{C_1 V_1 + C_2 V_2}{C_1 + C_2}$ (2½ marks)

(b) P.E. before sharing $= \dfrac{1}{2}C_1 V_1^2 + \dfrac{1}{2}C_2 V_2^2$

P.E. after sharing $= \dfrac{1}{2}C_1 V^2 + \dfrac{1}{2}C_2 V^2 = \dfrac{1}{2}(C_1 + C_2)V^2$

$= \dfrac{1}{2}(C_1 + C_2)\left[\dfrac{C_1 V_1 + C_2 V_2}{C_1 + C_2}\right]^2 = \dfrac{1}{2}\dfrac{(C_1 V_1 + C_2 V_2)^2}{(C_1 + C_2)}$

$\therefore$ Loss of energy $= \dfrac{1}{2}C_1 V_1^2 + \dfrac{1}{2}C_2 V_2^2$

$- \dfrac{1}{2}\dfrac{(C_1 V_1 + C_2 V_2)^2}{(C_1 + C_2)}$

$= \dfrac{1}{2(C_1 + C_2)} [(C_1 V_1^2 + C_2 V_2^2)(C_1 + C_2)$

$- (C_1 V_1 + C_2 V_2)^2]$

$= \dfrac{1}{2(C_1 + C_2)} [C_1^2 V_1^2 + C_1 C_2 V_1^2 + C_1 C_2 V_2^2 + C_2^2 V_2^2$

$- C_1^2 V_1^2 - C_2^2 V_2^2 - 2C_1 C_2 V_1 V_2]$

$= \dfrac{1}{2(C_1 + C_2)} C_1 C_2 (V_1^2 + V_2^2 - 2V_1 V_2)$

$= \dfrac{C_1 C_2}{2(C_1 + C_2)}(V_1 - V_2)^2 = \text{Positive}$ (2½ marks)

$\therefore$ Energy is lost due to sharing of charges.

32. (i) Faraday gave two laws of electromagnetic induction.

First law : *Whenever there is change in the magnetic flux associated with a circuit, an e.m.f. is induced in the circuit. This is also known as **Neumann's law***

Second law : *The magnitude of the induced e.m.f. (e) is directly proportional to the time rate of change of the magnetic flux through the circuit.*

i.e., $e \propto \dfrac{\Delta\phi}{\Delta t}$ or, $e = k\dfrac{\Delta\phi}{\Delta t}$ (2 marks)

(a) (i) When coil A is placed parallel to B and near to it, due to mutual induction an e.m.f is induced in B and the bulb lights up.

(b) When the coil B is moved upwards, distance between A and B increases. Hence the magnetic flux linked with B decrease and mutual induction decreases and hence the bulb gets dimmer.

OR

(a) **Lenz's law and conservation of energy:** Lenz's law is according to law of conservation of energy because when N-pole of a magnet is moved towards the coil, the upper face of the coil acquires north polarity. So work has to be done against the force of repulsion in bringing the magnet closer to the coil.

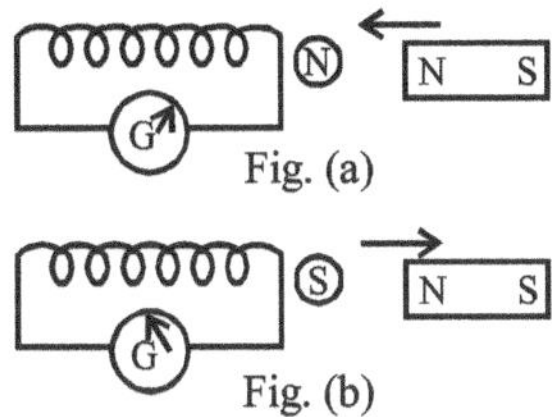

When the N-pole is moved away, south polarity is developed on the upper face of the coil. Therefore, work has to be done against the force of attraction in taking the magnet away from the coil. (2 marks)

∴ Mechanical work done is converted into electrical energy of the coil.

When the magnet does not move work done is zero, so no electrical energy is produced.

(b) (i) Since

where, I = Strength of current through the coil at any time

ϕ = Amount of magnetic flux linked with all turns of the coil at that time

and, L = Constant of proportionality called coefficient of self induction

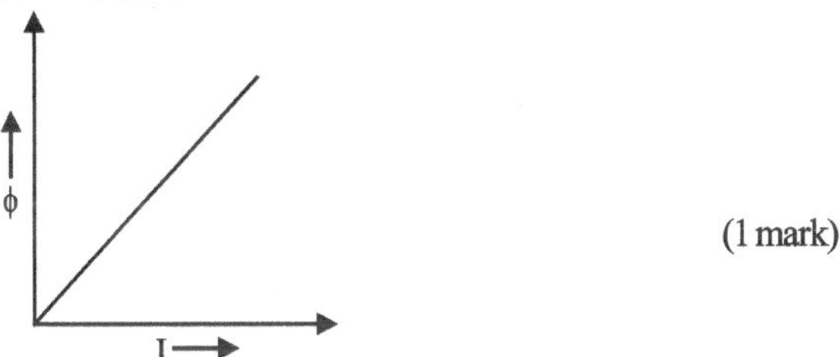

(1 mark)

(ii) Induced emf,

$$e = \frac{-d\phi}{dt} = \frac{-d}{dt}(LI)$$

i.e., $e = -L\dfrac{dI}{dt}$ (1 mark)

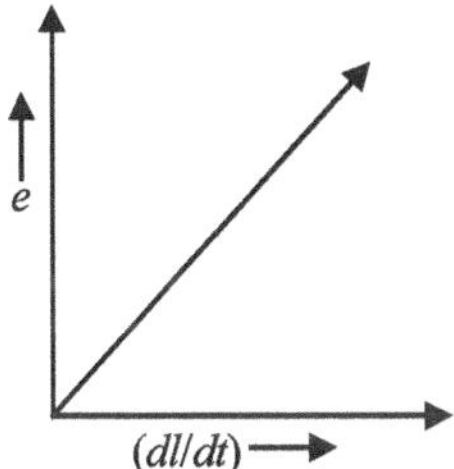

[The graph is drawn considering only magnitude of e]

(iii) Since magnetic potential energy is given by, $U = \dfrac{1}{2}LI^2$

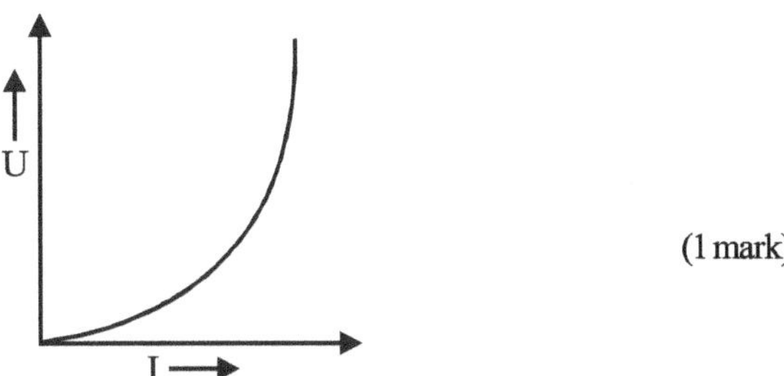

(1 mark)

33. According to the band theory, each atom has two bands, valence band (energy E_V) and conduction band (energy E_C) consisting of closely spaced energy levels. Their difference is called energy gap or band gap E_g (fig. (Q-1)).

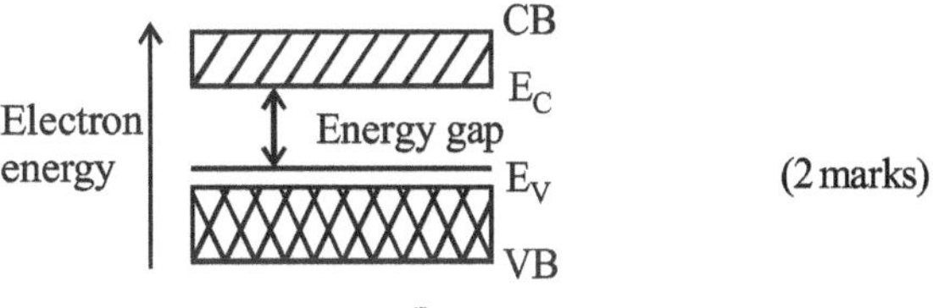

(2 marks)

Case 1: When both bands overlap (fig. (ii)), electrons in valence orbit are free to move in conduction band and cause current to flow (Eg ≈ 0). These are **metals.**

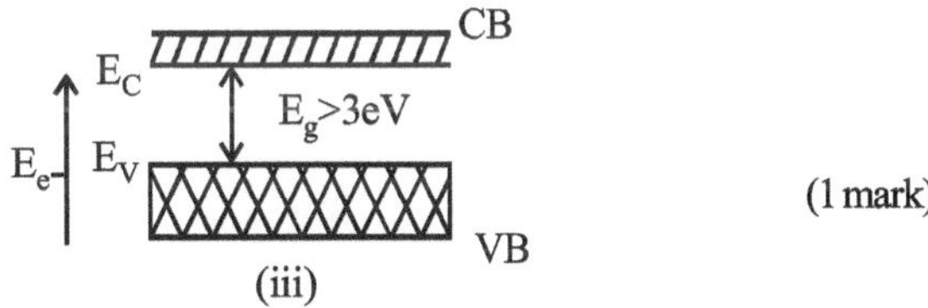

(1 mark)

Case 2: When band gap is large, the electrons in valence band are bound and cannot move to conduction band ($E_g > 3$ eV). These materials donot not carry current. They are **insulators** (fig. (iii)).

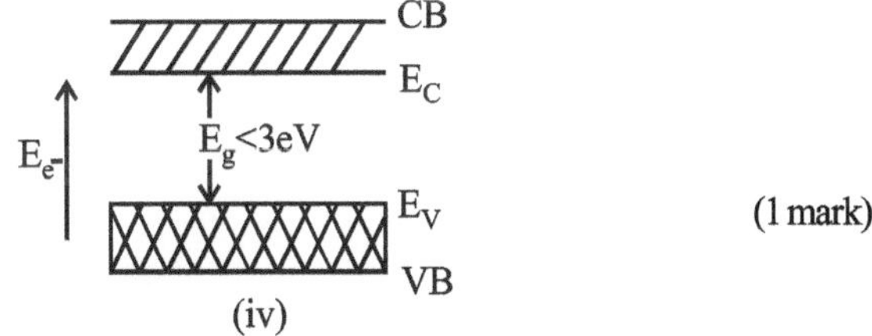

(1 mark)

Case 3: When band gap is finite but small ($E_g < 3$ eV) then electron from valence band can easily pick external energy (heat or voltage) and go to conduction band. Such materials have resistance lower than insulators and are called semiconductors.

(1 mark)

OR

The energy band structure of a semiconductor has donor or acceptor energy states after doping, which are given by E_D or E_A respectively. In n–type semiconductor, donor energy level E_D is slightly below the bottom E_C of the conduction band and electrons from this level can easily move into the conduction band with very small amount of energy.

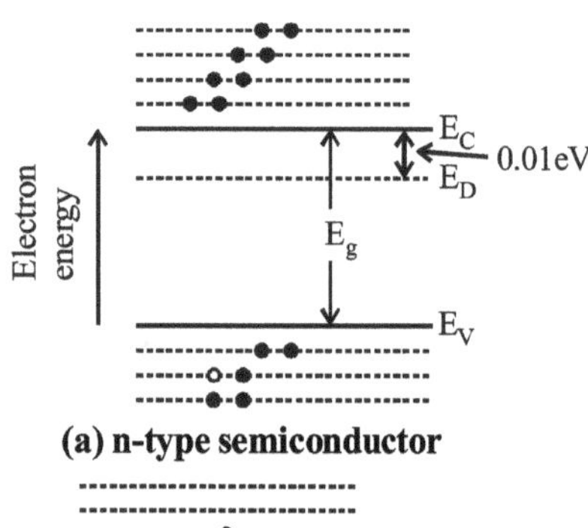

(a) n-type semiconductor

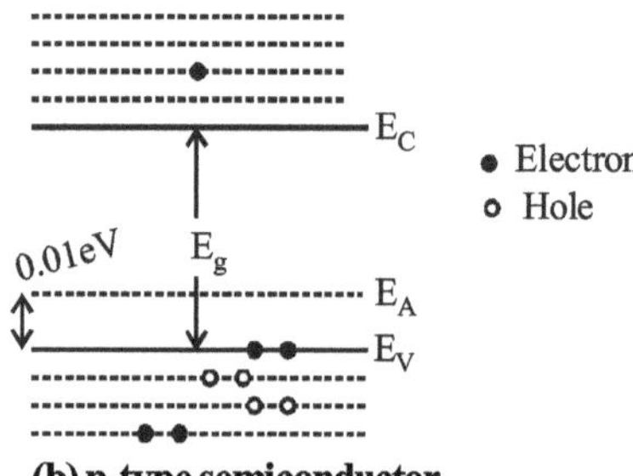

(b) p-type semiconductor

At room temperature most donar atoms are ionised but very few Si atoms are ionised so that conduction band has mostly donor electrons. For p–type semiconductor, the acceptor energy level E_A is slightly above valence band so that electrons from valence band can easily jump to this level E_A and ionise acceptor atom, thus leaving a hole in the valence band. At room temperature, most of acceptor atoms get ionised leaving holes in the valence band which conduct charge. The electron and hole concentration in a semiconductor is given by $n_e \, n_h = n_i^2$ **(5 marks)**

---

34. **(i)** $\tau = m\beta \sin\theta = 0.75 \times 0.20 = 0.15 \, \text{Nm}$ **(1 mark)**

(ii) Work done by external torque,
$W = MB \, (1 - \cos\theta)$
$= 0.75 \times 0.2 \, (1 - \cos 180°)$
$= 0.15 \, (1 + 1) = 0.3 \, \text{J}$ **(2 marks)**

(iii) Magnetic moment $= NIA$ **(1 mark)**

OR

(iii) Torque $= IAB$
$= 10 \times 0.02 \times 0.2 = 0.04 \, \text{Nm}$ **(1 mark)**

35. **(i)** $\Delta E = \dfrac{12400}{4.500 \text{Å}} = 2.75 \, \text{eV}$ **(1 mark)**

For photoelectric effect, $\Delta E > W_0$ (work function). Barium or Lithium can be used to produce electrons.

(ii) $h\upsilon = W_{ex} + $ maximum kinetic energy
$h\upsilon_0 = 8 \, \text{eV} = W_{ex} + 2 \, \text{eV} \Rightarrow W_{ex} = 6 \, \text{eV}$
For incoming radiation, energy is
$h \times 1.25 \, \upsilon_0 = 10 \, \text{eV}, W_{ex} = 6 \, \text{eV}$
$\therefore$ Kinetic energy (maximum) $= 4 \, \text{eV}$. **(1 mark)**

(iii) For photoelectric emission, photoelectric current, incident light frequency should be greater than threshold frequency.

Light of frequency 1.5 times the threshold frequency v_0 incident.

$$v = \frac{3}{2} v_0$$

If frequency is halved,

$$\therefore v' = \frac{v}{2} = \frac{3}{4} v_0 \qquad \because v' < v_0$$

$\therefore$ No photoelectric emission will take place. **(2 marks)**

OR

(iii) Moment of photon $= p = \dfrac{h}{\lambda} \quad \because E = mc^2$

But, $p = mc \qquad \therefore E = mc.c$ So, $E = pc$ or $E = \dfrac{hc}{\lambda}$

$\therefore \dfrac{hc}{\lambda} = pc$ or $p = \dfrac{h}{\lambda}$ and $\lambda = \dfrac{c}{f}$

$\therefore p = \dfrac{hf}{c}$ **(2 marks)**

1. **(b)** Here, $q_1 = 1 \times 10^{-7}$C, q_2 and 2×10^{-7} C,
$r = 20$ cm $= 20 \times 10^{-2}$ m

$$F = \frac{q_1 q_2}{4\pi\varepsilon_0 r^2} = \frac{9\times10^9 \times 1\times10^{-7} \times 2\times10^{-7}}{(20\times10^{-2})^2}$$

$$= 4.5\times10^{-3} \ N \qquad \text{(1 mark)}$$

2. **(d)** The coil of a moving coil galvanometer is wound over metallic frame to provide electromagnetic damping so it becomes dead beat galvanometer. (1 mark)

3. **(c)** Let P is the observation point at a distance r from $-2q$ and at $(L+r)$ from $+8q$.
Given now, net EFI at $P = 0$

$\therefore \vec{E}_1 =$ EFI (Electric Field Intensity) at P due to $+8q$

$\vec{E}_2 =$ EFI (Electric Field Intensity) at P due to $-2q$

$$\left|\vec{E_1}\right| = \left|\vec{E_2}\right| \quad \therefore \frac{k(8q)}{(L+r)^2} = \frac{k(2q)}{r^2} \ \therefore \frac{4}{(L+r)^2} = \frac{1}{(r)^2}$$

$4r^2 = (L+r)^2 \Rightarrow 2r = L+r$ (1 mark)
$r = L \qquad \therefore$ P is at $x = L + L = 2L$ from origin

4. **(a)** Given that all capacitors are connected in parallel so, the equivalent capacitance will be $C_{eq} = C_1 + C_2 + C_3 + C_4$
$= 1+2+4+3 = 10 \ \mu F$
Voltage of battery V = 20 V
We have, $Q = CV = 10 \ \mu F \times 20 = 200 \ \mu C$ (1 mark)

5. **(a)** Current flowing through the conductor,
$I = n \, e \, v \, A$. Hence

$$\frac{4}{1} = \frac{nev_{d_1}\pi(1)^2}{nev_{d_2}\pi(2)^2} \text{ or } \frac{v_{d_1}}{v_{d_2}} = \frac{4\times1}{1} = \frac{16}{1}. \qquad \text{(1 mark)}$$

6. **(a)** According to Kirchhoff's first law
At junction A, $i_{AB} = 2+2 = 4$ A
At junction B, $i_{AB} = i_{BC} - 1 = 3$A

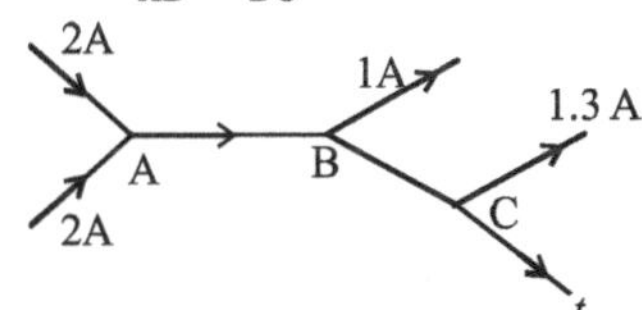

At junction C, $i = i_{BC} - 1.3 = 3 - 1.3 = 1.7$ amp (1 mark)

7. **(d)** When the temperature of a magnetic material decreases, the magnetization remains the same in a diamagnetic material. (1 mark)

8. **(c)** As I increases, ϕ increases
$\therefore$ I_i is such that it opposes the increases in ϕ.
Hence, ϕ decreases (By Right Hand Rule). The induced current will be counter clockwise. (1 mark)

9. **(b)** $\varepsilon = M\dfrac{di}{dt}$ or $8 = M\left[\dfrac{(4-2)}{0.05}\right]$

$\therefore \ M = \dfrac{8\times0.05}{2} = 0.2$ henry (1 mark)

10. **(b)** The wave having highest energy, has lowest wavelength as,

$E_\gamma > E_{x-rays} > E_{visible} > E_{microwave}$
$\Rightarrow \lambda_\gamma < \lambda_{x-rays} < \lambda_{visible} < \lambda_{microwave}$ (1 mark)

11. **(b)** We know that frequency of electromagnetic radiation remains the same when it changes the medium. Further

$$\mu = \frac{\text{wavelength of light in vacuum}}{\text{wavelength of light in medium}} = \frac{\lambda_v}{\lambda_m}$$

$$\lambda_m = \frac{\lambda_v}{\mu} = \frac{\lambda}{\mu} \qquad \text{(1 mark)}$$

Similarly, $\mu = \dfrac{\text{velocity of light in vacuum}}{\text{velocity of light in medium}}$

$$\lambda_m = \frac{v}{\mu}$$

12. **(d)** $P_2 = P - P_1 = \dfrac{100}{80} - \dfrac{100}{20} = -3.75$ D (1 mark)

13. **(d)** Average BE/nucleon increases first, and then decreases, as is clear from BE curve. (1 mark)

14. **(a)** Isotones means equal number of neutrons *i.e.*, $(A-Z)$
$= 74 - 34 = 71 - 31 = 40.$ (1 mark)

15. **(b)** Donar energy (fermi) level lies just below the conduction band in n-type semiconductor. (1 mark)

16. **(c)** Assertion is correct. The induced field cancels the external field. Reason is false. When a current is set up in a conductor, there exists an electric field inside it. (1 mark)

17. **(a)** $R = R_0 (A)^{1/3}$ (1 mark)

18. **(b)** $\theta_c = \sin^{-1}\left(\dfrac{1}{\mu}\right)$ and $\mu \propto \dfrac{1}{\lambda}$ (1 mark)

19. Given $N_P = 200$, $N_s = 1000$, $P_{output} = 10$ kW $= 10^4$ W,
$E_P = 200$ V.
For an ideal transformer $P_{output} = P_{input} = 10^4$ W

$$\Rightarrow E_s I_s = E_P I_P \Rightarrow \frac{E_s}{E_P} = \frac{N_s}{N_P}$$

$$\therefore E_s = \frac{N_s}{N_P} \times E_P = \frac{1000}{200} \times 200 = 1000 \text{ V.} \qquad \text{(1 mark)}$$

Input power $= E_P I_P = 10^4 \Rightarrow I_P = \dfrac{10^4}{200} = 50$ A (1 mark)

20. **(i)** The fringe-width of interference pattern increases with the decrease in separation between $S_1 S_2$ as $\beta \propto \dfrac{1}{d}$
(1 mark)
(ii) The fringe-width decrease as wavelength gets reduced when interference set up is taken from air to water.
(1 mark)

21. **(i)** The figure is shown below.

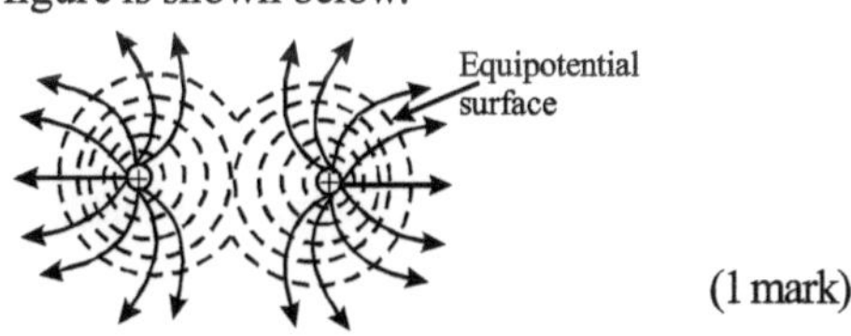

(1 mark)

Equipotential surfaces of two
identical positive charges

(ii) By definition, electric potential energy of any charge q placed in the region of electric field is equal to the work done in bringing charge q from infinity to that point and given by

$$U = qV$$

Expression for Potential energy,

$$U = q_1V_1 + q_2V_2 = \frac{1}{4\pi\varepsilon_0} \cdot \frac{q_1q_2}{|r_2 - r_1|} \qquad \text{(1 mark)}$$

OR

(i) $\because$ Electric field intensity and potential difference are related as

$$E = -\frac{\Delta V}{\Delta r}$$

$$\Rightarrow \quad \Delta V = -E\Delta r$$

$$\Rightarrow \quad V_A - V_C = -(2+2)E$$

$$V_A - V_C = -4E$$

$$V_C - V_A = 4E \qquad \text{(1 mark)}$$

(ii) As $V_C - V_A = 4E$, is positive

$$\therefore \quad V_C > V_A$$

Potential is greater at point C than point A, as potential decreases along the direction of electric field. (1 mark)

22. (i) Mutual induction: It is the phenomenon in which a change of current in one coil induces an emf in another coil placed near it. The coil in which the current changes is called the primary coil and the coil in which the emf is induced is called the secondary coil.

(ii) As we know, $e = -M\dfrac{dI}{dt}$

$$e = -1.5 \times \frac{20 - 0}{0.5} = -60\,V$$

So, the flux linked with the other coil is given by

$$\Delta\phi = e \times \Delta t = -60 \times 0.5 = -30\,Wb \qquad (2 \times 1 = 2\text{ marks})$$

23. $\because$ Fringe width, $(\beta) = \dfrac{D\lambda}{d}$

$$\Rightarrow \quad \frac{\beta_1}{\beta_2} = \frac{\lambda_1}{\lambda_2} \qquad (\because \text{ D and d are same})$$

Here, $\beta_1 = 7.2 \times 10^{-3}\,m$

$$\beta_2 = 8.1 \times 10^{-3}\,m$$

and $\lambda_1 = 630 \times 10^{-9}\,m$ (1 mark)

Wavelength of another source of laser light

$$\Rightarrow \quad \lambda_2 = \frac{\beta_2}{\beta_1} \times \lambda_1 = \frac{8.1 \times 10^{-3}}{7.2 \times 10^{-3}} \times 630 \times 10^{-9}\,m$$

or $\lambda_2 = 708.75 \times 10^{-9}\,m$

$\therefore \quad \lambda_2 = 708.75\,nm$ (1 mark)

24. (a) In the nuclear reaction, for example

$$_1^2H + {_1^2}H \longrightarrow {_2^3}He + {_0}n^1 + 3.27\,MeV$$

Total number of nucleons is conserved.

i.e. number of neutrons + protons of the reactants is equal to the number of neutrons + protons of the products.

But the sum of the masses of the reactants and the sum of the masses of the products is not the same i.e. there is some mass defect (Δm). Energy equivalent to the mass defect is released in the nuclear reaction.

According to Einstein's mass energy equivalence relation,

$$\Delta E = \Delta mc^2 \qquad \text{(1 mark)}$$

(b) Let A be the mass number and R the radius of the nucleus.

Then mass of the nucleus $= A$ amu

$$M = A \times 1.6 \times 10^{-27}\,kg$$

Now, $R = R_0 A^{1/3}$

where R_0 is a constant whose numerical value is (1.2×10^{-15})

$\therefore$ Volume of the nucleus $= \dfrac{4}{3}\pi R^3 = \dfrac{4}{3}\pi R_0^3 A$

$\therefore$ Density of the nucleus

$$= \frac{M}{V} = \frac{A \times 1.6 \times 10^{-27}\,kg \times 3}{4 \times 3.14 \times \left(1.2 \times 10^{-15}\right)^3 \times A}$$

$$= 2.2 \times 10^{17}\,kg\,m^{-3} \text{ which is independent of A. (1 mark)}$$

25. Given : $f_0 = 75$ cm, $f_e = 5$ cm.

minimum magnifying power, $m = \dfrac{f_0}{f_e} = \dfrac{75}{5} = 25$ (1 mark)

Max. magnifying power,

$$m = \frac{f_0}{f_e}\left(1 + \frac{d}{f_e}\right) = \frac{75}{5} \times \left(1 + \frac{25}{5}\right) = 25 \times (1+5)$$

$$= 25 \times 6 = 150 \qquad \text{(1 mark)}$$

OR

Apparent depth.

$$d = \frac{d_1}{n_1} + \frac{d_2}{n_2} = \frac{40}{1.6} + \frac{30}{1.5} = 25 + 20 = 45\,cm. \quad (2\text{ marks})$$

26.

	N-type semicoductor		P-tpye semiconductor
1.	Intrinsic semiconductor is doped by pentavalent atoms e.g. As, Sb etc.	1.	Intrinsic semiconductor is doped by trivalent atoms e.g. Al, B etc.
2.	It has an extra electron from the impurity.	2.	It has an extra hole from the impurity.
3.	Dopant atom is positively charged.	3.	Dopant atom is negatively charged.
4.	Electrons are majority charge carriers.	4.	Holes are majority charge carriers.
5.	n_e (no. of electron) $\gg n_h$ (no. of holes)	5.	n_h (no. of holes) $\gg n_e$ (no. of electron)
6.	Donar energy level is close to conduction band.	6.	Acceptor level is close to valence band. $(6 \times \frac{1}{2} = 3\text{ marks})$

27. If E is the emf of the cell, r is the internal resistance of the cell and I is the current through the circuit. Then Terminal voltage 'V' of the cell is $V = E - Ir$

So, $V = -Ir + E$ (1 mark)

Comparing with the equation of a straight line $y = mx + c$, we get: $y = V$; $x = I$; $m = -r$; $c = E$

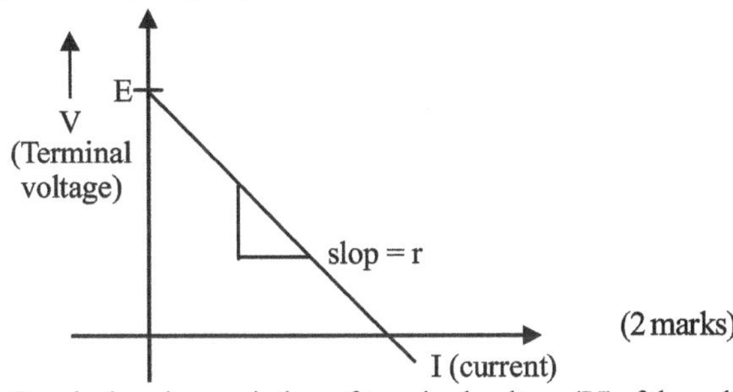

(2 marks)

Graph showing variation of terminal voltage 'V' of the cell versus the current 'I'

Where, Emf of the cell = Intercept on V axis

Internal resistance = slope of line. (1 mark)

28. (a) de-Broglie wavelength of a charged particle is given by $\lambda \propto \dfrac{1}{\sqrt{mq}}$

$2m_p$ and e are mass and charge of a deuteron respectively, and, $4m_p$ and $2e$ are mass and charge of an alpha particle respectively.

$$\frac{\lambda_D}{\lambda_\alpha} = \sqrt{\frac{m_\alpha q_\alpha}{m_D q_D}} = \sqrt{\frac{(4m_p)(2e)}{(2m_p)(e)}} = \frac{2}{1}$$

Thus, de-Broglie wavelength associated with deutron is twice of the de-Broglie wavelength of alpha particle.

(2 marks)

(b) (For same accelerating potential K.E $\propto q$)

Charge of a deuteron is less as compared to an alpha particle. So, deuteron will have less value of K.E.

(1 mark)

OR

(i) Energy of a photon is given by
$E = h\nu$

Number of photons emitted per second, $n = \dfrac{P}{E}$ where,

P = Power emitted

On putting the values, we get,

$n = 3 \times 10^{-3} / 6.63 \times 10^{-34} \times 5 \times 10^{14}$

$\quad = 9.05 \times 10^{15}$ (2 marks)

(ii) The photoelectric current is known to be directly proportional to the intensity of incident light with fixed frequency. So, the plot will be a straight line shown as,

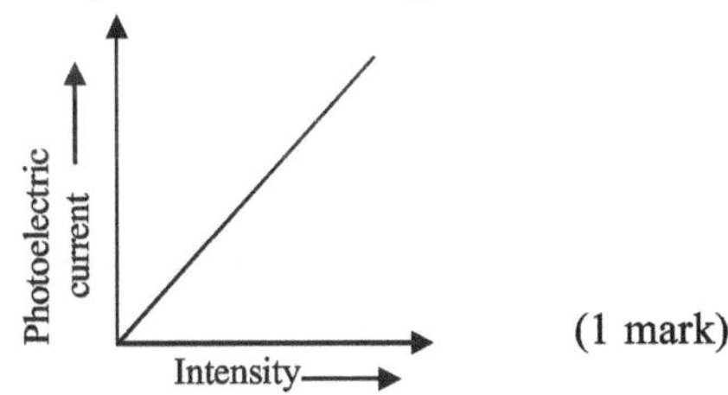

(1 mark)

29. (i) Ray diagram : (ii)

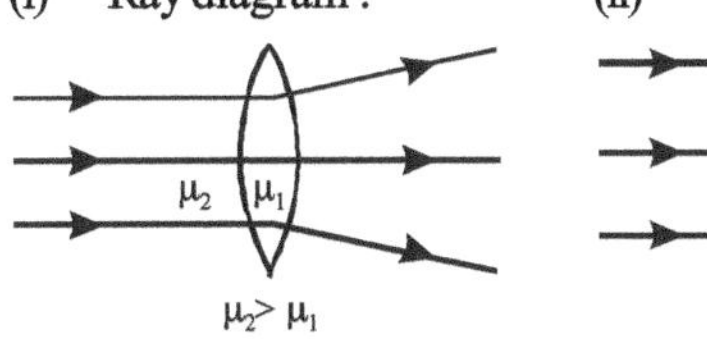

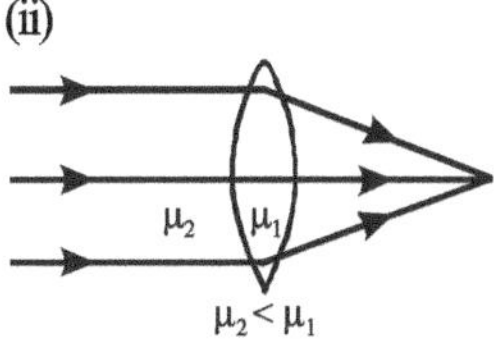

$(2 \times 1 = 2 \text{ marks})$

As the lens is equiconvex, therefore,

$R_1 = R_2 = R$,

Using the expression

$$\frac{f_L}{f_a} = \frac{\left(_a\mu_g - 1\right)}{\left(\dfrac{_a\mu_g}{_a\mu_L} - 1\right)} = \frac{\mu_1 - 1}{\left(\dfrac{\mu_1}{\mu_2} - 2\right)}$$

or, $f_L = \dfrac{(\mu_1 - 1)\mu_2}{(\mu_1 - \mu_2)} \times f_a$ (1 mark)

30. An intrinsic semiconductor at 0 K is like an insulator because all its electrons are in the valence band in form of bound electrons and hence not free to conduct current. At T > 0 K, some of these electrons pick up thermal energy and move to conduction band.

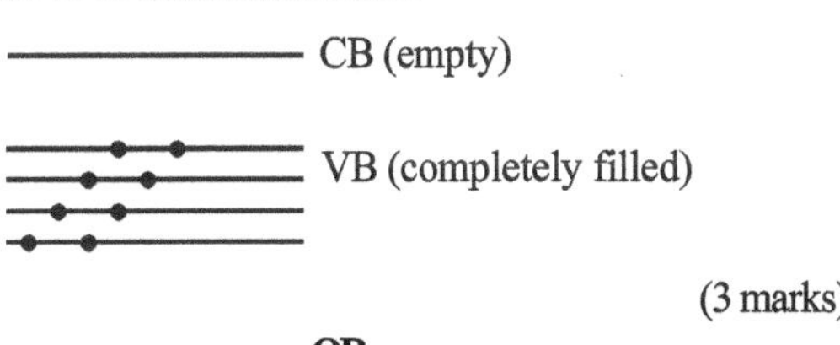

(3 marks)

OR

Here we use two diodes to rectify voltage corresponding to both positive and negative half of the a.c. cycle. Here, the p–side of the two diodes are connected to ends of secondary which is centre tapped in this transformer. For positive half cycle, D_1 is forward biased and conducts and for negative half cycle D_2 conducts. (1 mark)

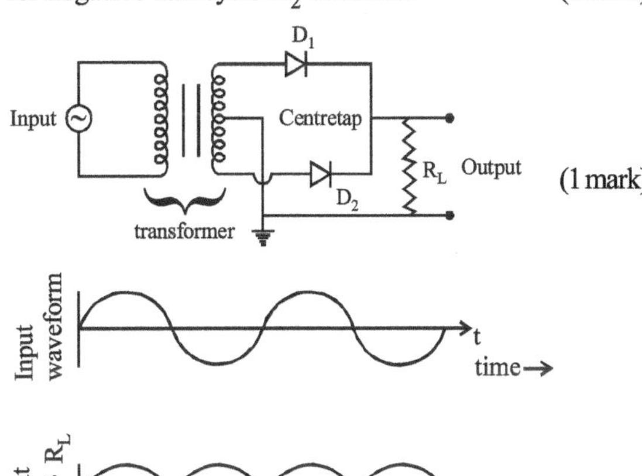

(1 mark)

The output across load is a continuously, varying pulse of the shape of half sinusoids. (1 mark)

31. (a) The outward electric flux due to charge $+Q$ is independent of the shape and size of the surface, which encloses it because :

(i) Number of electric field lines coming out from a closed surface enclosing the charge depends on the charge enclosed by the surface,

(ii) Number of electric field lines coming out from a closed surface enclosing the charge is independent of the position of the charge inside the closed surface.

$$(2 \times 1 = 2 \text{ marks})$$

(b) Let us consider two positively charged thin parallel sheets A and B with uniform surface densities of charge σ_1 and σ_2 respectively.

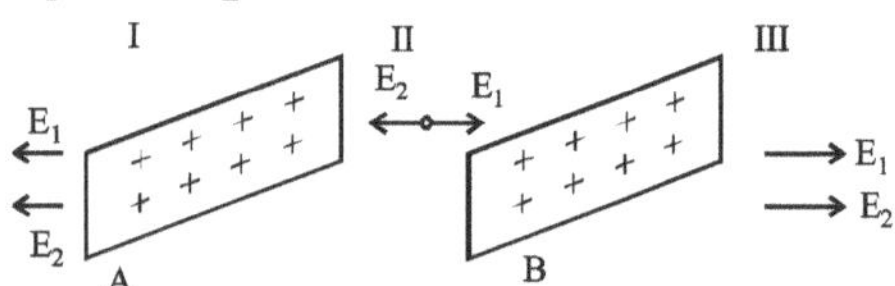

Let $\sigma_1 > \sigma_2 > 0$

In region I, $E_I = -E_1 - E_2 = \dfrac{-\sigma_1}{2\varepsilon_0} - \dfrac{\sigma_2}{2\varepsilon_0}$

$\Rightarrow \quad E_I = -\dfrac{1}{2\varepsilon_0}(\sigma_1 + \sigma_2)$

In region II, $E_{II} = E_1 - E_2$

$$= \dfrac{\sigma_1}{2\varepsilon_0} - \dfrac{\sigma_2}{2\varepsilon_0} = \dfrac{\sigma_1 - \sigma_2}{2\varepsilon_0}$$

In region III, $E_{III} = E_1 + E_2$

$$= \dfrac{\sigma_1}{2\varepsilon_0} + \dfrac{\sigma_2}{2\varepsilon_0} = \dfrac{\sigma_1 + \sigma_2}{2\varepsilon_0}$$

In $\sigma_1 = \sigma$ and $\sigma_2 = -\sigma$ then $E_I = 0$, $E_{III} = 0$

$E_{II} = \dfrac{2\sigma}{2\varepsilon_0} = \dfrac{\sigma}{\varepsilon_0} = $ constant

Clearly, field (i) between the sheets

$E_{II} = \dfrac{\sigma}{\varepsilon_0} = $ constant and

(ii) outside the sheets $E_I = E_{III} = 0$ (3 marks)

OR

(a) Electric dipole moment is defined as the product of either charge of the dipole and the distance between them.

i.e. $\vec{p} = q \times \overline{2l}$, where $\overline{2l}$ is the vector distance from the $-$ve to $+$ve charge

It is a vector quantity.   (1 mark)

Expression for the electric field of a dipole at a point on the equatorial plane of the dipole :

Let there be a point P (on the equatorial plane of the dipole) at a distance r from the centre of a dipole formed by two charges $-q$ and $+q$ and having dipole moments $\vec{p} = 2\,\vec{ql}$.

We have to find the electric field intensity at point P.

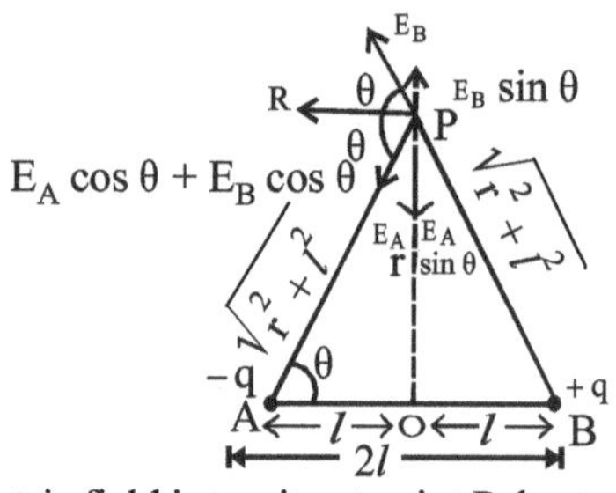

The electric field intensity at point P due to $+q$ (at B)

$$E_A = \dfrac{1}{4\pi\,\epsilon_0} \cdot \dfrac{q}{\left(r^2 + l^2\right)} \text{ along BP}$$

and electric field intensity at P due to $-q$ charge (at A)

$$E_B = \dfrac{1}{4\pi\,\epsilon_0} \cdot \dfrac{q}{\left(r^2 + l^2\right)} \text{ along PA}$$

Clearly, $E_A = E_B$ in magnitude.   (1 mark)

E_A and E_B can be resolved into two rectangular components.

Components of E_A

(i) $E_A \cos\theta$ along PX

(ii) $E_A \sin\theta$ along PY

Components of E_B

(i) $E_B \cos\theta$ along PX

(ii) $E_B \sin\theta$ along YP

Vertical components being equal and opposite cancel each other.

Therefore, net electric field intensity along PX

$E = E_A \cos\theta + E_A \cos\theta \quad (\because E_A = E_B)$

$\quad = 2E_A \cos\theta$ along PX

$$= 2 \cdot \dfrac{1}{4\pi\,\epsilon_0} \cdot \dfrac{q}{\left(r^2 + l^2\right)} \cdot \dfrac{1}{\sqrt{r^2 + l^2}}$$ (1 mark)

or, $E = \dfrac{1}{4\pi\,\epsilon_0} \cdot \dfrac{p}{\left(r^2 + l^2\right)^{3/2}}$ along PX $(\because p = q \times 2l)$

If $l << r$ so that it can be neglected, then

$E = \dfrac{1}{4\pi\,\epsilon_0} \cdot \dfrac{p}{r^3}$ along PX

$\therefore \quad E \propto \dfrac{1}{r^3}$ (1 mark)

(b) Equipotential surfaces due to an electric dipole.

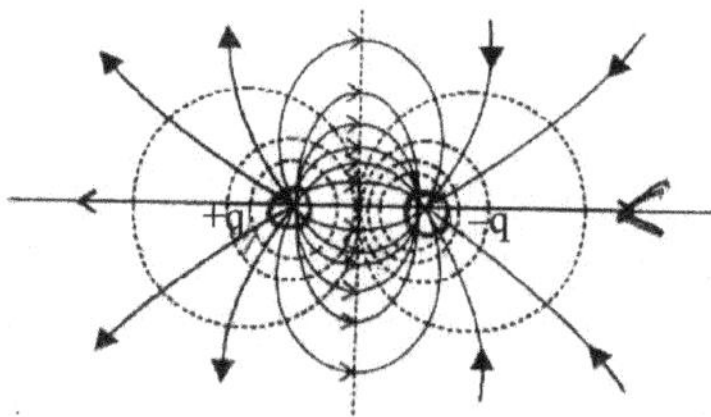

Potential due to the dipole is zero at the line bisecting the dipole length.   (1 mark)

32. Let a charged particle is moving in the magnetic field with a velocity $\vec{v}$ making angle θ with $\vec{B}$.

The component of $\vec{v}$ along $\vec{B}$ is $v\cos\theta$, due to which no force will act on the particle, so it will cover a distance

along the magnetic field with a constant speed.
The perpendicular component v sin θ will provide a force,
F = qBvsinθ which provide the necessary centripetal force
for the circular motion of the charged particle

$$\therefore \quad Bqv\sin\theta = \frac{m(v\sin\theta)^2}{r} \Rightarrow v\sin\theta = \frac{Bqr}{m} \quad \text{(1 mark)}$$

and r = radius of the path $= \dfrac{mv\sin\theta}{Bq}$ (1 mark)

If sin θ = 1, i.e. θ = 90° then $r = \dfrac{mv}{Bq}$ (1 mark)

Angular velocity of rotation of the particle in magnetic

field $\omega = \dfrac{v\sin\theta}{r} = \dfrac{Bq}{m}$

$\therefore$ Time taken to complete one revolution $T = \dfrac{2\pi}{\omega}$

$\Rightarrow \quad T = \dfrac{2\pi m}{Bq}$ (1 mark)

which is independent of its speed.
Under the combined action of both the velocities the
charged particle will undergo a linear as well as a circular
motion. So the resultant path will be a helix. (1 mark)

OR

Consider a straight conductor XY lying in the plane of
paper. Consider a point P at a perpendicular distance '*a*'
from straight conductor.

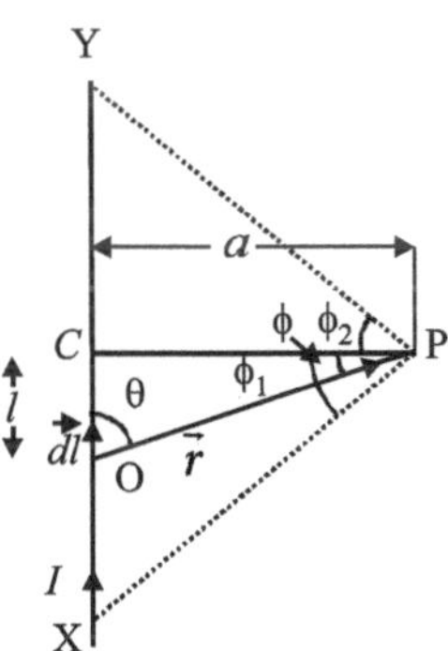

Now Magnetic field induction at a point P due to current
I passing through conductor XY is given by

$$B = \frac{\mu_0 I}{4\pi a}\left[\sin\phi_1 + \sin\phi_2\right] \quad \text{(1 mark)}$$

At the centre of the infinite long wire,

$\phi_1 = \phi_2 = 90°$

$\therefore \quad B = \dfrac{\mu_0 I}{4\pi a}\left[\sin 90° + \sin 90°\right]$

$\Rightarrow \quad B = \dfrac{\mu_0}{4\pi}\dfrac{2I}{a}$ ....(1) (1 mark)

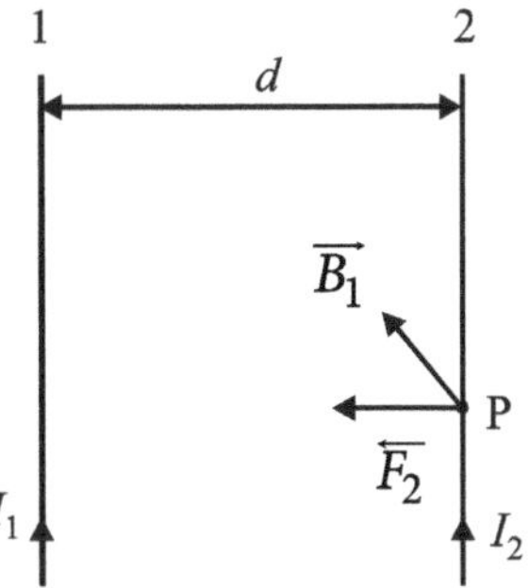

Consider two infinite straight conductors 1 and 2. Let I_1
and I_2 current flowing through the conductor 1 and 2
and they are *d* distance apart from each other.
The magnetic field induction (B) at a point P on
conductor 2 due to current I_1 passing through conductor

1 is given by $B_1 = \dfrac{\mu_0 2I_1}{4\pi d}$

According to right hand rule, the direction of this
magnetic field is perpendicular to the plane of the paper
inward.
Now force experienced (F_2) by unit length of conductor
2 will be F$_2$ = $B_1 I_2 \times 1$ = B$_1 I_2$

$\therefore \quad F_2 = \dfrac{\mu_0}{4\pi}\dfrac{2I_1 I_2}{d}$ (1 mark)

Conductor 1 also experiences the same amount of force,
directed towards the conductor 2. Hence, conductor 1
and conductor 2 attract each other. Thus, two linear
parallel conductors carrying currents in the same direction
attract and repel each other when the current flows in
the opposite direction.
Let $I_1 = I_1 = 1A; r = 1\ m$

Then, $F_1 = F_2 = F = 10^{-7}\ \dfrac{2\times 1\times 1}{1}$

$\Rightarrow \quad F = 2 \times 10^{-7}$ N/m (1 mark)

Definition of one ampere : One ampere is that value of
constant current which when flowing through each of
the two parallel uniform long linear conductors placed in
free space at a distance of 1 m from each other will
attract or repel each other with a force of 2×10^{-7} N per
metre of their length. (1 mark)

33. (a) The phenomenon of spreading of light waves as they
pass through a narrow opening is called diffraction of light.
(1 mark)

(b) In the region of central maximum, the intensity is
maximum because the path difference between the waves
arising from all parts of the slit is zero.

(c) The position of secondary maxima are at θ

$= \left(n+\dfrac{1}{2}\right)\dfrac{\lambda}{a}$ and secondary minima are at θ

$= \dfrac{n\lambda}{a}$

where n = ± 1, ± 2,.... and a is the slit width.

For secondary maxima, consider an angle, $\theta = \dfrac{3\lambda}{2a}$

(by putting n = 1). Now divide the slit into three equal parts. The first two halves of the slits will have a path difference of $\dfrac{\lambda}{2}$. Therefore waves coming out from these two halves will cancel each other. Only the remaining one third of the slit contributes to the intensity at a point between two minima. Consequently the intensity at the secondary maxima becomes less than that of central maximum.

(3 marks)

OR

(i) Consider a point P on the screen at which wavelets travelling in a direction, making angle θ with CO, are brought to focus by the lens.

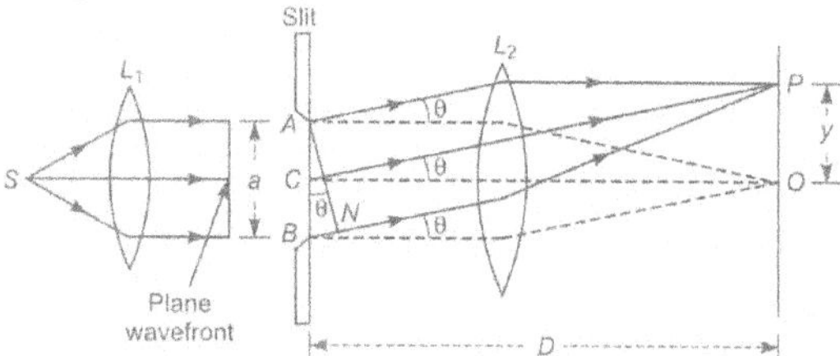

The wavelets from points A and B will have a path difference equal to BN.

From the right-angled ΔANB, we have

BN = AB sin θ

BN = a sin θ ..... (i)   (1 mark)

Suppose, BN = λ and $\theta = \theta_1$

Then, the above equation gives

λ = a sin θ_1

$\Rightarrow \quad \sin\theta_1 = \dfrac{\lambda}{a}$ ..... (ii)

Such a point on the screen will be the position of first secondary minimum.

If, BN = 2λ and $\theta = \theta_2$, then

2λ = a sin θ_2,

$\sin\theta_2 = \dfrac{\lambda}{a}$ ..... (iii)

Such a point on the screen will be the position of first secondary minimum.

In general, for nth minimum at point P,

$\sin\theta_n = \dfrac{n\lambda}{a}$ ..... (iv)   (1 mark)

If y_n is the distance of the nth minimum from the centre of the screen, then from right-angled ΔCOP, we have

$\tan\theta_n = \dfrac{OP}{CO} = \dfrac{y_n}{D}$.   .... (v)

In case of θ_n is small sin $\theta_n \approx \tan\theta_n$

There Eqs, (iv) and (v) are given

$\dfrac{y_n}{D} = \dfrac{n\lambda}{a} \Rightarrow y_n = \dfrac{n\lambda D}{a}$

If, BN = $\dfrac{3\lambda}{2}$ and $\theta = \theta_1'$, then from Eq. (i), we have

$\sin\theta_1' = \dfrac{3\lambda}{2\lambda}$

Such a point on the screen will be the position of the first secondary maximum. Corresponding to path difference.

If, BN = $\dfrac{5\lambda}{2}$ and $\theta = \theta_2'$ the second secondary maximum is produced

In general, for the nth maximum at point P,

$\sin\theta_n' = \dfrac{(2n+1)\lambda}{2a}$ ..... (vi)   (1 mark)

where n = 1, 2, 3, ... an integer.

If y_n is the distance of nth maximum from the centre of the screen, then the angular position of the nth maximum is given by,

$\tan\theta_n' = \dfrac{y_n}{D}$ ..... (vii)

In case of θ_n' is small, $\sin\theta_n' = \tan\theta_n'$

$\Rightarrow \quad Y_n' = \dfrac{(2n+1)\lambda D}{2a}$ For n = 1, $\theta' = \dfrac{3\lambda}{2a}$

[From Eq. (vi), small angle approximation,

$\sin\theta' = \theta' = \dfrac{(2n+1)\lambda}{2a}$]

The angle is midway between the two dark fringes. Divide the slit into three equal parts. If we take the first two-third part of the slit, the path difference between the two ends would be

$\dfrac{2}{3}a \times \theta' = \lambda$

The first two-third is divided into two halves which have path difference $\dfrac{\lambda}{2}$. The contribution due to these two halve is 180° out of phase and gets cancel.   (1 mark)

Only the remaining one-third part of the slit contribute to the intensity at a point between the two minima which will be much weaker than the intensity of central maxima. Thus, with increase in the intensity, the maxima gets weaker.

(ii) (a) Size of central diffraction band is inversely proportional to the slit width i.e., size of central diffraction band $= \dfrac{2\lambda}{d}$ (½ mark)

(b) The light waves are diffracted by the edge of the tiny circular obstacle. These waves interfere constructively at the centre of shadow and appears as bright spot. (½ mark)

34. (i) Given that

$E_1 = -15.6\text{ eV}, E_\infty = 0\text{ eV}.$

Ionization energy of the atom :

$E_\infty - E_1 = 0 - (-15.6\text{ eV}) = 15.6\text{ eV}$

So, ionization potential = 15.6 V   (1 mark)

(ii) For short wavelength limit of the series terminating at $n = 2$, a transition must take place from $n = \infty$ state to n

= 2 state. For this, $\Delta E = 5.30 \, eV$

$$\lambda = \frac{12400}{\Delta E(eV)} \mathring{A} = \frac{12400}{5.30} \mathring{A} = 2339 \mathring{A} \qquad \text{(2 marks)}$$

(iii) The excitation energy for the $n = 3$ state is

$$\Delta E = E_3 - E_1 = 15.6 - 3.08 = 12.52 \, eV$$

Excitation potential $= 12.52 \, V$ $\qquad$ (1 mark)

OR

(iii) $\lambda = \dfrac{12400}{E_3^z - E_1^z} = \dfrac{12400}{12.52} \mathring{A} = 990 \mathring{A}$

Wave number

$$= \frac{1}{\lambda} = \frac{1}{990 \times 10^{-10} \, m} = 1.009 \times 10^7 \, m^{-1}$$

35. (i) Since the south pole of the magnet is approaching towards the loop, so by Lenz's law the induced current in the loop should be in such a direction that it should oppose the approach of the S-pole. So another S-pole should be produced at the near end of the coil. Therefore, the current should be in clockwise direction when viewed from the magnet side. $\qquad$ (2 marks)

(ii) Induced current will be clockwise in both the coils, when viewed from the magnet side as the N-pole is moving away from coil AB so a S-pole should be created at the end B. The S-pole is approching towards CD, hence another S-pole should be produced at the end C to provent its approach. $\qquad$ (1 mark)

(iii) As soon as the switch S is closed, an e.m.f. is induced in the ring R and it is repelled. $\qquad$ (1 mark)

OR

(iii) When the magnet falls, the magnetic flux linked through the metal ring changes, so current is induced in the ring will be in such a direction according to Lenz's law that it opposes the motion of the magnet, so its acceleration will be less than g.

1. **(d)** To get effective capacitance of 6 μF two capacitors of 4 μF each connected in series and one of 4 μF capacitor in parallel with them.

Two capacitors in series

$$\therefore \frac{1}{C} = \frac{1}{C_1} + \frac{1}{C_2} = \frac{1}{4} + \frac{1}{4} = \frac{1}{2}$$

1 capacitor in parallel

$$\therefore C_{eq} = C_3 + C = 4 + 2 = 6\,\mu F \qquad \text{(1 mark)}$$

2. **(c)** Equating magnetic force to centripetal force,

$$\frac{mv^2}{r} = qvB\,\sin 90^\circ$$

Time to complete one revolution,

$$T = \frac{2\pi r}{v} = \frac{2\pi m}{qB} \qquad \text{(1 mark)}$$

3. **(b)** $\dfrac{F}{\ell} = \dfrac{\mu_0 i_1 i_2}{2\pi d} = \dfrac{\mu_0 i^2}{2\pi d}$

(1 mark)

(attractive as current is in the same direction)

4. **(d)** All other statements except (iv) are incorrect. The electric field over the Gaussian surface remains continuous and uniform at every point. (1 mark)

5. **(c)** Current sensitivity of a galvanometer = deflection per unit current. (1 mark)

6. **(c)** Here, $N = 100$
$R = 9$ cm $= 9 \times 10^{-2}$ m, and $I = 0.4$ A

Now, $B = \dfrac{\mu_0 NI}{2R} = \dfrac{2\pi \times 10^{-7} \times 100 \times 0.4}{9 \times 10^{-2}}$

$$= \frac{2 \times 3.14 \times 0.4}{9} \times 10^{-3}$$

$$= 0.279 \times 10^{-3}\,\text{T} = 2.79 \times 10^{-4}\,\text{T} \qquad \text{(1 mark)}$$

7. **(c)** Equipotential surfaces are normal to the electric field lines. The following figure shows the equipotential surfaces along with electric field lines for a system of two positive charges.

(1 mark)

8. **(a)** $n_d \sin i_c = n_r \sin 90^\circ$ ($\because$ From Snell's law)

$$\sin i_c = \frac{n_r}{n_d} = \frac{v_d}{v_r} \quad \left(\therefore v = \frac{c}{n} \right)$$

$$\sin i_c = \frac{1.5 \times 10^8}{2 \times 10^8} = \frac{1.5}{2}$$

$$\sin i_c = \frac{3}{4} \quad \tan i_c = \frac{3}{\sqrt{4^2 - 3^2}} \Rightarrow \frac{3}{\sqrt{7}}$$

The critical angle between them, $i_c = \tan^{-1}\left(\dfrac{3}{\sqrt{7}}\right)$

(1 mark)

9. **(d)** Diffraction on a single slit is equivalent to interference of light from infinite number of coherent sources contained in the slit. (1 mark)

10. **(c)** A slit would give divergent; a biprism would give double; a glass slab would give a parallel wavefront. Edge is downward. (1 mark)

11. **(b)** If $R_1 = R, R_2 = -2R$

$$\frac{1}{f} = (\mu - 1)\left(\frac{1}{R_1} - \frac{1}{R_2} \right)$$

$$\frac{1}{6} = (1.5 - 1)\left(\frac{1}{R} + \frac{1}{2R} \right) = \frac{0.5 \times 3}{2R}$$

$R = 4.5$ cm (1 mark)

12. **(b)** Transition from higher states to $n = 2$ lead to emission of radiation with wavelengths 656.3 nm and 365.0 nm. These wavelengths fall in the visible region and constitute the Balmer series. (1 mark)

13. **(b)** In p-type semiconductor, trivalent impurities are added to intrinsic semiconductor, which creates holes which are majority charge carriers. (1 mark)

14. **(d)** $M_{microscope} \Rightarrow$ decrease
$M_{telescope} \Rightarrow$ increase (1 mark)

15. **(c)** μ_{ferro} is maximum (1 mark)

16. **(c)** $X_L \propto V$ (1 mark)

17. **(a)** Different types of electromagnetic waves have different frequencies. Also, they travel through vacuum with same speed. (1 mark)

18. **(b)** (1 mark)

19. Here, $n = 200, A = 900\,mm^2 = 900 \times 10^{-6}\,m^2, I = 2A, B = 0.5\,T$

(i) Magnetic moment of the coil $M = nIA$
$= 200 \times 2 \times 900 \times 10^{-6} = 36 \times 10^{-2}\,Am^2$ (1 mark)

(ii) Torque acting on the coil $\tau = MB \sin \theta$
$= 36 \times 10^{-2} \times 0.5 \times 0 = 0$ [$\theta = 0^\circ$] (1 mark)

20.

Intrinsic Semiconductor	Extrinsic Semiconductor
1. It is pure semiconducting material and no impurity atoms are added to it.	**1.** It is prepared by doping a small quantity of impurity atoms to the pure semiconducting material.
Examples are crystalline forms of pure silicon and germanium.	Examples are silicon and germanium crystals with impurity atoms of arsenic, antimony, phosphorous etc. or indium, boron, aluminium etc.
2. The number of free electrons in conduction band and the number of holes in valence band is exactly equal and very small indeed.	**2.** The number of free electrons and holes is never equal. There is excess of electrons in n-type semiconductors and excess of holes in p-type semiconductors.
3. Its electrical conductivity is low.	**3.** Its electrical conductivity is high.
4. Its electrical conductivity is a function of temperature alone.	**4.** Its electrical conductivity depends upon the temperature as well as on the quantity of impurity atoms doped in the structure.

(½ × 4 = 2 marks)

21. Potential difference between the plates

$\Delta V = 10 - 0 = 10\ V$ (B is grounded so its potential is zero)

(i) $E = \dfrac{\Delta V}{d} = \dfrac{10}{10^{-2}} = 10^3\ V/m$ (1 mark)

(ii) Plate A is an equipotential surface.

Hence work done in moving a charge of 10 μC from X to Y is zero. (1 mark)

22. Characteristics of electromagnetic waves:

(i) They travel in free space with the same speed equal to $c = 3 \times 10^8$ m/s

(ii) Electromagnetic waves are transverse in nature. Velocity of electromagnetic waves in any medium is given by

$v = \dfrac{1}{\sqrt{\mu\varepsilon}}$,

where μ is the permeability and ε is the permittivity of the medium (2 × 1 = 2 marks)

OR

(i) Microwaves

(ii) Radio waves

(iii) Gamma rays

(iv) X-rays. (½ × 4 = 2 marks)

23. (i) **Lenz's law :** Whenever the magnetic flux linked with a circuit changes, an induced emf is produced and the direction of the induced current is such that it opposes the cause which produces it. (1 mark)

(ii) Yes, emf will be induced in the metallic rod because there will be a change of magnetic flux. The metallic rod will cut the magnetic lines of the earth's magnetic field. (1 mark)

OR

As $\Delta I = -2\ A$

$\Delta t = 10 \times 10^{-3}$ s

$V = 200\ V$

As we know, $e = -L\dfrac{\Delta I}{\Delta t}$

$\therefore 200 = -L\left(\dfrac{-2}{10 \times 10^{-3}}\right)$

$200 = L \times 2 \times 10^2$

$L = 1H$

(2 × 1 = 2 marks)

24. (a) Angular width, $\Delta\theta = \dfrac{\beta}{D} = \dfrac{(\lambda D / d)}{D} = \dfrac{\lambda}{d}$

$\therefore\ d = \dfrac{\lambda}{\Delta\theta} = \dfrac{6000 \times 10^{-10}(m)}{1° \times \pi / 180(rad)}$

$= 3.44 \times 10^{-5}$ m $= 0.0344$ mm (1 mark)

(b) The frequency and wavelength of reflected wave will not change.

The refracted wave will have same frequency.

The velocity of light in water is given by,

$v = \lambda f$ (1 mark)

where, v = velocity of light

λ = wavelength of light

f = frequency of light

If velocity will decrease, wavelength (λ) will also decrease.

25. Here, $\mu = \sqrt{2}$, A = 60°

As, $r_1 + r_2 = A$ for minimum deviation

$r_1 = r_2 = \dfrac{A}{2} = \dfrac{60°}{2} = 30°$ (1 mark)

As, $\mu = \dfrac{\sin i_1}{\sin r_1} = \sqrt{2} \times \sin 30° = \sqrt{2} \times \dfrac{1}{2} = \dfrac{1}{\sqrt{2}}$

$\sin i_1 = \sin 45°\ \therefore i = 45°$ (1 mark)

26. Let a current I flows through the outer coil of radius R. The magnet field at the centre of the coil is

$B = \dfrac{\mu_0 I}{2R}$ (1 mark)

As $r \ll R$, hence B may be considered to be constant over the centre cross-sectional area of inner coil of radius r. Hence, magnetic flux linked with the smaller coil will be

$\phi_1 = BA_1 = \dfrac{\mu_0 I}{2R}\pi r^2$ (1 mark)

As we know, $\phi_1 = M_{12}I_2$

Now mutual inductance $M_{12} = \dfrac{\phi_1}{I_2} = \dfrac{\mu_0 r^2}{2R}$

But, $M_{12} = M_{21} =$ suppose, M

$\therefore \quad M = \dfrac{\mu_0 \pi r^2}{2R}$ (1 mark)

OR

Magnetic field at a point inside the solenoid is $B = \dfrac{\mu_0 NI}{\ell}$

Where N is the total number of turns of the solenoid and l is its length. B is constant throughout the length of the solenoid.

Magnetic flux through each turn = B × area of each turn.

$\therefore \quad \phi_1 = \mu_0 \dfrac{N}{\ell} I \times A$ (1 mark)

where A is the area of each turn.

$\therefore \quad$ Total magnetic flux linked with the solenoid $= \phi$

$= \mu_0 \dfrac{N}{\ell} IA \times N$ (1 mark)

But from the definition of self inductance (L), $\phi = LI$.

$\therefore \quad LI = \mu_0 \dfrac{N}{\ell} IA \times N \Rightarrow L = \dfrac{\mu_0 N^2 A}{\ell}$ (1 mark)

27. E.m.f of a cell is defined as the maximum potential difference between the two electrodes of the cell when no current is drawn from the cell (ie, in open circuit). (1 mark)

The e.m.f of a cell depends upon the nature of electrodes, concentration and nature of electrolyte and its temperature. (1 mark)

Consider a cell of emf E, internal resistance r connected to an external resistor R. Total resistance of the circuit $= R + r$ ....(1)

$\therefore \quad$ Current flowing in the circuit

$I = \dfrac{E}{R+r}$ ....(2)

Potential difference across internal resistance
$r = Ir$ ....(3)

$\therefore \quad$ Terminal potential difference
$V = E - Ir$ ....(4)

or, $V = \dfrac{E}{R+r} R$ (Since $V = IR$) ....(5)

(1 mark)

From (4) we can see that emf is more than potential difference.

28. The electric dipole moment of dipole has the magnitude
$p = ql = 2 \times 10^{-6} \times 10^{-2} = 2 \times 10^{-8}$ C-m (1 mark)

The electric field at the point P on the axis of dipole has the magnitude

$E = \left(\dfrac{1}{4\pi\varepsilon_0}\right)\left(\dfrac{2p}{r^3}\right) = (9\times 10^9)\left(\dfrac{2\times 2\times 10^{-8}}{1^3}\right)$

$= 360$ N/C (1 mark)

The electric field at the point P on the equator of dipole has the magnitude

$E = \left(\dfrac{1}{4\pi\varepsilon_0}\right)\left(\dfrac{p}{r^3}\right) = (9\times 10^9)\left(\dfrac{2\times 10^{-8}}{1^3}\right) = 180$ N/C

(1 mark)

29. Here, $Z = 80$, $KE = K = 8$ MeV
$= 8 \times 10^6 \times 1.6 \times 10^{-19}$ J

$\because \quad$ Energy conservation law,

$K = \dfrac{(Ze)(2e)}{4\pi\varepsilon_0 r_0}$ (1 mark)

where $r_0 =$ distance of closest approach.

$r_0 = \dfrac{2Ze^2}{4\pi\varepsilon_0 (K)}$

$= \dfrac{(9\times 10^9 \times 2\times 80\times 0.6\times 10^{-19})^2}{8\times 10^6 \times 1.6\times 10^{-19}}$

$r_0 = 2.88 \times 10^{-19}$ m $= \dfrac{1}{K}$ (1 mark)

If KE gets doubled, distance of closest approach reduces to half. (1 mark)

OR

Let there be an electron revolving in an orbit of radius 'r' with velocity v. The orbit is equivalent to a magnetic shell of magnetic moment
$M = IA$ ... (i)

(1 mark)

Where I is the current and A is the area of the orbit.
Now, I is given by

$I = \dfrac{e}{T} = \dfrac{ev}{2\pi r}$ ... (ii)

From eqs.(i) and (ii)

$M = \dfrac{ev}{2\pi r} \times \pi r^2 = \dfrac{evr}{2}$ ...(iii)

(1 mark)

According to Bohr's theory angular momentum

$mvr = \dfrac{nh}{2\pi}$ or $vr = \dfrac{nh}{2\pi m}$ ... (iv)

From equations (iii) and (iv),

$M = \dfrac{neh}{4\pi m}$ ... (v)

For the ground state $n = 1$

Therefore magnetic moment, $M = \dfrac{eh}{4\pi m}$ (1 mark)

30. Density of water $= 10^3$ kg/m$^3 = \rho_w$

Density of a nucleon $= \dfrac{mass}{volume} = \rho_n$

$\rho_n = \dfrac{m}{\dfrac{4}{3}\pi R_0^3} = \dfrac{1.67\times 10^{-27}}{\dfrac{4}{3}\times 3.14\times (1.2\times 10^{-15})^3}$

(1 mark)

$= \dfrac{1.67\times 10^{-27}}{4.185\times 1.2\times 1.2\times 1.2\times 10^{-45}}$

$$= \frac{1.67}{7.23} \times 10^{18} = 0.23 \times 10^{18} = 23 \times 10^{16} \qquad \text{(1 mark)}$$

$$\text{Ratio } \frac{\rho_n}{\rho_w} = \frac{23 \times 10^{16}}{10^3} = 23 \times 10^{13} = 2.3 \times 10^{14}. \qquad \text{(1 mark)}$$

31. (a) Let there be an electric dipole of length $2a$ and having charges $+q$ and $-q$. We have to find potential on the axial line at point P at a distance $OP = x$ from the centre O of the dipole.

Potential at point P

$$V = \frac{1}{4\pi\varepsilon_0} \frac{q}{x-a} + \frac{1}{4\pi\varepsilon_0} \frac{-q}{x+a} \qquad \text{(1 mark)}$$

$$\text{or} \quad V = \frac{q}{4\pi\varepsilon_0}\left(\frac{1}{x-a} - \frac{1}{x+a}\right)$$

$$= \frac{q}{4\pi\varepsilon_0}\left(\frac{2a}{x^2-a^2}\right)$$

$$V = \frac{p}{4\pi\varepsilon_0\left(x^2-a^2\right)} \quad (\because p = q \times 2a) \qquad \text{(1 mark)}$$

(b) When there is no dielectric, then capacitance

$$C = \frac{\varepsilon_0 lb}{d}$$

For the first capacitor, capacitance

$$C' = \frac{K\varepsilon_0 lb}{d} = KC \qquad \qquad \text{... (i)}$$
$$\text{(1 mark)}$$

In second case two capacitors connected in parallel

$$C_1 = \frac{K_1\varepsilon_0 lb}{2d} \text{ and } C_2 = \frac{K_2\varepsilon_0 lb}{2d}$$

$$\therefore \quad C'' = C_1 + C_2 = \frac{K_1\varepsilon_0 lb}{2d} + \frac{K_2\varepsilon_0 lb}{2d}$$

$$\text{or} \quad C'' = C\frac{(K_1+K_2)}{2} \qquad \qquad \text{.....(ii)}$$
$$\text{(1 mark)}$$

If the capacitance in each case be same, then from equ.(i) and (ii)

$$K = \left(\frac{K_1+K_2}{2}\right) \qquad \text{(1 mark)}$$

OR

This work is stored as P.E. of the capacitor.

$$C_0 = \frac{\varepsilon_0 A}{d}, \quad C = \frac{k \in_0 A}{d} \text{ and } Q = C_0 V$$

$$\text{Here, } C = 10\,C_0 \qquad (\because k = 10)$$

$$\therefore \quad Q' = CV = 10Q \qquad \text{(2 marks)}$$

(i) $E = \dfrac{V}{d}$, as potential (V) and distance between the plates (d) is not changed, E also does not change. (1 mark)

(ii) $E_{\text{initial}} = \dfrac{1}{2}C_0 V^2$

$$E_{\text{final}} = \frac{1}{2}(10 C_0)V^2 = 10 \times \frac{1}{2}C_0 V^2$$

$$= 10 E_{\text{initial}} \qquad \text{(2 marks)}$$

32. (a) When light wave is incident on photoelectric material, the photoelectrons should be emitted (after a long time) if work function is large. But no photoelectron is emitted by incident radiations if the frequency is less than the threshold frequency. The energy of the ejected electrons also has no relevance with the intensity of incident light, although according to the wave nature, it should be there. If the light is incident for a longer interval of light, the energy should also have increased. That is why photoelectric effect is not explained on the basis of wave nature of light. (2 marks)

(b) Basic features of photon picture :

(i) A photon of frequency ν is a packet of energy $E = h\nu$, where h is a planck's constant.

(ii) While interacting with matter photons behave as if they are all particles.

(iii) All photons travel in vacuum with the same velocity. However, their velocity in different media is different.

(iv) There is no charge on a photon. They are not deflected by electric and magnetic fields.

(v) The energy of a photon does not depend upon the intensity of radiation.

(vi) When it interacts with a photoelectric material, it is completely absorbed and loses its identity.

(vii) Its collisions with the electron in the photoelectric material is elastic i.e., total energy and momentum are conserved during the collision. (3 marks)

OR

Einstein's photoelectric equation

$$h\nu = h\nu_0 + \frac{1}{2}mv^2$$

$$h\nu = h\nu_0 + eV_s, \qquad \text{(1 mark)}$$

where v is the velocity of the ejected electrons and V_s is the stopping potential.

This equation is based on the following properties of photons:

(i) A photon is a packet of energy. It frequency and h plank's constant.

(ii) When a photon is incident on a photoelectric material, it is completely absorbed by the electron. The energy of the photon is used in ejecting electron and the balance if any is used up in imparting kinetic energy to the electron.
$$(\tfrac{1}{2} \times 2 = 1 \text{ mark})$$

Two important observation which can be explained by the equation :

(i) The photoelectric emission takes place only if the incident light has a frequency greater than the threshold frequency v_0. If $v < v_0$, then $\frac{1}{2}mv^2$ will be –ve, which is not possible. Hence, electron will not be emitted. (1 mark)

(ii) When the frequency of the incident light increases, then $\frac{1}{2}mv^2$ i.e., kinetic energy of electron increases because work function $= hv_0$ is fixed. With increase in frequency more and more energy is available to the electron ejected and hence stopping potential also increases.

According to the photoelectric equation.

$$K_{max} = \frac{1}{2}mv_{max}^2 = hv - \phi_o$$

$$K_{max} = \frac{hc}{\lambda_1} - \phi_0 \ \dots\dots (i)$$

Let the maximum kinetic energy for the wavelength of the incident λ_2 be K_{max}

$$K_{max} = \frac{hc}{\lambda_2} - \phi_0 \ \dots\dots (ii) \qquad \text{(1 mark)}$$

From equations (i) and (ii) we have

$$\frac{hc}{\lambda_2} - \phi_0 = 2\left(\frac{hc}{\lambda_1} - \phi_0\right)$$

$$\Rightarrow \ \phi_0 = hc\left(\frac{2}{\lambda_1} - \frac{1}{\lambda_2}\right) \Rightarrow hv_0 = hc\left(\frac{2}{\lambda_1} - \frac{1}{\lambda_2}\right)$$

$$\Rightarrow \ \frac{c}{\lambda_0} = c\left(\frac{2}{\lambda_1} - \frac{1}{\lambda_2}\right) \Rightarrow \frac{1}{\lambda_0} = \left(\frac{2}{\lambda_1} - \frac{1}{\lambda_2}\right)$$

$$\Rightarrow \ \lambda_0 = \frac{\lambda_1\lambda_2}{2\lambda_2 - \lambda_1} \qquad \text{(1 mark)}$$

33. (a) The necessary conditions to obtain sustained interference fringes are:

(i) The two sources of light must be coherent.

(ii) The two sources should preferably be monochromatic.

(iii) The coherent sources must be very close to each other. (1 mark)

(b) The fringe width in Young's double slit experiment is given by

$$\beta = \frac{\lambda D}{d}$$

where λ = wavelength of source

D = distance between the slits and screen

d = distance between the slits

$$\Rightarrow \ \beta \propto D \qquad \text{(1 mark)}$$

The variation of fringe width with distance of screen from the slits is given by the graph shown below:

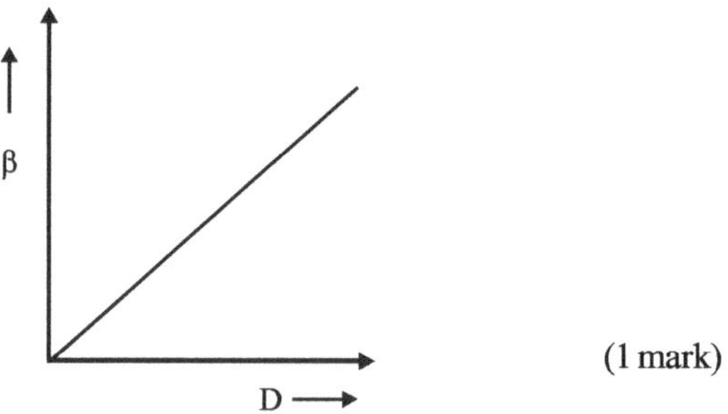

(1 mark)

It is a linear graph with slope equal to λ/d, So. for the fringe width to vary linearly with distance of screen from the slits, the ratio of wavelength to distance between the slits should remain constant. Therefore, it is advised to take wavelengths of incident light nearly equal to the width of the slit. (1 mark)

(c) Fringe width is given by

$$\beta = \frac{\lambda D}{d}$$

Hence, if the distance between the slits is reduced then the width of the fringes increases. (1 mark)

OR

(a)

	Diffraction		Interference
1	The diffraction pattern has a central bright maximum which is twice as wide as other maxima.	1	The interference has a number of equally spaced bright and dark bands
2	The diffraction pattern is a superposition of waves originating from each point on a single slit.	2	The interference pattern is due to the superposition of waves emanating from the two narrow slits.

$(2 \times 1 = 2 \text{ marks})$

(b) Given: $a = 1 \times 10^{-4}$ m, $D = 1.8$ m,

$\lambda_1 = 590$ nm $= 590 \times 10^{-9}$ m,

$\lambda_2 = 596$ nm $= 596 \times 10^{-9}$ m

To obtain first maxima, phase difference,

$$a\sin\theta = (2n+1)\frac{\lambda}{2} \qquad \text{(1 mark)}$$

for $n = 1$ $a\sin\theta = 3\frac{\lambda}{2}$

or $a \cdot \frac{y}{D} = 3\frac{\lambda}{2} \Rightarrow y = \frac{3}{2}\lambda\frac{D}{a}$ (1 mark)

Separation between the positions of the first maxima

$$= y_2 - y_1 = \frac{3}{2}\frac{D}{a}\lambda_2 - \frac{3}{2}\frac{D}{a}\lambda_1 \qquad = \frac{3}{2}\frac{D}{a}(\lambda_2 - \lambda_1)$$

$$= \frac{3}{2} \times \frac{1.8}{1 \times 10^{-4}} \times (596 - 590) \times 10^{-9}$$

$$= 16.2 \times 10^{-5}\,\text{m} \hspace{3cm} \text{(1 mark)}$$

34. (i) Av. electric field energy (1 mark)

$$= \left(\frac{1}{2}CV_{rms}^2\right) = 25 \times 10^{-3}\,\text{J}$$

$$\therefore \quad \frac{1}{2}C \times (I_{rms}X_C)$$

$$\therefore \quad \frac{1}{2} \times C.I_{rms}^2 \times \frac{1}{4\pi^2 v^2 c^2} = 25 \times 10^{-3}\,\text{J}$$

$$\therefore \quad C = 20\mu F \hspace{3cm} \text{(1 mark)}$$

(ii) Av. magnetic energy $\left(\dfrac{1}{2}LI_{rms}^2\right)$

$$\therefore \quad L = \frac{2 \times 5 \times 10^{-3}}{(.10)^2} \Rightarrow L = 1\,\text{henry} \hspace{1cm} \text{(1 mark)}$$

(iii) The sum for rms voltage across C, rms voltage across R and rms voltage across L is not equal to rms voltage across ideal ac source. (1 mark)

OR

(iii) At resonance inpedence Z = R

35. (i) $V_B = I\,(R_D + R)$ (1 mark)

$$\Rightarrow 5 = 1 \times 10^{-3}\left(\frac{0.7}{10^{-3}} + R\right)$$

$$\Rightarrow R = 4.3\,k\Omega$$

(ii) $V_B = I\,(R_D + R)$ (1 mark)

$$\Rightarrow 5 = 5 \times 10^{-3}\left(\frac{0.7}{5mA} + R\right)$$

$$\Rightarrow 1\,k\Omega = 180\Omega + R$$

$$\Rightarrow R = 860\Omega \hspace{2cm} \text{(1 mark)}$$

(iii) Power $= VI = (6 - 0.7) \times 5 \times 10^{-3}$ W

$$= 26.4\,\text{mW} \hspace{3cm} \text{(1 mark)}$$

OR

(iii) p-n junction diode

1. **(b)** We have $E_a = \dfrac{2kp}{r^3}$ and $E_e = \dfrac{kp}{r^3}$; $\therefore E_a = 2E_e$

(1 mark)

2. **(b)** At equipotential surface, every point has same potential. So, potential difference is zero. (1 mark)

3. **(b)** The charge particle will follow helical path if its velocity vector makes an angle other than 0° or 90° (1 mark)

4. **(d)** The ratio of intensity of magnetisation and magnetising field is called magnetic susceptibility.

(1 mark)

5. **(b)** $\theta = \dfrac{NiAB}{C} \Rightarrow \theta \propto N$ [Number of turns]

(1 mark)

6. **(b)** $F \propto i_1 i_2$, so force on B due to C will be greater than that due to A. Hence net force on B acts towards C.

(1 mark)

7. **(b)** In normal adjustment,

$M = \dfrac{f_0}{f_e} = 20$, $f_e = \dfrac{f_0}{20} = \dfrac{60}{20} = 3$ cm (1 mark)

8. **(c)** de-Broglie's relation, $\lambda = \dfrac{h}{p}$

momentum $p = \sqrt{2mE}$

$\Rightarrow \lambda = \dfrac{h}{\sqrt{2mE}} = \dfrac{h}{\sqrt{2mK}}$ $(\because E = K)$ (1 mark)

9. **(c)** Nucleus does not contain electron. (1 mark)

10. **(a)** Focal length of lens

$\dfrac{1}{f} = (\mu - 1)\left(\dfrac{1}{R_1} - \dfrac{1}{R_2}\right)$ (1 mark)

11. **(c)** We use the formula,
$R = R_0 A^{1/3}$
This represents relation between atomic mass and radius of the nucleus.
For berillium, $R_1 = R_0 (9)^{1/3}$
For germanium, $R_2 = R_0 A^{1/3}$
$\dfrac{R_1}{R_2} = \dfrac{(9)^{1/3}}{(A)^{1/3}} \Rightarrow \dfrac{1}{2} = \dfrac{(9)^{1/3}}{(A)^{1/3}}$

$\Rightarrow \dfrac{1}{8} = \dfrac{9}{A} \Rightarrow A = 8 \times 9 = 72$. (1 mark)

12. **(b)** In case of Proton-Proton Electrostatic repulsive force is also present which reduces the net force. (1 mark)

13. **(c)** (1 mark)

14. **(d)** $\dfrac{I_{max}}{I_{min}} = \dfrac{25}{9}$ or $\left(\dfrac{a_1 + a_2}{a_1 - a_2}\right)^2 = \dfrac{25}{9}$

where a denotes amplitude.

$\dfrac{a_1 + a_2}{a_1 - a_2} = \dfrac{5}{3}$ or $5a_1 - 5a_2 = 3a_1 + 3a_2$

or, $5a_1 - 5a_2 = 3a_1 + 3a_2$ or $2a_1 = 8a_2$

or, $\dfrac{a_1}{a_2} = 4$ or $\left(\dfrac{a_1}{a_2}\right)^2 = 16 = \dfrac{I_1}{I_2}$. (1 mark)

15. **(d)** $\because \sin\theta = \dfrac{1.22\lambda}{D}$, where D is opening diameter.

When opening size diameter of the pinhole is increased, the diffraction size decreases but intensity increases.

(1 mark)

16. **(d)** The photoelectric current depends on the intensity of light. (1 mark)

17. **(b)** According to Bohr's model, when the electron is in one of its stationary circular orbits, it does not radiate energy, hence the atom is stable. (1 mark)

18. **(c)** Only moving charge particle produces magnetic field.

(1 mark)

19. (i) Interference arises due to the superposition of waves from two coherent sorces. Diffraction pattern is obtained due to waves arising from different parts of the same wavefront.

(ii) In intereference pattern, all the bright fringes are of the same intensity. However, in the diffraction pattern, all bright fringes are not of the same intensity. $(2 \times 1 = 2 \text{ marks})$

20. $C_o = \dfrac{\varepsilon_0 A}{d} = \dfrac{8.85 \times 10^{-12} \times 6 \times 10^{-3}}{3 \times 10^{-3}}$

$= 17.7 \times 10^{-12} = 17.7$ pF
$Q = C_0 V = 17.7 \times 10^{-12} \times 100$
$= 17.7 \times 10^{-10}$ C.

(a) $C = k C_0 = 6 \times 17.7 = 106.2$ pF. (1 mark)

(b) After the voltage supply is disconnected
$Q = 17.7 \times 10^{-10}$ C.
$C = 106.2 \times 10^{-12}$ F

$V = \dfrac{Q}{C} = \dfrac{17.7 \times 10^{-10}}{106.2 \times 10^{-12}} = 0.166 \times 10^2$

$= 166.6$ volt. (1 mark)

21. (a) Reverse biased as P-crystal of the diode is earthed i.e., at lower potential and N-crystal is at higher potential (5V)

(b) **P-N junction diode as a full wave rectifier :** The circuit uses two diodes connected to the ends of a centre tapped transformer. The voltage rectified by the two diodes is half of the secondary voltage i.e., each diode conducts for half cycle of input but alternately so that net output across load comes as half sinusoids with positive values only.

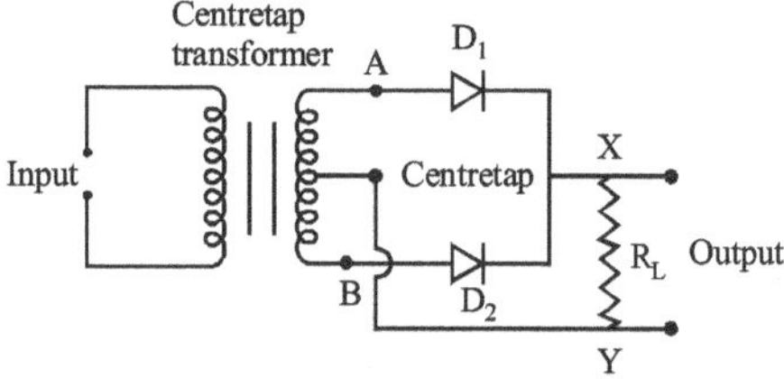

For positive cycle diode D_1 conducts (FB) but D_2 is being out of phase is reverse biased and does not conduct. Thus output across R_L is due to D_1 only. In negative cycle of input D_1 is R.B. but D_2 is F.B. and conducts as with respect to centretap point A is negative but B is positive. Hence output across R_L is due to D_2.

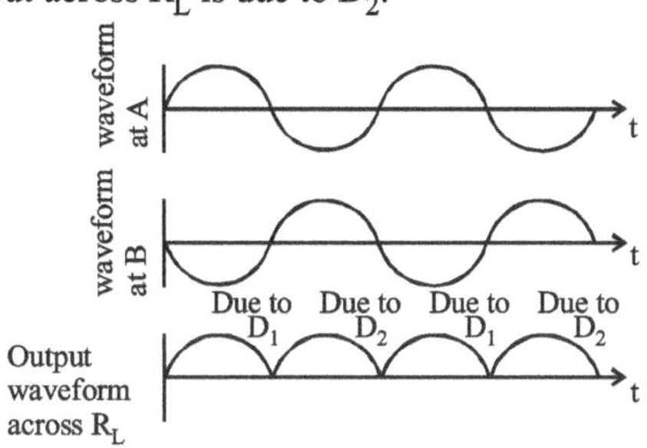

(2 marks)

OR

(i) Width of depletion layer's decreases in forward bias.
(ii) Width depletion layer increases in reverse bias.

(2 marks)

22. Given : $h = 60$ cm, $\mu = 4/3 = 1.33$, $A = \pi r^2 = ?$,

$$\frac{\sin\theta_c}{\sin 90°} = \frac{1}{\mu} \quad \therefore \sin\theta_c = \frac{1}{\mu}$$

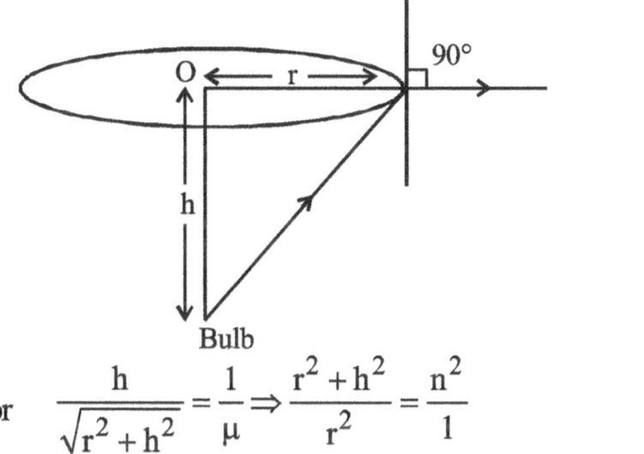

or $\quad \dfrac{h}{\sqrt{r^2+h^2}} = \dfrac{1}{\mu} \Rightarrow \dfrac{r^2+h^2}{r^2} = \dfrac{n^2}{1}$

$\Rightarrow \quad 1 + \dfrac{h^2}{r^2} = \mu^2 - 1 \Rightarrow r^2 = \dfrac{h^2}{\mu^2 - 1}$

or, $\quad r = \dfrac{h}{\sqrt{\mu^2 - 1}}$ (1 mark)

$\therefore \quad r = \dfrac{60}{\sqrt{(1.33)^2 - 1}} = 70.3\,\text{cm}$

Therefore, area of the surface of water through which light comes out
$A = \pi r^2 = 3.14 \times (70.3)^2 = 1.55\,\text{m}^2$ (1 mark)

23. Since threshold voltage is 0.7 V, the diode doesn't conduct till then. Again, it doesn't conduct after voltage falls to 0.7V. The half wave rectification would be, (1 mark)

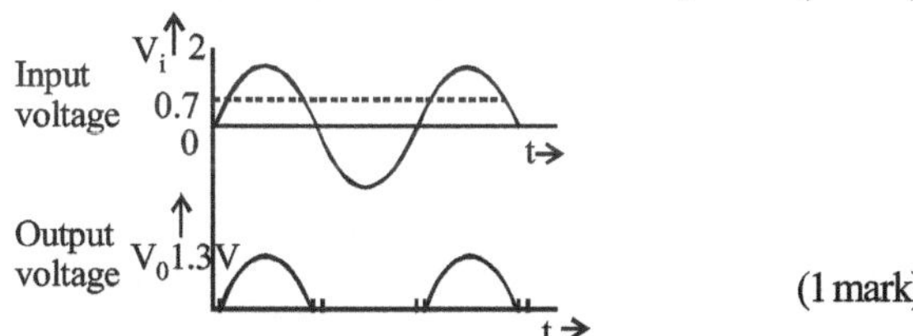

(1 mark)

24. The angle of deviation δ for a ray of light in a prism is given by
$$\delta = i + e - A$$

where $\quad i$ = Angle of incidence of ray
$\quad e$ = Angle of emergence and
$\quad A$ = Angle of prism

$\Rightarrow \delta = 2i - A \quad (\because e = i)$

Given : $\quad i = e = \dfrac{3}{4}A$ (1 mark)

$\therefore \delta = 2 \times \dfrac{3}{4}A - A = \dfrac{1}{2}A$

As the prism is equilateral, $\angle A = 60°$

$\therefore \delta = \dfrac{1}{2} \times 60° = 30°$ (1 mark)

OR

According to Snell's Law, we know $\quad \mu = \dfrac{1}{\sin C}$

$\therefore \dfrac{c}{v} = \dfrac{1}{\sin C} \quad \left(\because \mu = \dfrac{C}{V}\right)$

$\Rightarrow v = \sin C \times c \Rightarrow v = \sin 45° \times 3 \times 10^8$

$\Rightarrow v = 2.12 \times 10^8$ (1 mark)

Therefore, speed of light in the medium is 2.12×10^8 ms^{-1}. We know that the critical angle of the medium depends on its refractive index and the refractive index μ of a medium is inversely proportional to the wavelength of incident light. So, the critical angle of the medium also depends upon the wavelength of incident light. (1 mark)

25. In an electromagnetic wave, the electric field vector, the magnetic field vector and the wave propagation vector are perpendicular to each other. So, if the wave propagation vector is along Z-direction, then electric field vector can be along X-direction and the magnetic field vector will be along Y-direction. (1 mark)

$\therefore \quad$ Wavelength $= \lambda = \dfrac{c}{v} = \dfrac{3 \times 10^8}{12 \times 10^6} = 10$ m.

(1 mark)

26. Production of induced e.m.f. in a coil due to the change of current in a neighbouring coil, is called mutual induction.

(1 mark)

Suppose a current i is passed through the inner solenoid S_1. A magnetic field $B = \mu_0 n_1 i$ is produced inside S_1, whereas the field outside it is zero.

The flux through each turn S_2 is
$$B\pi r_1^2 = \mu_0 n_1 i\pi r_1^2$$ (1 mark)

The total flux through all the turns in a length l of S_2 is
$$\phi = (\mu_0 n_1 i\pi r_1^2)n_2 l = (\mu_0 n_1 n_2 \pi r_1^2 l)i$$
$$\Rightarrow M = \mu_0 n_1 n_2 \pi r_1^2 l$$ (1 mark)

OR

No e.m.f. will be produced between the ends of a metallic pole falling vertically through the plane of magnetic meridian as the falling pole does not cut any magnetic lines of force. (3 marks)

27. The average time difference between two successive collisions of drifting electrons inside the conductor under the influence of electric field is known as relaxation time.

(1 mark)

Drift speed and relaxation time are related as:

$$V_d = -\frac{eE\tau}{m}$$

As current $I = -ne\,Av_d$

$$I = -neA\left(-\frac{eE\tau}{m}\right)$$

$$I = \frac{ne^2 A\tau}{m}\left(\frac{V}{l}\right)\left(\because E = \frac{V}{l}\right) \qquad \text{(1 mark)}$$

$$\Rightarrow \quad \frac{V}{I} = \frac{ml}{ne^2 A\tau} = \rho\frac{l}{A} = R$$

$$\rho = \frac{m}{ne^2\tau} \qquad \text{(1 mark)}$$

28. (i) Stopping potential = 0 at a higher frequency for B. Hence, it has a higher work function.

(1 mark)

(ii) $\text{Slope} = \dfrac{h}{e} = \dfrac{2}{(10-5)\times10^{14}}$ for A.

$$= \frac{2.5}{(15-10)\times10^{14}} \text{ for B.} \qquad \text{(1 mark)}$$

$$h = \frac{1.6\times10^{-19}}{5}\times2\times10^{-14} = 6.04\times10^{-34}\,\text{Js for A}$$

$$= \frac{1.6\times10^{-19}\times2.5\times10^{-14}}{5} = 8\times10^{-34}\,\text{Js for B}$$

Since h works out differently, experiment is not consistent with the Einstein's theory. (1 mark)

29. (i) As, radius of electron's nth orbit in hydrogen atom

$$r_n = \frac{\varepsilon_0 h^2}{\pi m e^2}n^2 \;\Rightarrow\; r_n \propto n^2 \qquad \text{(1½ marks)}$$

(ii) Also, the total energy of an electron belonging to nth orbits,

$$E_n = -\frac{me^2}{8\varepsilon_0^2 n^2 h^2} \;\Rightarrow\; |E_n| \propto \frac{1}{n^2} \qquad \text{(1½ marks)}$$

i.e., total energy of electron increases as $\dfrac{1}{n^2}$.

OR

Basic assumption of Rutherford atomic model are given below

(i) Atom consists of small central core, called atomic nucleus in which whole mass and positive charge is assumed to be concentrated.

(ii) The size of the nucleus is much smaller than size of the atom.

(iii) The nucleus is surrounded by electrons. Atoms are electrically neutral as total negative charge of electrons surrounding the nucleus is equal to total positive charge on the nucleus.

(iv) Electrons revolves around the nucleus in various circular orbits and necessary centripetal force is provided by electrostatic force of attraction between positively charged nucleus and negatively charged electrons.

(2 marks)

Stability of atom : When an electron revolves around the nucleus, then it radiates electromagnetic energy and hence, radius of orbit of electron decreases gradually. Thus, electron revolve on spiral path of decreasing radius and finally, it should fall into nucleus, but this does not happen. Thus, Rutherford atomic model cannot account for stability of atom. (1 mark)

30. **Conductors :** (i) In conductors, the valence band is completely filled and the conduction band is either partially filled with an extremely small energy gap between the valence and conduction bands or empty, with the two bands overlapping each other.

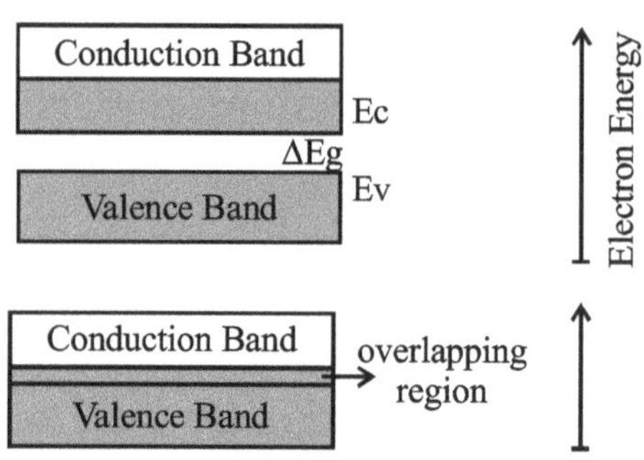

(ii) On applying an even small electric field, conductors can conduct electricity. (1 mark)

Semiconductors: (i) In semiconductors the energy band structure is similar to that of insulators, but in this case, the size of forbidden energy gap is much smaller than that of the insulators, as shown,

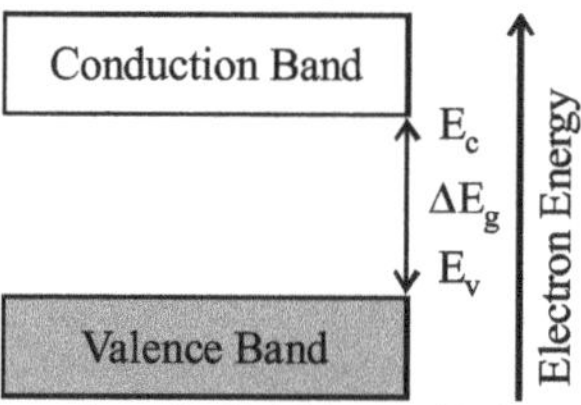

(ii) When an electric field is applied to a semiconductor, the electrons in the valence band find it comparatively easier to shift to the conduction band. So, the conductivity of semiconductors lies between the conductivity of conductors and insulators. (1 mark)

Insulators: (i) In insulators, the energy gap between the conduction and valence band is very large. Also, the conduction band is practically empty.

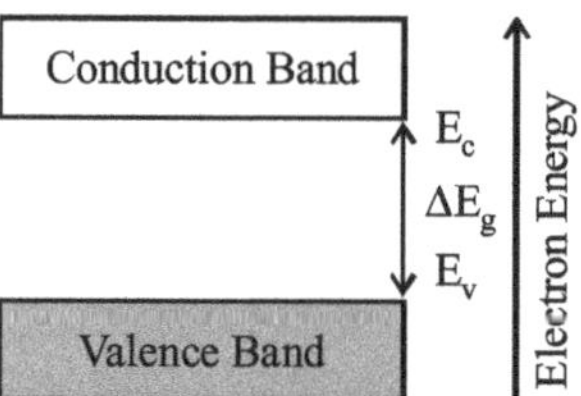

(ii) When an electric field is applied across such a solid, the electrons find it difficult to acquire such a large amount of energy to reach the conduction band. Thus, conduction band continues to be empty. That is why no current flows through insulators. (1 mark)

31. Gauss's law states that the total electric flux through a closed surface is equal to $\dfrac{1}{\varepsilon_0}$ times the charge enclosed by it.

i.e., $\phi = \dfrac{q}{\varepsilon_0}$ (1 mark)

Now, the electric field $E = Cx\hat{i}$ is in X-direction only. So faces with surface vector perpendicular to this field would give zero electric flux i.e., $\phi = E\,ds\cos 90° = 0$,
So, flux would be due to only two surfaces,

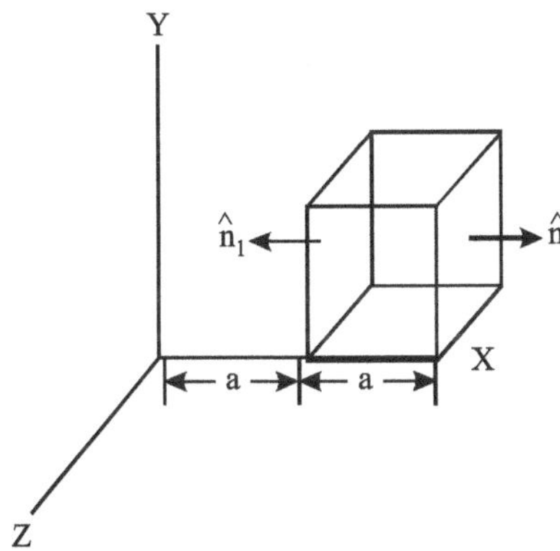

Magnitude of E at left face
$E_L = Cx = Ca$ [x = a at left face]
Magnitude of E at right face
$E_R = Cx = C2a = 2aC$ [x = 2 a at right face]
     (1 mark)

Thus,

$\phi_L = E_L \cdot dS$

$= -aC \times a^2 = -a^3 C$ [As $\theta = 180°$]

$\phi_R = E_R \cdot dS = 2aC\,dS\,\cos\theta$

$= 2aCa^2 = 2a^3 C$ (1 mark)

(i)   Net flux through cube is

     $= \phi_L + \phi_R$

     $= -a^3 C + 2a^3 C$

     $= a^3 C \; N\text{-}m^2 C^{-1}$ (1 mark)

(ii)   Net charge inside the cube
     By Gauss's law

     $\phi = \dfrac{q}{\varepsilon_0}$

     $q = a^3 C\varepsilon_0$ (1 mark)

OR

(i)   Given : $\vec{E} = 20x\,\hat{i}$
     $A = 20\,cm^2 = 20 \times 10^{-4}\,m^2$

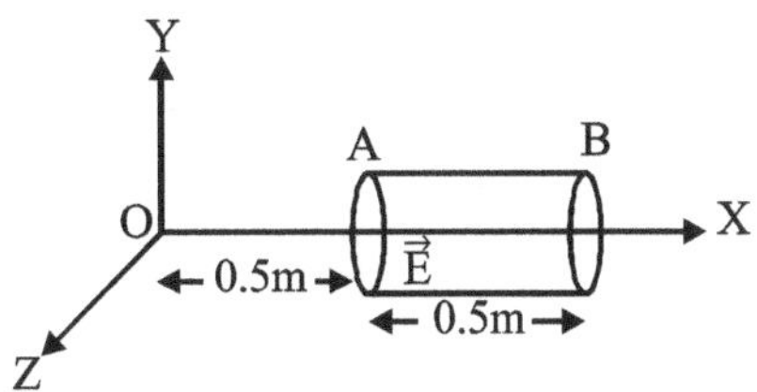

Since the electric field $\vec{E} = 20x\,\hat{i}$ is directed along the x-axis, there is no any flux across curved surface.   (1 mark)
Flux through the face A of the cylinder

$\phi_1 = \oint \vec{E} \cdot \overrightarrow{ds}$

$= Es \cos 180°$

$= 20 \times 0.5 \times (-1) \times 20 \times 10^{-4}$

$= -200 \times 10^{-4} = -2 \times 10^{-2}\,NC^{-1}\,m^2$ (1 mark)

Flux through the face B of the cylinder

$\phi_2 = \oint \vec{E} \cdot \overrightarrow{ds}$

$= EA \cos \theta$

$= 20 \times 20 \times 10^{-4} \times 1$

$= 400 \times 10^{-4}\,NC^{-1}\,m^2$

$= 4 \times 10^{-2}\,NC^{-1}\,m^2$ (1 mark)

Therefore net flux through the cylinder   (1 mark)

$\phi = \phi_1 + \phi_2$

$= 4 \times 10^{-2} - 2 \times 10^{-2}$

$= 2 \times 10^{-2}\,NC^{-1}\,m^2$ (1 mark)

(ii)   According to Gauss's theorem

     $\phi = \int \vec{E} \cdot \overrightarrow{ds} = \dfrac{Q}{\epsilon_0}$

or, $2 \times 10^{-2} = \dfrac{Q}{\epsilon_0}$

or, $Q = 2 \times 10^{-2} \times 8.854 \times 10^{-12} = 1.7708 \times 10^{-3}$ C

Hence the charge enclosed by the cylinder is
1.7708×10^{-13} C   (1 mark)

32. The variation of current with angular frequency for the two resistances R_1 and R_2 shown in the graph below.

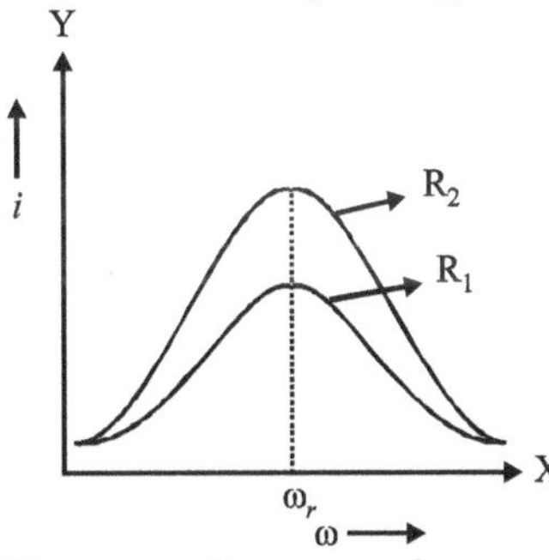

Here, $\omega_r =$ Resonance frequency   (2 marks)

(a) From the graph, we can see that resonance for the resistance R_2 is sharper than for R_1 because resistance R_2 is less than resistance R_1. Therefore, at resonance, the value of peak current will rise more abruptly for a lower value of resistance. (1 mark)

(b) Power associated with the resistance is given by

$$P = E_v I_v \qquad \text{(1 mark)}$$

From the graph, we can say that the current in case of R_2 is more than the current in case of R_1. Hence, the power dissipation in case of the circuit with R_2 is more than that with R_1. (1 mark)

OR

In a series LCR circuit, the impedance of the circuit is given by $Z = \sqrt{\left(L\omega - \dfrac{1}{c\omega}\right)^2 + R^2}$, where ω is the angular frequency. Clearly, as ω varies Z also varies and hence the current also varies. At a certain frequency (resonant frequency) $\omega = \omega_0$, Z becomes minimum and the current becomes maximum.

Plot showing variation of current with frequency:

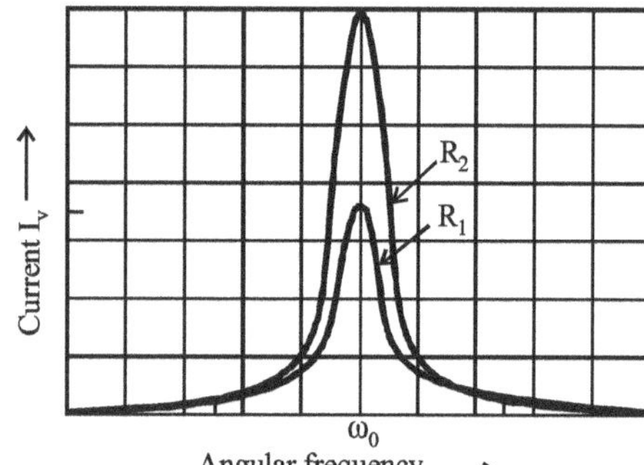

(2 marks)

Current at resonance

$$i_v = \frac{E_v}{Z} = \frac{E_v}{R} \quad \left(\text{as } L\omega_0 = \frac{1}{C\omega_0}\right) \qquad \text{(1 mark)}$$

Smaller the value of R_2, sharper the resonance curve.

Q-factor of the circuit is defined as the ratio of inductive reactance at resonance to the resistance R in the circuit (1 mark)

$$\text{i.e., } Q = \frac{L\omega_0}{R} = \frac{1}{C\omega_0 R} \quad \text{i.e., } Q \propto \frac{1}{R}$$

Significance of Q-factor : The Q-factor of an LCR circuit is a measure of the sharpness of the resonance. Larger the value of Q-factor sharper is the resonance curve. (1 mark)

33. Distance between the two sources

$$d = 0.15 \text{ mm} = 1.5 \times 10^{-4} \text{ m}$$

Wavelength, $\lambda = 450 \text{ nm} = 4.5 \times 10^{-7} \text{ m}$

Distance of screen from source, $D = 1 \text{ m}$

(i) (a) The distance of nth order bright fringe from central fringe is given by $y_n = \dfrac{Dn\lambda}{d}$

For second bright fringe, $y_2 = \dfrac{2D\lambda}{d}$

$$y_2 = \frac{2 \times 1 \times 4.5 \times 10^{-7}}{1.5 \times 10^{-4}} = 6 \times 10^{-7+4}$$

$$y_2 = 6 \times 10^{-3} \text{ m}$$

The distance of the second bright fringe $y_2 = 6 \text{ mm}$ (2 marks)

(b) The distance of nth order dark fringe from central fringe is given by $y_n' = (2n-1)\dfrac{D\lambda}{2d}$

For second dark fringe $n = 2$

$$y_n' = (2 \times 2 - 1)\frac{D\lambda}{2d} = \frac{3D\lambda}{2d}$$

$$= \frac{3}{2} \times \frac{1 \times 4.5 \times 10^{-7}}{1.5 \times 10^{-4}}$$

The distance of the second dark fringe, $y_n' = 4.5 \text{ mm}$ (2 marks)

(ii) With increase of D, fringe width increases as

$$\beta = \frac{D\lambda}{d} \text{ or } \beta \propto D \qquad \text{(1 mark)}$$

OR

(a) Let XY be the surface separating the denser medium and the rarer medium. Let:

v_1 = Speed of lightwave in the denser medium

v_2 = Speed of light wave in the rarer medium

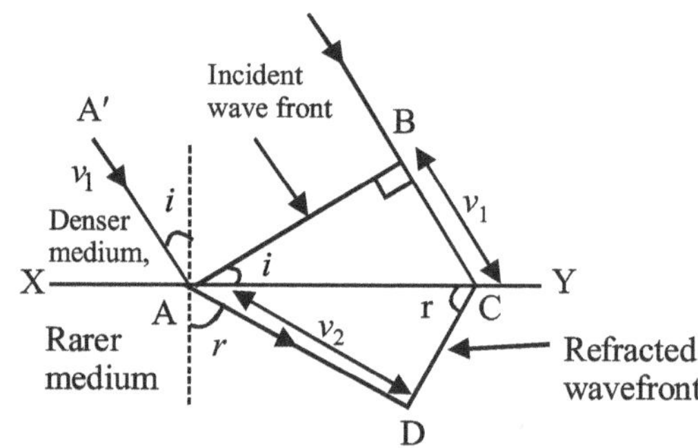

(2 marks)

Let us consider a plane wavefront AB. Let this wavefront incident on the interface at an angle of incidence i.

Let t be the time taken by the wavefront to travel the distance BC in denser medium.

$$\Rightarrow \quad BC = v_1 t$$

To determine the shape of refracted wavefront, we will draw a sphere of radius $v_2 t$ from point A in the rarer medium. Let CD represent a tangent plane drawn from point C onto the sphere.

Now, $\quad AD = v_2 t$

Here, CD would represent the refracted wavefront. Considering the triangles ABC and ADC, we get

$$\sin i = \frac{BC}{AC} = \frac{v_1 t}{AC} \qquad\qquad \text{(1 mark)}$$

$$\sin r = \frac{AD}{AC} = \frac{v_2 t}{AC}$$

$$\Rightarrow \quad \frac{\sin r}{\sin i} = \frac{v_2}{v_1} \qquad ....(1) \qquad \text{(1 mark)}$$

Since $r > i$, the speed of light in the rarer medium (v_2) will be greater than the speed of light in the denser medium (v_1).

Now, $\mu_1 = \dfrac{c}{v_1}$; $\mu_2 = \dfrac{c}{v_2}$

where

μ_1 = Refractive index of denser medium

μ_2 = Refractive index of rarer medium

Further, (1) can be written as $\mu_1 \sin i = \mu_2 \sin r$

This is the Snell's law of refraction. (1 mark)

34. (i) Drift velocity $v_d = \dfrac{\rho E \tau}{m}$

With increase in temperature, relaxation time (τ) decreases.

$\therefore$ Drift velocity also decreases. (1 mark)

(ii) $|v_d| = \dfrac{eE\tau}{m} = \dfrac{e\tau}{m} \cdot \dfrac{V}{\ell}$ when l is doubled, the drift speed becomes half. (1 mark)

(iii) $v_d = \dfrac{eE\tau}{m} = \dfrac{e\tau}{m}\left(\dfrac{V}{\ell}\right) \qquad \therefore v_d \propto V$

$\therefore$ Drift velocity will be double if the voltage becomes 2V. (2 marks)

OR

(iii) Let n be the number of free electrons per unit volume of the conductor.

Volume of the conductor = $A\ell$

Number of free electrons of the conductor = n

Total free charge of the conductor = $nA\ell e$, where e is the charge of an electron.

If t be the time taken to cover a distance ℓ by this change,

then $t = \dfrac{\ell}{v_d}$

$\therefore \quad I = \dfrac{q}{t} = \dfrac{nAe\ell}{\ell / v_d} = nAev_d \Rightarrow v_d = \dfrac{I}{enA} \quad \therefore v_d \propto I$

(2 marks)

35. (i) (i) $L = \mu_0 \dfrac{N^2}{\ell} A \qquad \therefore L \propto N^2$

If number of turns (N) of one coil is decreased, self inductance (L) also decreases.

(ii) If an iron core is introduced in the coil, the permeability (μ) increases. So self inductance also increases. (1 mark)

(ii) Self-inductance $L \propto N^2$, so when the number of turns is doubled, self-inductance will become 4 times. (1 mark)

(iii) Iuduced e.m.f. $= e = -L\dfrac{di}{dt}$

$$\therefore \quad L = \left|\dfrac{e}{di / dt}\right| = \dfrac{40 \times 10^{-3}}{2}$$
$$= 20 \times 10^{-3}\,H = 20\,\text{mH}. \qquad \text{(2 marks)}$$

OR

(iii) Relative permeability $\mu_r = \dfrac{L_{medium}}{L_{air}} = \dfrac{10\,\text{mH}}{0.01\,\text{mH}} = 1000.$

(2 marks)

1. **(d)** Force, $F = qVB = \dfrac{mv^2}{R}$ $\therefore R = \dfrac{mv}{Bq}$ (1 mark)

2. **(a)** Magnetic susceptibility χ for dia-magnetic materials only is negative and low $|\chi| = -1$; for paramagnetic substances low but positive $|\chi| = 1$ and for ferromagnetic substances positive and high $|\chi| = 10^2$. (1 mark)

3. **(b)** Wattless current flow in a circuit only when circuit is resistanceless i.e. circuit is purely capacitive or inductive. (1 mark)

4. **(c)** Field at the center of a circular coil of radius r is

$$B = \dfrac{\mu_0 I}{2r}$$ (1 mark)

5. **(c)** Radio waves has the longest wavelength in the electromagnetic spectrum. (1 mark)

6. **(a)** $\dfrac{f_0}{f_e} = 9$, $\therefore f_0 = 9 f_e$

Also $f_0 + f_e = 20$ ($\because$ final image is at infinity)

$9f_e + f_e = 20$, $f_e = 2$ cm, $\therefore f_0 = 18$ cm (1 mark)

7. **(c)** Converging spherical (1 mark)

8. **(a)** The energy in electromagnetic wave is divided equally between the electric and magnetic field.

So, in an electromagnetic wave, half of the intensity is provided by the electric field and half by the magnetic field.

Hence, required ratio should be 1 : 1. (1 mark)

9. **(a)** Wavefront is the locus of all points, where the particles of the medium vibrate with the same phase. (1 mark)

10. **(c)** $I_{max} = I + 4I + 2\sqrt{I \times 4I} = 9I$,

and $I_{min} = I + 4I - 2\sqrt{I \times 4I} = I$. (1 mark)

11. **(d)** $qV = \dfrac{1}{2}mv^2$ or $mv = \sqrt{2qVm}$;

So $\lambda = \dfrac{h}{mv} = \dfrac{h}{\sqrt{2qVm}}$ i.e., $\lambda \propto \dfrac{1}{\sqrt{qm}}$;

so $\dfrac{\lambda_p}{\lambda_\alpha} = \sqrt{\dfrac{q_\alpha m_\alpha}{q_p m_p}} = \sqrt{2 \times 4} = 2\sqrt{2}$ (1 mark)

12. **(b)** $R = R_0(A)^{1/3}$

$\therefore \dfrac{R_1}{R_2} = \left(\dfrac{A_1}{A_2}\right)^{1/3} = \left(\dfrac{27}{125}\right)^{1/3} = \dfrac{3}{5}$

$R_2 = \dfrac{5}{3} \times 3.6 = 6$ fermi (1 mark)

13. **(d)** $E = \Delta m.c^2 \Rightarrow E = \dfrac{0.3}{1000} \times (3 \times 10^8)^2 = 2.7 \times 10^{13} J$

$= \dfrac{2.7 \times 10^{13}}{3.6 \times 10^6} = 7.5 \times 10^6 \, kWh.$ (1 mark)

14. **(d)** 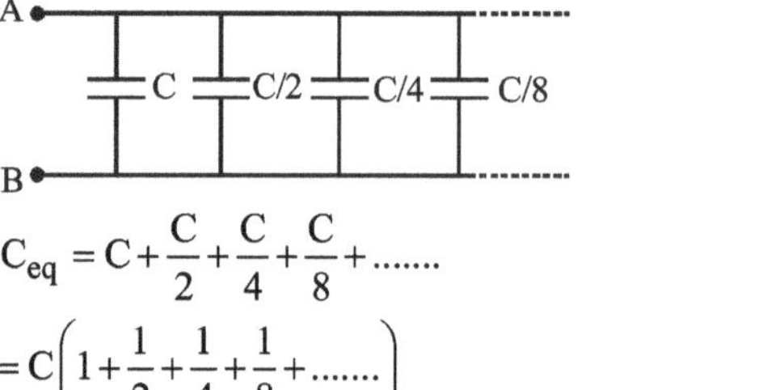

In forward bias, $V_1 > V_2$ i.e., in figure (d) p-type semiconductor is at higher potential w.r.t. n-type semiconductor. (1 mark)

15. **(b)** 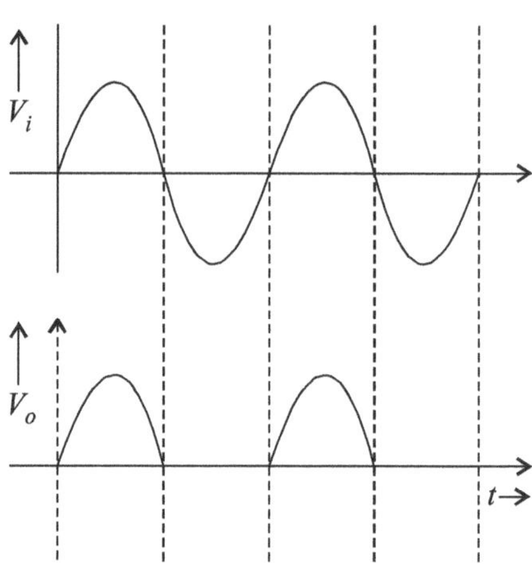

We can see from graph, of input and output of Half Wave Ractifier

$T_{input} = T_{output} \Rightarrow f_{input} = f_{output}$ $\left[\because T = \dfrac{1}{f}\right]$ (1 mark)

16. **(c)** Electric field at any point depends on presence of all charges. (1 mark)

17. **(c)** Diffraction takes place for all types of wave. (1 mark)

18. **(a)** Maximum number of bright fringe is inversely proportional to wavelength of light used. (1 mark)

19. **(i)** Magnetic field at centre due to circular current carrying coil (B) $= \dfrac{\mu_0 NI}{2r}$ (1 mark)

(ii) Magnetic moment $M = NIA = NI(\pi r^2)$

$M = \pi NIr^2$ (1 mark)

20. Combining the capacitances in series in the each branch between the points A and B and then, combining them in parallel, we get

$C_{eq} = C + \dfrac{C}{2} + \dfrac{C}{4} + \dfrac{C}{8} + \dots$

$= C\left(1 + \dfrac{1}{2} + \dfrac{1}{4} + \dfrac{1}{8} + \dots\right)$

$= C\left(\dfrac{1}{1 - 1/2}\right) = 2C = 2\mu F$ (2 marks)

OR

Let the potential difference across the plates of a parallel plate capacitor be V and d is the distance between them

A = area of the plates

Then electric field E_0 between them is given by

$$E_0 = \dfrac{V}{d} = \dfrac{Q}{A\epsilon_0}$$

When a slab of thickness $t = \dfrac{2}{3}d$ and dielectric constant K is introduced between the plates

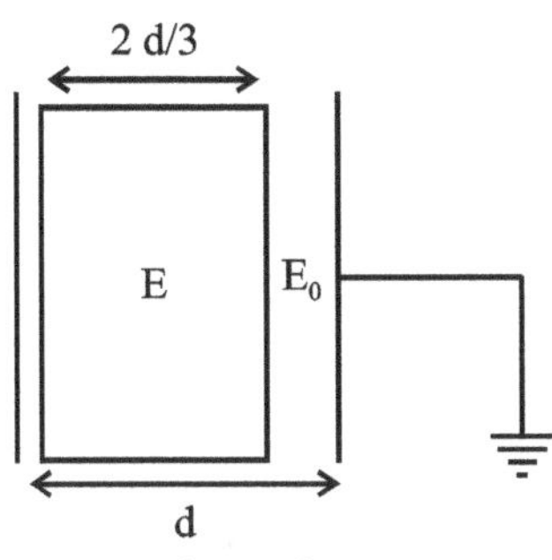

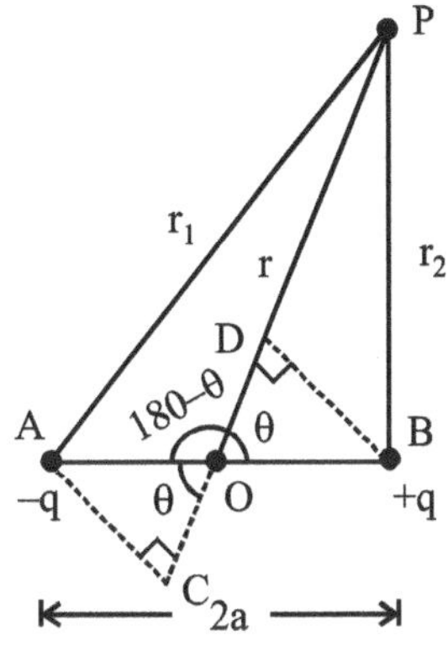

Then $V = E_0\left(d - \dfrac{2d}{3}\right) + E \times \dfrac{2d}{3}$ (1 mark)

$$= E_0\,\dfrac{d}{3} + \dfrac{E_0}{K}\,\dfrac{2d}{3} = E_0\,\dfrac{d}{3}\left[1 + \dfrac{2}{K}\right]$$

or $V = \dfrac{Q}{A\,\epsilon_0}\,\dfrac{d}{3}\left[1 + \dfrac{2}{K}\right]$ $\left(\because E_0 = \dfrac{Q}{A\,\epsilon_0}\right)$

Therefore capacitance

$$C = \dfrac{Q}{V} = \dfrac{3A\,\epsilon_0}{d\left(1 + \dfrac{2}{K}\right)}$$ (1 mark)

This is the required expression.

21. The masses of the three isotopes are 19.99u, 20.99u and 21.99u.

Their abundance are 90.51%, 0.27% and 9.22%

$\therefore$ Average atomic mass of neon is

$$\dfrac{90.51 \times 19.99 + 0.27 \times 20.99 + 9.22 \times 21.99}{90.51 + 0.27 + 9.22}$$

$$= \dfrac{2017.7}{100} = 20.17\,u.$$ (2 marks)

22. Here, $r = 30\,\Omega$, $R = 970\,\Omega$, $V_{rms} = 50V$,

$V_0 = \sqrt{2}\,V_{rms} = \sqrt{2} \times 50 = 70.7V$

Max. load current $I_0 = \dfrac{V_0}{r+R} = \dfrac{70.7}{30+970}$

$$= \dfrac{70.7}{1000} = 70.7 \times 10^{-3}\,A = 70.7\,mA.$$ (1 mark)

(i) Mean load current,

$$I_m = \dfrac{2I_0}{\pi} = \dfrac{2 \times 70.7\,mA}{3.14} = 45\,mA$$ (½ mark)

(ii) r.m.s. value of load current,

$$I_{rms} = \dfrac{I_0}{\sqrt{2}} = \dfrac{70.7}{\sqrt{2}} = \dfrac{70.7}{1.414} = 50\,mA.$$ (½ mark)

23. Let P be the point where the potential due to the dipole has to be calculated.

Dipole moment $= p = q \times 2a$

$OP = r$, $\angle BOP = \theta$; $AP = r_1$, $BP = r_2$

Draw $AC \perp PO$ produced and $BD \perp PO$.

In $\triangle AOC$, $\cos\theta = \dfrac{OC}{OA} = \dfrac{OC}{a}$

$\therefore$ $OC = a\cos\theta$ and $OD = a\cos\theta$

$\therefore$ Potential at P due to $AB = V$

$$= \dfrac{kq}{r_2} - \dfrac{kq}{r_1} = kq\left[\dfrac{1}{r_2} - \dfrac{1}{r_1}\right]$$ (1 mark)

$r_1 = AP \simeq CP = OP + OC = r + a\cos\theta$;

$r_2 = BP = DP = OP - OD = r - a\cos\theta$

$\therefore$ $V = kq\left[\dfrac{1}{r - a\cos\theta} - \dfrac{1}{r + a\cos\theta}\right]$

$$= kq\left[\dfrac{r + a\cos\theta - r + a\cos\theta}{r^2 - a^2\cos^2\theta}\right]$$

$$= \dfrac{kq \times 2a\cos\theta}{r^2 - a^2\cos^2\theta} = \dfrac{kq \times 2a\cos\theta}{r^2 - a^2\cos^2\theta}$$

$$= \dfrac{kp\cos\theta}{r^2 - a^2\cos^2\theta},$$

where $p = 2aq$ = dipole moment

When P lies on the axial line of the dipole

$\theta = 0°$, $\cos\theta = 1$

$\therefore$ $V = \dfrac{kp}{r^2 - a^2}$ If $a \ll r$, $V = \dfrac{kp}{r^2}$

When P lies on the equatorial line of the dipole, $\theta = 90°$, $\cos 90° = 0$ $\therefore V = 0.$ (1 mark)

OR

The torque acting on a dipole placed in a uniform electric field at an angle θ is

$\tau = pE\sin\theta$

(i) When the dipole is parallel to the field, $\overrightarrow{p}$ is along $\overrightarrow{E}$

$\therefore$ $\theta = 0$

$\therefore$ $\tau = pE\sin\theta = 0$ (1 mark)

(ii) When the dipole is perpendicular to the field is perpendicular to $\overrightarrow{E}$

$\therefore$ $\theta = 90°$

$\therefore$ Torque acting on it is maximum .

$\therefore$ $\tau_{max} = pE$ (1 mark)

24. (a) The necessary conditions for the phenomenon of total internal reflection to occur are :

(i) The light rays must pass from the denser medium to rarer medium.

(ii) The angle of incidence in the denser medium must be greater than the critical angle C.   ($\frac{1}{2} \times 2 = 1$ mark)

(b) If $^a\mu_b$ is the refractive index of the denser medium (b) w.r.t. the rarer medium (a) and C be the critical angle, then

$$^a\mu_b = \frac{1}{\sin C} \qquad \text{(1 mark)}$$

25. (a) Since, the current and the voltage are in phase in X so X is resistance and in Y current leads the voltage by $\pi/2$ so it is capacitor.   (1 mark)

(b) In X, resistance $= R = \dfrac{V}{I} = \dfrac{220}{0.5} = 440\ \Omega$

$\because$ The current is same through Y for the same voltage, so the reactance of Y is same as that of X.

$$X_C = 440\ \Omega$$

For series combination of X and Y, Impedance

$$= Z = \sqrt{R^2 - X_C^2} = \sqrt{440^2 + 440^2} = 440\sqrt{2}$$

$\therefore$ Current through the series combination,

$$I = \frac{V}{Z} = \frac{220}{440\sqrt{2}} = \frac{220\sqrt{2}}{440 \times 2} = \frac{\sqrt{2}}{4} = \frac{1.414}{4}$$

$$= 0.35\ A \qquad \text{(1 mark)}$$

26. The equivalent circuit is

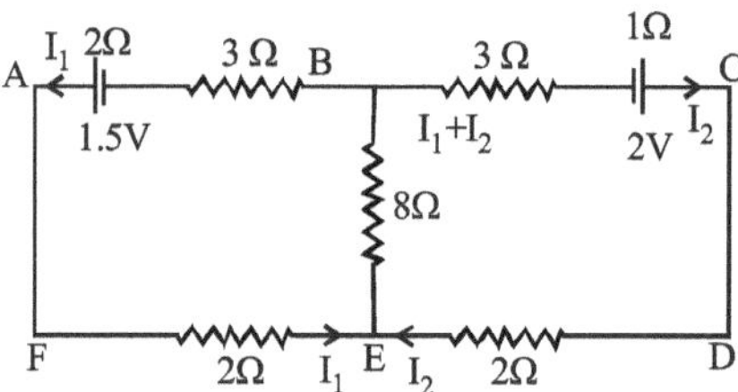

For the loop ABEFA,

$$-1.5 = -(2 + 3 + 2)I_1 - 8(I_1 + I_2)$$

$$\frac{15}{10} = 7I_1 + 8I_1 + 8I_2$$

$$\Rightarrow\ 15I_1 + 8I_2 = \frac{15}{10}\ ....(1) \qquad \text{(1 mark)}$$

For the loop BCDEB,

$$2 = (3 + 1 + 2)I_2 + 8(I_1 + I_2)$$

$$2 = 6I_2 + 8I_1 + 8I_2 \Rightarrow 8I_1 + 14I_2 = 2$$

$$\Rightarrow\ 4I_1 + 7I_2 = 1 \qquad ....(2) \qquad \text{(1 mark)}$$

Solving we get $I_1 = \dfrac{5}{146}$ A and $I_2 = \dfrac{9}{73}$ A

$\therefore$ Potential difference across $8\ \Omega\ (I_1 + I_2)$

$$= 8\left(\frac{5}{146} + \frac{9}{73}\right) = 8 \times \frac{23}{146} = \frac{92}{73}\ V. \qquad \text{(1 mark)}$$

27.

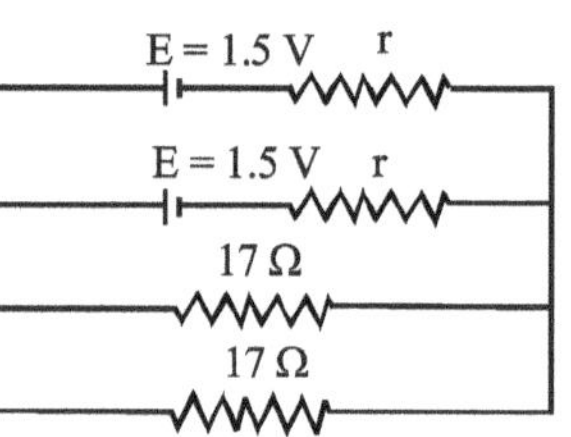

Let the internal resistance of each cell is r.

E = 1.5 volt, V = 1.4 volt.

The equivalent resistance of two 17 Ω in parallel is

$$R = \frac{17 \times 17}{17 + 17} = \frac{17}{2} = 8.5\ \Omega \qquad \text{(1 mark)}$$

$$\therefore\quad I = \frac{E}{R + \dfrac{r}{2}} \text{ and } V = IR$$

$$\therefore\quad R + \frac{r}{2} = \frac{E}{I} = \frac{ER}{V} \qquad \text{(1 mark)}$$

$$\therefore\quad \frac{r}{2} = \frac{E}{V}R - R = \left(\frac{E}{V} - 1\right)R$$

$$\Rightarrow\ r = 2\left(\frac{E}{V} - 1\right)R = 2\left(\frac{1.5}{1.4} - 1\right)8.5 = 1.21\ \Omega. \text{ (approx.)}$$

$$\text{(1 mark)}$$

OR

(i)

For detailed circuit ABCFA / FCDEF:

$$\text{(1 mark)}$$

(ii) Applying Kirchhoff's 1st law at point F,

$$I_1 + I_2 = I_3 \qquad .....(1)$$

For the loop ABCFA, applying Kirchhoff's 2nd law, $12 - 6 = -1I_1 + 2I_2$

$$\Rightarrow\ 6 = 2I_2 - I_1 \ ....(2)$$

For the loop FCDEF applying Kirchhoff's 2nd law,

$$-12 = -2I_2 - 15I_3$$

$$12 = 2I_2 + 15(I_1 + I_2)$$

$$12 = 2I_2 + 15I_1 + 15I_2$$

$$12 = 15I_1 + 17I_2 \qquad .....(3)$$

Solving we get, $I_1 = -\dfrac{78}{47}$ A, $I_2 = \dfrac{102}{47}$ A and

$$I_3 = \frac{24}{47}\ A$$

Potential difference across the 15 Ω resistance

$$= 15 \times I_3 = 15 \times \frac{24}{47} = 7.66\ V. \qquad \text{(2 marks)}$$

28. (i) The central bright fringe is white.

(ii) When the source is moved closer to the double-slits, the interference pattern becomes less sharp and if the source is too close to the slits the fringes disappear.

(iii) Due to the increase in the widths of the two slits, the brightness of fringes increase.   ($3 \times 1 = 3$ marks)

29. According to Bohr's theory of hydrogen atom, energy of photon released, $E_2 - E_1 = h\nu$

Given, $E_1 = -1.151\,\text{eV}$

$$E_2 = -0.85$$
$$E_2 - E_1 = -0.85 - (-1.51) = 1.51 - 0.85$$
$$E_2 - E_1 = 0.66\,\text{eV}$$
$$\therefore \quad E = E_2 - E_1 = 0.66\,\text{eV} \qquad \text{(1 mark)}$$

So, the wavelength of emitted spectral line,

$$\lambda = \frac{1242\,\text{eV} - nm}{E\,(\text{in eV})} = \frac{1242\,\text{eV} - nm}{0.66\,\text{eV}}$$

$$\lambda = 1.88 \times 10^{-6}\,\text{m} \qquad \text{(1 mark)}$$

As here, $\lambda = 1.88 \times 10^{-6}\,\text{m} \approx 18751 \times 10^{-10}\,\text{m}$

The wavelength belongs to Paschen series of hydrogen spectrum. (1 mark)

30. In an intrinsic semiconductor, each of the 4 valence electrons is between two atoms (Si or Ge) in a shared covalent bond. It is bound at low temperatures, but at high temperatures it can pick thermal energy and move out of the valence band and into the interstitial space. This electron is free to conduct. The vacancy left behind by it is called a **hole** and it also conducts charge.

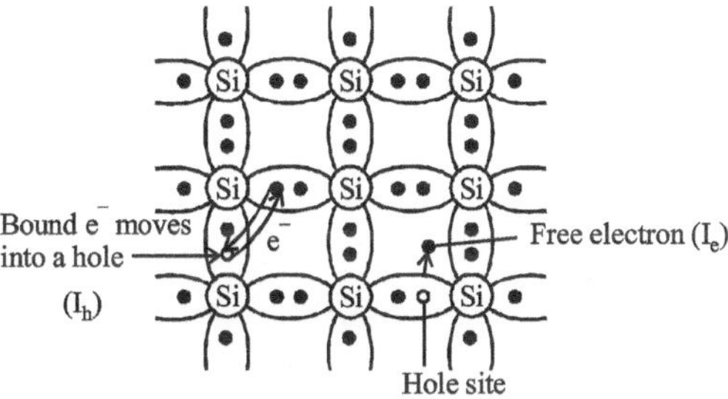

Another electron from a different band can come and occupy this vacancy, hence creating a vacancy elsewhere and causing motion of bound electrons. These holes move towards the negative potential giving rise to hole current I_h. The total current I, is sum of hole current I_h and electron current I_e. (3 marks)

OR

$$1\,\text{ppm} = 1\,\text{part per million} = \frac{1}{10^6}$$

$$\therefore \quad \text{No. of As atoms} = \frac{5 \times 10^{28}}{10^6} = 5 \times 10^{22}/\text{m}^3 \quad \text{(1 mark)}$$

One As atom gives one free electron.

$$\therefore \quad n_e = 5 \times 10^{22}/\text{m}^3$$

Now $n_i^2 = n_e\,n_h \Rightarrow n_h = \dfrac{n_i^2}{n_e} = \dfrac{(1.5 \times 10^{16})^2}{5 \times 10^{22}}$ (1 mark)

(intrinsic Si concentration $= 1.5 \times 10^{16}/\text{m}^3$)

$$\Rightarrow \quad n_h = 4.5 \times 10^9/\text{m}^3. \qquad \text{(1 mark)}$$

31. The resistivity of the material of a conductor is defined as the resistance of unit length and unit area of cross-section of the conductor. The S. I unit of resistivity is ohm metre (Ωm).

Resistivity of a material, $\rho = \dfrac{m}{ne^2\tau}$ or $\rho \propto \dfrac{1}{n\tau}$ Where m is

the mass of electron, n is the number density of electron and τ is the average relaxation time. This shows that the resistivity is related to two parameters of the material namely n and τ. (2 marks)

The variation of resistivity with temperature is different in different materials.

(i) For metallic conductors

The temperature dependence of resistivity of a metal is given by the relation,

$$\rho = \rho_0[1 + \alpha(T - T_0)] \qquad ......(1)$$

Where ρ and ρ_0 are the resistivity at temperature T and T_0 respectively and α is called temperature coefficient of resistivity.

$$\therefore \quad \alpha = \frac{\rho - \rho_0}{\rho_0(T - T_0)} = \frac{d\rho}{\rho_0} \cdot \frac{1}{dT} \quad ......(2)$$

The resistivity of a conductor increases with increase in temperature since α is positive. The variation of resistivity of copper with temperature is as shown.

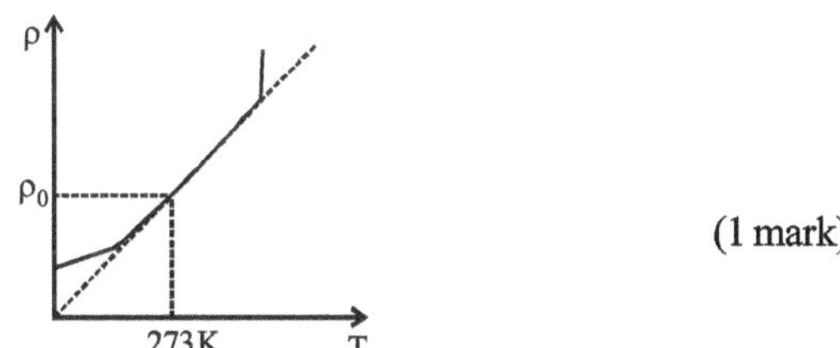

(1 mark)

(ii) For Semiconductors

For Semiconductors, the resistivity decreases as temperature increases since the value of α is negative.

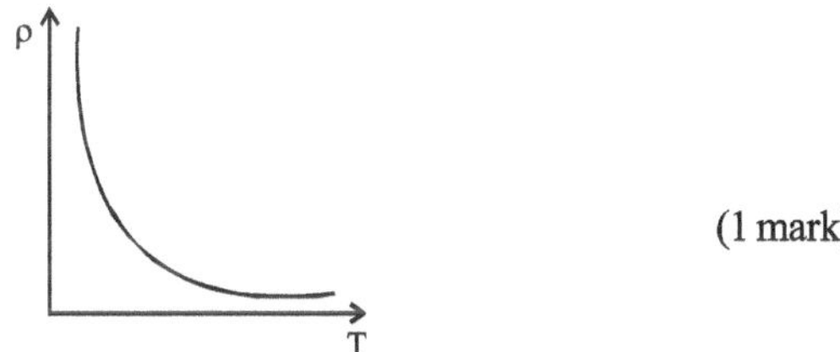

(1 mark)

(iii) For insulators

The resistivity increases exponentially with decrease in temperature. It becomes infinitely large at temperatures near absolute zero. (1 mark)

OR

(i) Kirchhoff's Ist rule or junction rule The algebraic sum of electric currents at any junction of electric circuit is equal to zero i.e.,

Kirchhorff's IInd rul or Voltage Law in any closed mesh of electrical circuit, the algebraic sum of emfs of cells and the product of currents and resistances is always equal to zero.

i.e., $\sum E + \sum IR = 0$

(ii) Let $6I$ current be drawn from the cell. Since the paths AA', AD and AB are symmetrical, current through them is same. ($2 \times 1 = 2$ marks)

As per Kirchhoff's junction rule, the current distribution is shown in the figure.

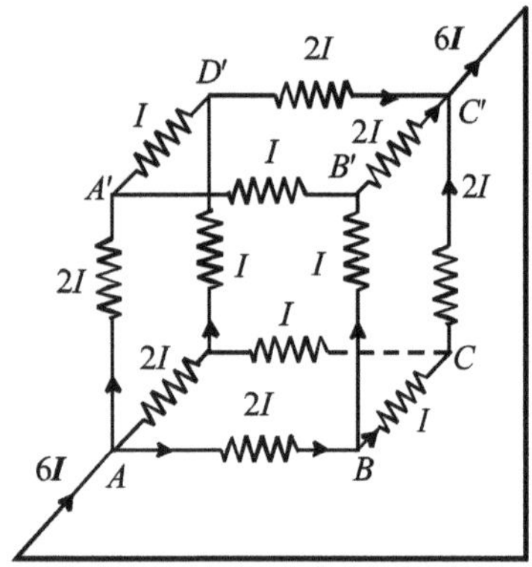

Let the equivalent resistance across the combination be R.

$$E = V_A - V_B = (6I)R \Rightarrow 6IR = 10 \quad [\because E = 10V] \quad \ldots(i)$$

(1 mark)

Applying Kirchhoff's second rule in loop $AA'B'C'A$

$$-2I \times 1 - I \times 1 - 2I \times 1 + 10 = 0 \Rightarrow 5I = 10$$

$$I = 2\text{A}$$

Total current in the network $= 6I$

$$= 6 \times 2 = 12\text{ A} \qquad (1\text{ mark})$$

From Eq. (i), $6IR = 10$

$$6 \times 2 \times R = 10$$

$$R = \frac{10}{12} = \frac{5}{6}\Omega = \frac{5}{6}\Omega \qquad (1\text{ mark})$$

32. (a) Magnetic moment associated with a current carrying circular coil of radius r having N turns, (1 mark)

$$\vec{M} = NI(\pi r^2)\,\hat{n}$$

(b)

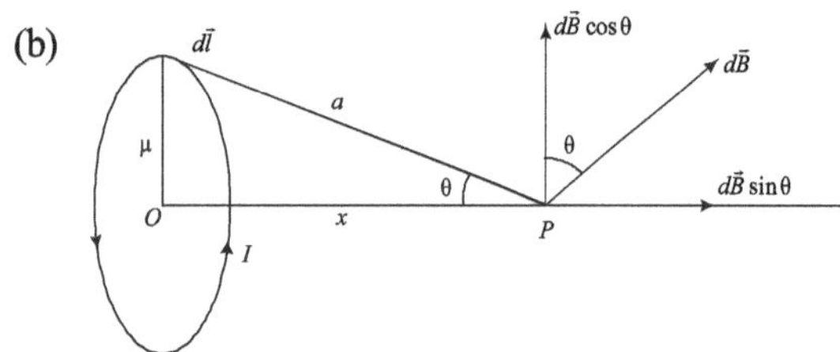

From Biot-savart law, the magnetic field at point $P(x, 0, 0)$ due to current element $\vec{dl}$,

$$\vec{dB} = \frac{\mu_0}{4\pi}\frac{I\,dl\sin 90°}{a^2} \qquad (2\text{ marks})$$

Now, the vertical component $\cos\theta$ will cancel out for entire coil. So,

$$\vec{B} \text{ at } P \Rightarrow B = \int dB\sin\theta$$

$$B = \frac{\mu_0 I}{4\pi a^2}\sin\theta\int dl$$

Now $\int dl = 2\pi r \therefore B = \frac{\mu_0 I}{4\pi a^2}\times\frac{r}{a}\times 2\pi r \left[\because \sin\theta = \frac{r}{a}\right]$

$$B = \frac{\mu_0 I r^2}{2a^3} = \frac{\mu_0 I r^2}{2(r^2 + x^2)^{3/2}}\,\hat{i}.$$

For coil having N turns, $= \frac{\mu_0 I N r^2}{2(r^2 + x^2)^{3/2}}\,\hat{i}.$ (2 marks)

OR

(a) Current sensitivity

It is defined as the deflection produced in the galvanometer when a unit current flows through it.

Current sensitivity $I_C = \dfrac{NBA}{K}$

Where $N =$ no. of turns in the coil

$B =$ Magnetic field

$A =$ area of coil of galvanometer. (1 mark)

(b) (i)

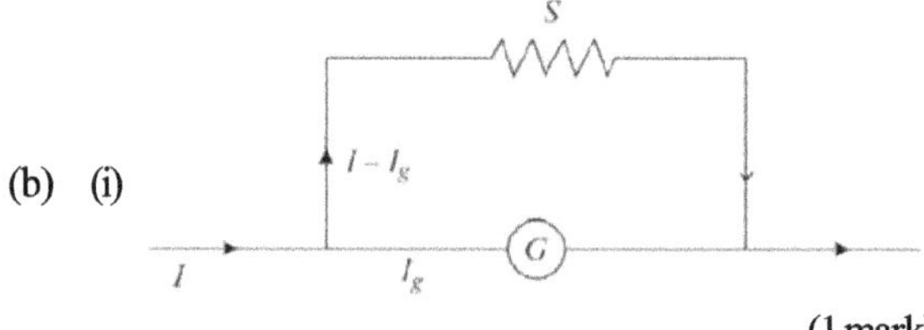

(1 mark)

Galvanometer can be converted into ammeter by connecting a shunt (small resistance) S with parallel to galvanometer.

As galvanometer and shunt are connected in parallel, so,

Potential across $G =$ Potential across the S

$$I_g G = (I - I_g)S \therefore S = \frac{I_g}{I - I_g}G. \qquad (2\text{ marks})$$

(ii) Effective resistance of this ammeter will be

$$\frac{1}{R_A} = \frac{1}{G} + \frac{1}{S}$$

$$R_A = \frac{GS}{G + S}. \qquad (1\text{ mark})$$

33. From the lens maker formula, we have

$$\frac{1}{f} = (\mu - 1)\left(\frac{1}{R_1} - \frac{1}{R_2}\right)$$

Let f_1 anf f_2 be the focal lengths of the two mediums.

Then, $\dfrac{1}{f_1} = (\mu_1 - 1)\left[\dfrac{1}{R} - \left(-\dfrac{1}{R}\right)\right] \Rightarrow \dfrac{1}{f_1} = (\mu_1 - 1)\left(\dfrac{2}{R}\right)$

$$\frac{1}{f_2} = (\mu_2 - 1)\left[\left(-\frac{1}{R}\right) - \frac{1}{\infty}\right]$$

$$\Rightarrow \frac{1}{f_2} = (\mu_2 - 1)\left(-\frac{1}{R}\right) \qquad (1\text{ mark})$$

(a) If f_{eq} is the equivalent focal length of the combination, then

$$\frac{1}{f_{eq}} = \frac{1}{f_1} + \frac{1}{f_2} \Rightarrow \frac{1}{f_{eq}} = \frac{2(\mu_1 - 1)}{R} - \frac{(\mu_2 - 1)}{R}$$

$$\Rightarrow \frac{1}{f_{eq}} = \frac{2\mu_1 - \mu_2 - 1}{R}$$

$$\Rightarrow f_{eq} = \frac{R}{2\mu_1 - \mu_2 - 1} \qquad (2\text{ marks})$$

(b) For the combination to behave as a diverging lens, $f_{eq} < 0$

$$\Rightarrow \quad \frac{R}{2\mu_1 - \mu_2 - 1} < 0 \Rightarrow 2\mu_1 - \mu_2 - 1 < 0$$

$$\Rightarrow \quad \mu_1 < \frac{(\mu_2 + 1)}{2} \qquad \text{(1 mark)}$$

which is the required condition

(c) For $\mu_1 > (\mu_2 + 1)/2$. the combination will behave as the converging lens. So, an object placed far away from the lens will form image at the focus of the lens.

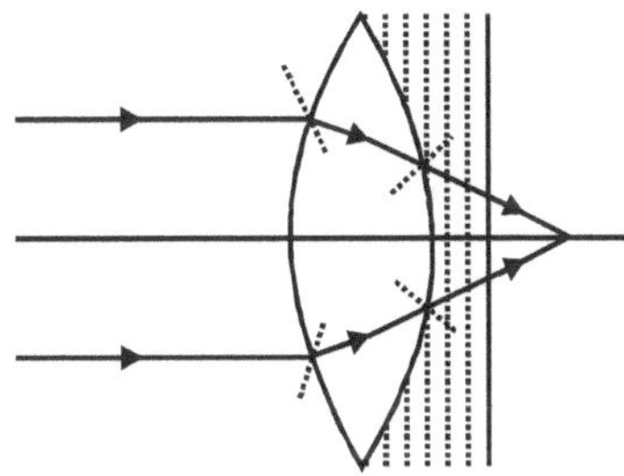

The image so formed will be real and diminished in nature. (1 mark)

OR

(i) (1 mark)

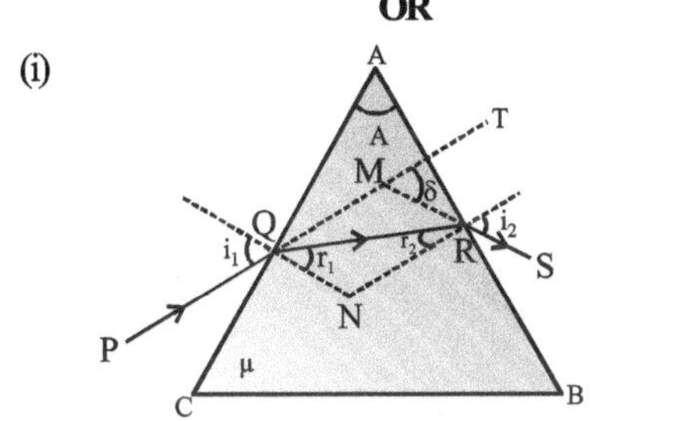

Let, PQ and RS are incident and emergent rays. Let, incident ray get deviated by δ by prism i.e.,

$$\angle TMS = \delta$$

Suppose, δ_1 and δ_2 are deviation produced at refractors taking place at AB and AC respectively.

$$\therefore \quad \delta = \delta_1 + \delta_2$$
$$\delta = (i_1 - r_1) + (i_2 - r_2)$$
$$\delta = (i_1 + i_2) - (r_1 + r_2) \qquad ..... \text{(i)} \qquad (\text{1 mark})$$

Also, in quadilateral, AQNR,

$$A + \angle QNR = 180°$$

$[\because$ QN and RN are normal on two surfaces$]$

Also, in $\triangle QNR$,

$$\angle QNR + r_1 + r_2 = 180°$$
$$\Rightarrow \quad A = r_1 + r_2 \qquad ..... \text{(ii)} \qquad \text{(1 mark)}$$

From eqs. (i) and (ii), we get,

$$\delta = (i_1 + i_2) - A z \qquad ..... \text{(iii)}$$

Angle of deviation produced by prism varies with angle of incidence.

When prism is adjusted at angle of minimum deviation, then

$$i_1 = i_2 = i$$

At $\delta = \delta_{m'} \Rightarrow r_1 = r_2 = r$

From eqs, (i) and (ii), we have

$$\delta_m = 2i - 2r \text{ and } 2r = A \Rightarrow i = \frac{A + \delta_m}{2} \quad r = \frac{A}{2}$$

$\therefore$ Refractive index of material of prism

$$\mu = \frac{\sin i}{\sin r} = \frac{\sin\left(\dfrac{A + \delta_m}{2}\right)}{\sin\dfrac{A}{2}} \qquad \text{(1 mark)}$$

(ii) When light is incident on one end of the optical fibre at an angle of incidence greater than the critical angle for the glass cladding pair of media. The light suffers repeated total internal reflections and light travels through the optical fibre without any loss of energy from one place to other inside the optical fibre. (1 mark)

34. (i) Energy of incident photon

$$E = \frac{hc}{\lambda} = \frac{6.6 \times 10^{-34} \times 3 \times 10^8}{3300 \times 10^{-10}} = 3.75 \text{ eV}$$

A will not emit photoelectrons because energy of incident photon is less than work function of A. (2 marks)

(ii) $eV_0 = h(v - v_0)$

When $V_0 = 0$, $v = v_0$, the threshold frequency.

From the graph it follows that

$$v_0 = 4 \times 10^{15} \text{ Hz}$$

Therefore, work function is

$$\phi = hv_0 = 6.6 \times 10^{-34} \times 4 \times 10^{15} = 16.5 \text{ eV} \qquad \text{(1 mark)}$$

(iii) $eV_0 = hv - hv_0$

$$V_0 = \frac{h}{e}v - \frac{h}{e}v_0$$

$$Y = mn + e$$

$$\text{Slope} = \frac{h}{e} \qquad \text{(1 mark)}$$

OR

(iii) Magnitude of saturation photoelectric current depends on intensity of incident radiation. (1 mark)

35. We know that $r = \dfrac{mV}{qB}$

$$\therefore \quad V > \frac{qBl}{m}$$

(i) If $V = \dfrac{qBl}{m}$ then particle will cover semi circular path

in this condition the path length of the particle in region II is maximum. (2 marks)

(ii) Nature of orbit is helix. (1 mark)

(iii) $F = q(\vec{V} \times \vec{B})$ if $V \parallel B$, then $\vec{F} = 0$ (1 mark)

OR

(iii) Pair of vectors always right angle are $\vec{F}$ and $\vec{v}$, $\vec{F}$ and $\vec{B}$. (1 mark)

1. **(a)** Power, $P = \dfrac{V^2}{R} \Rightarrow R = \dfrac{V^2}{P}$

   i.e., $R \propto \dfrac{1}{P}$

   i.e., the resistance of 25 W bulb is greater than 100 W bulb.
   Heat produced by the bulbs, $H = I^2 Rt$.
   Since the bulbs are connected in series, current remains same.
   i.e., $H \propto R$
   i.e., The heat produced by 25 W bulb is greater and hence it will glow brighter. (1 mark)

2. **(a)** $\mu_r < 1$ and $\varepsilon_r > 1$. (1 mark)

3. **(b)** As we know,

   $\vec{E} \times \vec{B} = \vec{V}$

   $(E\hat{j}) \times (\vec{B}) = V\hat{i}$ ($\because$ Electric field vector is along +y axis)

   So, $\vec{B} = B\hat{k}$ (1 mark)
   i.e., direction of magnetic field vector is along +z direction.

4. **(b)** For radial distance $r = a/2$

   $B_1 = \dfrac{\mu_0 i r}{2\pi a^2} \Rightarrow B_1 = \dfrac{\mu_0 i}{4\pi a}$

   For radial distance $r = 2a$

   $B_2 = \dfrac{\mu_0 i}{4\pi a} \quad \therefore \dfrac{B_1}{B_2} = 1$ (1 mark)

5. **(a)** The conduction electrons collides with each other more. the specific resistance of a conductor increases with temperature according to the reaction $\rho_T = \rho_0{}^{eEg/kgT}$ where ρ_0 is the specific resistance at $0°$ C, E_g = energy of the gap between the valence and the conduction band, k_B is the Boltzmann constant and T, the temperature of the resistor. (1 mark)

6. **(c)** We know that

   $V = \dfrac{1}{\sqrt{\mu\varepsilon}}$ and $C = \dfrac{1}{\sqrt{\mu_0\varepsilon_0}}$

   So, $\dfrac{V}{C} = \dfrac{\sqrt{\mu_0\varepsilon_0}}{\sqrt{\mu\varepsilon}} = \dfrac{\sqrt{\mu_0\varepsilon_0}}{\sqrt{\mu_0\varepsilon_0\,\mu_r\varepsilon_r}} = \dfrac{1}{\sqrt{\mu_r\varepsilon_r}}$

   $V = \dfrac{C}{\sqrt{\mu_r\varepsilon_r}}$ (1 mark)

7. **(d)** Current sensitivity of moving coil galvanometer

   $I_s = \dfrac{NBA}{C}$ ...(i)

   Voltage sensitivity of moving coil galvanometer,

   $V_s = \dfrac{NBA}{CR_G}$ ...(ii)

   Dividing eqn. (i) by (ii)
   Resistance of galvanometer

   $R_G = \dfrac{I_s}{V_s} = \dfrac{5 \times 1}{20 \times 10^{-3}} = \dfrac{5000}{20} = 250\,\Omega$ (1 mark)

8. **(b)** The position of nth dark fringe. So position of first dark fringe in $x_1 = \lambda D / 2d$.
   $d = 20$ cm, $D = 0.1$ mm, $\lambda = 5460$ Å, $x_1 = 0.16$ (1 mark)

9. **(a)** Energy of a H-like atom in it's n^{th} state is given by

   $E_n = -Z^2 \times \dfrac{13.6}{n^2}\,eV$

   For, first excited state of He^+, $n = 2$, $Z = 2$ (1 mark)

   $\therefore \quad E_{He^+} = -\dfrac{4}{2^2} \times 13.6 = -13.6\,eV$

10. **(b)** Mass defect $\Delta m = 0.02866$ a.m.u.
    Energy $= 0.02866 \times 931 = 26.7$ MeV
    As $_1H^2 + {}_1H^2 \longrightarrow {}_2He^4$
    Energy liberated per a.m.u $= 13.35/2$ MeV
    $\qquad\qquad = 6.675$ MeV (1 mark)

11. **(c)** Binding energy is lower for both light and heavy nuclei. (1 mark)

12. **(a)** If two ends of a p-n junction are joined by a wire, there will not be a steady current in the circuit. (1 mark)

13. **(d)** $n_i^2 = n_e n_h$
    $(1.5 \times 10^{16})^2 = n_e(4.5 \times 10^{22})$
    $\Rightarrow n_e = 0.5 \times 10^{10}$
    or $n_e = 5 \times 10^9$
    Given $n_h = 4.5 \times 10^{22}$
    $\Rightarrow n_h \gg n_e$
    $\therefore$ Semiconductor is p-type and
    $n_e = 5 \times 10^9\,m^{-3}$. (1 mark)

14. **(c)** By doping, the band gap reduce from 1eV to 0.3 to 0.7 eV & electron can achieve this energy (0.3eV to 0.7eV) at room temperature & reach in C.B (conduction band). (1 mark)

15. **(b)** $\lambda = \dfrac{hc}{E} = \dfrac{6.62 \times 10^{-34} \times 3 \times 10^8}{(60 \times 10^{-3} \times 1.6 \times 10^{-19})} = 2.07 \times 10^{-5}$ m (1 mark)

16. **(b)** Study of junction diode characteristics shows that the junction diode offers a low resistance path, when forward biased and high resistance path when reverse biased. This feature of the junction diode enables it to be used as a rectifier. (1 mark)

17. **(b)** $I_{max} = \left(\sqrt{9I_0} + \sqrt{4I_0}\right)^2 = 25I_0$

    $I_{min} = \left(\sqrt{9I_0} - \sqrt{4I_0}\right)^2 = I_0$ (1 mark)

    $\therefore \dfrac{I_{max}}{I_{min}} = 25$

18. **(c)** The wavelength of these wave ranges between 4000 Å to 100 Å that is smaller wavelength and higher frequency. They are absorbed by atmosphere and convert oxygen into ozone. They cause skin diseases and they are harmful to eye and cause permanent blindness. (1 mark)

19. The S.I. unit of magnetic field is tesla. (T)

The strength of magnetic field at a point is said to be 1T if a charge of 1C while moving at right angles to a magnetic field, with a velocity of 1 m/s experiences a force of 1 N at that point.

The force on a moving charged particle is F

$= qBv\sin\theta$

If $\theta = 90°$, i.e. the particle moves at right angles to the magnetic field, $F = qBv$ which provides the necessary centripetal force for the circular motion of the particle. There is no linear acceleration. So no increase in linear velocity and hence in kinetic energy. **(2 marks)**

20. (i) In interference, all the bright frings have same intensity i.e., are equally bright while in diffraction, all the bright fringes are not of the same intensity i.e., are not equally bright.

(ii) In interference, there is a good contrast between the bright and the dark fringes while in diffraction, there is a poor contrast between the dark and the the bright fringes.

$(1 \times 2 = 2 \text{ marks})$

21. The potential at points C and D will be same, so no charge will flow through the 3 μF capacitor.

$\therefore$ The equivalent circuit is

1 μF and 2 μF are connected in series,

$\therefore \quad C_1 = \dfrac{2 \times 1}{2+1} = \dfrac{2}{3}\mu F, \ C_2 = \dfrac{2}{3}\mu F$ **(1 mark)**

Two $\dfrac{2}{3}$ μF capacitors are connected in parallel,

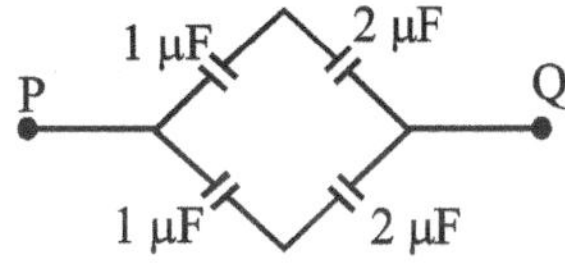

$\therefore \quad C_{eq} = C_1 + C_2 \Rightarrow C_{eq} = \dfrac{2}{3} + \dfrac{2}{3} = \dfrac{4}{3}\mu F$ **(1 mark)**

22. As we know, $I \propto v_d$ and $v_d \propto E$ and $E \propto V$

$\therefore I \propto V = $ which is ohm's law.

$v_d = -\dfrac{eE\tau}{m}$ and $E = -\dfrac{V}{\ell}$ $\quad \therefore v_d = \dfrac{eV\tau}{m\ell}$ and I

$= nAev_d$ **(1 mark)**

$\therefore I = neA\left(\dfrac{eV}{m\ell}\right)\tau = \left(\dfrac{ne^2A\tau}{m\ell}\right)V = \dfrac{1}{R}V$

or $V = IR$ where $R = \dfrac{m\ell}{nAe^2\tau}$ is a constant for a particular conductor at a particular temperature and is called the resistance of the conductor. **(1 mark)**

OR

Let n be the number of free electrons per unit volume of the conductor.

Volume of the conductor $= A\ell$

Number of free electrons of the conductor $= n$

Total free charge of the conductor $= nA\ell e$, where e is the charge of an electron.

If t be the time taken to cover a distance ℓ by this change, then $t = \dfrac{\ell}{v_d}$

$\therefore I = \dfrac{q}{t} = \dfrac{nAe\ell}{\ell / v_d} = nAev_d \Rightarrow v_d = \dfrac{I}{enA}$

$\therefore v_d \propto I$ **(2 marks)**

23. Energy separation $= 57 \times 10^{-3}$ eV

$= 57 \times 10^{-3} \times 1.6 \times 10^{-19}$ J **(1 mark)**

$\text{Energy} = \dfrac{hc}{\lambda} \Rightarrow \lambda = \dfrac{hc}{E}$

$= \dfrac{6.6 \times 10^{-34} \times 3 \times 10^8}{57 \times 10^{-3} \times 1.6 \times 10^{-19}}$

$= 2.177 \times 10^{-5}$ m $=$ maximum wavelength to create a hole.

(1 mark)

24.

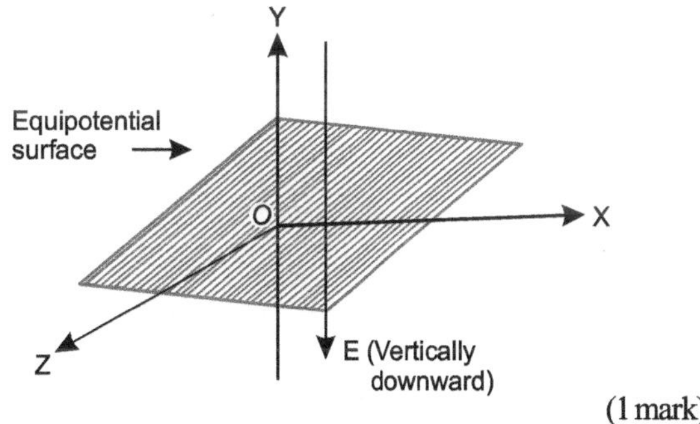

Negative q charge experiences force in a direction opposite to the direction of electric field.

$\therefore$ Negative q charge balances when

$qE = mg$

$E = \dfrac{mg}{q}$ **(1 mark)**

The direction of electric field is along vertically downward direction.

The equipotential surface between the plates is:

(1 mark)

OR

Force on q due to 4q charge, $\quad F_A = \dfrac{k\,4q.q}{(x/2)^2} = \dfrac{k\,4q^2}{(x/2)^2}$ **(1 mark)**

Force on q due to Q, $F_B = \dfrac{k.Qq}{(x/2)^2}$

Net force on q $= 0$ if $F_B = F_A$

i.e. $\dfrac{k\,Qq}{(x/2)^2} = \dfrac{k\,4q^2}{(x/2)^2} \Rightarrow Q = 4q$ **(1 mark)**

25. An accelerated or retarded charge or an oscillating LC circuit can be a source of electromagnetic waves. (1 mark)

Electric and magnetic field vectors are perpendicular to each other and perpendicular to the direction of propagation of the wave.

The speed of all electromagnetic waves is same in vacuum. (1 mark)

OR

Electromagnetic waves consist of time varying sinusoidal electric and magnetic fields in perpendicular direction. (1 mark)

It's velocity in vacuum is given by $c = \dfrac{1}{\sqrt{\mu_0 \varepsilon_0}}$ and it doesn't depend on any factor, as it is same for all electromagnetic waves in vacuum. (1 mark)

26. Let PQ be a conductor of length ℓ.

I be the current through the conductor.

$\overrightarrow{B}$ is the magnetic field intensity. $\overrightarrow{v_d}$ is the drift speed of electrons. θ is the angle between $\overrightarrow{B}$ and I.

n be the no. of electrons per unit volume of the conductor. A is the cross-sectional area of the conductor.

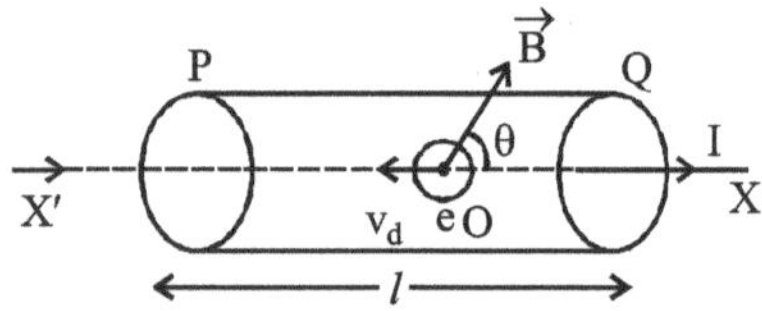

Total no. of free electrons in the conductor $N = nA\ell$

Magnetic Lorentz force on each electron $\overrightarrow{f} = -e\left(\overrightarrow{v_d} \times \overrightarrow{B}\right)$

$\therefore$ Total force of all free electrons

$\overrightarrow{F} = N\overrightarrow{f} = -nA\ell e\left(\overrightarrow{v_d} \times \overrightarrow{B}\right)$

But $I = nAev_d$

$\therefore$ $I\ell = nA\ell ev_d$

$\overrightarrow{I\ell}$ is called current element vector and is opposite to $\overrightarrow{v_d}$

$\therefore$ $\overrightarrow{I\ell} = -nA\ell e\overrightarrow{v_d}$

$\therefore$ $\overrightarrow{F} = \overrightarrow{I\ell} \times \overrightarrow{B}$

$\therefore$ $|\overrightarrow{F}| = I|\overrightarrow{\ell} \times \overrightarrow{B}| \Rightarrow F = I\ell B \sin\theta$ (3 marks)

27. (i) Graph between terminal voltage V and resistance (R)

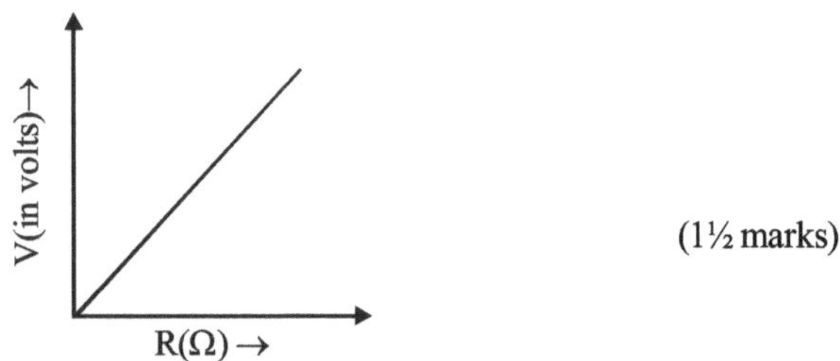

(1½ marks)

(ii) Graph between terminal voltage (V) and current (I)

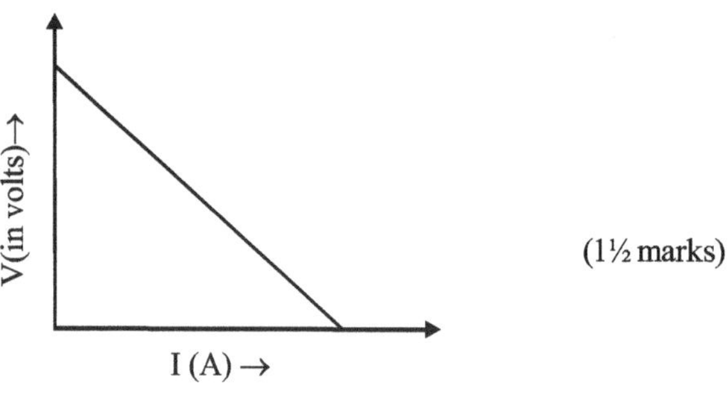

(1½ marks)

28. The de-Broglie wavelength of a particle is given by

$$\lambda \propto \dfrac{1}{\sqrt{mq}}$$

If m_p and q are mass and charge of a proton respectively, and m_α and $2q$ are mass and charge of a alpha particle respectively. Then,

According to question

$\lambda_p = \lambda_\alpha$

(i) For accelerating potential,

$\lambda = \dfrac{12.27}{\sqrt{V}}$

$\lambda_p = \dfrac{12.27}{\sqrt{V_p}}$ or $V_P = \left(\dfrac{12.27}{\lambda_p}\right)^2$

and $\lambda_\alpha = \dfrac{12.27}{\sqrt{v_\alpha}}$ or $V_\alpha = \left(\dfrac{12.27}{\lambda_\alpha}\right)^2$

Now, $\dfrac{V_p}{V_\alpha} = \dfrac{(12.27/\lambda_p)^2}{(12.27/\lambda_\alpha)^2}$

$\dfrac{V_p}{V_\alpha} = \left(\dfrac{\lambda_\alpha}{\lambda_p}\right)^2$ $(\because \lambda_p = \lambda_\alpha)$ (1½ marks)

$V_p : V_\alpha = 1.$

(ii) For, speed

$\lambda = \dfrac{h}{p} = \dfrac{h}{mv}$

Now, $\lambda_p = \dfrac{h}{m_p v_p}$ or $= v_p = \dfrac{h}{m_p \lambda_p}$

and $\lambda_\alpha = \dfrac{h}{m_\alpha v_\alpha}$ or $v_\alpha = \dfrac{h}{m_\alpha \lambda_\alpha}$

$\dfrac{v_p}{v_\alpha} = \dfrac{h/m_p \lambda_p}{h/m_\alpha \lambda_\alpha}$

$\dfrac{v_p}{v_\alpha} = \dfrac{m_p \lambda_p}{m_p v_p}$ $(\because \lambda_p = \lambda_\alpha$ and $m_\alpha = 4m_p)$

$\Rightarrow \dfrac{v_p}{v_\alpha} = \dfrac{4m_p}{m_p}$

$v_p : v_\alpha = 4 : 1$ (1½ marks)

OR

(i) Energy of a photon is given by, ν

$$E = h\nu$$

Number of photons emitted per second,

$$n = \frac{P}{E} \text{ where, P = power emitted} \qquad \text{(1 mark)}$$

On putting the values, we get,

$$n = \frac{2.0 \times 10^{-3}}{6.63 \times 10^{-34} \times 6.0 \times 10^{14}} = 5.03 \times 10^{15} \qquad \text{(1 mark)}$$

(ii) The photoelectric current is known to be directly proportional to the intensity of incident light with fixed frequency. So, the plot will be a straight line shown as,

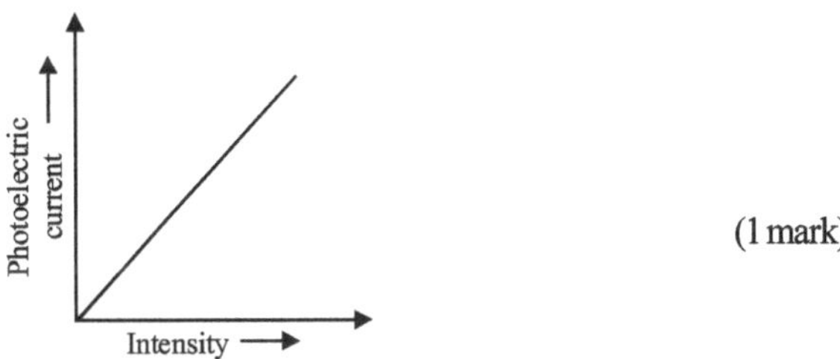

(1 mark)

29. Let an electron of mass m, carrying a charge e revolving around the nucleus of hydrogen atom carrying a charge +e. Let r_n be the radius of the orbit and v_n is the speed of the electron in that orbit. The necessary centripetal force to revolve the electron is provided by the electrostatic force between the electron and hydrogen nucleus

$$\therefore \quad k\frac{e^2}{r_n^2} = m\frac{v_n^2}{r_n}, \text{ where } k = \frac{1}{4\pi \epsilon_0}$$

$$\therefore \quad r_n = \frac{ke^2}{mv_n^2} \qquad ...(i)$$

$$\text{or,} \quad mv_n^2 = \frac{ke^2}{r_n} \qquad ...(ii) \qquad \text{(1 mark)}$$

According to the angular momentum postulate

$$mv_n r_n = \frac{nh}{2\pi} \text{ or } v_n = \frac{nh}{2\pi m r_n} \qquad ...(iii)$$

Putting the value of v_n from (iii) into (i), we have

$$r_n = \frac{ke^2}{m.n^2 h^2} 4\pi^2 m^2 r_n^2$$

$$\text{or} \quad r_n = \frac{n^2 h^2}{4\pi^2 ke^2 m} \qquad ....(iv)$$

KE of the electron $= \frac{1}{2}mv_n^2 = \frac{1}{2}\frac{ke^2}{r_n}$

$$= \frac{1}{2}\frac{ke^2}{n^2 h^2}.4\pi^2 kme^2 = \frac{2\pi^2 k^2 me^4}{n^2 h^2} \qquad ....(v)$$

Potential energy of the electron

$$PE = -\frac{kq_1 q_2}{r} = -\frac{k.e.e}{r_n} = -\frac{ke^2}{r_n} = \frac{-ke^2}{n^2 h^2}4\pi^2 ke^2 m$$

$$PE = \frac{-4\pi^2 k^2 e^4 m}{n^2 h^2}$$

$\therefore$ Total energy of the electron $= \frac{2\pi^2 k^2 me^4}{n^2 h^2} - \frac{4\pi k^2 me^4}{n^2 h^2}$

$$\text{or, } E_n = \frac{-2\pi^2 k^2 me^4}{n^2 h^2} \qquad \text{(1 mark)}$$

If E_{ni} and E_{nf} are the energies of the electron for which $n = n_i$ and n_f

$$\therefore \quad E_{ni} = \frac{-2\pi^2 k^2 me^4}{n_i^2 h^2} \text{ and } E_{nf} = \frac{-2\pi^2 k^2 me^4}{n_f^2 h^2}$$

If $h\nu$ is the energy of the photon when the electron jumps from $n = n_i$ to $n = n_f$, then

$$h\nu = \frac{2\pi^2 k^2 me^4}{h^2 n_f^2} + \frac{-2\pi^2 k^2 me^4}{h^2 n_i^2}$$

$$\Rightarrow \quad h\nu = \frac{2\pi^2 k^2 me^4}{h^2}\left[\frac{1}{n_f^2} - \frac{1}{n_i^2}\right]$$

$$\text{or, } \quad \nu = \frac{2\pi^2 k^2 me^4}{h^3}\left[\frac{1}{n_f^2} - \frac{1}{n_i^2}\right] \qquad \text{(1 mark)}$$

Spectral series when the transition of the electron takes place from

$$n_i = 4 \text{ to } n_f = 3 \rightarrow \text{Paschen series}$$
$$n_i = 4 \text{ to } n_f = 2 \rightarrow \text{Balmer series}$$
$$n_i = 4 \text{ to } n_f = 1 \rightarrow \text{Lyman series}$$

OR

According to Bohr's theory, when an electron jumps from inner to outer orbits it absorbs energy and when it jumps from outer to inner orbits it emits energy. The energy of the emitted radiation is equal to the difference of the two energy levels involved and the total number of energies of electron in different orbits of an atom are diagrammatically represented by the energy level diagram. Total energy of electron in n^{th} orbit is given by

$$E = \frac{-2\pi^2 mk^2 e^4}{n^2 h^2} \text{ where } k = \frac{1}{4\pi\varepsilon_0} \text{ and hence}$$

$$E = \frac{-13.6 eV}{n^2} \text{ for H-atom} \qquad \text{(1 mark)}$$

Also the number of waves given per unit length is

$$\bar{\nu} = RZ^2\left[\frac{1}{n_1^2} - \frac{1}{n_2^2}\right] \qquad \text{(1 mark)}$$

For hydrogen, $Z = 1$ $\therefore$ $\bar{\nu} = R\left[\frac{1}{n_1^2} - \frac{1}{n_2^2}\right]$

Where n_1 and n_2 are n^{th} orbit numbers and $R = 1.097 \times 10^7 \text{ m}^{-1}$ is Rydberg constant.

(i)   When electron jumps from outer orbit to

n = 1 orbit then $\bar{v}_1 = R\left[\dfrac{1}{1^2} - \dfrac{1}{k^2}\right]$ where

k = 2, 3, 4 etc. is Lyman series for energy
$E_1 = -13.6$ eV of the electron in n = 1 orbit.

(ii)   When electron jumps from outer to second orbit then

$\bar{v}_2 = R\left[\dfrac{1}{2^2} - \dfrac{1}{k^2}\right]$ where k = 3, 4, 5....... and energy of

electron is $E_2 = \dfrac{-13.6}{2^2}$

$= -3.4$ eV. This is Balmer Series.

(iii)   When electron jumps from any outer orbit to third orbit then

$\bar{v}_3 = R\left[\dfrac{1}{3^2} - \dfrac{1}{k^2}\right]$ where k = 4, 5, 6........ is **Paschen series**

and energy is

$E_3 = \dfrac{-13.6}{3^2} = -1.51$ eV

Similarly, for $n_1 = 4$ and $n_2 = 5, 6, 7......$ we get **Brackett series** whose electron energy is $E_4 = -0.85$ eV.

We get Pfund Series for $n_1 = 5$ and $n_2 = 6, 7 ....$ where electron in stationary orbit has energy

$E_5 = -0.54$ eV. As n increases, E_n increases until at n = ∞, E = 0. (1 mark)

The energy level diagram is drawn in figure 4.

30. $R = R_0 A^{1/3}$ where R_0 = constant, A mass number of a nucleus. Considering, nucleus to be nearly spherical.

Volume of nucleus = constant × R^3

= constant × $R_0^3 A$ = constant × A

Density = $\dfrac{mass}{volume}$ for a nucleus, mass = A,

∴ Density = $\dfrac{A}{const. \times A} = \dfrac{1}{const.}$

∴ Density = constant, independent of A. (3 marks)

31.   Let us consider charge +q is uniformly distributed over a spherical shell of radius R. Let electric field is to be obtained at P lies outside of spherical shell.

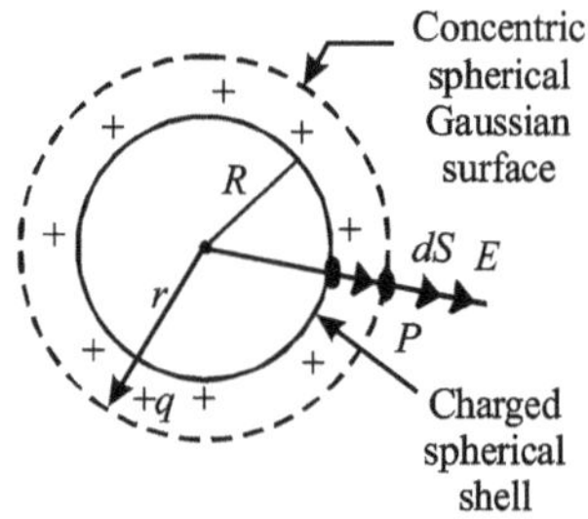

E at any point is radially outward and has same magnitude at all points which lies at the same distance (r) from centre of spherical shell. Therefore, consider a Gaussian surface of radius r such that r > R.

Gaussian surface enclosed charge q inside it.

By Gauss's theorem,

$$\oint E.dS = \frac{q}{\varepsilon_0}$$

$$\oint E.dS \cos 0° = \frac{q}{\varepsilon_0} \quad [\because E \text{ and } dS \text{ are along the same direction}]$$

$$E\oint dS = \frac{q}{\varepsilon_0}$$

$$E \times 4\pi r^2 = \frac{q}{\varepsilon_0}$$

$$E = \frac{1}{4\pi\varepsilon_0} \cdot \frac{q}{r^2}$$

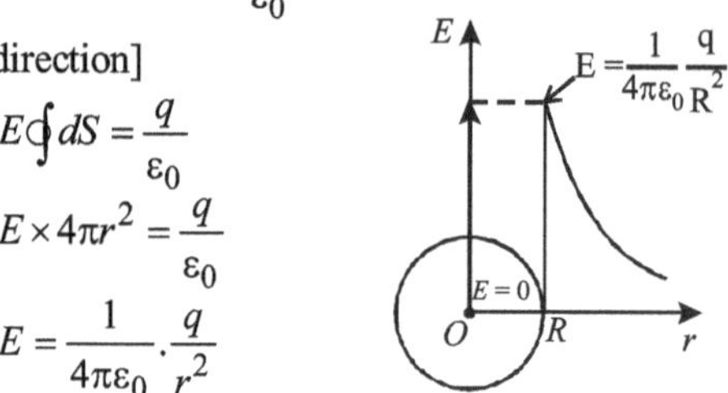

Variation of E with r for a charged spherical shell.

(5 marks)

OR

(a) A parallel plate capacitor consists of two large plane parallel conducting plates separated by a small distance.

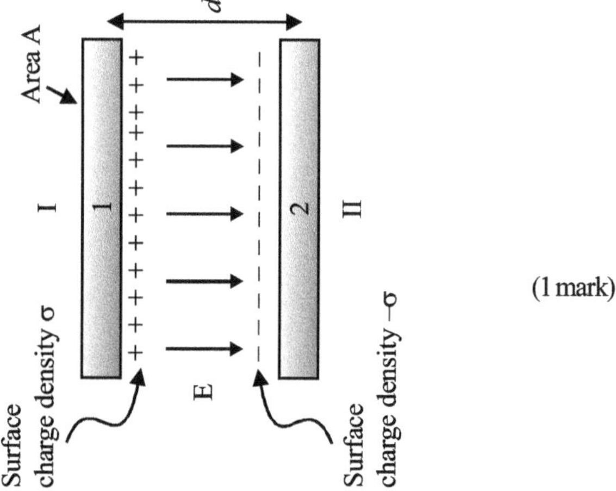

(1 mark)

Let A be the area of each plate and d be the separation between them. The two plates have charges Q and –Q. Plate 1 has surface charge density, σ = Q/A,
And plate 2 has a surface charge density –σ.
Electric field in, Outer region I,

$$E = \frac{\sigma}{2\varepsilon_0} - \frac{\sigma}{2\varepsilon_0} = 0$$

In outer region II,

$$E = \frac{\sigma}{2\varepsilon_0} - \frac{\sigma}{2\varepsilon_0} = 0$$

(1 mark)

In the inner region between plates 1 and 2, the electric fields due to the two charged plates add up.

$$E = \frac{\sigma}{2\varepsilon_0} + \frac{\sigma}{2\varepsilon_0} = \frac{\sigma}{\varepsilon_0} = \frac{Q}{\varepsilon_0} = \frac{Q}{\varepsilon_0 A}$$

(1 mark)

The direction of electric field is from positive to the negative plate. For uniform electric field, potential difference is simply the electric field times the distance between the plates.

$$V = E\,d = \frac{1}{\varepsilon_0}\frac{Qd}{A}$$

Capacitance (C) of the parallel plate capacitor, $C = \dfrac{Q}{V} = \dfrac{\varepsilon_0 A}{d}$

(1 mark)

(b) The surface charge density for a spherical conductor is given by, $\sigma = \dfrac{Q}{4\pi r^2}$

For spherical conductor R_1, the surface charge density is given by, $\sigma_1 = \dfrac{q_1}{4\pi R_1^2}$

Similarly, for spherical conductor R_2, the surface charge density is given by, $\sigma_2 = \dfrac{q_2}{4\pi R_2^2}$

$\therefore \quad \dfrac{\sigma_1}{\sigma_2} = \left(\dfrac{q_1}{q_2}\right)\left(\dfrac{R_2^2}{R_1^2}\right)$

Since the two conductors are connected, we have,

$q_1 = q_2$

$\therefore \quad \dfrac{\sigma_1}{\sigma_2} = \dfrac{R_2^2}{R_1^2} = \left(\dfrac{R_2}{R_1}\right)^2$ (1 mark)

32. (i) Faraday's laws of electromagnetic induction:

First law: Wherever there is a change in magnetic flux associted with a coil, an e.m.f. is induced in the coil. It last so long as the change continues. (1 mark)

Second law: The induced e.m.f. is directly proportional to the rate of change of magnetic flux of the coil and has a direction opposite to that of the change of magnetic flux. Mathematically, (1 mark)

$$e \propto -\dfrac{d\phi}{dt} \ \Rightarrow \ e = -k\dfrac{d\phi}{dt}$$

$$[k = 1 \text{ for all system of units}]$$

$\therefore \quad e = -\dfrac{d\phi}{dt}$ (1 mark)

(ii) When the switch is closed the flux associated with L changes, an e.m.f. is induced in L which will oppose the growth of current in Q. But no such induced e.m.f. will be produced in R. So P will light up faster. (2 marks)

OR

When current flowing in one of two nearby coil is charged, the magnetic flux linked with the other coil changes, due to which an emf is induced in the other coil. This phenomenon is called mutual induction. The coil in which current is changed is called primary coil and the coil in which emf is induced is called secondary coil.

I_1 B   S   P   S

(1 mark)

Suppose there are two coils P and S. The current I_1 is flowing in primary coil P due to which an effective magnetic flux ϕ_2 is linked with secondary coil S.

By experiment, $\phi_2 \propto I_1 \qquad \therefore \phi_2 = MI_1$

Where M is a constant, called coefficient of mutual induction or mutual inductance.

$\therefore M = \dfrac{\phi_2}{I_1}$ If $I_1 = 1$ A, then $M = \phi_2$

$\therefore$ Mutual inductance between two coils is numerically equal to the effective flux linkage with secondary coil, when current flowing in primary coil is 1A.

From Faraday's law,

induced e.m.f in secondary coil $= e_2 = -\dfrac{d\phi_2}{dt}$

$\Rightarrow e_2 = -\dfrac{d}{dt}(MI_1) = -M\dfrac{dI_1}{dt}$ (1 mark)

$\therefore \quad M = -\dfrac{e_2}{\dfrac{dI_1}{dt}}$

If $dI_1/dt = 1$ A/s $\qquad \therefore M = e_2$ (numerically)

$\therefore$ Mutual inductance between two coils is numerically equal to the emf induced with secondary coil, when rate of change of current in primary coil is 1 A/s. (1 mark)

Mutual inductance of a solenoid:

Consider a long solenoid of length l and number of turns N_1. At its central part, a coil of N_2 number of turns is wound. If I_1 is the current flowing in long solenoid, the magnetic field produced within the solenoid is $B_1 = \dfrac{N_1 I_1}{\ell}$

$\therefore$ Flux linked with each turn of secondary coil $= \phi_2 = B_1 A$, where A is the cross-sectional area of the solenoid.

$\therefore$ Total flux linked with secondary coil of N_2 number of turns $= \phi_2' = N_2\phi_2 = N_2 B_1 A$

$= N_2\left(\dfrac{\mu_o N_1 I_1}{\ell}\right) A$ (1 mark)

$\therefore \ \phi_2' = \dfrac{\mu_0 N_1 N_2}{\ell} A I_1$

$\therefore$ Mutual inductance $= M = \dfrac{\phi_2'}{I_1} = \dfrac{\mu_o N_1 N_2 A}{\ell}$

(1 mark)

33. The magnifying power of a telescope is equal to the ratio of the visual angle subtended at the eye by final image formed at least distance of distinct vision to the visual angle subtended at naked eye by the object at infinity. (1 mark)

when final image is at D.

Magnifying power $M = \dfrac{f_o}{f_e}\left(1 + \dfrac{f_e}{D}\right)$

In normal adjustment $M = -\dfrac{f_o}{f_e}$ (1 mark)

Focal length of objective lens $f_o = 150$ cm

Focal length of eye lens $f_e = 5$ cm

When final image forms at $D = 25$ cm

$\therefore \quad$ Magnification $M = -\dfrac{f_o}{f_e}\left(1 + \dfrac{f_e}{D}\right)$

$= -\dfrac{150}{5}\left(1 + \dfrac{5}{25}\right) = -\dfrac{150}{5} \times \dfrac{6}{5}$ (1 mark)

Let height of final image is h cm $\quad \therefore \tan\beta = \dfrac{h}{25}$

β = visual angle formed by final image at eye

α = visual angle substended by object at objective

$\tan\alpha = \dfrac{100\ m}{3000\ m} = \dfrac{1}{30}$

But $M = \dfrac{\tan\beta}{\tan\alpha}$ $-36 = \dfrac{\left(\dfrac{h}{25}\right)}{\left(\dfrac{1}{30}\right)} = \dfrac{h}{25}\times 30$

$-36 = \dfrac{6h}{5}$ (1 mark)

$h = -\dfrac{36\times 5}{6} = -30\,\text{cm}$ (1 mark)

OR

(i) Given : $i = e = 3A/4$, $A = 60°$
From formula,
$i + e = A + \delta$
or, $3A/4 + 3A/4 = A + \delta$

$\Rightarrow \dfrac{A}{2} = \delta$ or $\dfrac{60°}{2} = \delta$

$\Rightarrow \delta = 30°$ (2½ marks)

(ii) Since $i = e$, the prism is in the minimum deviation position, therefore, the refractive index of the prism

$\mu = \dfrac{\sin(A + \delta_m)/2}{\text{Sin}A/2}$

$= \dfrac{\sin(60° + 30°)/2}{\sin(60°/2)}$

$= 0.707/0.5 = 1.414$ (2½ marks)

34. (i) The flux leakage in a transformer can be reduced by winding the primary and secondary coils one over the other. (1 mark)

(ii) The magnetisation of the core is repeatedly reversed by the alternating magnetic field which results in loss of energy as heat. (1 mark)

(iii) In steady current, the phenomenon of mutual induction does not take place. (2 marks)

OR

(iii) There are three assumptions:–
(i) The primary resistance and current are small.
(ii) The same flux links both the primary and the secondary as very little flux escapes from the core. (2 marks)
(iii) The secondary current is small.

35. (i) From lens formula,

$\dfrac{1}{f} = (\mu - 1)\left(\dfrac{1}{R_1} - \dfrac{1}{R_2}\right)$

$\dfrac{1}{f_1} = (1.5 - 1)\left(\dfrac{1}{8} + \dfrac{1}{R}\right) \Rightarrow f_1 = 2R$

$\dfrac{1}{f_2} = (1.7 - 1)\left(\dfrac{1}{-R} - \dfrac{1}{R}\right) \Rightarrow f_2 = \dfrac{-5R}{7}$

$\dfrac{1}{f_3} = (1.5 - 1)\left(\dfrac{1}{R} + \dfrac{1}{8}\right) \Rightarrow f_3 = 2R$

$\dfrac{1}{f_{eq}} = \dfrac{1}{2R} - \dfrac{7}{5R} + \dfrac{1}{2R}$

$\Rightarrow F_{eq} = -2.5R = -50\,\text{cm}$ (2 marks)

(ii) Cutting a lens in transverse direction doubles their focal length i.e., $2f$.
Using the formula of equivalent focal length.

$\dfrac{1}{f} = \dfrac{1}{f_1} + \dfrac{1}{f_2} + \dfrac{1}{f_3} + \dfrac{1}{f_4}$

We get equivalent focal length as $\dfrac{f}{2}$. (1 mark)

(iii) $P = \dfrac{1}{f} = (\mu_1 - \mu_2)\left(\dfrac{1}{R_1} - \dfrac{1}{R_2}\right)$

(μ_1 is refractive index of lens and μ_2 is of surrounding medium)

$\Rightarrow 1.25 = (1.5 - \mu_2)\left(\dfrac{1}{0.2} + \dfrac{1}{0.4}\right)$

$\Rightarrow \dfrac{1.25 \times 0.08}{0.6} = (1.5 - \mu_2) \Rightarrow \mu_2 = \dfrac{4}{3}$ (1 mark)

OR

(iii) We have power $P = \dfrac{1}{f} = (\mu - 1)\left(\dfrac{1}{R_1} - \dfrac{1}{R_2}\right)$

$= (1.5 - 1)\left(\dfrac{1}{20} - \dfrac{1}{-20}\right) \times \dfrac{1}{10^{-2}}$

$= 0.5 \times \dfrac{2}{20} \times 100 = +5\,\text{D}$ (1 mark)

1. **(a)** $\underset{r}{Q_1 \rule{3cm}{0.4pt} Q_2} \quad K = 5 \qquad F = \dfrac{1}{4\pi\varepsilon_0 k}\dfrac{Q_1 Q_2}{r^2}$

$Q_1 \rule{3cm}{0.4pt} Q_2$ force in the charges in the air is

$F' = \dfrac{1}{4\pi\varepsilon_0}\dfrac{Q_1 Q_2}{r^2} = K F = 5 F$ (1 mark)

2. **(a)** Torque, $\tau = pE\sin\theta$

$\tau = pE \sin 90°$

$= pE$ (Maximum) (1 mark)

3. **(a)** E = 500 V/m   V = 3000 V.

We know that electric field $(E) = 500 = \dfrac{V}{d}$

or $d = \dfrac{3000}{500} = 6\,\text{m}$ (1 mark)

4. **(b)** The rate of generation of heat, for a given potential difference is, $P = V^2/R$ (1 mark)

5. **(b)** Resistance of a wire is given by $R = \rho\dfrac{l}{a}$

If the length is increased by 10% then new

length $l' = l + \dfrac{1}{10} = \dfrac{11}{10}l$

In that case, area of cross-section of wire would decrease by 10%

∴ New area of cross-section

$A' = A - \dfrac{A}{10} = \dfrac{9}{10}A \qquad \therefore R' = \rho\dfrac{l'}{A'} = \rho\dfrac{\frac{1}{10}l}{\frac{9}{10}A}$

$R' = \dfrac{11}{9}\rho\dfrac{l}{R} \qquad\qquad R' = 1.21R$

Thus the new resistance increases by 1.21 times. The specific resistance (resistivity) remains unchanged as it depends on the nature of the material of the wire. (1 mark)

6. **(b)** Let ℓ be length of wire

Ist case : $\ell = 2\pi r \Rightarrow r = \dfrac{\ell}{2\pi}$

$B = \dfrac{\mu_0 I}{2\pi r} = \dfrac{\mu_0 I}{\ell}$

2nd Case : $\ell = 2(2\pi r') \Rightarrow r' = \dfrac{\ell}{4\pi}$

$B' = \dfrac{\mu_0 In}{2\pi\frac{\ell}{4\pi}} = \dfrac{2\mu_0 I}{\frac{\ell}{2}}$ (where n = 2)

on putting the value of $B \Rightarrow B' = 4\left(\dfrac{\mu_0 I}{l}\right) = 4B$ (1 mark)

7. **(a)** Given, length of wire X, $\ell_1 = 50\,\text{cm} = 0.5\,\text{m}$

Length of wire Y, $\ell_2 = 5\,\text{m}$

Distance between two wire, $r = 5\,\text{cm} = 5 \times 10^{-2}\,\text{m}$

Force of interaction $= I_1 \ell_1 B_{12}$

$= \dfrac{\mu_0 I_1 I_2}{2\pi r} \qquad \left(\therefore B_{12} = \dfrac{\mu_0 I_2}{2\pi r}\right)$

$= \dfrac{4\pi \times 10^{-7} \times 6 \times 0.5}{2\pi \times 5 \times 10^{-2}} = 1.2 \times 10^{-5}$ towards X (1 mark)

8. **(a)** Diamagnetic substance do not obey Curie's law and χ_m is independent of T. (1 mark)

9. **(a)** The phase angle between voltage V and current I is $\pi/2$. Therefore, power factor $\cos\phi = \cos(\pi/2) = 0$. Hence the power consumed is zero. (1 mark)

10. **(d)** In forward biasing, the diode conducts. For ideal junction diode, the forward resistance is zero; therefore, entire applied voltage occurs across external resistance R *i.e.*, there occur no potential drop, but potential across R is V in forward biased. (1 mark)

11. **(c)** The electromagnetic waves of all wavelengths travel with the same speed in space which is equal to velocity of light. (1 mark)

12. **(c)** Let magnifying power of eye and objective is m_e and m_0. therefore, $m = m_0 \times m_e \Rightarrow 32 = 8 \times m_e$

$\Rightarrow m_e = 4$ (1 mark)

13. **(d)** $\sin C = \dfrac{1}{\mu} = \dfrac{1}{\sqrt{2}} \qquad \therefore C = \sin^{-1}\left(\dfrac{1}{\sqrt{2}}\right) = 45°$

Now $\dfrac{\sin C}{\sin r} = \dfrac{1}{\mu}$ or $\dfrac{\sin 45°}{\sin r} = \dfrac{1}{\sqrt{2}}$

$\sin r = 1$ or $r = 90°$ (1 mark)

14. **(d)** Convex mirror always forms, virtual, erect and smaller image. (1 mark)

15. **(b)** According to principle of diffraction, $a\sin\theta = n\lambda$

where, n = order of secondary minimum

or, $a\sin 30° = 1 \times (6500 \times 10^{-10})$

or, $a = 1.3 \times 10^{-6}\,\text{m}$, or, $a = 1.3$ micron. (1 mark)

16. **(b)** Capacitive reactance $= \dfrac{1}{\omega c} = \dfrac{1}{2\pi fc}$

Here, f = frequency of source of emf

For direct current, $f = 0$

∵ capacitive reactance $= \infty$ (1 mark)

17. **(b)** Assertion (A) is true. Reason (R) is true and is the correct explanation of Assertion (A). (1 mark)

18. **(a)** Lenz's law (that the direction of induced emf is always such as to oppose the change that cause it) is direct consequence of the law of conservation of energy. (1 mark)

19. Total e.m.f $= nE$, Total resistance $= R + \dfrac{nr}{m}$

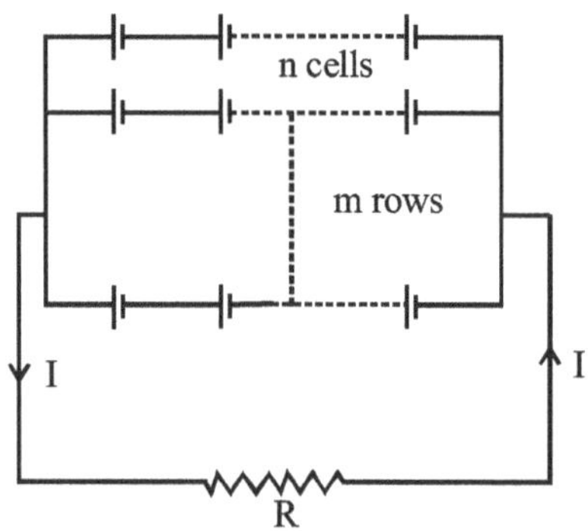

$$\left[\because \text{ Total internal resistance} \right.$$

$$\frac{1}{r_p} = \frac{1}{nr} + \frac{1}{nr} + \dots\dots\dots \text{ m times} = \frac{m}{nr} \quad \therefore \ r_p = \frac{nr}{m}\left.\right]$$

$$\therefore \quad \text{Current} = I = \frac{nE}{R + \dfrac{nr}{m}} \Rightarrow I = \frac{mnE}{mR + nr}$$

I will be maximum if $mR + nr$ is minimum.   (1 mark)

That is possible if $mR = nr$ i.e. $R = \dfrac{nr}{m}$

i.e. External resistance of the circuit = Total internal resistance of all the cells.   (1 mark)

OR

Graph of variation of resistivity with temperature for nichrome

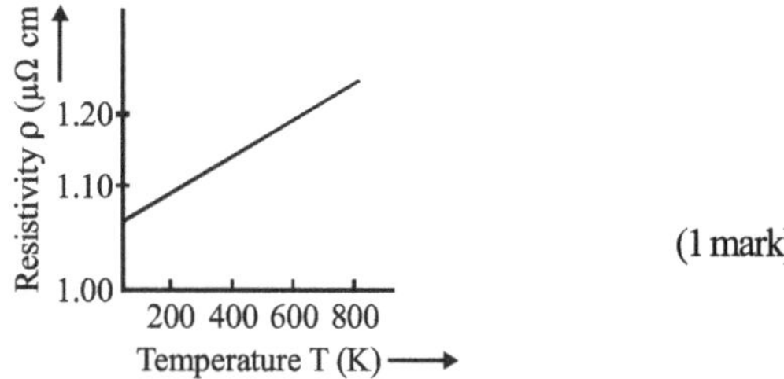

   (1 mark)

Property of nichrome used to make standard resistance coils : Its low temperature coefficient of resistance. (1 mark)

20. Two identical capacitors C_1 and C_2 gets fully charged with 5V battery initially.

So, the charge and potential difference on both capacitors becomes

$q = CV = 2 \times 10^{-6} \times 5V = 10\ \mu C$

and $V = 5V$

On introduction of dielectric medium of $K = 5$.   (1 mark)

For C_1 (Continue to be connected with battery) potential difference of C_1, $(V') = 5V$

Capacitance of $C_1' = KC = 5 \times 2\mu F = 10\ \mu F$

Charge $q' = C'V; = (10\ \mu F)(5\ V) = 50\ \mu C$ (½ mark)

For C_2 (Disconnected with battery)

Charge $q' = q = 10\ \mu C$

Potential difference

$$V' = \frac{V}{K} = \frac{5}{5} = 1\ V \qquad\qquad (½\text{ mark})$$

OR

In series combination,

$$C_s = \frac{C}{n}$$

In parallel combination,

$$\Rightarrow \quad C_p = nC$$

According to problem,

$$C = nC_s = 3 \times 1\mu F = 3\mu F$$

In parallel combination,

$$C_p = nC = 3 \times 3 = 9\mu F$$
$$C_p = 9\mu F \qquad\qquad (1\text{ mark})$$

For same voltage,

Energy stored, $U \propto C$

$$\therefore \quad \frac{U_s}{U_p} = \frac{C_s}{C_p} \Rightarrow \frac{U_s}{U_p} = \frac{1}{9}$$

or, $U_s : U_P = 1 : 9$ (1 mark)

21. (a) Microwaves are suitable for radar system in aircraft navigation.

(b) X-rays are produced by bombarding a metal target by high speed electrons. $(2 \times 1 = 2\text{ marks})$

22. $\angle i$ = angle of incidence

$\angle e$ = angle of emergence

δ = angle of deviation

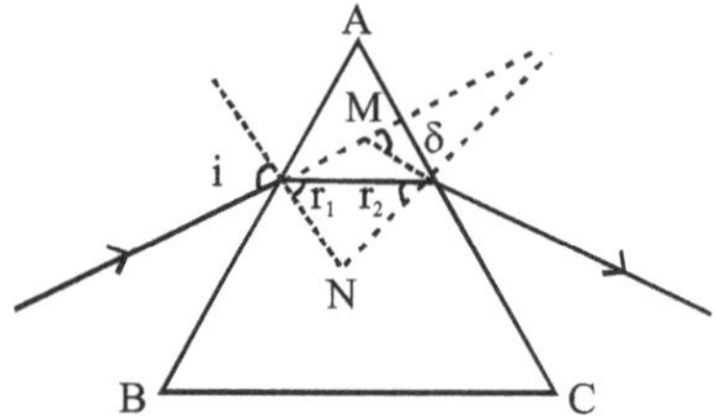

In the quadrilateral AQNR,

$\angle A + \angle QNR = 180°$ ...(i)

In the traingle QNR

$r_1 + r_2 + \angle QNR = 180°$ ...(ii)

$\therefore r_1 + r_2 = \angle A$ ...(iii)

The angle of deviation,

$\delta = (i - r_1) + (e - r_2) = i + e - (r_1 + r_2)$

$\therefore \delta = i + e - A$ ...(iv)   (1 mark)

According to snell's law, $\dfrac{\sin i}{\sin r_1} = n_{21}$

or, $\dfrac{i}{r_1} = n_{21}$ (since angles are small)

$\therefore i = r_1 \cdot n_{21}$

Also, $\dfrac{\sin e}{\sin r_2} = n_{21} \Rightarrow \dfrac{e}{r_2} = n_{21} \quad \therefore e = r_2 . n_{21}$

using the equation (iv)

$\delta = r_1 . n_{21} + r_2 . n_{21} A = (r_1 + r_2) n_{21} A = A . n_{21} A$

$\therefore \delta = (n_{21} - 1) A$ (1 mark)

23. (a) Spherical.

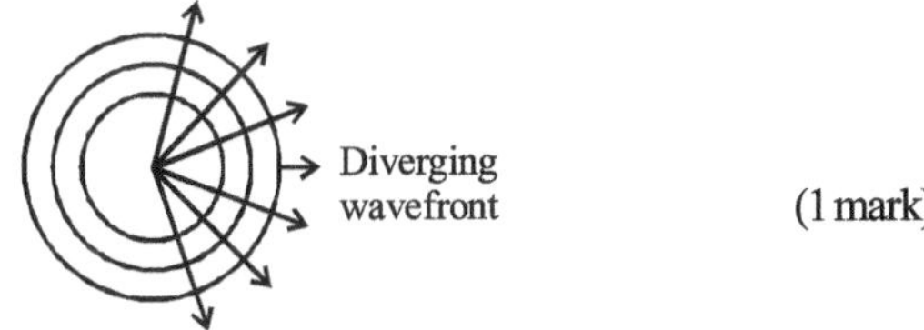

       (1 mark)

(b) Plane.

When a point source is placed at the focus of a convex lens, the emergent rays are parallel, hence the wavefont is plane.   (½ mark)

(c) Plane.

As the star is very far away, therefore the wavefront reacting us is a very large sphere and a small area on the surface of a large sphere is nearly plannar.   (½ mark)

24. **P-N junction diode as a full wave rectifier :** The circuit uses two diodes connected to the ends of a centre tapped transformer. The voltage rectified by the two diodes is half of the secondary voltage i.e., each diode conducts for half cycle of input but alternately so that net output across load comes as half sinusoids with positive values only.

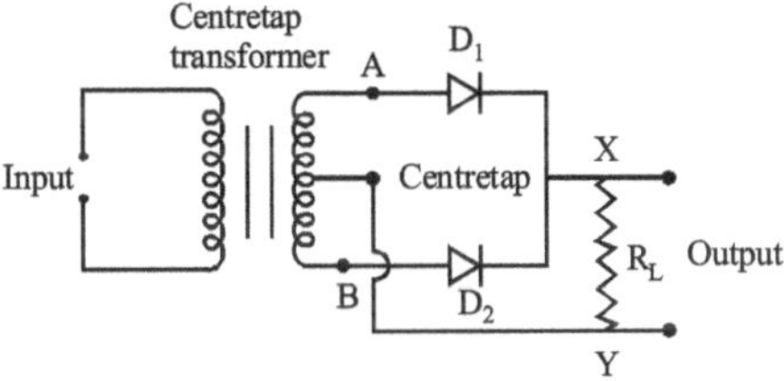

For positive cycle diode D_1 conducts (FB) but D_2 is being out of phase is reverse biased and does not conduct. Thus output across R_L is due to D_1 only. In negative cycle of input D_1 is R.B. but D_2 is F.B. and conducts as with respect

to centretap point A is negative but B is positive. Hence output across R_L is due to D_2.

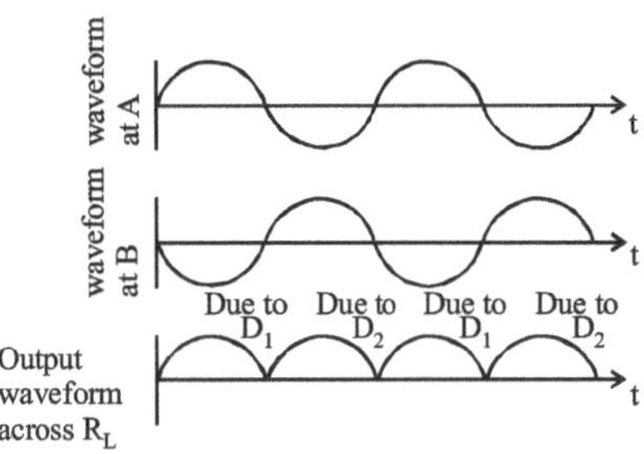

     (2 marks)

OR

In an intrinsic semiconductor, each of the 4 valence electrons is between two atoms (Si or Ge) in a shared covalent bond. It is bound at low temperatures, but at high temperatures it can pick thermal energy and move out of the valence band and into the interstitial space. This electron is free to conduct. The vacancy left behind by it is called a **hole** and it also conducts charge.

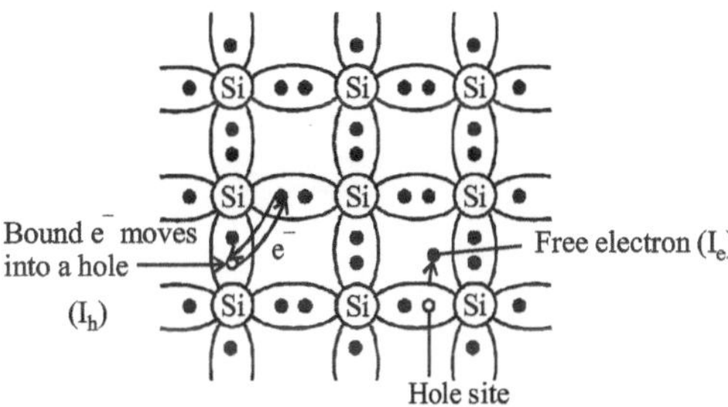

Another electron from a different band can come and occupy this vacancy, hence creating a vacancy elsewhere and causing motion of bound electrons. These holes move towards the negative potential giving rise to hole current I_h. The total current I, is sum of hole current I_h and electron current I_e.   (2 marks)

25.

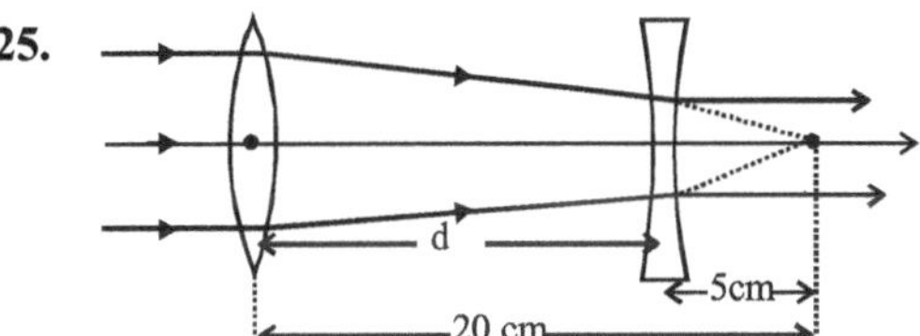

As the parallel beam of light is incident on convex lens,

$u = -\infty$, $f = 20$ cm

$\dfrac{1}{v} - \dfrac{1}{u} = \dfrac{1}{f} \Rightarrow \dfrac{1}{v} - \dfrac{1}{-\infty} = \dfrac{1}{20} \Rightarrow \dfrac{1}{v} = \dfrac{1}{20} \quad \therefore v = 20 \text{cm}$

     (1 mark)

In the absence of concave lens, the image would have been formed at a distance of 20 cm. This image acts as an object for concave lens which, formes its image at infinity.

∴ d = distance between the convex lens and concave lens

∴ virtual object distance for concave lens
$= (20 - d)$ cm.

$v = \infty$, $f = -5$ m.

As, $\dfrac{1}{v} - \dfrac{1}{u} = \dfrac{1}{f}$ ∴ $\dfrac{1}{\infty} - \dfrac{1}{(20-d)} = \dfrac{1}{-5}$

$\Rightarrow (20 - d) = 5 \Rightarrow 20 - 5 = d$ ∴ $d = 15$ cm   (1 mark)

26. Magnetic field at a point inside the solenoid is

$$B = \frac{\mu_0 NI}{\ell}$$

Where N is the total number of turns of the solenoid and *l* is its length. B is constant throughout the length of the solenoid.

Magnetic flux through each turn = B × area of each turn.

∴ $\phi_1 = \mu_0 \dfrac{N}{\ell} I \times A$

where A is the area of each turn.

∴   Total magnetic flux linked with the solenoid

$= \phi = \mu_0 \dfrac{N}{\ell} IA \times N$

But from the definition of self inductance (L), $\phi = LI$.

∴ $LI = \mu_0 \dfrac{N}{\ell} IA \times N \Rightarrow L = \dfrac{\mu_0 N^2 A}{\ell}$ (3 marks)

27. Given : $I_1 = 0.5$ A, $R_1 = 12$ ohm, $I_2 = 0.25$ A, $R_2 = 25$ ohm

From formula, $I = \dfrac{E}{(R + r)}$ or $E = I(R + r)$ (1 mark)

$0.5 \times (12 + r) = 0.25 \times (25 + r)$ (1 mark)

Solving we get, r = 1 ohm and emf,

$E = 0.5 (12 + 1) = 6.5$ V   (1 mark)

OR

Relation between current (I) and drift velocity (v_d) :

$I = V_d enA$

$I = \dfrac{e^2 VnA}{mL} \tau$ $\left(\because V_d = \dfrac{eV}{mL} T \right)$ (1½ mark)

It is clear from this expression that with the rise in temperatue τ decreases, this decreases the current in the circuit, which in turn increases the resistance of the conductor.   (1½ mark)

28. Let $I = I_0 \sin \omega t$ is the alternating current flowing through a resistance R in a small time dt.

∴ Heat produced = $dH = I^2 R dt$ ...(i)

If $I_{r.m.s}$ be the r.m.s value of current then by definition, heat produced in time t,

$$H = I_{r.m.s}^2 RT$$ ..(ii)   (1 mark)

Comparing equations (i) and (ii),

$$I_{r.m.s}^2 RT = \int_0^T I^2 R\,dt = R\int_0^T I^2\,dt = R\int_0^T I_0^2 \sin^2 \omega t\,dt$$

$$I_{r.m.s}^2 T = \frac{I_0^2}{2}\int_0^T 2\sin^2 \omega t\,dt = \frac{I_0^2}{2}\int_0^T (1 - \cos 2\omega t)\,dt$$

$$= \frac{I_0^2}{2}\left| t - \frac{\sin 2\omega t}{2\omega} \right|_0^T = \frac{I_0^2}{2}\left[t - \frac{1}{2\omega}\left(\sin 2 \times \frac{2\pi}{T} t \right) \right]_0^T$$

   (1 mark)

$$= \frac{I_0^2}{2}\left[t - \frac{1}{2\omega}\left(\sin 4\pi - \sin 0 \right) \right] = \frac{I_0^2 T}{2}$$

∴ $I_{rms}^2 = \dfrac{I_0^2}{2}$ ∴ $I_{rms} = \dfrac{I_0}{\sqrt{2}}$ (1 mark)

OR

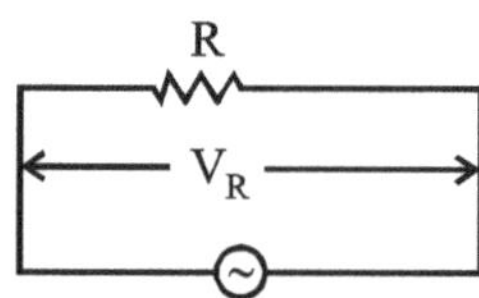

Let V_R be the instantaneous voltage drop across R. E is the applied alternating e.m.f. to the circuit. E_0 is the maximum voltage.

∴ $E = E_0 \sin \omega t = IR$

∴ $I = \dfrac{E_0}{R} \sin \omega t = I_0 \sin \omega t$ (1 mark)

where $I_0 = \dfrac{E_0}{R}$ = Maximum value of current.

∴   Current and voltage are in phase with each other.

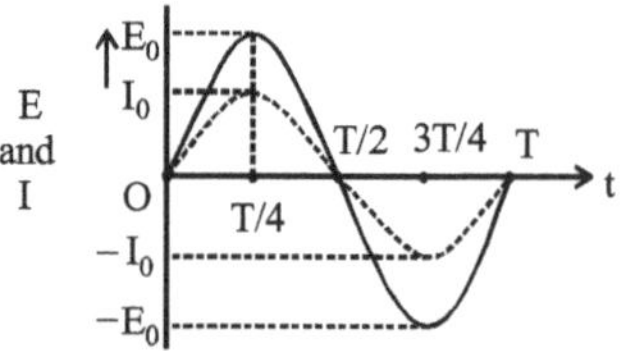

Graphical representation of voltage and current

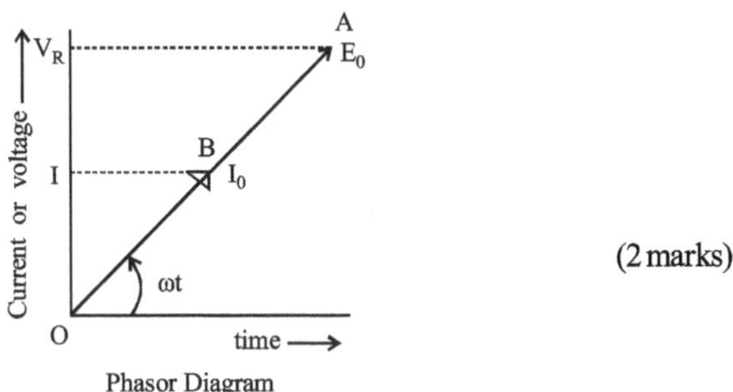

Phasor Diagram

(2 marks)

The reflections of E_0 and I_0 on y-axis gives the instantaneous voltage drop across R (V_R). ωt is called the phase angle.

29. The situation is shown in figure.

The square can be considered as one of the faces of a cube of each side 10 cm, enclosing the point charge inside it. The cube surface will act as Gaussian surface. (1 mark)

Given, $q = 10\,\mu C = 10 \times 10^{-6}\,C$,

$\varepsilon_0 = 8.854 \times 10^{-12}\,C^2 N^{-1} m^2$ (taken)

By Gauss's law for whole closed surface,

$$\phi = q/\varepsilon_0 = \frac{10 \times 10^{-6}}{8.854 \times 10^{-12}}$$

$$= 1.13 \times 10^6\,Nm^2/C \qquad \text{(1 mark)}$$

As one face area is *one-sixth* of total surface area of the cube,

$$\text{Flux through one face} = \frac{\phi}{6} = \frac{1.13 \times 10^6}{6}$$

$$= 1.88 \times 10^5\,Nm^2/C \qquad \text{(1 mark)}$$

30. (a) The isotope $^6_3 Li$ has abundance 7.5% and $^7_3 Li$ has 92.5%. $m\,(^6_3 Li) = 6.01512\,u$ $m\,(^7_3 Li) = 7.01600\,u$

Average mass of Li

$$= \frac{6.01512 \times 7.5 + 7.01600 \times 92.5}{7.5 + 92.5}$$

$$= \frac{45.1140 + 648.98}{7.5 + 92.5} = \frac{694.094}{100} = 6.94000\ \text{u. (1½ marks)}$$

(b) $m\,(^{10}_5 B) = 10.01294\,u;\ m\,(^{11}_5 B)$

$= 11.00931\,u;\ m\,(B)$

$= 10.811\,u.$

Let abundance of $^{10}_5 B$ be x% thus abundance of $^{11}_5 B$ will be $(100-x)\%$

Average mass of Boron

$$= \frac{10.01294x + 11.00931(100-x)}{100} = 10.811\,u$$

$\Rightarrow\quad 10.01294x + 1100.931 - 11.00931x = 1081.1$

$\Rightarrow\quad 0.996x = 19.831$

$\Rightarrow\quad x = 19.91\% = $ abundance of $^{10}_5 B$; and $(100-x)$

$= (100 - 19.91) = 80.1\%$ abundance of $^{11}_5 B$ (1½ marks)

31. Here $PQ = RS = \ell = $ length of the coil

$QR = SP = b = $ breadth of the coil

θ is the angle between plane of the coil and $\vec{B}$.

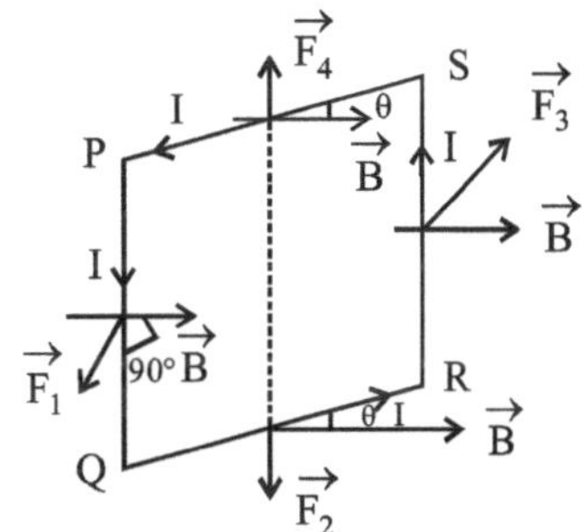

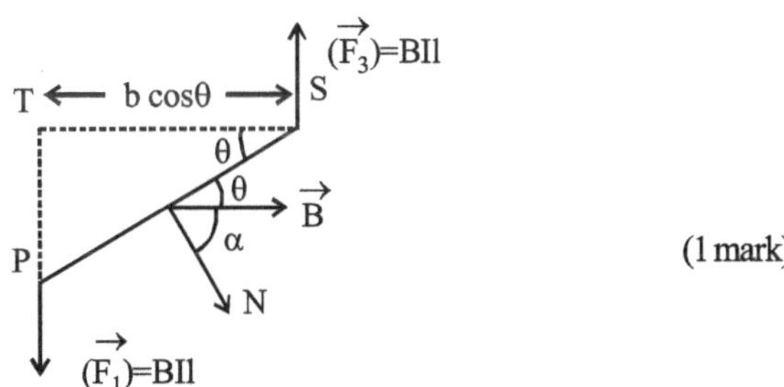

(1 mark)

$\vec{F_1}, \vec{F_2}, \vec{F_3}, \vec{F_4}$ are forces on four arms PQ, QR, RS and SP respectively.

$$\vec{F_4} = I(\vec{SP} \times \vec{B})$$

$\Rightarrow\quad IB\,(SP)\sin(180° - \theta) = IbB\sin\theta$

$$\vec{F_2} = I(\vec{QR} \times \vec{B}) \Rightarrow F_2 = IB\,(QR)\sin\theta = IbB\sin\theta \quad \text{(1 mark)}$$

They are equal in magnitude but opposite in direction, and will cancel each other.

$\vec{F_1} = I(\overrightarrow{PQ} \times \vec{B}) \Rightarrow F_1 = IB\,(PQ)\sin 90°$

$= I\ell B\,(\because \overrightarrow{PQ} \perp \vec{B})$

This is perpendicular to the plane of the coil and directed outwards.

$\vec{F_3} = I(\overrightarrow{RS} \times \vec{B}) \Rightarrow F_3 = I(RS)\,B\sin 90°$

$= I\ell B\ (\because \overrightarrow{RS} \perp \vec{B})$ (1 mark)

This is perpendicular to the plane of the coil and directed inwards.

They are equal, parallel but oppositely directed along their line of action, so they will form a couple which will try to rotate the coil in anticolockwise direction about its axis.

Torque on the coil = moment of the couple $= \vec{F} \times \vec{r}$

$\Rightarrow \quad \tau = I\ell B \times b\cos\theta$ [$\because$ perpendicular distance between the force = $b\cos\theta$]

$\Rightarrow \tau = IBA\cos\theta$ where $A = \ell b$ = area of the coil (1 mark)

If the coil has n number of turns, $\tau = nIBA\cos\theta$.

If the angle between the normal on the plane of the coil and $\vec{B}$ is α then $\theta + \alpha = 90° \Rightarrow \theta = 90° - \alpha$

$\Rightarrow \quad \cos\theta = \cos(90° - \alpha) = \sin\alpha$

$\therefore \quad \tau = nIBA\sin\alpha = MB\sin\alpha = |\vec{M} \times \vec{B}|$

Where M = magnetic dipole moment of the coil = nIA

    (1 mark)

OR

When a charged particle with charge q moves inside a magnetic field $\vec{B}$ with velocity v, it experiences a force, which is given by:

$\vec{F} = q(\vec{v} \times \vec{B})$ (1 mark)

Here, $\vec{v}$ is perpendicular to $\vec{B}$ and $\vec{F}$ is the force on the charged particle which acts as the centripetal force and makes it move along a circular path.

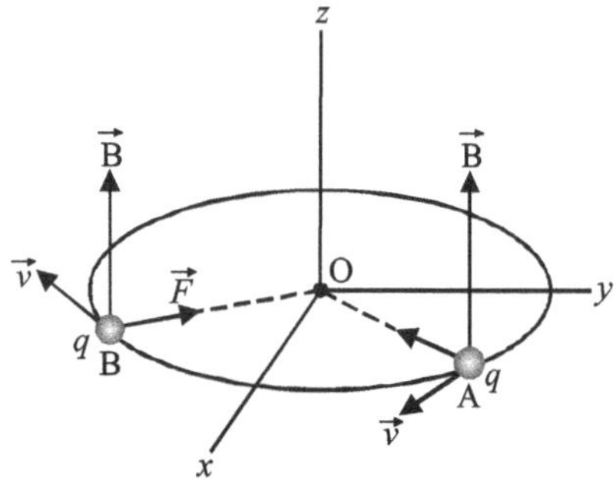

Let m be the mass of the charged particle and r be the radius of the circular path.

$q(\vec{v} \times \vec{B}) = \dfrac{mv^2}{r}$ (1 mark)

Since, v and B are perpendicular to each other.

$\therefore \quad qvB = \dfrac{mv^2}{r} \quad \boxed{r = \dfrac{mv}{Bq}}$ (1 mark)

Time period of circular motion of the charged particle can be calculated as shown below:

$T = \dfrac{2\pi r}{v} = \dfrac{2\pi}{v}\dfrac{mv}{Bq}$

$T = \dfrac{2\pi m}{Bq}$ (1 mark)

$\therefore$ Angular frequency is

$\omega = \dfrac{2\pi}{T} \quad \boxed{\therefore \omega = \dfrac{Bq}{m}}$

Therefore, the frequency of the revolution of the charged particle is independent of the velocity or the energy of the particle.   (1 mark)

32. **Cut-off voltage :** The minimum negative voltage (V_0) applied an anode plate with respect to the cathode for which photocurrent in the circuit reduces to zero.   (1 mark)

Threshold frequency : The minimum frequency of incident radiation which is required for photoelectric, effect or the ejection of photoelectrons from metal surface.   (1 mark)

Einstein's photo-electric equation,

$h\nu = h\nu_0 + KE_{max} = h\nu_0 + eV_0$

$V_0 = \dfrac{h}{e}(\nu - \nu_0)$

The variation of cut-off potential with frequency of incident radiation is shown below

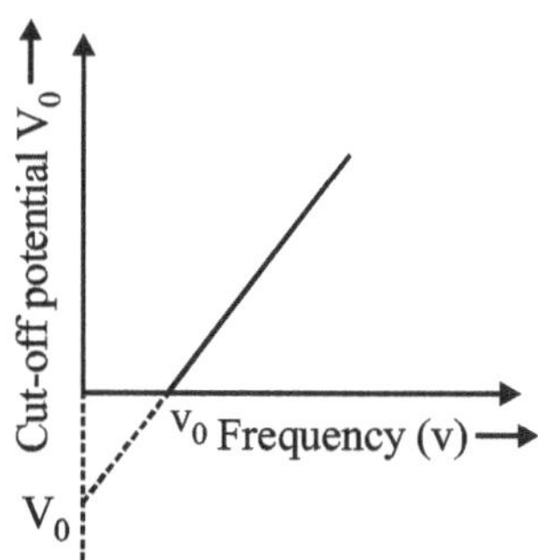

From this graph, we can calculate the value of threshold frequency (point of intersection of frequency axis) and stopping potential (point of intersection on potential axis).

(3 marks)

OR

(a) de-Broglie wavelength of a charged particle is given by, $\lambda \propto \dfrac{1}{\sqrt{mq}}$

If m_p and e are mass and charge of a proton respectively, and, m_D and e are mass and charge of a deutron respectively, then

$$\frac{\lambda_p}{\lambda_D} = \sqrt{\frac{m_D q_D}{m_p q_p}} = \sqrt{\frac{(2m_p)(e)}{(m_p)(e)}} = \sqrt{2}$$

$$\lambda_p = \sqrt{2}\lambda_D$$

Thus, de-broglie wavelength associated with proton is $\sqrt{2}$ times of the de-broglie wavelength of deutron and hence it is more. (2½ marks)

(b) Momentum, is given by, $P = \dfrac{h}{\lambda}$ or, $p \propto \dfrac{1}{\lambda}$

where, h = plank's constant

Since the wavelength of a proton is more than that of deutron thus, the momentum of a proton is lesser than that of deutron. Hence, the momentum of proton is less.

(2½ marks)

33. (a) As the resultant intensity at a point,

$$I = I_1 + I_2 + 2\sqrt{I_1 I_2}\,\cos\phi \qquad \text{(1 mark)}$$

When the path difference $= \lambda$,

phase difference $= 0°$

$\therefore\ I_R = I + I + 2\sqrt{I \times I}\,\cos 0°$

$= 2I + 2\sqrt{I^2} \times 1 = 2I + 2I = 4I = K.$ (1 mark)

When the path difference $= \dfrac{\lambda}{3}$, phase difference $\phi = \dfrac{2\pi}{3}$

$\therefore\ I'_R = I + I + 2\sqrt{I.I}.\cos\left(\dfrac{2\pi}{3}\right)$

$= 2I + 2\sqrt{I^2} \times \left(-\dfrac{1}{2}\right) = 2I - \dfrac{2I}{2} = I$ (1 mark)

$\therefore\ \ I' = \dfrac{K}{4}$ (½ marks)

(b) Angular width $\theta = \dfrac{\lambda}{d}$

$$0.1° = \frac{0.1}{180}\pi = \frac{6\times10^{-7}}{d}$$

$$d = \frac{6\times180\times10^{-7}}{0.1\times\pi} = 3.44 \times 10^{-4}\,\text{m} \qquad \text{(1½ marks)}$$

OR

Here $d = 2$ mm, $D = 1.2$ m, $\lambda_1 = 650$ nm, $\lambda_2 = 520$ nm

(a) Distance of third bright fringe from the central maximum for the wavelength 650 nm.

$$y_3 = \frac{3\lambda D}{d} = \frac{3\left(650\times10^{-9}\right)1.2}{2\times10^{-3}} = 1.17\,\text{m} \qquad \text{(2 marks)}$$

(b) Let at linear distance 'y' from center of screen the bright fringes due to both wavelength coincides. Let n_1 number of bright fringe with wavelength λ_1 coincides with n_2 number of bright fringe with wavelength λ_2.

We can write

$y = n_1\beta_1 = n_2\beta_2$

$n_1 = \dfrac{\lambda_1 D}{d} = n_2\dfrac{D\lambda_2}{d}$

or $\quad n_1\lambda_1 = n_2\lambda_2$ ...(i) (1 mark)

Also at first position of coincide the nth bright of one will coincide with $(n + 1)^{th}$ bright fringe of other.

If $\lambda_2 < \lambda_1$

So then $n_2 > n_1$

then $n_2 = n_1 + 1$ ...(ii) (1 mark)

Using equation (ii) in equation (i)

$n_1\lambda_1 = (n_1 + 1)\lambda_2$

$n_1(650) \times 10^{-9} = (n_1 + 1)\,520 \times 10^{-9}$

$65\,n_1 = 52\,n_1 + 52$ or $12\,n_1 = 52$ or $n_1 = 4$

So, the fourth bright fringe of wavelength 520 nm coincides with 5th bright fringe of wavelength 650 nm. (1 mark)

34. (i) For hydrogen or hydrogen like atoms

$$E_n = \frac{-13.6\,Z^2}{n^2}\,\text{eV}/\text{atom}$$

For hydrogen atom $\qquad\qquad E_1 = -13.6\,\text{eV (for } n = 1)$

$\qquad$ (Z = 1) $\qquad\qquad\qquad E_2 = -3.4\,\text{eV (for } n = 2)$

$\therefore \Delta E = E_2 - E_1 = -3.4 - (-13.6) = 10.2$ eV

i.e., When hydrogen comes to ground state from its first excited state it will release 10.2 eV of energy.

For He$^+$ ion $\quad$ $E_1 = -13.6 \times 4$ eV $= -54.4$ eV (for $n = 1$)
$(Z = 2)$ $\qquad\qquad$ $E_2 = -13.6$ eV (for $n = 2$)
$\qquad\qquad\qquad\qquad\quad$ $E_3 = -6.04$ eV (for $n = 3$)
$\qquad\qquad\qquad\qquad\quad$ $E_4 = -3.4$eV (for $n = 4$)

Here He$^+$ ion is in the first excited state i.e., possessing energy -13.6 eV. After receiving energy of $+10.2$ eV from excited hydrogen atom on collision, the energy of electron will be $(-13.6 + 10.2)$ eV $= -3.4$ eV. Hence the quantum number of the state finally populated in He$^+$ ions, $n = 4$.

$\hfill$ (2 marks)

(ii) Wavelength of visible light lies in the range,
$\lambda_1 = 4000$Å to $\lambda_2 = 7000$Å.
Therefore

$$E_1 = \frac{12375}{\lambda_1} = \frac{12375}{4000} = 3.09 \text{ eV}$$

$$E_2 = \frac{12375}{\lambda_2} = \frac{12375}{7000} = 1.77 \text{ eV}$$

For He$^+$ atom in transition from $n = 4$ to $n = 3$, energy of photon released will lie between E_1 and E_2.

$$E_4 - E_3 = -3.4 - (-6.04) = 2.64 \text{ eV}$$

$\therefore$ Wavelength of photon corresponding to this energy, (2.64 eV)

$$\lambda = \frac{12375}{2.64} \text{Å} = 4687.5 \text{ Å} = 4.68 \times 10^{-7} \text{ m} \hfill \text{(1 mark)}$$

(iii) Kinetic energy for hydrogen or hydrogen like atom K

$$K = \frac{-13.6Z^2}{n^2} \Rightarrow K \propto Z^2$$

$$\frac{K_H}{K_{He^+}} = \left(\frac{Z_H}{Z_{He^+}}\right)^2 = \left(\frac{1}{2}\right)^2 = \frac{1}{4} \hfill \text{(1 mark)}$$

OR

(iii) The value of x = 0.
The product of linear momentum and angular momentum is independent of value of n. $\hfill$ (1 mark)

35. **(i)** $\quad$ Ratio = 1 $\hfill$ (1 mark)
$\quad$ **(ii)** $\quad$ Boron $\hfill$ (1 mark)
$\quad$ **(iii)** Conductivity increases $\hfill$ (2 marks)

OR

(iii) Output frequency = 2×60 Hz $= 120$ Hz $\hfill$ (2 marks)